5900

Taking Sides:
Clashing Views in
Educational Psychology, 7/e

by Leonard Abbeduto
Frank Symons

http://create.mcgraw-hill.com

ISBN-10: 0078047986   ISBN-13: 9780078047985

Contents

Preface

The field of educational psychology seems to be constantly enmeshed in controversy. Some of the controversies are ongoing; occasionally, a controversy may die down a bit only to return in full force again, perhaps in a slightly different form. Other controversies are more short-lived; either they are resolved or they are abandoned as intractable. From the outside it may seem that these controversies reflect inefficiency and a lack of progress in the field of educational psychology and even that "educational psychologists just like to argue." But are these controversies really as counterproductive as they appear?

In fact, controversies provide the foundation for deeper understanding of the educational issues involved, thereby leading to progress. This is not merely our personal belief. There is considerable empirical evidence from research in educational psychology and cognitive science to support this claim. It is not too difficult to see why this is the case. When we engage in discussion of a controversy, we are forced to muster evidence to support our position and to fully develop in a systematic fashion all of its implications. This can lead us to see gaps in our evidence and fallacies in our reasoning, or to recognize previously unrealized implications. As a result, we may decide to gather additional evidence, modify our position, or even abandon it entirely. It is this spirit of controversy and argumentation that is the basis of this textbook.

Book Organization

This book addresses current controversies in educational psychology, each of which has elicited sharply divergent responses from scholars and practitioners. We have organized these issues into three parts. In the first part, we focus on issues that concern the impact of the diverse needs and characteristics of the students found in most classrooms in U.S. schools today: gender equity, student failure, inclusion of students with special educational needs, the achievement gap between ethnic and racial majority and minority students, and the digital and technology needs of the current generation of students. In the second part of the book, we focus on issues that concern the theoretical foundations of teaching and learning in the classroom: the value of constructivism, the educational implications of Howard Gardner's theory of multiple intelligences, the need for and value of teaching students self-control, the pedagogical implications of recent work on brain development and function, and the role of video games as contributors to student violence. The final part of the book features issues surrounding the effectiveness of teaching and assessment in the classroom: the need for and value of schools adopting a standard core curriculum, the appropriateness of character, or moral, education as part of the school curriculum, the value of

homework, the impact of grades on student performance, the impact of class size on student outcomes, and the amount of time students should spend in school.

Each issue is stated as a question and is represented by two previously published articles, the first supporting a yes answer to the question and the second arguing a no response. Each issue is preceded by a set of learning objects and an introduction, which provides background and a context for evaluating the articles. Each issue ends with questions to encourage critical reflection and an "Is There Common Ground" section, which briefly summarizes the complexities of the controversy and possible routes to resolution. We also include additional readings and Internet resources.

Leonard Abbeduto
University of California, Davis

Frank Symons
University of Minnesota

Editors of This Volume

Leonard Abbeduto, PhD, is the director of the MIND Institute, the Tsakopoulos-Vismara Endowed Chair, and professor of psychiatry and behavioral sciences at the University of California, Davis. Dr. Abbeduto's research is focused broadly on the development of language across the lifespan in individuals with neurodevelopmental disorders, such as Down syndrome and autism, and the family context for language development. He was previously on the faculty of the Department of Educational Psychology at the University of Wisconsin–Madison. He earned his PhD in psychology from the University of Illinois at Chicago in 1982.

Frank Symons, PhD, is a professor of educational psychology in the College of Education and Human Development at the University of Minnesota. Dr. Symons's research is focused on understanding the severe behavior problems of children and adults with special needs, primarily those with developmental disabilities and emotional or behavioral disorders. He earned his PhD in education and human development form Vanderbilt University in 1996.

Acknowledgments

This book would not have been possible without the encouragement, boundless understanding, and good humor of my wife, Terry, and my sons, Jackson and Mack. They have shaped everything I do. I also am indebted to my mother, Dorothy, for a lifetime of unwavering support. Finally, I dedicate this volume to my late friend and mentor, Sheldon Rosenberg; I am forever in his debt.

Leonard Abbeduto

I am very thankful to Alicia Vegell for her assistance on this volume and her enduring patience with me. Thanks to my friends and colleagues in the Special Education Program and the Department of Educational Psychology at the University of Minnesota for an intellectually inspiring academic environment. Gratitude goes to my family—Stacy, Stewart, and Elisabeth—from whom I learn about clashing views and for which I continue to be grateful. Last, I would like to dedicate this volume to Red and the early enriched environment created for me.

Frank Symons

Academic Advisory Board Members

Members of the Academic Advisory Board are instrumental in the final selection of articles for *Taking Sides* books and ExpressBooks. Their review of the articles for content, level, and appropriateness provides critical direction to the editor(s) and staff. We think that you will find their careful consideration reflected in this book.

Beverly Bohn
Park University

Li Cao
University of West Georgia

Monica Glina
Montclair State Univeristy

Aaron J. Lawler
Benedictine University

Jeffrey Liew
Texas A&M University

Glen D. McClary
D'Youville College

John R. McClure
Northern Arizona University

Nancy Meadows
Texas Christian University

Anne Marie Rakip
South Carolina State University

Terry Salem
Lake Land College

Thomas R. Scheira
Buffalo State College

Elizabeth G. Siemanowski
Wesley College

Ervin F. Sparapani
Saginaw Valley State University

Correlation Guide

The *Taking Sides* series presents current issues in a debate-style format designed to stimulate student interest and develop critical-thinking skills. Each issue is thoughtfully framed with an issue summary, an issue introduction, learning outcomes, and key end-of-issue instructional and discussion tools. The pro and con essays—selected for their liveliness and substance—represent the arguments of leading scholars and commentators in their fields.

Taking Sides: Clashing Views in Educational Psychology, 7/e is an easy-to-use reader that presents issues on important topics such as *diversity in the classroom, theories of learning, effective teaching and evaluation,* and more. For more information on *Taking Sides* and other *McGraw-Hill Create™ Contemporary Learning Series* titles, visit www .mcgrawhillcreate.com.

This convenient guide matches the issues in **Taking Sides: Educational Psychology, 7/e** with the corresponding chapters in two of our best-selling McGraw-Hill Educational Psychology textbooks by Santrock and Bohlin et al.

Taking Sides: Educational Psychology, 7/e	Educational Psychology, 5/e by Santrock	EdPsych: Modules, 2/e by Bohlin et al.
Are Single-Gender Classes Necessary to Create Equal Opportunities for Boys and Girls?	**Chapter 3:** Social Contexts and Socioemotional Development **Chapter 4:** Individual Variations **Chapter 5:** Sociocultural Diversity	**Chapter 1:** Today's Diverse Classrooms **Chapter 3:** Social Development **Chapter 4:** Emotional Development **Chapter 18:** Creating a Productive Learning Environment **Chapter 19:** Understanding and Managing Student Behavior **Chapter 21:** Grouping Practices
Should Struggling Students Be Retained?	**Chapter 6:** Learners Who Are Exceptional **Chapter 11:** Learning and Cognition in the Content Areas **Chapter 12:** Planning, Instruction, and Technology **Chapter 13:** Motivation, Teaching, and Learning **Chapter 15:** Standardized Tests and Teaching **Chapter 16:** Classroom Assessment and Grading	**Chapter 1:** Today's Diverse Classroom **Chapter 2:** Contexts of Development **Chapter 4:** Emotional Development **Chapter 21:** Grouping Practices **Chapter 26:** Assessing Student Learning **Chapter 28:** Performance Assessment
Is Full Inclusion Always the Best Option for Children with Disabilities?	**Chapter 6:** Learners Who Are Exceptional **Chapter 12:** Planning, Instruction, and Technology **Chapter 13:** Motivation, Teaching, and Learning **Chapter 14:** Managing the Classroom	**Chapter 1:** Today's Diverse Classroom **Chapter 2:** Contexts of Development **Chapter 18:** Creating a Productive Learning Environment **Chapter 19:** Understanding and Managing Student **Chapter 21:** Grouping Practices **Chapter 24:** Cognitive Disabilities **Chapter 25:** Emotional, Social, and Behavioral Disabilities
Are Schools Closing the Achievement Gap between Students from Different Ethnic and Racial Backgrounds?	**Chapter 1:** Educational Psychology: A Tool for Effective Teaching **Chapter 4:** Individual Variations **Chapter 5:** Sociocultural Diversity **Chapter 12:** Planning, Instruction, and Technology **Chapter 13:** Motivation, Teaching, and Learning **Chapter 15:** Standardized Tests and Teaching **Chapter 16:** Classroom Assessment and Grading	**Chapter 1:** Today's Diverse Classroom **Chapter 18:** Creating a Productive Learning Environment **Chapter 19:** Understanding and Managing Student **Chapter 20:** Instruction: Behavioral, Cognitive, and Constructivist Approaches **Chapter 26:** Assessing Student Learning **Chapter 27:** Test Construction and Use **Chapter 28:** Performance Assessment **Chapter 29:** Standardized Testing **Chapter 30:** Issues in Standardized Testing
Does the Current Generation of Students Require Digital Tools for Learning?	**Chapter 1:** Educational Psychology: A Tool for Effective Teaching **Chapter 2:** Cognitive and Language Development **Chapter 4:** Individual Variations **Chapter 8:** The Information-Processing Approach **Chapter 9:** Complex Cognitive Processes **Chapter 12:** Planning, Instruction, and Technology	**Chapter 6:** The Brain and Development **Chapter 11:** Information Processing **Chapter 12:** Metacognition **Chapter 13:** Transfer of Skills and Knowledge **Chapter 14:** Critical Thinking and Problem Solving **Chapter 20:** Instruction: Behavioral, Cognitive, and Constructivist Approaches

(Continued)

Taking Sides: Educational Psychology, 7/e	Educational Psychology, 5/e by Santrock	EdPsych: Modules, 2/e by Bohlin et al.
Is a Constructivist Approach to Teaching Effective?	**Chapter 2:** Cognitive and Language Development **Chapter 3:** Social Contexts and Socioemotional Development **Chapter 4:** Individual Variations **Chapter 10:** Social Constructivist Approaches **Chapter 11:** Learning and Cognition in the Content Areas **Chapter 12:** Planning, Instruction, and Technology **Chapter 13:** Motivation, Teaching, and Learning	**Chapter 2:** Contexts of Development **Chapter 3:** Social Development **Chapter 4:** Emotional Development **Chapter 5:** Moral Development **Chapter 10:** Social Cognitive Theory **Chapter 11:** Information Processing **Chapter 13:** Transfer of Skills and Knowledge **Chapter 14:** Critical Thinking and Problem Solving **Chapter 20:** Instruction: Behavioral, Cognitive, and Constructivist Approaches **Chapter 28:** Performance Assessment **Chapter 29:** Standardized Testing **Chapter 30:** Issues in Standardized Testing
Can Howard Gardner's Theory of Multiple Intelligences Transform Educational Practice?	**Chapter 4:** Individual Variations **Chapter 8:** The Information-Processing Approach **Chapter 9:** Complex Cognitive Processes **Chapter 11:** Learning and Cognition in the Content Areas **Chapter 15:** Standardized Tests and Teaching **Chapter 16:** Classroom Assessment and Grading	**Chapter 6:** The Brain and Development **Chapter 7:** Cognitive Development **Chapter 8:** Language Development **Chapter 10:** Social Cognitive Theory **Chapter 11:** Information Processing **Chapter 12:** Metacognition **Chapter 13:** Transfer of Skills and Knowledge **Chapter 14:** Critical Thinking and Problem Solving **Chapter 20:** Instruction: Behavioral, Cognitive, and Constructivist Approaches **Chapter 22:** Intelligence **Chapter 23:** Giftedness and Creativity **Chapter 26:** Assessing Student Learning
Should Schools Teach Students Self-Control?	**Chapter 3:** Social Contexts and Socioemotional Development **Chapter 4:** Individual Variations **Chapter 7:** Behavioral and Social Cognitive Approaches **Chapter 13:** Motivation, Teaching, and Learning **Chapter 14:** Managing the Classroom	**Chapter 2:** Contexts of Development **Chapter 3:** Social Development **Chapter 4:** Emotional Development **Chapter 9:** Behavioral Learning Theories **Chapter 10:** Social Cognitive Theory **Chapter 15:** Behavioral Theory **Chapter 19:** Understanding and Managing Student
Do Recent Discoveries About the Brain Have Implications for Classroom Practice?	**Chapter 1:** Educational Psychology: A Tool for Effective Teaching **Chapter 4:** Individual Variations **Chapter 8:** The Information-Processing Approach **Chapter 9:** Complex Cognitive Processes **Chapter 12:** Planning, Instruction, and Technology	**Chapter 6:** The Brain and Development **Chapter 7:** Cognitive Development **Chapter 8:** Language Development **Chapter 11:** Information Processing **Chapter 12:** Metacognition
Do Video Games Promote Violent Behavior in Students?	**Chapter 1:** Educational Psychology: A Tool for Effective Teaching **Chapter 3:** Social Contexts and Socioemotional Development **Chapter 6:** Learners Who Are Exceptional **Chapter 8:** The Information-Processing Approach **Chapter 14:** Managing the Classroom	**Chapter 1:** Today's Diverse Classroom **Chapter 2:** Contexts of Development **Chapter 3:** Social Development **Chapter 4:** Emotional Development **Chapter 5:** Moral Development **Chapter 6:** The Brain and Development **Chapter 9:** Behavioral Learning Theories **Chapter 10:** Social Cognitive Theory **Chapter 11:** Information Processing
Should Schools Adopt a Common Core Curriculum?	**Chapter 2:** Cognitive and Language Development **Chapter 3:** Social Contexts and Socioemotional Development **Chapter 4:** Individual Variations **Chapter 5:** Sociocultural Diversity **Chapter 11:** Learning and Cognition in the Content Areas **Chapter 12:** Planning, Instruction, and Technology **Chapter 15:** Standardized Tests and Teaching **Chapter 16:** Classroom Assessment and Grading	**Chapter 1:** Today's Diverse Classroom **Chapter 9:** Behavioral Learning Theories **Chapter 10:** Social Cognitive Theory **Chapter 11:** Information Processing **Chapter 13:** Transfer of Skills and Knowledge **Chapter 18:** Creating a Productive Learning Environment **Chapter 20:** Instruction: Behavioral, Cognitive, and Constructivist Approaches **Chapter 26:** Assessing Student Learning **Chapter 30:** Issues in Standardized Testing

Taking Sides: Educational Psychology, 7/e	Educational Psychology, 5/e by Santrock	EdPsych: Modules, 2/e by Bohlin et al.
Should Character Education Define the Values We Teach Students?	**Chapter 3:** Social Contexts and Socioemotional Development **Chapter 4:** Individual Variations **Chapter 5:** Sociocultural Diversity **Chapter 13:** Motivation, Teaching, and Learning **Chapter 14:** Managing the Classroom	**Chapter 1:** Today's Diverse Classroom **Chapter 2:** Contexts of Development **Chapter 3:** Social Development **Chapter 4:** Emotional Development **Chapter 5:** Moral Development **Chapter 25:** Emotional, Social, and Behavioral Disabilities **Chapter 26:** Assessing Student Learning **Chapter 28:** Performance Assessment
Does Homework Lead to Improved Student Achievement?	**Chapter 1:** Educational Psychology: A Tool for Effective Teaching **Chapter 3:** Social Contexts and Socioemotional Development **Chapter 11:** Learning and Cognition in the Content Areas **Chapter 13:** Motivation, Teaching, and Learning **Chapter 16:** Classroom Assessment and Grading	**Chapter 1:** Today's Diverse Classroom **Chapter 13:** Transfer of Skills and Knowledge **Chapter 14:** Critical Thinking and Problem Solving **Chapter 15:** Behavioral Theory **Chapter 16:** Cognitive Theories **Chapter 17:** Self Theories **Chapter 18:** Creating a Productive Learning Environment **Chapter 28:** Performance Assessment
Does Grading Help Students Learn?	**Chapter 12:** Planning, Instruction, and Technology **Chapter 13:** Motivation, Teaching, and Learning **Chapter 15:** Standardized Tests and Teaching **Chapter 16:** Classroom Assessment and Grading	**Chapter 15:** Behavioral Theory **Chapter 16:** Cognitive Theories **Chapter 17:** Self Theories **Chapter 18:** Creating a Productive Learning Environment **Chapter 26:** Assessing Student Learning **Chapter 27:** Test Construction and Use **Chapter 28:** Performance Assessment
Should Schools Decrease Class Size to Improve Student Outcomes?	**Chapter 1:** Educational Psychology: A Tool for Effective Teaching **Chapter 12:** Planning, Instruction, and Technology **Chapter 13:** Motivation, Teaching, and Learning **Chapter 14:** Managing the Classroom	**Chapter 1:** Today's Diverse Classroom **Chapter 2:** Contexts of Development **Chapter 3:** Social Development **Chapter 18:** Creating a Productive Learning Environment **Chapter 21:** Grouping Practices **Chapter 26:** Assessing Student Learning
Should Student Time in School Be Changed?	**Chapter 1:** Educational Psychology: A Tool for Effective Teaching **Chapter 2:** Cognitive and Language Development **Chapter 3:** Social Contexts and Socioemotional Development **Chapter 12:** Planning, Instruction, and Technology **Chapter 14:** Managing the Classroom	**Chapter 1:** Today's Diverse Classroom **Chapter 2:** Contexts of Development **Chapter 6:** The Brain and Development **Chapter 15:** Behavioral Theory **Chapter 16:** Cognitive Theories **Chapter 17:** Self Theories

Topic Guide

Achievement Gap

Are Schools Closing the Achievement Gap between Students from Different Ethnic and Racial Backgrounds?
Does the Current Generation of Students Require Digital Tools for Learning?

Classrooms

Should Schools Decrease Class Size to Improve Student Outcomes?
Should Student Time in School Be Changed?

Constructivism

Is a Constructivist Approach to Teaching Effective?

Curriculum

Should Character Education Define the Values We Teach Students?
Should Schools Adopt a Common Core Curriculum?

Diversity

Are Schools Closing the Achievement Gap between Students from Different Ethnic and Racial Backgrounds?
Are Single-Gender Classes Necessary to Create Equal Opportunities for Boys and Girls?
Does the Current Generation of Students Require Digital Tools for Learning?
Is Full Inclusion Always the Best Option for Children with Disabilities?
Should Struggling Students Be Retained?

Educational Neuroscience

Can Howard Gardner's Theory of Multiple Intelligences Transform Educational Practice?
Do Recent Discoveries About the Brain Have Implications for Classroom Practice?

Effective Teaching

Does Grading Help Students Learn?
Does Homework Lead to Improved Student Achievement?
Should Schools Teach Students Self-Control?

Evaluation of Teaching

Does Homework Lead to Improved Student Achievement?

Gender & Education

Are Single-Gender Classes Necessary to Create Equal Opportunities for Boys and Girls?

Placement

Are Single-Gender Classes Necessary to Create Equal Opportunities for Boys and Girls?
Is Full Inclusion Always the Best Option for Children with Disabilities?
Should Struggling Students Be Retained?

School Reform

Does Grading Help Students Learn?
Should Schools Decrease Class Size to Improve Student Outcomes?
Should Student Time in School Be Changed?

Standards

Are Single-Gender Classes Necessary to Create Equal Opportunities for Boys and Girls?
Does Grading Help Students Learn?

Teacher Preparation

Does Grading Help Students Learn?
Does Homework Lead to Improved Student Achievement?
Is a Constructivist Approach to Teaching Effective?
Should Schools Teach Students Self-Control?

Technology

Do Recent Discoveries About the Brain Have Implications for Classroom Practice?
Do Video Games Promote Violent Behavior in Students?
Does the Current Generation of Students Require Digital Tools for Learning?

Theories of Learning

Can Howard Gardner's Theory of Multiple Intelligences Transform Educational Practice?
Do Recent Discoveries About the Brain Have Implications for Classroom Practice?
Do Video Games Promote Violent Behavior in Students?
Is a Constructivist Approach to Teaching Effective?
Should Schools Teach Students Self-Control?

Introduction

What Is Educational Psychology?

Educational psychology has traditionally been defined as the application of psychological theories, methods, and findings to the study of learning and teaching. This has led educational psychologists to study such topics as the development of particular academic skills (e.g., reading); the ways in which children acquire and represent knowledge in particular substantive domains (e.g., mathematics) and how those representations can be supported by classroom instruction; individual differences in intelligence and achievement and their relation to classroom instruction; how student motivation is related to learning and to different pedagogical practices; the relationships among different domains of ability and functioning, including the relationship between the cognitive and social domains; how best to assess ability, achievement, and teaching effectiveness; and how to change the beliefs and practices of teachers.

Such a diverse range of interests has always required an eclectic approach. Thus, educational psychologists have traditionally drawn on the concepts and tools of many of the subdisciplines of psychology: developmental psychology, psychometrics, cognitive psychology, clinical psychology, learning science, and social psychology, to name but a few. In recent years, moreover, educational psychologists have begun to more fully understand the complexity of the factors and systems at play in teaching and learning. This has led them to cross disciplinary boundaries and draw on theories, methods, and findings from other disciplines, including cultural anthropology, linguistics, philosophy, educational administration, political science, sociology, social work, and neuroscience. In turn, educational psychologists have begun to ask questions and examine variables that have not previously been seen as within their purview, such as the relationship between family functioning and academic performance, the role of cultural identity in student achievement, the relationships between economic conditions and pedagogical practices, the impact of changing societal conceptions of juvenile crime on the educational process, the role of the school in the life of a community, and the interaction between experience and the biological processes underlying brain structure, function, and development. Educational psychologists have also begun to see the need to more fully understand the domains that form the subject matter of schools, which has led them to address questions about the nature of expertise in domains such as mathematics and science. And finally, educational psychologists have come to view themselves as the agents of educational reform.

In short, traditional boundaries between educational psychology and other disciplines concerned with children, families, learning, education, and social change have begun to blur. This expansion of scope and crossing of disciplinary boundaries, however, has meant that educational psychologists have become enmeshed in an increasing number of controversies.

Controversies in Educational Psychology: Where They Come from and How They Can Be Resolved

In this text, we have framed each of the current controversies in educational psychology as a question, such as *Is full inclusion always the best option for children with disabilities?* This approach is useful because, at its most basic level, educational psychology is the science of providing answers to questions about teaching and learning. Sometimes these questions arise from outside the field of educational psychology or even from outside the field of education, as when business leaders turn to educators with questions about how to prepare children for the technological workplace they will face as adults, or when political leaders ask educational psychologists whether or not the inclusion of students with disabilities within the regular classroom is "working." At other times, the questions come from within the field of educational psychology itself, as in the case of questions about whether a constructivist approach (child-centered and discovery-oriented rather than teacher-controlled and scaffolded) is effective in promoting student mastery of academic content. Whatever the sources of these questions, it often happens that educational psychologists and other stakeholders in the educational process end up holding sharply different views about the answers. What creates these controversies? Why do experts in the field hold contrasting theories and beliefs? Analyzing some of the causes of controversies in educational psychology may allow us to understand the paths that must be taken to resolve them.

Empirical Data

Many questions become controversial because the empirical data needed to supply the answer are lacking. In some cases, the lack of data simply reflects the fact that the question has been asked only recently and thus, there has not been sufficient time to conduct the necessary research. In other cases, however, the question has become controversial *because* of the data that have been collected. That is, the data generated have been inconsistent across studies or can be interpreted as providing support for conflicting theories. Such ambiguity often occurs when the question has been addressed through a *correlational* approach rather than through an *experimental* approach.

In a correlational study, an investigator examines the relationship that exists naturally between two or more variables. In this approach, the scientist does not control or manipulate nature but rather, measures it, or at least parts of it. Consider, for example, a hypothetical controversy between the relative effectiveness of two approaches to teaching reading (A and B). One way to address this controversy would be to find schools that adopted the different approaches and ask whether students' reading achievement scores are better for schools adopting approach A or approach B. At first glance, this seems likely a relatively straightforward way to decide the controversy. The interpretive problem for such a study, as for any correlational study, is that there may be other differences between the two types of schools in addition to their approaches to teaching reading, and these unmeasured differences may really be responsible for any differences in student achievement that are observed. These differences between the schools might include differences in family demographics (e.g., socioeconomic status, race, and ethnicity), resources available to the schools, level of parental commitment, and so on.

Such alternative interpretations could be ruled out by adopting an experimental approach. In an experiment, the researcher exerts control over the variables of interest. In a true experiment, participants (e.g., students, classes, or schools) are assigned at random to the various *conditions* of interest (e.g., instructional approach A and approach B in our example). The value of such random assignment is that, given a large enough sample of participants, we can be confident that the conditions being compared are similar on all variables except those being studied. So, for example, if we have a large number of schools in our sample and we assign them randomly to Approach A and Approach B, we will end up, on average, with about the same number of affluent and economically disadvantaged schools in each condition, the same number of ethnically diverse and ethnically homogeneous schools in each condition, the same number of initially high-achieving and low-achieving schools in each condition, and so on. Such similarity across conditions makes for unambiguous results. In this example, an experimental approach would entitle us to conclude unambiguously that any differences in student achievement observed between the two types of schools had been caused by the difference in their approaches to teaching reading.

If the experimental approach allows for unambiguous interpretation and the correlational approach does not, it would seem sensible to always opt for the experimental approach and thereby avoid any controversy about what the data say. Unfortunately, it is not that simple. For many questions about teaching and learning, it is not possible to do an experiment. Either the situation does not allow the researcher to control the relevant variables or control can be achieved only by creating such an artificial version of the phenomenon to be studied that the possibility of generalizing from the results of the experiment to the "real world" seems remote. Examining the relative effectiveness of gender-segregated and coeducational classes provides an example of a question that does not easily lend itself to an experimental approach. In particular, it is likely that many students, parents, teachers, and school administrators will feel strongly about whether gender segregation is a good idea or not. This means that it is highly unlikely that they will submit to being randomly assigned to a gender-segregated or coeducational class. And if random assignment is not possible, neither is the experimental approach. In this case, we might need to be content with comparisons among naturally formed classes (i.e., the correlational approach), trying to rule out some of the alternative interpretations by recourse to other statistical or logical means.

In each of the controversies we consider in this volume, we have tried to briefly summarize the empirical data that are available and discussed whether or not these data have helped to fuel the controversy (see the section entitled "Is There Common Ground?"). Much of what we have had to say in this regard hinges on the distinction between the correlational and experimental approaches. We also have made suggestions, when possible, about the studies needed to resolve the controversies, as well as pointing out the difficulties that might be encountered in such studies.

Theoretical Perspectives

Questions can also become controversial because different theories can lead to different answers. The role of theory in advancing scientific understanding is frequently misunderstood. This misunderstanding most often takes the form of a statement (or an attitude) such as "It's only a theory" (meaning "as opposed to a fact or objective truth"). But it would be impossible for any science, including the science of educational psychology, to advance very far without theories. Theories serve three purposes:

1. Theories specify which observations are relevant and which are irrelevant to understanding the phenomena of interest. By way of illustration, consider the task of understanding children's cognitive development. Think of all the things that a child does in his or her very busy day. Although the child engages in many behaviors, not all will be relevant to understanding how his or her cognitive skills develop. We might easily dismiss behaviors such as sneezing, blinking, coughing, giggling, and a host of other seemingly irrelevant behaviors. But what about cases in which the child talks to himself or herself while trying to figure out how a toy works? Or how about the length of time he or she stares at a math problem before beginning to work on it with pencil and paper? For these and a host of other behaviors, theories tell us whether these behaviors are relevant or irrelevant to understanding cognitive development.

2. Theories help to explain the observations that have been collected about the phenomena of interest. In the theory of Jean Piaget, for example, preschool-age children's self-talk (i.e., talking aloud to the self) is relevant to understanding cognitive development because it reflects the child's egocentrism, or self-centeredness. Egocentrism prevents the child from recognizing flaws in his or her reasoning about other people and about problems in the physical world. In Piaget's theory, self-talk is a behavior to be overcome by development and helps to explain the limitations of the preschooler's thinking and behaving.

3. Theories generate predictions that can then be tested by collecting new observations. If the predictions are supported, then we can have more confidence in the theory. If the predictions are not supported, then we must either revise the theory or abandon it. Consider, for example, the explanation of the infant's formation of an attachment to its parent. Behaviorist theories traditionally proposed that the infant "learns" to become attached to its mother, not because of any quality of the mother or infant, but because the mother typically provides food and, thus, comes to have reinforcing properties. One of the predictions of such a theory is that the failure of a mother to provide food should preclude the infant's attachment to her. In fact, this prediction was not supported either by experimental work with nonhuman primates or by correlational studies involving humans. Hence, behaviorist theories have been largely abandoned by researchers seeking to understand attachment.

Although theories serve valuable roles, typically the process of theory testing is a protracted one. Seldom do the results of a single empirical study lead to the rise of one theory and the downfall of another. In part, this is because theories often can be revised to accommodate inconsistent results, although at some point the revisions may become so extensive as to render the theory useless. In addition, different theories often lead their proponents to examine very different sorts of observations (i.e., those depicted as relevant by the theory), which means that direct comparison of the predictions of contrasting theories is sometimes difficult or impossible. Whatever the reasons, the fact is that different theories, each of which attempts to explain the same phenomena (e.g., classroom learning), can coexist and enjoy support, which, of course, ensures controversy. Eventually, however, these controversies will be resolved as evidence accumulates in favor of one theory and against the others.

The role of theory in generating (and resolving) controversy is an important theme throughout this book. In fact, the controversies in Unit 2 of this book are motivated almost entirely by theoretical disputes. The reader will see that often the controversies emerge from the clash of formal theories built within, and explicitly recognized by, a particular academic discipline, such as educational psychology. In some instances, however, the reader will see that the controversy is fueled by informal theories that are held tacitly by the people involved (e.g., teachers, parents, lawmakers) and that are the product of the contexts in which they themselves have lived and grown.

Contextual Influences on the Stakeholders in the Educational Process

Many of the controversies that arise in educational psychology are not the product of vagaries in empirical data or of the existence of competing theories. Instead, many controversies result from contextual influences on the various stakeholders in the educational process (i.e., students, teachers, administrators, parents, civic leaders, and politicians). The late William Kessen, who was a professor at Yale University, was among the first to draw attention to the influence of context on children and on those who care for and study children. He outlined these influences in the provocatively entitled article "The American Child and Other Cultural Inventions," *American Psychologist* (October 1979). Three of Kessen's points are particularly important for understanding the source (and the potential resolution) of many of the controversies considered in the present volume.

1. *Children's lives and development are shaped by the contexts in which they live.* These contexts are multidimensional and can be defined by, among other things, physical variables (e.g., whether or not children are exposed to lead paint through living in an older home), family variables (e.g., whether they live in a two-parent or single-parent home), economic variables (e.g., whether their families are economically disadvantaged or affluent), social variables (e.g., whether they live in a safe or high-crime neighborhood), institutional variables (e.g., whether they are required to attend school or to hold down a job), cultural variables (e.g., parental beliefs and practices related to disciplining children), and historical variables (e.g., whether they happen to live during a time of war or peace). When we think about children attending schools in the United States today, for example, we need to remember that those children are living in very different contexts than were children living during, for example, the early part of the twentieth century. We should also remember—especially as we compare today's students in the United States to those attending schools in other countries—that the contexts for children in the United States may differ in important respects from those of children in Japan or in South Africa. And finally, we should remember that not all children attending U.S. schools today are growing up in precisely the same contexts. Unfortunately, far

too many children come to school carrying the scars of homelessness, abuse, and racial discrimination, scars that may interfere with their ability to derive maximum benefit from the educational opportunities afforded them. In other words, Kessen argued that the diverse circumstances of children's lives—diversity across historical time, across cultures or nations, and even within a culture or nation—can lead to a diversity of outcomes.

Many of the questions considered in this text have arisen in part because of such contextually determined diversity. Concerns about the diversity within any classroom with regard to student background, preparation, and needs have led to a host of questions about whether and how to accommodate such diversity in the classroom. In fact, it is questions of the latter sort that form Unit 1 of this book. Questions about contextually determined diversity have become controversial in part because of empirical data. They also have become controversial, however, because of two other types of contextual influences identified by Kessen.

2. *The views and behaviors of those who care for children are also shaped by the contexts in which they have lived.* By this, Kessen meant that the parents, teachers, community leaders, politicians, and other adults who directly or indirectly influence children's lives are themselves the product of the contexts in which they have lived. As a result, the attitudes they have about the nature of children (e.g., whether children are born inherently willful or inherently loving), about appropriate child-rearing practices (e.g., whether or not children should be spanked), about the developmental outcomes that are optimal (e.g., whether it is better for children to grow into compliant and conforming adults or into autonomous and critical adults), and, of course, about education will differ depending on the contexts of their own lives. In short, the answers that teachers, administrators, civic leaders, and politicians arrive at when faced with questions about education are sometimes determined more by the contexts of their lives than by any formal theory or the results of any empirical investigations.

Many of the questions considered in this text have become controversial precisely because of this type of contextual influence. Consider, for example, the controversy surrounding the inclusion of students with disabilities in classrooms alongside their peers without disabilities (as opposed to being in separate classrooms). For many advocates of inclusion, the issue is rooted in questions about the civil rights of students with disabilities. In fact, these advocates see the issue as the same as that faced in the 1950s and 1960s when racial segregation was battled on the grounds that "separate" social institutions and systems preclude "equal" opportunities.

3. *The views and behaviors of scholars who study children, development, and education are also shaped by the contexts in which they have lived.* Kessen was among the first to chastise education researchers and theorists for their rather "superior attitude"; that is, the assumption that somehow they were immune from the same influences that affect parents, teachers, and the rest of the public, and the assumption that somehow their scientific objectivity transcended historical time and place. Kessen was not simply arguing that scholars have incomplete knowledge and that somehow, as they learn more, they get closer to the truth and less susceptible to contextual influence. Instead, he argued that scholars are people too and that they can never escape the influence of the contexts in which they have lived. Some of the controversies considered in this text have arisen from these types of contextual influence. We see this, for example, in a tendency of researchers to have an almost blind devotion to a particular investigative approach or method of measurement; one in which they see only the advantages and none of the disadvantages.

Throughout this book, we have endeavored to point out various contextual influences on the controversies considered. It is our hope that by doing so, we take a step toward clarifying these influences and thereby move closer to resolving the controversies. Identifying these contextual influences, however, is a difficult and ad hoc process. It is also, of course, a subjective process, shaped by our own contexts. We urge the reader to look critically at the ways in which context shapes the views of the writers of these selections. We urge the reader also to examine how his or her own context may be affecting how he or she regards the data and theories presented in these selections.

Leonard Abbeduto
University of California, Davis

Frank Symons
University of Minnesota

Unit 1

UNIT

Meeting the Diverse Needs of a Diverse and Changing Classroom

*T*oday, *it seems that schools in the United States are being asked to do more and more. Indeed, the scope of education for any individual student is more inclusive than ever before. Schools must now meet not only the needs of students in traditional academic domains, such as mathematics and science, but also the needs they have in the social and emotional domains. At the same time, there has been an increased recognition of the diversity that characterizes the student population and an increased effort to tailor the curriculum to the unique needs of various subgroups. This has led, for example, to separate science and math classes for male and female students in some schools and to calls for greater attention to the disparate academic outcomes often seen for students of different ethnicities and races. Some of these attempts to expand the educational agenda have been legislated, as in the case of the inclusion of students with disabilities in regular classrooms. Other attempts have emerged from changes in the characteristics of the students being served, as in the dramatic increases in ethnic and racial diversity and the widespread availability of digital technologies. These changes in the educational agenda, however, have been fraught with controversy. In the articles of this section, we consider the controversies that have arisen as schools have tried to meet the diverse needs of a rapidly changing classroom.*

Selected, Edited, and with Issue Framing Material by:
Leonard Abbeduto, *University of California, Davis*
and
Frank Symons, *University of Minnesota*

ISSUE

Are Single-Gender Classes Necessary to Create Equal Opportunities for Boys and Girls?

YES: **Frances R. Spielhagen**, from "How Tweens View Single-Sex Classes," *Educational Leadership* (April 2006)

NO: **Kelley King and Michael Gurian**, from "Teaching to the Minds of Boys," *Educational Leadership* (September 2006)

Learning Outcomes

After reading this issue, you will be able to:

- Summarize the achievement differences between male and female students.
- Discuss the views of students who have participated in both single- and mixed-gender classrooms.
- Describe the strategies used to support student learning in single- and mixed-gender classrooms.

ISSUE SUMMARY

YES: Frances R. Spielhagen, a postdoctoral research fellow at the Center for Gifted Education at the College of William and Mary, argues that single-gender classes are viewed as more conducive to learning than are coeducational classes by students, especially younger students.

NO: Kelley King and Michael Gurian argue that coeducational classrooms can be made to be more accommodating to the learning profiles of both boys and girls, and they illustrate this approach through the example of classrooms that became more "boy friendly" through the inclusion of experiential and kinesthetic activities around literacy.

Despite changing attitudes and the enactment of laws designed to ensure that males and females are afforded equal educational opportunities, gender-related differences in academic achievement still exist. In reading and language arts, girls score higher on achievement tests and are less likely to be referred for remedial programs than are boys. In math and science, boys maintain an advantage. Although gender differences in academic achievement are relatively small, and certainly less than the differences observed among males or among females, they are important because of their influence on the career paths available to men and women.

Gender-related differences in academic achievement are due, in part, to the beliefs that children bring to school and to their behavior in the classroom. Importantly, there is considerable evidence that differences in academic preparation and behavior are largely the result of the environment rather than of direct biological influences on development.

Parents are an important part of the environment that serves to push boys and girls down different academic paths. The role of the media has also been much debated. Unfortunately, teachers and the culture of most U.S. schools are at fault as well. Consider the following:

1. In preschool and early elementary school years, the physical arrangement of the classroom often segregates boys and girls and reinforces the differences between them. For example, a pretend kitchen and associated role-playing materials are typically used in a different location than are blocks and other building materials.
2. Teachers attend more to boys than to girls, are more likely to ask boys questions (especially open-ended, thought-provoking questions), and give boys more constructive criticism. Such behaviors are especially evident in traditionally male domains, such as science.
3. Teachers are more tolerant of interruptions from boys than from girls and encourage the latter to wait their turn.
4. Teachers are more likely to provide help to girls during difficult academic tasks, including during experiments and other hands-on science

activities, while encouraging boys to resolve difficulties on their own.

5. Teachers spend more time with girls during reading and language arts classes but more time with boys during math classes.

6. Teachers are less likely to assign girls than similarly achieving boys to high-math-ability groups. In general, girls are less likely than boys to be identified for inclusion in programs for gifted students.

How can schools be reformed to ensure that they help children to break free of gender stereotypes rather than maintain and even exacerbate achievement differences between boys and girls? Much of the debate surrounding the question of reform has focused on the achievement gaps in math and science, which appear to have the greatest potential for limiting career options. Two approaches to reform have been advocated. In the first, and certainly more popular, approach, scholars and policymakers, assuming that coeducational classrooms are a fact of life, have made suggestions for changing the culture and practices of these classrooms. Proponents of the second, more controversial, approach argue that gender-segregated classes are necessary to allow girls or boys the opportunity to learn in a climate that is suited to their characteristics and needs.

The following two selections weigh in on this issue of gender-segregated classes. In the first, Frances R. Spielhagen presents excerpts from interviews with middle-school students. In general, the students support single-gender classes, seeing them as containing fewer distractions and more supports for learning, although an interest in romantic relationships leads older students to "overlook" the shortcomings of coeducational classrooms. In the second selection, Kelly King and Michael Gurian argue that gender-equitable education is possible within the context of a coeducational classroom provided that the curriculum and pedagogical activities are adapted to meet the unique needs and challenges of students of both genders.

YES

Frances R. Spielhagen

How Tweens View Single-Sex Classes

Have you ever heard that saying, 'Time flies when you're having fun?' All-boy classes are fun! James, a 6th grader, cheerfully offered this opinion of the single-sex academic classes at Hudson Valley Middle School.[1] He quickly added, "I will probably want to be with girls when I am in high school."

Melissa, 13, expressed an older adolescent's point of view: "You can say what you want in all-girl classes and not be afraid of being teased, but sometimes we just want to be with the guys."

James and Melissa are part of the majority of students at this middle school in the rural Hudson Valley of upstate New York who have chosen to attend single-sex classes in language arts, math, science, and social studies. Hudson Valley Middle School, a public school whose 600 students come mostly from low-income backgrounds, has offered voluntary single-sex academic classes to its 6th, 7th, and 8th grade students for the last three years. Students remain in mixed groups for nonacademic classes and at lunchtime so they are not isolated from opposite-gender peers. In the first year of this reform, approximately 75 percent of the school's students chose to take single-sex classes; during the last two years, the majority of those students continued with that choice.

As part of my research into single-sex education (Spielhagen, 2005), I interviewed 24 Hudson Valley students a combination of 6th, 7th, and 8th graders who had attended single-sex classes for at least one academic year. Their comments offer insights into the minds of tweens who have sampled single-sex learning. Their perspectives indicate that voluntary single-sex classes can be a viable option for middle school students, but that such arrangements are most effective when classes are designed to address students' developmental needs. The younger students were more likely to find being in a single-sex class a positive experience; as students got older, they expressed more desire to be in mixed classes, even when that choice entailed potential problems.

Why Try Single-Sex Learning?

Concern over state standardized test scores prompted Hudson Valley Middle School to create voluntary single-sex classes. The school hoped that providing an environment free of the distraction caused by mixed-gender social interaction would lead to higher scores.

In the 19th century, single-sex schools were common, especially in grades 7 through 12. However, because classes for girls did not include academic subjects that would lead to higher education, early feminists urged that schools give *all* students access to the entire academic curriculum. Coeducational schools soon became the preferred model of public education, opening the doors to college enrollment for substantial numbers of girls.

Even then, secondary schools continued to maintain single-sex physical education classes until 1975. In that year, the provisions of Title IX (Tyack & Hansot, 2002) specifically forbade separate-gender physical education classes. According to Salomone (2003), many school districts misunderstood Title IX as a ban on all single-sex classes. Either way, emphasis on coeducational physical education classes quickly led to coeducation as the norm for public schools.

Meanwhile, over the last 20 years, education policymakers have noted the need to reverse declines in achievement among both boys and girls. Researchers agree that the middle school years are crucial to forming sound study habits (Clewell, 2002), but they have mixed opinions as to whether a return to single-sex classes would enhance the achievement of young adolescents.

For example, in 1995, Sadker and Sadker claimed that coeducational schools shortchange girls. At the same time, the American Association of University Women (AAUW) endorsed single-sex arrangements as a means of promoting female achievement, particularly in mathematics and science. Within a few years, however, the AAUW (1998) reversed its stance and concluded that single-sex classes could lead to programming decisions that discriminated against girls. In terms of boys, Sommers (2002) believes that single-sex arrangements are advantageous for boys who lag in academic areas, particularly reading and writing.

Listening to Student Voices

From ages 9 through 13, young adolescents experience tremendous physical, emotional, and cognitive development, so it is not surprising that the responses of students with whom I talked varied according to their ages. I asked students about their classroom choices, their perceptions of the classroom environment in single-sex as compared with mixed-gender groups, and their satisfaction level. The majority of the students had positive feelings about single-sex classes, with 62 percent stating that they could focus better without the opposite sex present. In general, the younger the student, the more enthusiastic the praise of the single-sex arrangement.

The 6th Grade Perspective

Sixth grade students' comments revealed a pre-adolescent viewpoint that the behavior of the other sex was a problem. Both boys and girls in 6th grade referred to their opposite-gender peers as "noisy" and "annoying."

James, a slightly built 11-year-old, responded energetically to questions about being in all-boy classes. He admitted that his favorite class was gym "because you get to play games using your skills," but noted that he didn't pay much attention to the girls in the mixed gym classes because he and his friends (all boys) liked to be on teams together. James also said that he felt "more challenged" in his all-boy classes because he enjoyed the competition with other boys:

> I want to try to beat them. I didn't try to beat the girls [when I was in mixed classes] because I didn't think I could beat the top girls, so why bother?

The comments of 6th grade girls reinforced the conventional wisdom that girls experience more freedom in single-sex academic classes, particularly math and science. Alison, 11, said she "loves all-girl classes," especially math classes, because she's "good at math." She emphasized that in all-girl classes, "you don't have to worry about boys making fun of you." Twelve-year-old Becky echoed Alison's concerns about intellectual safety in mixed classes. When asked why she chose all-girl classes, she replied,

> The boys always picked on me because I am smarter than they are. In all-girl classes, the teachers word things better and say them differently. In mixed classes, they say things more simply for the boys.

She added that all-girl classes are fun and the students get more accomplished, even though the girls "get loud and ask too many questions."

7th and 8th Grade Perspectives

Although by 7th grade many students' attitudes had begun to shift toward typically adolescent emotional and social concerns, 7th graders consistently remarked on their ability to focus better in their single-sex classes. Mary, a 13-year-old 7th grader, reported that she had meant to try all-girl classes for just a year but had decided to stay with the arrangement. She reported a definite improvement in her grades, noting that "I can concentrate better. I am not afraid to raise my hand."

Another 7th grader, Nancy, reported that

> In mixed classes, you are too nervous to ask a question and be wrong and the boys might laugh

at you. We get higher grades because we pay attention more and don't get distracted.

On the other hand, Heather, 13, complained that she was in an all-girl class because "my mom decided to torture me." Heather went along with her mother's choice because she was curious. She conceded that she liked the all-girl classes because they made it easier to relate to her girlfriends but added that the situation allowed girls to "help each other with guy problems." Heather was clearly becoming more interested in mixed-gender social pairing. She offered another adolescent insight, noting,

> In some ways it's really nice to be with your friends, but sometimes the girls get catty, and it is hard to get space away from them.

The 7th and 8th grade boys were less enthusiastic than the girls about single-sex classes. Bullying seemed to become more of a problem with only boys present. Danny, 13, noted that he had been curious about all-boy classes, but that after two years in such classes, he planned to choose mixed-gender classes for 8th grade. In the all-boy classes, Danny reported, he could talk more about sports with his friends and "just hang out," but that "boys try to act tougher" in that environment. Eighth grader Jim, also 13, admitted that he had been picked on by other boys in mixed classes in 7th grade, but that mistreatment was worse in the all-boy classes. He explained, "The guys who pick on us would be more interested in impressing the girls" in a mixed-gender group. Jim added that he missed being with his female friends.

What Are the Students Telling Us?

From these tweens' perspective, single-sex classes can clearly contribute to a comfortable yet intellectually challenging middle school experience. Such arrangements work as long as students can choose whether or not to participate.

Students in all grades reinforced the importance of emotional, intellectual, and physical safety perennial concerns in the middle grades. The problem of bullying reared its head among the 7th and 8th grade boys, but the students did not agree on which arrangement might be less bully-prone. However, caution dictates that schools take measures to ensure that a *Lord of the Flies* scenario does not emerge from a policy that keeps boys in the same single-sex grouping during all three years of middle school. Sorting students into different all-male configurations for different years might address this problem.

The overwhelmingly positive responses from the girls in this study suggest that single-sex classes are particularly beneficial to middle school girls. Even 8th grade girls supported the notion that greater concentration is possible in all-girl classes. As the girls grew older, they became more assertive about their interest in boys. Unlike the boys, however, they expressed a feeling of bonding with their female classmates and enjoyed discussing issues about boys together.

Students experienced the distraction presented by the opposite gender in different ways as they grew older. Younger kids complained about the noisiness of their opposite-sex peers, whereas older students simply referred to the social distractions of having the opposite sex in their classrooms. However, older students loudly and clearly stated their preference for facing those distractions.

Offering Multiple Options

Turning Points 2000 (Jackson & Davis, 2000), a landmark document on middle school reform, recommended that middle schools organize learning climates that promote intellectual development and shared academic purpose. According to the students in my study, single-sex classes in public middle schools support these goals. *Turning Points 2000* also called for middle schools to offer multiple options to students. Hudson Valley Middle School displays innovative programming by restricting single-sex classes to the academic core courses so that students can experience the benefits of both single-sex classes and day-to-day interaction with students of the other sex. Offering subject-specific single-sex classes in each grade might provide even more flexibility, as long as the curriculum remains identical for both genders.

Providing optional single-sex environments for young adolescents with the existing public middle school framework would offer cost-effective school choice for parents, involving them as stakeholders in the education of their children. For many tweens, single-sex classes provide an enviable situation in which learning time flies because students are having fun.

Note

1. All names in this article are pseudonyms.

References

American Association of University Women. (1998). *Separated by sex: A critical look at single-sex education for girls.* Washington, DC: Author.

Clewell, B. (2002). Breaking the barriers: The critical middle school years. In E. Rassen, L. Iura, & P. Berkman (Eds.), *Gender in education* (pp. 301–313). San Francisco: Jossey-Bass.

Jackson, A., & Davis, G. (2000). *Turning points 2000: Educating adolescents in the 21st century.* New York: Carnegie Corporation.

Sadker, M., & Sadker, D. (1995). *Failing at fairness: How our schools cheat girls.* New York: Simon & Schuster.

Salomone, R. (2003). *Same, different, equal: Rethinking single-sex schooling.* New Haven, CT: Yale University Press.

Sommers, C. (2002). Why Johnny can't, like, read and write. In E. Rassen, L. Iura, & P. Berkman (Eds.), *Gender in education* (pp. 700–721). San Francisco: Jossey-Bass.

Spielhagen, F. (2005). *Separate by choice: Single-sex classes in a public middle school.* Unpublished manuscript.

Tyack, D., & Hansot, E. (2002). Feminists discover the hidden injuries of coeducation. In E. Rassen, L. Iura, & P. Berkman (Eds.), *Gender in education* (pp. 12–50). San Francisco: Jossey-Bass.

FRANCES R. SPIELHAGEN is an associate professor of education at Mount Saint Mary College.

**Kelley King and
Michael Gurian**

 **NO**

Teaching to the Minds of Boys

Boys who don't read or write as well as we'd like come in all kinds. There's Garrett, who's perpetually in motion, his fingers drumming the desk. He's not focusing on his reading and pokes the student in front of him. He's becoming a discipline problem. There's Jared, who stares into space, failing to fill more than a few short lines with words. There's Dan, who turns in rushed and sloppy work and receives failing grades. When it comes to fulfilling the kinds of assignments that we call "literacy," boys are often out of their chairs rather than in them.

At Douglass Elementary School, in Boulder, Colorado, a significant literacy gap existed among the 470 students. On the 2005 Colorado State Assessment Program (CSAP), boys attending Douglass underperformed the girls in grades 3–5 (the boys' scores ranged from 6–21 points lower, with a 13-point gap overall). Because boys represented at least half the student population at every grade level—and 75 percent of the special education population—it was clear that the gender gap had powerful implications for the school as a whole and for the futures of the students.

In looking closely at these statistics, the staff suspected that Douglass was not alone in facing classrooms full of boys who were not learning to read and write as well as the girls were. In fact, all over the world boys are struggling in school, with lower grades, more discipline problems, more learning disabilities, and more behavior disorders than girls (Gurian & Stevens, 2005). As experienced teachers of boys, as parents of sons, and as professionals charged with solving a specific and compelling problem, the educators at Douglass went to work. They discovered that recent brain research backed up many of their intuitions about gender and learning styles (see Gurian, Henley, & Trueman, 2001).

By introducing more boy-friendly teaching strategies in the classroom, the school was able to close the gender gap in just one year. At the same time, girls' reading and writing performance improved.

On the Colorado State Assessment Program, Douglass Elementary students experienced an overall net percentage gain of 21.9, which was the highest achievement gain of any school in the Boulder Valley School District. Moreover, Douglass reversed the typical trend of girls outperforming boys: The boys experienced a 24.4 percentage point gain in reading and writing; the girls a 19 percentage point gain, which constituted three times the gain of girls

in other district elementary schools. Most remarkably, Douglass special education students achieved 7.5 times the average gain for this population of students in the district, coming in with a 50-point gain.

A Look Into Boy-Friendly Classrooms

How did Douglass manage these successes? Using a theory developed by one of the authors (Gurian et al., 2001; Gurian & Stevens, 2005), the school analyzed the natural assets that both girls and boys bring to learning (see "The Brain: His and Hers," p. 59). Douglass realized that its classrooms were generally a better fit for the verbal-emotive, sit-still, take-notes, listen-carefully, multitasking girl. Teachers tended to view the natural assets that boys bring to learning—impulsivity, single-task focus, spatial-kinesthetic learning, and physical aggression—as problems. By altering strategies to accommodate these more typically male assets, Douglass helped its students succeed, as the following vignettes illustrate.

Increasing Experiential and Kinesthetic Learning Opportunities

Today's assignment in Mrs. Hill's 4th grade class is to arrange words and punctuation marks into a sentence that makes sense and is grammatically correct. Instead of relying on worksheets or the overhead, which might have bored students like Alexander, the teacher directs the students to arrange cards representing the sentence parts across the classroom floor. The task-oriented discussion and interaction, the physical movement, and the orientation in space access the boys' neurological strengths, keeping them energized and attentive. Alexander and his group are working hard to complete their grammatical challenge before the other groups do.

These male-friendly elements have also energized the girls. Many of them like a good debate, competition, and moving around.

Supporting Literacy Through Spatial-Visual Representations

Across the hall in Mrs. Johnston's 3rd grade classroom, the students are writing. Timothy has great ideas and is always trying to please, but at the beginning of the year, he had great difficulty writing even a single paragraph. Formulating his ideas into well-organized thoughts, coupled with sitting still and the fine-motor task of writing, often overwhelmed him. His mother testified to his frequent meltdowns at home.

Realizing the need for nonverbal planning tools, especially in males, to help bridge the gap between what students are thinking and what they're able to put down on paper, Mrs. Johnston now asks Timothy and his classmates to create storyboards, a series of pictures with or without words that graphically depict a story line. The pictures on the storyboard prompt the brain to remember relevant words, functioning for these learners as first-stage brainstorming. Now when Timothy writes, he describes what he has previously drawn and then adds to that foundation. His spatial-visual assets are helping him to write.

Letting Boys Choose Topics That Appeal to Them

Although parents and educators are quick to point out to students the more practical relevance of reading—you need to read to get through high school and college so you can get a job—this kind of reasoning works more readily for girls than for boys. Said one 6th grade boy, "The only reading that's a *must* is reading what's on the computer or in a football manual. There's no point in reading a book for pleasure."

Many teachers are familiar with this kind of response. Boys often seem to think that what they read in language arts class is irrelevant. Mrs. Vanee decided to innovate in this area. In her 2nd grade classroom, most of the boys read and write about such topics as NASCAR racing, atomic bombs, and football or about such situations as a parrot biting a dad through the lip. Many of the girls write about best friends, books, mermaids, and unicorns.

When asked why he thought he was writing about superheroes whereas Brittany was writing about her best friend, 8-year-old Luke replied, "Because boys have more R-rated minds than girls do," with "R-rated" referring to a preference for aggression scenarios, competition, action, and superhero journeys. Brittany concurred as she rolled her eyes in a "Yes."

Although Mrs. Vanee is aware of the potential for excess here, she now understands how relevant this focus on action and heroism is to males, and she sees that letting boys write on these topics has improved their papers. It has also provided her with numerous opportunities to teach lessons on character, nonviolence, and civility. Moreover, giving students greater choice in what they read and write has improved writing among both boys and girls.

Helping Boys with Homework

One of the primary reasons that some boys get Ds and Fs in school is their inattention to homework. This was true for 5th grader Todd, who generally did his homework in a shoddy way—or not at all.

Douglass teachers now request that parents sign homework assignments. Homework with no signature requires an explanation. This way, the school gets parents involved, encouraging them to supervise homework and cut out distractions that their children may be experiencing, such as TV and video games, until the homework is completed. This policy also keeps parents apprised of the quality of the homework that their child is turning in.

Todd's grades have improved since this policy was started. He's now getting *B*s instead of *D*s on his language arts assignments. His teacher, Mrs. Steposki, is especially vigilant, meeting with him regularly to see whether he's gotten his homework signed and supporting his parents in keeping him focused. Although Todd still doesn't enjoy a lot of his homework—much of it feels like busywork to him—he does feel pride in getting a *B*. "Things are better now," he says.

Offering Single-Gender Learning Environments

One of the innovations that teachers can use in targeted ways in coeducational classes is single-gender grouping. Mrs. Holsted has decided to divide her 2nd grade class today to give the students a choice in reading material. The girls choose several *American Girls* doll books; the boys choose Lynne Reid Banks's *The Indian in the Cupboard* (HarperTrophy, 1999).

Soon the girls are on the floor with a giant piece of chart paper and markers. They label each of three circles of a Venn diagram with the name of a female book character and then they write down adjectives to describe that character. Meanwhile, in the boys' group, Ryan and David are writing lines for a play about the novel they've chosen, happy to be able to act out the battle scene. A lot of what these students need to learn "sticks" because of this approach. Tomorrow, the students will return to their coed groupings, and some will note that they like being back together.

Making Reading and Writing Purposeful

Quite often, boys do their best work when teachers establish authentic purpose and meaningful, real-life connections. In his 4th grade classroom, Mr. Hoyt talks to 10-year-old Clayton about his narrative fiction piece. Clayton doesn't feel the need to do any more work on his D+ paper. When Mr. Hoyt asks who his audience is, Clayton replies, "Just the class and you." "What if you were reading this to someone else?" asks Mr. Hoyt. "Say, a high school basketball player you like?" Clayton ponders this. "Think about an older guy you respect," Mr. Hoyt suggests. "Write this for him to read." Clayton thinks of just the right person—his older brother—and starts the paper over again.

Garrett sits across the room. His real-life project is to draw to scale a map of the school and playground and then annotate it. From there, he'll develop a proposal for a new playground layout and present it to the school's landscape design architect and the playground revitalization committee.

Meanwhile, Greg is designing a Web site on which students can post their writing projects for others to read. In fact, to create a greater sense of the importance of writing, Mr. Hoyt suggested that Douglass Elementary start providing opportunities for all students to share their writing in front of large audiences—at monthly school assemblies, for example. Competition and the opportunity to earn public respect have helped motivate many undermotivated students—especially the boys.

Seeking Out Male Role Models

Douglass Elementary recognizes the special insight and impact of teachers like Mr. Hoyt, who serve as valuable role models for boys. The school actively encourages men to visit classrooms to share their own writing and speak about their favorite books. This is an area in which the school successfully partnered with parents. Several of the students' fathers write professionally as journalists, screenwriters, authors, or lyricists. Appealing to fathers to be role models for literacy has yielded many special guest speakers and several weekly "regulars" in the classroom.

Getting Serious About Gender Learning

There's nothing revolutionary about the strategies that we have suggested. Teachers have already used many of them in their classrooms, but perhaps they haven't used them in an organized and scientific way. Teacher training at Douglass, which focused on the gender learning work conducted by the Gurian Institute, connected brain science to classroom practice. Teachers learned that good science supported many of their personal observations about how boys and girls learn.

By incorporating new theories from gender science into classroom practice, teachers *can* close gender gaps and significantly improve learning. Douglass Elementary school provided the action research that proves just that. But to bring about these improvements, teachers need to ask themselves some key questions:

- As teachers, do we fully understand the challenges that boys face in education today?

- Do we realize that there is a scientific basis for innovating on behalf of both girls and boys as disaggregated groups?
- Does my school incorporate boy-friendly and girl-friendly learning innovations in full knowledge of how essential they are in accommodating the structural and chemical gender differences built into the human brain?
- Do the educators in my school realize that many behaviors typical of either boys or girls are neurologically based?

Although tackling these questions is challenging, acting on what we have learned can lead to rewards for everyone—for teachers, parents, communities, and especially our students.

References

Blum, D. (1997). *Sex on the brain: The biological differences between men and women.* New York: Viking.

Havers, F. (1995, March 2). Rhyming tasks male and female brains differently. *The Yale Herald.*

Gurian, M. (1996). *The wonder of boys.* New York: Tarcher/Putnam.

Gurian, M., Henley, P., & Trueman, T. (2001). *Boys and girls learn differently: A guide for teachers and parents.* San Francisco: Jossey–Bass.

Gurian, M., & Stevens, K. (2005). *The minds of boys: Saving our sons from falling behind in school and life.* San Francisco: Jossey-Bass.

Rich, B. (Ed.). (2000). *The Dana brain daybook.* New York: The Charles A. Dana Foundation.

Sax, L. (2005). *Why gender matters.* New York: Doubleday.

Taylor, S. (2002). *The tending instinct.* New York: Times Books.

KELLEY KING is the former principal of Douglass Elementary School in the Boulder Valley School District, Boulder, Colorado.

MICHAEL GURIAN is a marriage and family counselor in private practice, author, and cofounder of the Gurian Institute, which is nonprofit foundation supporting educational research and training.

EXPLORING THE ISSUE

Are Single-Gender Classes Necessary to Create Equal Opportunities for Boys and Girls?

Critical Thinking and Reflection

1. Summarize the findings from Spielhagen's study of same-sex middle-school classrooms. What are the strengths of the study? What are its weaknesses or limitations?
2. Briefly summarize King and Gurian's suggestions for ensuring a boy-friendly classroom. Do you think that the accommodations suggested for boys may put girls at a disadvantage? Why?
3. Imagine that you are the teacher for an all-boys math class. How would you organize and conduct the class? How would it be similar to and different from the class described by King and Gurian? Why?

Is There Common Ground?

Can we rely on empirical research to decide whether or not single-gender classes ensure that boys and girls have equal chances to succeed in all academic fields? In principle, the answer is yes. It should be possible, for example, to compare the math or science achievement of girls enrolled in girls-only classes to that of girls enrolled in coeducational classes. Do the former have higher achievement than the latter? Does their achievement equal that of boys? In fact, several studies suggest that achievement is higher for girls in single-gender classes than in coeducational classes. See "The Effects of Sex-Grouped Schooling on Achievement: The Role of National Context," by David P. Baker, Cornelius Riordan, and Maryellen Schaub, *Comparative Education Review* (November 1995).

Unfortunately, interpreting such comparisons is often not a straightforward matter because researchers have been content largely with comparisons of "naturally occurring" classes, that is, classes over which they had little or no control in terms of the assignment of students and teachers to classes or the curriculum. As a result, the classes that were compared may have differed in many ways, including in parental beliefs about innate differences between boys and girls, the motivation of the students to master the subject in question, the intensity and content of the instruction, and the extent to which single-gender classes are perceived to have high status or prestige by the community. This makes it difficult to determine whether differences in achievement between girls in girls-only classes and girls in coeducational classes are due to the gender composition of the classes (and the associated

differences in climate) or to one or more of these "confounding" factors. Controlled experiments are needed to show the full impact of single-gender classes on the achievement of girls and boys.

Create Central

www.mhhe.com/createcentral

Additional Resources

Dara E. Babinski, Margaret H. Sibley, J. Megan Ross & William E. Pelham, "The Effects of Single Versus Mixed Gender Treatment for Adolescent Girls with ADHD," *Journal of Clinical Child & Adolescent Psychology* (2013, 42:2, 243–250, DOI: 10.1080/15374416.2012.756814).

Christy Belcher, Andy Frey, and Pamela Yankeelov, "The Effects of Single-Sex Classrooms on Classroom Environment, Self-Esteem, and Standardized Test Scores," *School Social Work Journal* (Fall 2006).

Deborah A. Garrahy, "Three Third-Grade Teachers' Gender-Related Beliefs and Behavior," *The Elementary School Journal* (vol. 102, 2001).

Marlon C. James., "Never Quit: The Complexities of Promoting Social and Academic Excellence at a Single-Gender School for Urban African American Males," *Journal of African American Males in Education* (vol. 1, no. 3, 2010).

Internet References . . .

The Gurian Institute

http://gurianinstitute.com/

American Association of University Women

http://www.aauw.org/

The Myra Sadker Foundation

http://www.sadker.org/

Selected, Edited, and with Issue Framing Material by:
Leonard Abbeduto, *University of California, Davis*
and
Frank Symons, *University of Minnesota*

ISSUE

Should Struggling Students Be Retained?

YES: Jon Lorence and Anthony Gary Dworkin, from "Elementary Grade Retention in Texas and Reading Achievement among Racial Groups: 1994–2002," *Review of Policy Research* (September 2006)

NO: Nancy Frey, from "Retention, Social Promotion, and Academic Redshirting: What Do We Know and Need to Know?" *Remedial and Special Education* (November/December 2005)

Learning Outcomes
After reading this issue, you will be able to: • Articulate the disctinction among grade retention, social promotion, and academic "red shirting." • Describe what the range of alternative is for students failing to achieve at grade level. • Discuss the conflict created by social promotion and academic accountability policy.

ISSUE SUMMARY

YES: Jon Lorence, an associate professor of sociology, and Anthony G. Dworkin, a professor of sociology, both cofounders of the Sociology of Education Research Group at the University of Houston, argue that although the majority of educational researchers contend that making low-performing students repeat a grade is ineffective, careful analysis of primary-grades data from school districts in Texas shows persistent positive effects of retention on academic performance over time.

NO: Nancy Frey, an associate professor of literacy in the School of Teacher Education at San Diego State University, argues that the policy of retention and associated procedures such as social promotion and academic "redshirting," in which there is purposeful delayed entry into kindergarten, are largely flawed with little compelling evidence to support their practice.

"**D**o no harm" is part of the oath taken by practitioners of medicine. Increasingly, the majority of educational researchers and leaders are concluding that the requirement to have academically low-performing students repeat a grade is not only inappropriate, but may, in fact, be a harmful educational practice. When students fail to achieve by the end of a school year, the question is a very basic one to all educators—what should be done for students whose learning and achievement falls well below expectations? Historically and continuing through the present the main options have been either to retain or promote the student. From a professional perspective, organizations such as the National Association of School Psychologists (NASP) view the practice of grade retention as seriously deficient urging "schools and parents to seek alternatives to retention" (NASP, 2003). From a research perspective, educational researchers such as Mantzicopoulos and Morrison writing in the *American Educational Research Journal* (Volume 29, 1992) contend

that "Unlike mixed empirical evidence on other educational issues, research on elementary school nonpromotion [i.e., retention] is unequivocal . . . retention is not an effective policy" (p. 183).

Unfortunately or, perhaps, fortunately, depending on your perspective, there is disagreement among educational researchers and policymakers regarding how compelling the evidence is concerning the deleterious effects of retention for low-achieving students. There is also no firm agreement on alternatives which range from extending the school day to extending the school year to summer school and individualized tutoring. The lack of agreement is based, in part, on little firm evidence one way or the other about effective practice in the face of persistent underachievement, and as suggested by Nancy Frey, the field needs a new generation of studies focusing on the effectiveness of these practices and effective alternatives.

The practice of retention has its roots, at least in part, in the expansive nature of American public education as it progressed from local to mandatory with consequent massive increases in numbers and abilities. One structural adaptation to diversity, predicated by a philosophy of innate individual differences, was ability tracking and homogenous grouping of students. Along with tracking and grouping, retention emerged as a logical outcome for the remediation of students failing to sufficiently achieve the curricular goals for their chronological age and academic level. Partly as a result of tracking and ability grouping, but also because of the practice of social promotion (passing to the next grade level with one's peer despite failing grade-level academic requirements) retention rates dropped slowly but steadily over much of the course of the twentieth century. Near the end of the century, however, rates appeared to be on the rise, most likely tied to emergent policies on no or low tolerance for low achievement brought about by the current accountability movement.

Within the context of accountability, the practice of promoting students a grade level in the absence of academic mastery of grade-level material runs counter to the expectations of many including parents, educators, and policymakers. The movement relies on the implementation of so-called "high stakes" year-end testing determining student achievement of the expected standards. With this movement, as ElizaBeth McCay has pointed out, the issue has once again become dichotomized with the pendulum swinging back to retention applied rigidly in practice despite the lack of widespread support for its use among the educational research community. Another emerging contemporary educational phenomenon worth pointing out, "academic red-shirting," involves the parental practice of voluntarily delaying kindergarten entry. The logic of this practice is rooted in the notion of giving a child a competitive advantage in relation to academic achievement and ultimately high-stakes testing but, to date, there is little evidence it results in its intended effective and some concern about unintended effects, particularly on teacher expectations for kindergarten students.

YES

Jon Lorence and
Anthony Gary Dworkin

Elementary Grade Retention in Texas and Reading Achievement among Racial Groups: 1994–2002

Background

For over two decades public officials, the business community, and other interested individuals have subjected public schools to greater standards of accountability. Beginning with the publication of *A Nation at Risk* (National Commission on Excellence in Education, 1983) and culminating in passage of the No Child Left Behind Act of 2001 (2002), school administrators and teachers have been increasingly forced to address the needs of academically challenged students who struggle to learn an increasing amount of required material. Although there is overwhelming agreement that students failing their courses should be helped, there is little consensus as to which remediation strategies are best for enabling low-performing children to meet new accountability standards. A commonly used practice is to require students who fail a grade to repeat the grade in the next school year. Many educators believe that giving these children an additional year to learn the material they have failed will provide them an adequate foundation to proceed successfully through the remainder of their education. It is often assumed that students will be unable to learn the more advanced material in the next grade if they do not understand the subject matter of the current grade. Therefore, the long-run effect of grade retention should be to improve student academic outcomes. Conversely, researchers in colleges of education contend that making low-performing students repeat a grade is detrimental to their academic achievement. Retention is viewed as ineffective because gains in academic achievement during the repeated year are presumed to be either negligible or quickly fade if they do occur. Instead of requiring a failing student to repeat a grade, most educational researchers contend that it is better to place the child in the next grade, even if the student has not learned all the material required for promotion. Appropriate supplemental instruction during the year of promotion should enable low-performing students to catch up with their classmates who were not experiencing academic difficulty. This practice of "social promotion" is presumed to be more beneficial than grade retention because the child can remain with the same classmates and the student is not perceived as a failure. Proponents of social promotion argue that grade retention only damages the child's self esteem; the child becomes alienated and psychologically withdraws from school. In short, opponents of grade retention contend that making low-performing students repeat a grade is detrimental to their long-term educational progress and will eventually lead to dropping out of school (e.g., Jimerson, Anderson, & Whipple, 2002).

In spite of these warnings about the potential negative consequences of grade retention, given the demand for greater accountability, more state and local school districts have mandated that students in certain grades be held back if they do not meet mandated promotion criteria. For example, the Chicago Public Schools in 1996 ended the practice of social promotion by requiring all students in the third, sixth, and eighth grades to obtain a specified minimum score on the Iowa Test of Basic Skills before moving to the next grade (Roderick & Nagaoka, 2005). Beginning in 2003, Texas required that third graders receive a minimum score on the state's mandated reading test before promotion to grade four. Starting in 2005, Texas fifth graders were required to meet predetermined scores in reading and mathematics before being allowed to proceed to the sixth grade. Because the implementation of high-stakes testing promotional standards has been relatively recent, few educational systems have sufficient data to evaluate the impact of grade retention on academic performance. With few exceptions, almost all of the research assessing the impact of grade retention on academic achievement has pertained to teacher-initiated retention. That is, teachers and principals use their own judgmental criteria to make the decision to retain a pupil, rather than being forced to make students repeat a grade largely on the basis of a standardized test score. The current article focuses on the patterns of academic achievement among academically challenged students who were either retained or socially promoted at the discretion of their teachers and principals. We examine whether the effects of teacher-initiated grade retention vary across racial/ethnic groups. An investigation of the variables predicting grade retention is also presented. We first briefly summarize the literature on the academic impact of making students repeat a grade. A description of the data and analytical strategy to be used then follows. After presenting the findings we speculate on their implications for educational policy.

From *Review of Policy Research*, vol. 23, no. 5, 2006, pp. 999–1005, 1010, 1011, 1014, 1016, 1021, 1026–1033 (tables omitted). Copyright © 2006 by Policy Studies Organization and American Political Science Association. Reprinted by permission of Wiley-Blackwell.

Prior Findings Regarding the Effect of Grade Retention

Conflicting Conclusions

The overwhelming consensus among researchers in colleges of education is that requiring low-achieving students to repeat a grade is an inappropriate educational practice. To illustrate, Mantzicopoulos and Morrison (1992, p. 183) contend that "Unlike mixed empirical evidence on other educational issues, research on elementary school non-promotion is unequivocal. It supports the conclusion that retention is not an effective policy." Some opponents of grade retention argue that "retention worsens rather than improves the level of student achievement in years following the repeat year" (Shepard & Smith, 1990, p. 88). These strong beliefs about the ineffectiveness of grade retention are primarily derived from two reviews examining the impact of making students repeat a grade. Two meta-analyses are frequently cited as definitive studies that demonstrate that requiring low-performing students to repeat a grade is a futile educational practice. Holmes (1989) aggregated findings from 63 separate retention studies from 1960 to 1987. More recently, Jimerson (2001) reviewed 22 research articles published largely during the 1990s. Both authors concluded their summaries demonstrated that requiring students to repeat a grade is an ineffective strategy to improve student learning. However, Alexander, Entwisle, and Dauber (2003) questioned the conclusions from both the Holmes and Jimerson meta-analyses and argued that a large number of the retention studies were flawed, resulting in erroneous interpretations based on "bad science."

Whereas Alexander et al. (2003) pointed out general shortcomings of the literature examining the effect of grade retention, Lorence (2006) systematically examined the individual published studies pertaining to educational achievement that compose the two major meta-analyses on the retention literature. His reexamination of the retention literature utilized multiple criteria to assess the quality of the listed studies. Published studies were assumed to be of higher quality than unpublished convention papers, master's theses, or dissertations. The extent to which research designs controlled for rival hypotheses was also assessed by examining the comparability of matched students or the use of statistical controls. The basis of comparisons (usually age or grade) between retained and nonretained students was also investigated. Comparability in the measurement scales of tests given to promoted and retained pupils was assessed when evaluating the impact of making students repeat a grade. The size of samples and their effect on statistical power were also considered in the evaluation of the meta-analysis papers. On the basis of these criteria, Lorence (2005) found the methodological adequacy of the vast majority of studies cited in the Holmes (1989) to be highly suspect. Only 10 of the 63 retention studies Holmes cited had been subjected to

a peer review process. Of these, six studies lacked appropriate controls for initial differences between retained and promoted students prior to retention. These studies did not have initial measures of student outcomes or did not statistically adjust for earlier indicators of student ability when students were retained. Results from the four studies that had more adequate controls for initial differences in abilities between students prior to retention were mixed. Two studies (Dobbs & Neville, 1967; Niklason, 1987) concluded against making low-performing students repeat a grade, but the extent of initial similarity between promoted and retained students was uncertain. Further, same-age comparisons were made that likely biased the results in favor of the promoted students who had covered an additional year of more advanced material. Conversely, two studies which controlled for student differences existing prior to retention found that the academically challenged students who repeated a grade outperformed their socially promoted peers (Chansky, 1964; Peterson, DeGracie, & Ayabe, 1987). The sample sizes were so small in the ten studies Holmes cited that statistical significance could not be reached even if the retained students obtained higher achievement scores than the promoted students. In only one of the ten studies was there more than 100 retained or promoted pupils. Contrary to the assertions of those who cite the Holmes meta-analysis to support their criticism of making students repeat a grade (e.g., Heubert & Hauser, 1999, p. 129; Shepard, 2000), there is no overwhelming body of evidence in the Holmes review showing that grade retention is an ineffective strategy to assist academically struggling students.

Many of the shortcomings observed in the Holmes review also pervade Jimerson's (2001) meta-analysis. Although Jimerson summarized 18 published studies examining academic achievement, few studies adequately adjusted for initial differences between retained and non-retained students. In addition, the sample sizes were so small in several studies that insufficient statistical power did not allow authors to reject a null hypothesis of no difference between retained and socially promoted students when retained pupils surpassed the academic performance of the promoted students. Even if low-performing retained students caught up with promoted students, most researchers concluded that making students repeat a grade was ineffective because the authors assumed that the retained pupils should outperform their nonretained classmates. Like the Holmes meta-analysis, Jimerson's review of grade retention studies does not conclusively demonstrate that retention is an ineffective remediation practice. However, one panel study meeting acceptable research standards analyzed academically challenged economically disadvantaged minority children in the Chicago Public Schools during the 1980s. Reynolds (1992) found that low-performing students who repeated a grade did no better than socially promoted students who were also struggling with school. Alternately, several studies indicated that making students repeat a grade seemed to boost their test scores or grades, at least temporarily (e.g., Alexander, Entwisle, & Dauber, 1994; Pierson & Connell, 1992). More recent retention studies of comparable research quality also indicate that retained students obtained higher test scores than low-performing socially promoted students (Jacobs & Lefgren, 2004; Karweit, 1999; Lorence, Dworkin, Toenjes, & Hill, 2002; Pomplun, 1988).

That researchers disagree on the impact of making low-performing students repeat a grade can also be illustrated by comparing the findings from two studies based on almost identical data from the Chicago Public Schools. Analyses by Jacobs and Lefgren (2004) suggest that making academically challenged Chicago elementary school students repeat third grade increased their academic achievement, but children repeating sixth grade obtained no benefit from retention. Conversely, Roderick and Nagoaka (2005) use the same set of test scores, but conclude that making students repeat third grade had no effect on test scores. Moreover, students who failed the required standardized sixth grade test and repeated the grade experienced less academic growth than their promoted counterparts. The different conclusions are unexpected because both analyses utilized a regression discontinuity design by examining students just below and above the preset cutoff criteria for promotion to the next grade. A partial explanation for the divergent conclusions may be that the two studies used somewhat different subsets of Chicago elementary children. Jacobs and Lefgren excluded students who were placed in special education whereas Roderick and Nagoaka kept special education students in their analyses. Another possible reason for the dissimilar findings is that the two studies used different procedures to gauge academic achievement. Jacob and Lefgren incorporated the initial third grade test scores during the base year prior to retention as a control variable. Roderick and Nagoaka, however, compared observed test scores after grade retention with predicted test scores derived from growth curve models of academic achievement beginning in first grade. The latter two authors believe their method better controls for regression to the mean artifacts; that is, the low-performing third graders who were retained had likely fallen below their true level of academic ability. Roderick and Nagoaka suggested that the positive effect of retention Jacobs and Lefgren reported was not attributable to repeating a grade, but instead occurred as a result of the retained children naturally rising back to their true levels of ability.

Contrary to the conventional wisdom among educational researchers, there is no overwhelming body of scientifically sound evidence demonstrating that making academically challenged students repeat a grade is ineffective or harmful to academic achievement. With only a few exceptions, the vast majority of studies that conclude that retention is an ineffective educational practice contain so many limitations that inferences from them are highly questionable if not unwarranted. It appears that, among the more methodologically sound studies, some find that grade retention may improve academic achievement while others report repeating the same grade has little effect, or may even result in negative educational outcomes. It appears as though the research findings evaluating the impact of making students repeat a grade are as inconclusive as they were in Jackson's (1975) seminal review of grade retention studies over 30 years ago.

The Inequitable Nature of Grade Retention

A major criticism of making elementary school pupils repeat a grade is that factors not directly related to academic performance have been found to be related to the retention decision. Critics of retention argue that children with specific social and demographic characteristics are more likely to be held back regardless of their cognitive abilities. Specifically, race/ethnicity, family social status, and gender have been hypothesized to influence grade progression, independent of student ability. Several studies examining bivariate relationships between social characteristics and nonpromotion show that racial and ethnic minorities exhibit higher probabilities of being retained than white students. For example, Abidin, Golladay, and Howerton (1971) reported that over one-half of the retained first and second graders in a southeastern urban school district were black. Similarly, minority students were overrepresented among nonpromoted students in two Utah school districts (Niklason, 1984). An examination of the National Education Longitudinal Study of 1988 found that retention rates were significantly higher among African American and Hispanic students when compared to whites (Meisels & Liaw, 1993). Jacobs and Lefgren (2004) also noted large percentages of African American and Hispanic students in Chicago have been required to repeat third and sixth grade.

Several of these studies have also suggested that students from lower socioeconomic backgrounds are also more likely to be held back in grade (Abidin et al., 1971; Meisels & Liaw, 1993). Further, these same studies found gender was associated with retention; boys were much more likely to repeat a grade than girls. Many of the earlier studies investigating the impact of student social background characteristics on grade retention, however, did not control for cognitive abilities and levels of academic performance. Analyses of Baltimore and Chicago public school students indicated that neither race nor family economic background were related to the likelihood of being required to repeat an early elementary grade after controlling for student cognitive skill levels and course grades (Dauber, Alexander, & Entwisle, 1993; Reynolds, 1992). But Karweit's (1999) analyses of a large nationally representative sample of first graders revealed that boys were significantly more likely to be held back in first grade than girls. Results from this national data set also indicated that more economically disadvantaged children evidenced higher retention rates, even after adjusting for student reading performance and other possible predictors of nonpromotion.

Critics of grade retention argue that, regardless of the net predictors of retention, requiring minorities to repeat a grade disadvantages them in several ways. Given that grade retention is presumed to be an ineffective remediation strategy, low-performing minority students will continue to fall behind their promoted classmates. Holmes (1989, p. 25) noted that studies suggesting retention was effective were based on white children and did not include black students, thus implying that grade retention will not help minority students. Reynolds (1992) examined only African American students and specifically argued against making minority students repeat a grade because retention would further impede their academic progress. These studies suggest that the effect of grade retention will vary by racial/ethnic group. Insofar as few studies have simultaneously examined the impact of grade retention on racially diverse groups of low-performing children, it is worthwhile to investigate whether students of specific racial/ethnic backgrounds are adversely affected by this educational practice.

The major focus of this article is to assess whether making academically challenged students repeat a grade is an ineffective remediation practice. We present findings from a panel of Texas elementary school children. Previous research on the effects of grade school retention in Texas have been described in reports to the Texas Education Agency, unpublished convention papers, and a book chapter (Dworkin et al., 1999; Dworkin & Lorence, 2003; Lorence, Dworkin, & Toenjes, 2000; Lorence et al., 2002). The findings presented extend our previous published analyses in several ways. First we investigate those factors associated with initial grade retention, a topic not examined in our earlier papers. The new findings are also based on outcome measures of student performance over a greater number of school years, which better enable us to assess the long term effect of grade retention on academic performance. Further, we investigate whether grade retention results in differential effects on student performance across racial/ethnic categories. . . .

To help gauge the possible impact of a bill pending in the state legislature to eliminate social promotion among low-performing elementary school students, the Texas Education Agency (TEA) initially provided anonymous annual individual-level data of all students enrolled in Texas public schools from 1994 through 1998. TEA later supplemented the initial data to include test information from the 1999–2000, 2000–2001, and 2001–2002 school years. A major advantage of the current dataset is that it contains the entire population of Texas public school children over a 9-year period. Most studies of grade retention have been able to examine the academic effects of non-promotion from only a limited number of students over a few years. The Texas state dataset is also large enough to enable comparisons of retention effects across broadly defined racial/ethnic segments of the school population. We focus on student reading performance because scores on the state's standardized reading examination became the basis for third grade retention beginning in 2003. During the academic years examined, the Texas Assessment of Academic Skills (TAAS) Test was required to be taken by all eligible students in the state public school system. We begin with 1994 reading scores because this was the year in which all Texas public school students in grades three through eight and grade ten began to be tested annually in the spring of the academic year.[1]

We analyze only those third grade students who failed the May, 1994 TAAS reading examination (i.e., they did not correctly answer 75% of the 44 questions asked). Following the progress of third graders in the 1993–1994 school year through tenth grade also maximizes the number of comparisons that can be made between retained and socially promoted low-performing students. The focal independent variable is grade retention. We compare the average reading scores of those failing students required to repeat third grade (the experimental group) with that of the socially promoted students who also did not have a passing third grade reading score (the control group). . . .

The percentages of children required to repeat the third grade were somewhat higher among Hispanic and African American students. Although about 50% of the children not exempted from taking the 1994 reading test were boys, boys were overrepresented among children failing to correctly answer 75% of the reading items, the designated passing cutoff. Hispanic and African American low-performing students were much more likely to be economically disadvantaged than non-Hispanic white children. More than three-quarters of the minority children qualified for the federal lunch program, compared to about 36% of the academically challenged non-Hispanic white students. Alternately, the proportion of students classified as being in special education among non-Hispanic whites was almost twice the magnitude of the minority children. Hardly any of the non-Hispanic white and African American students were listed as having difficulty with English, but over one-quarter of the Hispanic children were classified as having limited proficiency in English. . . .

Hispanic and African American boys were slightly more likely to be retained than girls; however, girls had somewhat higher retention rates among the non-Hispanic white students. Children who qualified for either a free or reduced-price lunch were somewhat more apt to be held back another year than children who did not participate in the federally subsidized program. Special education status appeared to be unrelated to grade retention among non-Hispanic white and Hispanic children. But it is noteworthy that African American students classified with a disability were less likely to be held back in grade than black children with no disability. Hispanic children with limited proficiency in English were somewhat less likely to be retained. Their teachers may have believed that the English of the LEP students would improve sufficiently to enable them to pass fourth grade. . . .

Effect of Retention on Reading Performance

We assess the impact of grade retention on academic performance when students were in the same grade. In this comparison, the reading results for the retained students are for the same grade as the socially promoted students; but the reading scores were obtained one year after that of the nonretainees. The socially promoted children are one grade ahead of the third grade repeaters even though both groups of students are of a similar age. Karweit (1999, pp. 43–44) argues that same-grade instead of same-year comparisons (i.e., students are of comparable ages but in different grades) should be utilized to assess the effect of retention. Examining mean differences in academic achievement between students in different grades is inappropriate because the promoted students have covered an additional year of curriculum than the retained students. The socially promoted have had more instruction over newer material and should therefore score higher than the retained students who are one grade behind. Same-grade comparisons are preferred because they capture differences in academic achievement between retained and promoted students who have covered the same material. . . .

After the year of repeating third grade, however, the average 1995 third grade reading score of the retained students (76.6) significantly surpassed the initial 1994 third grade reading score (61.1) of the children placed into grade four. Given that the retained students likely covered the same material twice, it is not surprising that they correctly answered more items at the end of their repeated grade than did the socially promoted low-achieving children who experienced third grade only once. More important is that, in fourth grade the average same-grade reading scores of the retained non-Hispanic white students (68.1) was greater than the fourth grade score of the socially promoted pupils (62.5). With the exception of grades eight and ten, the average same-grade reading scores of the retained third graders were significantly larger than those of the promoted children. Moreover, those non-Hispanic white students who repeated grade three in 1994–1995, on average, began passing the TAAS reading test after being held back in grade; socially promoted third graders, however, did not exceed the required level of proficiency until sixth grade.

A similar pattern occurred for both the Hispanic and African American students. Low-performing third grade students who repeated the grade markedly improved their TAAS reading scores by the end of their retention year. Although reading scores of the retained minority children fell after the year of retention, Hispanic and African American retainees in general correctly answered more questions than the socially promoted students. One exception arose among Hispanic students when in grade six. The retained Hispanic students, on average, slightly missed passing the required reading sixth grade test while the nonretained Hispanic adolescents barely obtained the mean minimum number of correct answers necessary to pass. Even though African American third grade retainees did not obtain average passing reading scores until eighth grade, the students required to repeat third grade usually answered more questions than the socially promoted African American pupils. Although the mean reading scores of the socially promoted African American pupils in sixth and eighth grade were slightly higher than those of the retained third graders. Third grade African American retainees, however, obtained significantly higher scores on the tenth grade reading test than did the nonretainees. . . .

The positive effect of grade retention was replicated within each of the minority groups. Once again, differences in initial ability, gender, special education classification, limited English proficiency, and economic status between the retained and socially promoted third graders were statistically adjusted using an analysis of covariance model. . . . The effect sizes derived from the adjusted mean differences between the retained and socially promoted students reveal that making low-performing minority students repeat a grade is associated with higher reading scores. Third grade retention allows failing students the opportunity to learn material they missed. Not only do the nonpromoted students catch up with the socially promoted pupils, but the mean adjusted reading scores indicate that the retainees evidence higher levels of reading ability in the following grades. As anticipated, the greatest relative gain in reading scores between the nonpromoted and socially promoted pupils occurs during the year of retention. At the end of the second year of third grade, the average reading score of the retained students is over one and one-half standard deviation larger than that of the previous year's third grade mean of the socially promoted. The gap between the retained and promoted third graders decreases somewhat in fourth and eight grades among Hispanic children. However, the retained students obtain reading scores that are statistically larger than their socially promoted counterparts. Moreover, after controlling for initial differences between the two groups, the retained Hispanic students begin passing the state reading test every year after being held back. The socially promoted Hispanic children did not meet minimum passing expectations until the fifth grade.

Among the African American students, retained children pass the reading test sooner than the nonretainees, once initial differences in student performance and other social background characteristics are adjusted. It is only in grade eight that the black pupils held back in third grade do not obtain significantly higher reading scores. Unlike the case for the non-Hispanic whites, Hispanic and African American third grade retainees on average correctly answer 6% more questions than the socially promoted minorities when in grade ten. The average tenth grade reading score of the retained minority third graders is about four-tenths of a standard deviation greater than that of the nonretained students, indicating that the effects of retention persisted during the sophomore year of high school. . . .

Summary and Discussion

Unlike many previous studies on grade retention that conclude that making students repeat a grade results in no academic benefit, the current findings reveal that requiring low-performing students to retake third grade is associated with increased reading performance. After repeating third grade, the reading scores of the retainees surpassed the initial third grade scores and remained comparable to those of the socially promoted. But after controlling for initial differences between the nonpromoted and socially promoted students, the advantage in academic performance became even more pronounced among the retained children. Comparing adjusted same-grade reading scores through six grades after retention revealed that socially promoted pupils lagged behind the reading ability of the retainees. The mean adjusted scores of the retained students were from 0.13 to 0.64 standard deviations larger than those of the socially promoted. Socially promoted students also took an extra grade of school before passing the state reading test. The positive association between retention and reading performance was replicated across the three largest racial/ethnic groups in the state. Making low-performing African American and Hispanic children repeat third grade also helped increase their reading levels when contrasted to test scores of their socially promoted classmates. There is no evidence in the data that making academically challenged children repeat a grade harms their academic progress. Indeed, retention seems to boost the ability of the initially low-performing minority readers over that of the socially promoted African American and Hispanic students who failed the state reading test. . . .

One reason this study found a positive relationship between retention and greater reading performance is that we examined the impact of holding students back a year in only third grade. The impact of retention may vary by specific grade level. For example, Alexander et al. (2003) reported more beneficial effects of retention when students repeated third and higher elementary grades. Children required to repeat first grade did not experience the same levels of achievement growth observed among students retained in later grades. The degree of educational improvement experienced after retention is likely related to the reasons for the retention. Young children are retained in first or second grade because of learning disabilities, emotional immaturity, or behavioral problems (e.g., Abidin et al., 1971; Caplan, 1973; Mantzicopoulos, Morrison, Hinshaw, & Carte, 1989). If children have severe learning problems, making them repeat a grade will probably not help them. Students retained in later grades may not have extensive learning difficulties or behavioral problems because they should have been retained in earlier grades. Children retained in third grade may need only additional exposure to class material in order to meet promotion criteria. Such students may be more likely to benefit from spending an extra year on the curriculum before moving up to the next grade. However,

critics of grade retention often cite studies in which middle school and high school students required to repeat a grade did not benefit from the extra year. Given the large number of low-performing third graders in the 1993–1994 Texas cohort, future analyses will allow us to ascertain the degree to which retention in later grades affects academic performance.

A major explanation for the positive effect of grade retention we observed pertains to the nature of instructional practices that occur during the repeated grade. Critics of grade retention argue that making low-performing students repeat a grade is ineffective because teachers do little to help students, except cover the same material from the previous year. For example, with respect to retention practices in Chicago, Reynolds, Temple, and McCoy (1997, p. 36) state that "Once students are retained, however, they usually get no special help with their schooling. They are often placed in low academic tracks only to repeat the previous year's instruction and ultimately disengage from school." Likewise, Roderick and Nagaoka (2005) report that children retained in the Chicago public schools probably received no additional educational assistance during the year of retention. If students are not given additional instruction to help them learn material missed in the previous year, there is little reason to expect simply repeating the curriculum will enhance student learning outcomes. However, a study based on the Mesa, Arizona, school district suggests that retention was successful when students received extra educational support during the retention year. Teachers prepared individual educational plans to address the academic shortcomings of students who repeated a grade (Peterson et al., 1987). Grade retention was associated with increased school performance under these circumstances.

Although we lack knowledge about the specific educational practices retained children experienced, individual and group interviews with teachers and administrators in the largest Texas metropolitan school districts indicate that children required to repeat a grade were often given considerable extra assistance, for example, more individualized attention and staff tutoring on specific areas of weakness (Hill et al., 1999). Third grade retainees received additional educational support to help them learn material they had failed in the previous school year. Texas students who repeated a grade may have outperformed the socially promoted because of greater access to supplemental educational resources. However, the aforementioned qualitative interviews further revealed that *students failing the TAAS reading test also received the same compensatory educational services provided to the retained children.* Remediation practices apparently did not differ between the low-performing retained and socially promoted students. The additional educational resources provided the socially promoted students may help explain why such a large number of the children failing the state's third grade reading test eventually began passing the TAAS without being retained. Had the learning needs of the socially promoted pupils been ignored, the positive effects of grade retention would likely have been even more pronounced. At a minimum, our findings contradict the negative view that "the effects of retention plus remediation approaches are likely to be disappointing" (McCoy & Reynolds, 1999, p. 295). One of the major limitations of retention research is that little information exists describing the nature of instruction retainees experience. Future studies should attempt to identify the specific curriculums and instructional practices both retained and socially promoted academically challenged students confront after not meeting promotional standards.

The current findings may be viewed as particularly relevant for policymakers, educational administrators, and teachers who must contend with the No Child Left Behind Act of 2001. The federal government's greater emphasis on making all students meet minimum academic standards has forced school districts to consider various strategies to help low-performing students become successful in school. Many states have implemented stringent promotion standards that require failing students to repeat the grade until able to demonstrate proficiency in the required subjects. Our results should not be interpreted to support the position that making poor-performing students repeat a grade will always enable them to catch up with regular performing classmates. In fact, earlier findings (Lorence et al., 2002) indicate that both low-performing retained and socially promoted third graders do not achieve the levels of reading proficiency observed among regular students. Nonetheless, our earlier and present findings suggest that repeating the school year *with* supplemental educational support enabled the failing third grade students to meet promotion standards. Further, the average reading scores of retained third grade students exceeded those of the socially promoted students.

It must be acknowledged that many of the socially promoted children eventually met minimum passing standards. Critics of retention could reasonably argue that promoting students to the next grade and providing them extra instructional support is equally effective. Assuming that the cost of retaining a student is $5,000, the figure usually mentioned by Texas educational administrators, the sum required to retain all of the 38,445 failing 1994 third graders we analyzed would have been slightly over $192 million. The question arises as to whether the cost is worth the benefit, especially when one considers that many of the socially promoted pupils eventually passed the TAAS reading test in later grades. The fact that the reading level of the socially promoted third grade students was one-half of a standard deviation larger than that of the retained children implies that students who answered less than 75% on the third grade reading test can pass later mandatory reading tests. The current findings indicate that the mandatory score for test success leading to annual progression in later grades could be lowered, perhaps to 70 or 65%. The data suggest that using a reading score of 75% correct as a cutoff point for identifying potentially academic failures may be overly stringent. However, we do not conclude that the automatic social promotion of academically challenged students will result in continual academic success. Unreported analyses reveal that about 10% ($n = 3,692$) of the socially promoted third graders were eventually retained prior to ninth grade and another 12% ($n = 4,607$) were required to repeat ninth grade.

Educational researchers (e.g., Darling-Hammond, 1998; Morris, 2001; Shepard, 2002, p. 62) have assumed that grade retention would be unnecessary if teachers correctly addressed students' learning gaps and additional resources like individual reading interventions and supplemental tutoring were made available to low-performing pupils. An examination of recent educational practices in Texas suggests that it may be unrealistic to presume that schools can provide all the services and additional instruction required to prevent retention. Texas elementary school teachers, particularly during the last four years, have used the strategies suggested for helping academically challenged children meet promotion standards. Teachers test their students at the beginning and middle of the academic year to assess areas of weakness and gaps in knowledge. Most third graders who have fallen behind their classmates have access to extended day programs, one-on-one instruction, pull-out programs, supplemental tutoring, summer school programs, and other remediation activities. Even with all of the effort devoted toward helping students progress to the next grade, 2.8% ($n = 8,924$) of the 2002–2003 Texas third graders were not allowed to proceed to the fourth grade (Texas Education Agency, 2004, Table 2). Critics of retention could argue that more money and staff are necessary to prevent students from failing. Our sense is that, unless seriously low-performing students are placed in an instructional setting with a teacher who has only a very limited number of students for the entire year, a small percentage of pupils will likely need to be retained in spite of the Herculean efforts of teachers and support staff. Some students begin the year so far behind their classmates that it will not be possible to raise them to the level of proficiency required for promotion. Many of the interviewed Texas educational personnel mentioned that students who entered Texas public schools after attending schools in other states often lagged behind the knowledge levels of children consistently enrolled in Texas (Hill et al., 1999).

We are doubtful that the current findings pertaining to the academic effects of grade retention and social promotion can be generalized to other states or school districts. It is important to stress that our results occurred within the context of a rigorous state educational accountability system. Not only does TEA require that all eligible students be tested annually, but test results are disaggregated by major sociodemographic categories. Test passage rates of various racial/ethnic and economic groups within individual schools and districts are available to the public and published in local newspapers. Public officials, businessmen, and parents pay particular attention to the percentage of students passing the TAAS in local schools. Consequently, administrators and schoolteachers are under intense pressure to ensure that all students, even those who are struggling, meet minimal levels of competency. It is no longer possible in Texas to ignore the academic performance of minority children and those who are economically disadvantaged. Few of the previous retention studies occurred in a high-stakes educational environment where administrators and teachers were held accountable for the performance of their students. In previous investigations, educators experienced neither positive nor negative consequences for the academic achievement of their pupils. The absence of any incentives for helping academically challenged students may also partially explain why students who repeated a grade demonstrated minimal, if any, improvement in school performance. Teachers could largely overlook children having trouble learning because there were no consequences for the educators. However, implementation of the No Child Left Behind Act of 2001 has resulted in the greater prevalence of disaggregated test results by various demographic groups across all states. Thus, the Texas results on grade retention may become less of an exception. As other states implement more rigorous accountability practices, researchers will have the opportunity to investigate whether retention, when contrasted to social promotion, yields the same sustained academic benefits observed among retained third grade children in Texas.

Note

1. Test scores are identified by the spring of the academic year. For example, test results from the spring of 1994 occurred in the 1993–1994 academic year.

References

Abidin, R. P., Golladay, W. M., & Howerton, A. L. (1971). Elementary school retention: An unjustifiable, discriminatory, and noxious educational policy. *Journal of School Psychology, 9*(4), 410–417.

Alexander, K. L., Entwisle, D. R., & Dauber, S. L. (1994). *On the success of failure: A reassessment of the effects of retention in the primary grades*. New York: Cambridge University Press.

Alexander, K. L., Entwisle, D. R., & Dauber, S. L. (2003). *On the success of failure: A reassessment of the effects of retention in the primary grades* (2nd ed.). New York: Cambridge University Press.

Bali, V. A., Anagnostopoulos, D., & Roberts, R. (2005). Toward a political explanation of grade retention. *Educational Evaluation and Policy Analysis, 27*(2), 133–155.

Campbell, D. T., & Kenny, D. A. (1999). *A primer on regression artifacts*. New York: Guilford Press.

Campbell, D. T., & Stanley, J. C. (1966). *Experimental and quasi-experimental designs for research*. Chicago: Rand McNally.

Caplan, P. J. (1973). The role of classroom conduct in the promotion and retention of elementary school children. *Journal of Experimental Education, 41*(3), 8–11.

Chansky, N. M. (1964). Progress of promoted and repeating grade 1 failures. *Journal of Experimental Education, 32*(3), 225–237.

Cohen, J. (1988). *Statistical power analysis for the behavioral sciences* (2nd ed.). Hillsdale, NJ: Erlbaum.

Darling-Hammond, L. (1998). Alternatives to grade retention. *The School Administrator, 55*(7), 18–21.

Dauber, S., Alexander, K. L., & Entwisle, D. R. (1993). Characteristics of early retainees and early precursors of retention in grade. *Merrill-Palmer Quarterly, 39*(3), 326–343.

Demaris, A. (1992). *Logit modeling: Practical applications*. Sage University Paper Series on Quantitative Applications in the Social Sciences, No. 07–086. Newbury Park, CA: Sage.

Dobbs, V., & Neville, D. (1967). The effect of nonpromotion on the achievement of groups matched from retained first graders and promoted second graders. *Journal of Educational Research, 60*(10), 470–475.

Dworkin, A. G., & Lorence, J. (2003). *Eight year longitudinal analyses of elementary school retention and social promotion in Texas: A final report*, prepared for the Texas Education Agency. Houston, TX: University of Houston, Department of Sociology.

Dworkin, A. G., Lorence, J., Toenjes, L. A., Hill, A. N., Perez, N., & Thomas, M. (1999). *Elementary school retention and social promotion in Texas: An assessment of students who failed the reading section of the TAAS*, prepared for the Texas Education Agency. Houston, TX: University of Houston, Department of Sociology.

Eide, E. R., & Showalter, M. H. (2001). The effect of grade retention of educational and labor market outcomes. *Economics of Education Review, 20*, 63–76.

Hauser, R. M. (1997). Indicators of high school completion and dropout. In R. M. Hauser, B. V. Brown, & W. R. Posser (Eds.), *Indicators of children's well being* (pp. 152–184). New York: Russell Sage Foundation.

Hauser, R. M. (2001). Should we end social promotion? Truth and consequences. In G. Orfield & M. Kornhaber (Eds.), *Raising standards or raising barriers? Inequality and high stakes testing in public education* (pp. 151–178). New York: Century Foundation.

Heckman, J. J. (1978). Dummy endogenous variables in a simultaneous equation system. *Econometrica, 46*(4), 931–961.

Heckman, J. (1979). Sample selection bias as a specification error. *Econometrica, 47*(1), 153–161.

Heubert, J. P., & Hauser, R. M. (1999). *High stakes: Testing for tracking, promotion, and graduation*. Washington, DC: National Academies Press.

Hill, A. N., Lorence, J., Dworkin, A. G., & Toenjes, L. A., Perez, N., Thomas, M., & Segvig, D. (1999). *Educational practices applied to Texas elementary students retained in grade,* prepared for the Texas Education Agency. Houston, TX: University of Houston, Department of Sociology.

Holmes, C. T. (1989). Grade level retention effects: A meta-analysis of research studies. In L. A. Shepard & M. L. Smith (Eds.), *Flunking grades: Research and policies on retention* (pp. 16–33). London: Falmer Press.

Hong, G., & Raudenbush, S. W. (2005). Effects of kindergarten retention policy on children's cognitive growth in reading and mathematics. *Educational Evaluation and Policy Analysis, 27*(3), 205–224.

Jackson, G. B. (1975). Research evidence on the effects of grade retention. *Review of Educational Research, 45*(4), 613–635.

Jacobs, B. A., & Lefgren, L. (2004). Remedial education and student achievement: A regression-discontinuity analysis. *The Review of Economics and Statistics, 86*(1), 226–244.

Jimerson, S. (2001). Meta-analysis of grade retention research: Implications for practice in the 21st century. *School Psychology Review, 30*(3), 420–437.

Jimerson, S., Anderson, G. E., & Whipple, A. D. (2002). Winning the battle and losing the war: Examining the relationship between grade retention and dropping out of high school. *Psychology in the Schools, 39*(4), 441–457.

Karweit, N. L. (1999). *Grade retention: Prevalence, timing, and effects* (Report No. 33). Baltimore: Johns Hopkins University, Center for Research on the Education of Students Placed at Risk.

Lorence, J. (2006). Retention research revisited. *International Education Journal, 7*(4).

Lorence, J., Dworkin, A. G., & Toenjes, L. A. (2000). *Longitudinal analyses of elementary school retention and promotion in Texas: A second year report,* prepared for the Texas Education Agency. Houston, TX: University of Houston, Department of Sociology.

Lorence, J., Dworkin, A. G., Toenjes, L. A., & Hill, A. N. (2002). Grade retention and social promotion in Texas, 1994–1999: Academic achievement among elementary school students. In D. Ravitch (Ed.), *Brookings papers on education policy 2002* (pp. 13–52). Washington, DC: Brookings Institution.

Mantzicopoulos, P., & Morrison, D. (1992). Kindergarten retention: Academic and behavioral outcomes through the end of second grade. *American Educational Research Journal, 29*(1), 107–121.

Mantzicopoulos, P., Morrison, D, Hinshaw, S. P., & Carte, E. T. (1989). Nonpromotion in kindergarten: The role of cognitive, perceptual, visual-motor, and demographic characteristics. *American Educational Research Journal, 26*(1), 107–121.

McCoy, A. R., & Reynolds, A. J. (1999). Grade retention and school performance: An extended investigation. *Journal of School Psychology, 37*(3), 273–98.

Meisels, S. J., & Liaw, F. (1993). Failure in grade: Do retained children catch up? *Journal of Educational Research, 87*(2), 69–77.

Morris, D. R. (2001). Assessing the implementation of high-stakes reform: Aggregate relationships between retention rates and test results. *National Association of Secondary School Principals Bulletin, 85*(629), 18–34.

National Commission On Excellence in Education. (1983). *A nation at risk: The imperative for educational reform.* Washington, DC: U.S. Government Printing Office.

Niklason, L. B. (1984). Do certain groups of children profit from a grade retention? *Psychology in the Schools, 21*(4), 485–499.

Niklason, L. B. (1987). Nonpromotion: A pseudoscientific solution. *Psychology in the Schools, 24*(4), 339–345.

No Child Left Behind Act of 2001, 20 U.S.C. § 6301 (2002).

Peterson, S. E., DeGracie, J. S., & Ayabe, C. R. (1987). A longitudinal study of the effects of retention/promotion on academic achievement. *American Educational Research Journal, 24*(1), 107–118.

Pierson, L., & Connell, J. P. (1992). Effect of grade retention on self-system processes, social engagement, and academic performance. *Journal of Educational Psychology, 84*(3), 300–307.

Pomplun, M. (1988). Retention, the earlier the better? *Journal of Educational Research, 81*(5), 281–287.

Reynolds, A. J. (1992). Grade retention and school adjustment: An explanatory analysis. *Educational Evaluation and Policy Analysis, 14*(2), 101–121.

Reynolds, A. J., Temple, J., & McCoy, A. (1997, September 17). Grade retention doesn't work. *Education Week,* p. 36.

Roderick, M., & Nagaoka, J. (2005). Retention under Chicago's high-stakes testing program: Helpful, harmful, or harmless? *Educational Evaluation and Policy Analysis, 27*(4), 309–340.

Rosenbaum, P. R., & Rubin, D. B. (1984). Reducing bias in observational studies using subclassification on the propensity score. *Journal of the American Statistical Association, 79*(387), 516–524.

Rosenbaum, P. R. & Rubin, D. B. (1985). Constructing a control group using multivariate matched sampling methods that incorporate the propensity score. *American Statistician, 39*(1), 33–38.

Schwager, M. T., Mitchell, D. E., Mitchell, T. K., & Hecht, J. B. (1992). How school district policy influences grade level retention in elementary schools. *Educational Evaluation and Policy Analysis, 14*(4), 421–438.

Shepard, L. (2000). Cited in Ending social promotion by Debra Viadero. *Education Week on the Web.* (March 15, 2000). . . . .

Shepard, L. (2002). Comment on grade retention and social promotion in Texas, 1994–1999: Academic achievement among elementary school students. In D. Ravitch (Ed.), *Brookings papers on education policy 2002* (pp. 56–63). Washington, DC: Brookings Institution.

Shepard, L. A., & Smith, M. L. (1990). Synthesis of research on grade retention. *Educational Leadership*, *47*(8), 84–88.

StatCorp. (2001). *Stata statistical software: Release 7.0.* College Station, TX: Stata Corporation.

Texas Education Association. (2004). *Grade-level retention in Texas public schools, 2002–2003.* (Document No. GE05 601 01). Austin, TX: Author.

Vella, F. (1998). Estimating models with sample selection bias: A survey. *Journal of Human Resources, 33*(1), 127–169.

Winship, C., & Morgan, S. L. (1999). The estimation of causal effects from observational data. In K. S. Cook & J. Hagan (Eds.), *Annual Review of Sociology*, Vol. 25 (pp. 659–707). Palo Alto, CA: Annual Reviews.

Jon Lorence is associate professor at the University of Houston. His research interests include determinants of academic achievement, teacher effectiveness, characteristics of effective schools, and educational measurement.

Anthony Gary Dworkin is Professor of Sociology at the University of Houston, where he has been on the faculty since 1973. He received an A.B. degree in sociology and psychology from Occidental College (Los Angeles, 1964), M.A. and Ph.D. degrees in sociology from Northwestern University (1966 and 1970, respectively). Dr. Dworkin's teaching and research have been in the areas of the sociology of education and race/ethnic relations, as well as sociological theory and quantitative research methods.

Nancy Frey

 **NO**

Retention, Social Promotion, and Academic Redshirting: What Do We Know and Need to Know?

"**H**eld Back." "Repeating." "Left Back." These euphemisms are used by adults to soften the blow to a child of being retained in grade. "Flunking" is the term used by children themselves to describe retention, an event so feared that they report they would rather "wet in class" than be retained (Byrnes & Yamamoto, 1985). Both the policy and the practice of retention of a child who is deemed to be faltering academically or socially are fraught with hopes for the best and fears of the worst.

The decision to retain a student has repercussions that extend well beyond the repeated year. However, educators, parents, and politicians have also criticized *social promotion* (i.e., the practice of sending a student to the next grade level despite his or her failing to achieve expectations) as anachronistic in an era of standards, school reform, and high accountability. Increasingly common among parents—especially more affluent ones—is the practice of delaying entry into kindergarten, referred to as *"academic redshirting."* This article provides a review of the history of retention and social promotion in the United States. Furthermore, longitudinal studies on the rates of retention, the characteristics of students who are most likely to repeat a year of schooling, and the academic and social effectiveness of retention are discussed. By extension, the association of retention and dropping out of high school is examined. The prevalence of delayed kindergarten enrollment is examined. Thus, the purpose of this article is to examine the aims of the teaching profession in the effort to determine what needs to occur next when a child fails to live up to expectations. Recommendations for future research are discussed.

The History of Retention

The history of retention as an educational practice for the remediation of students who fail to achieve has its roots in the schoolhouses of mid-19th-century America (Holmes & Matthews, 1984). Schools were first legislated in Massachusetts in 1647 to ensure that children learned to read the Bible as the way to thwart the devil (the "Ould Deluder" law), so that "learning may not be buried in the graves of our fathers in the church" (Monaghan & Barry, 1999, p. 4). Because settlements were small and likely to be distant from one another, children of all ages were taught as a single class in a one-room schoolhouse. Morality as a democratic ideal and religious mandate was emphasized over reading excellence; therefore, uncertain readers were merely absorbed into the classroom community. In fact, children were often taught to read and write at home, before they ever attended school—literacy acquisition per se was not regarded as a function of schooling (Pulliam & Van Patten, 1995).

As the population of the new nation increased in the 1800s, schools shed some—but not all—of their religious trappings in favor of education as a means of equalizing citizens and reorienting immigrants to the philosophy of democracy (Pulliam & Van Patten, 1995). Despite the shift away from religious training, schools changed little in their service delivery model, although the slightly larger schools could now afford to expand to two rooms—primary and secondary (Pulliam & Van Patten, 1995). Compulsory education was still a policy in only a few communities—never for African Americans, and rarely for girls or any children older than 10. Students who failed to achieve might simply withdraw from school to work on the family's behalf (Mondale & Patton, 2001).

The arrival of the Industrial Revolution and the influx of immigrants and freed slaves from the defeated South after the Civil War both fundamentally changed education and gave rise to the practice of retention. Compulsory education was founded to supply the educated workers needed to staff the factories and mills (Mondale & Patton, 2001). At the same time, the population in urban areas was growing rapidly, and schools became bigger. The increased enrollment allowed schools to specialize both in what was taught and in how it was taught. Thus, subjects like geography, history, and spelling were added to the curriculum, and children were placed in graded classrooms according to their chronological age (Pulliam & Van Patten, 1995). At the same time, the expansion of compulsory education laws and a new era of pluralism brought previously disenfranchised groups to the schoolhouse door—especially freed slaves, immigrants, and girls. For the first time, schools were organized in a physical and curricular layout that left some children behind.

The emergence of the philosophy of social Darwinism and the science of psychology in the latter half of the

From *Remedial and Special Education*, vol. 26, no. 6, November/December 2005, pp. 332–346. Copyright © 2005 by Hammill Institute on Disabilities and Sage in association with American Rehabilitation Counseling Association (ARCA). Reprinted by permission via Rightslink.

19th century ushered in a new set of beliefs about how people learn. Herbert Spencer's theory of social Darwinism set the stage for beliefs about "survival of the fittest" as a sociocultural phenomenon, not merely a biological mechanism of evolution (Hofstadter, 1955). In the meantime, William James was expanding the new science of psychology and promoting the perspective that all human thought could be constructed as conscious behavior. His influential *Talks with Teachers* (James, 1899) brought psychology into the classroom and fueled the emerging discipline of teacher education. . . .

The coupling of a renewed philosophy of difference among humans, based on purported scientific logic, and a pedagogy of learning driven by teacher stimulus and student response set the stage for retention as a widespread practice. All that was missing for retention to emerge was a way to further quantify and rank students. At the turn of the century, intelligence testing provided a mechanism for this.

The influence of intelligence testing on education is seen particularly in the way that intelligence scores (Binet & Simon, 1916) were used. The scientific approach to standardized measurement and evaluation of perceived ability was further evidenced in curriculum and instruction of reading and language arts through the establishment of practices of homogeneous grouping of students based on these assessments (Wheat, 1923). For example, in the New York City public schools, "Binet classes" were created for "the educationally retarded"—those students with IQ scores between 75 and 95 (Gates & Pritchard, 1942). Binet's original intent with intelligence testing had been to identify those children in need of specialized educational supports, not to use it as a device for irreversibly segregating low-performing students (Binet, 1969). Furthermore, Binet viewed intelligence not as a fixed and permanent construct but, rather, as one that could be influenced by instruction (Binet & Simon, 1916). The use of an "intelligence quotient" (so named because the student's chronological age is the denominator to compute an IQ score) to segregate students and limit their school and vocation options is an American idea, promoted chiefly by H. H. Goddard and Lewis Terman (Gould, 1996). Indeed, Goddard, the director of the Vineland (NJ) Training School for Feebleminded Boys and Girls, saw the use of IQ testing and subsequent placement of low-achieving students in proper vocations suitable for their abilities as the highest form of democracy. . . .

Terman held similarly strong opinions about the necessity of segregating low-achieving students and appeared to see segregation as a means to preserve a democratic way of life. He stated that segregated school placements of low-achieving students were necessary, and that without such educational engineering, low achievers would "drift easily into the ranks of the anti-social or join the army of Bolshevik discontents" (Terman, 1919, p. 285).

By some estimates, retention rates in the early part of this century were nearly 50%, and 20% of all students left school by eighth grade (Holmes & Matthews, 1984; Johnson, Merrell, & Stover, 1990). Retention had clearly become the intervention of choice for those who did not achieve. Many educators were alarmed with the high rates of failure among schoolchildren. The Russell Sage Foundation commissioned a study on "backward children" (the terminology then used to describe students who were past the age for their grade level), and the resulting work, *Laggards in Our Schools* (Ayres, 1909), made a case for differentiating expectations among students in order to foster their success. Ayres, a statistician and former superintendent, exposed school success figures that were tainted by unreported high retention and dropout rates.

Studies over the next 2 decades advocated homogeneous grouping within and across classrooms as an instructional arrangement that allowed the presentation of different material for high- and low-achieving students, although not all educators saw this as an improvement (Dewey, 1998). This pattern of grouping is perhaps most familiar from the practice of forming three reading groups within a class—the so-called "bluebirds, redbirds, and buzzards" plan. Although the overuse of homogeneous groups has also fallen into disfavor (e.g., Cunningham, Hall, & Defee, 1998), a positive outcome of homogeneous grouping in classrooms was a corresponding decline in retention rates from the 1930s through the 1960s (Johnson et al., 1990).

In the latter half of the twentieth century, interest in the efficacy and effects of retention has spurred research on policy and on the associated attitudes connected to the practice of nonpromotion. Determining the extent to which retention is used, and whether multiyear trends can be identified, has been a challenge.

Rates of Retention

The rate and number of students who are retained each year have been difficult to ascertain, in part because the method to collect these data has varied widely between districts and states. However, some reliable statistics can be projected from the various longitudinal studies conducted over the last decade. . . .

Retention Studies Focused on Primary Grades

A nationally representative sample of 9,240 students was tracked by the Center for Research on Students Placed At Risk at Johns Hopkins University from their entry in first grade in the fall of 1991 until the spring of 1994. During this span of 3.5 years, 18.4% of these students had been retained at least once (Karweit, 1999). Similar results were obtained in a smaller study of 190 children from the Minnesota Mother–Child Interaction Project, who have been studied for 21 years, since their mothers enrolled in a prenatal health clinic. By third grade, 16.8% of the cohort had been retained at least once (Jimerson, Carlson,

Rotert, Egeland, & Sroufe, 1997). It is important to note that the cohort from this study differs from that of the first study, as the families enrolled in the program qualified due to low income levels.

Multiyear Retention Studies

Since 1994, 120,000 seventh- to twelfth-grade students from 132 high schools in 80 communities have been participating in the National Longitudinal Study of Adolescent Health. This comprehensive study is examining influences on adolescent health behavior, including those in the home, school, and community. A stratified sample of 12,118 students from this database participated in a survey concerning aspects of their school life. Resnick et al. (1997) reported that 21.3% of all students had been retained at least once in their school career.

When the focus of a longitudinal study is on low-income, minority children, the retention rate is even higher. The Chicago Longitudinal Project has followed 1,164 children enrolled in Chicago public schools since 1986. These students were selected based on their socioeconomic status (SES) and ethnicity; 95% of the cohort is African American and 5% Hispanic. By the spring of 1994, when their age cohort had reached the eighth grade, 28% of the sample had been retained at least once (McCoy & Reynolds, 1999). Although individual studies vary in terms of the percentage of children retained in grade, they have consistently reported that the overall rate of retention hovers around 20% (Holmes & Saturday, 2000).

Rising Retention Rates

The yearly rate of retention appears to be rising, perhaps spurred by higher levels of accountability and the proliferation of "zero tolerance" policies regarding achievement in schools. The Center for Policy Research in Education reported in 1990 that 6% of schoolchildren were retained each year. In 1992, the annual rate of retention in the United States had nearly doubled to 11.1% (McMillen & Kaufman, 1993); by 1995, it had risen to 13.3% (Bureau of the Census, 1995). The National Association of School Psychologists has reported that grade retention has increased by 40% in the last 20 years (Dawson, 1998).

The proliferation of state policies that mandate high-stakes testing in order to progress to the next grade appears to be shifting the patterns of retention. Historically, the majority of retention events have occurred in kindergarten through third grade (Meisels & Liaw, 1993). However, a recent survey of 16 southern states revealed that the most common grade for retention is now ninth grade (Southern Regional Education Board, 2001). It has been suggested that this growth in ninth-grade retention rates is linked to high-stakes testing in tenth grade in these same states (Haney, 2001). Given the growth in retention rates in the early 1990s and the unavoidable lag in reports of statistical information, it is possible that studies released over the next 5 years will push these numbers even higher.

Who Is Retained?

Rates of retention appear to be related to gender, ethnicity, SES, and parental characteristics.

Ethnicity

Ethnicity has been identified as a predictor of retention. A large-scale study, the National Education Longitudinal Study of 1988 (NELS '88), followed 24,599 eighth-grade students from 1,000 schools. At the time of the study, it was the most comprehensive federal longitudinal study of its kind. Meisels and Liaw (1993) used the data from NELS '88 to analyze the characteristics of the students retained. Whereas the overall retention rate was 19.3% for all students, 29.9% of African Americans and 25.2% of Hispanics were held back, compared to only 17.2% of their European American peers (Meisels & Liaw, 1993). When gender and ethnicity are analyzed together, the variance increases. For example, the unbalanced range of retention rates in one study ranged from a low of 24% for White girls to a high of 47% for Hispanic/Latino boys at the end of eighth grade (Alexander, Entwisle, & Dauber, 1994). Using census data, Roderick (1995) reported a similar disparity at the end of ninth grade, ranging from a low of 15.8% for Hispanic girls to a high of 52% for African American boys.

Gender

The role of gender has been recognized as a factor in retention for at least 30 years (Abidin, Golladay, & Howerton, 1971; McCoy & Reynolds, 1999). In the South, boys are twice as likely to be retained as girls (Southern Regional Education Board, 2001). Similar figures have been derived from national studies. For instance, in the NELS '88 study, 24% of boys were retained, whereas only 15.3% of girls repeated a grade (Meisels & Liaw, 1993). Although it is not clear why boys are retained at higher rates, Meisels and Liaw have speculated that there may be a mismatch between expectations of school behavior and the typical development of male children. Another study probed the attitudes and beliefs of retained first-, third-, and sixth-grade boys and girls in an ethnically diverse community in the Southwest. Byrnes (1989) found that these children believed that retention was a punishment and felt stigmatized by it; 43% of the girls and 19% of the boys would not disclose to the researcher that they had been retained, even when directly questioned. Meisels and Liaw's (1993) evaluation of the NELS '88 data also confirmed the unique vulnerability of girls to the negative emotional effects of retention, which they speculated might be due to the need for affiliation and the establishment of identity.

Socioeconomic Status

Poverty is also a powerful predictor of retention. By some estimates, children from poor households are two to three times more likely to be retained (Southern Regional Education Board, 2001). The socioeconomic status (SES) of the students from the NELS '88 study was significantly related to retention: 33.9% of the students were in the lowest SES quartile, whereas only 8.6% lived in households from the highest SES quartile (Meisels & Liaw, 1993). The relationship between low SES schools and high rates of retention was confirmed in a study of 33 districts from the Council of Great City Schools (Gastright, 1989) and in an evaluation of retention patterns in Miami–Dade County, Florida (Morris, 2001). Nevertheless, in a 5-year analysis of retention rates in a midwestern school district with high-, middle-, and low-SES elementary schools, Gurewitz and Kramer (1995) found that individual differences in student performance could not account for disparate retention rates, and that middle SES schools had the highest retention rate. They theorized that low-SES students in middle-SES schools may appear more conspicuous. Other studies have further affirmed the compounded risk for those students who possess multiple predictive factors—especially African American boys living in poverty (Dauber, Alexander, & Entwisle, 1993).

Parental Factors

Characteristics of parents were found to be a factor influencing retention in several studies. In the aforementioned Minnesota Mother–Child Interaction Project, parent IQ, as measured by the *Wechsler Adult Intelligence Scale* (WAIS; Wechsler, 1997), was found to be significant at the $p < .05$ level, with mothers of retainees scoring lower on measures of cognitive functioning than the mothers of the promoted group. The researchers also reported that parent involvement at school was "the best predictor of children's promotion or retention status" (Jimerson et al., 1997, p. 21). This finding is consistent with the Chicago Longitudinal Study (Miedel & Reynolds, 1998). It is often assumed that all parents are aware of the type of literacy involvement that is expected of them. However, Lapp, Fisher, Flood, and Moore (2002) found that many low-income parents are not aware of this necessity, nor do they view early literacy training as their job. They do not believe that they have the knowledge or skills to assume this responsibility and, in fact, are concerned that they "might teach it wrong" (p. 275).

Exogenous factors—that is, variables present before the start of school—appear to weigh heavily on who is retained. In particular, boys, African American and Hispanic students, and students living in poverty (especially in urban environments) are most likely to be required to spend an extra year in school. This has raised concerns from educators, families, and policymakers, who have asked whether retention is effective.

Is Retention Effective?

A discussion of the effectiveness of retention as a practice for assisting students who do not achieve either academically or socially in a manner similar to their peers requires an explanation of the methodological limitations that have plagued some studies. The methodologies used in many retention studies have been criticized as flawed. Several researchers have analyzed dozens of early retention studies and found that many were too short in duration or lacked comparison groups (Holmes & Matthews, 1984; Jackson, 1975). The meta-analysis of Holmes and Matthews (1984) calculated effect sizes for 18 studies that did use a comparison group and found that retained students were significantly negatively affected, both academically and emotionally. In another meta-analysis, Holmes (1989) looked at 63 studies that met nominal research standards and found that 54 of them reported negative effects of retention. However, the dearth of rigorous studies highlighted the need for the examination of long-term effects of retention. Several longitudinal studies mentioned earlier in this article have attempted to do this, although limitations persist. A closer look at two such studies, the Minnesota Mother–Child Interaction Project and the Chicago Longitudinal Study, illustrates the current approaches to retention research.

Minnesota Mother–Child Interaction Project

The 190 children participating in this project were identified as at risk because of family poverty. One of the many purposes of the study was to determine the long-term effects of student retention in kindergarten through third grade. The 104 participants identified for the retention studies attended 120 different elementary schools (due to family mobility), and the results were published when the cohort was 10, 12, 14, 16, and 21 (Jimerson et al., 1997). Each student in the cohort was placed into one of three groups—never retained, retained once during primary grades, or socially promoted. However, it is important to note that these were comparison groups but not matched groups. Yearly achievement assessment batteries; interviews with teachers, mothers, and children; and measures of social and emotional well-being were conducted.

The researchers found that there were no significant differences between retained children and their socially promoted peers on achievement and intelligence measures. However, the two groups differed on behavioral, peer relation, and emotional measures. The researchers speculated that "perhaps retained children are perceived as poor students in large part because of their behavior in the classroom, since their school achievement does not distinguish them, but their behavior is distinctive" (Jimerson et al., 1997, p. 20).

The children from the Minnesota Mother–Child Interaction Project were followed throughout their high school years. Initially, retained students seemed to benefit in mathematics achievement, but this effect had disappeared by middle school (Jimerson & Schuder, 1996). No difference was found for reading comprehension or overall achievement, although retainees did continue to compare negatively to the rest of the cohort in both behavior and emotional health (Jimerson et al., 1997). Significantly, 52% of the socially promoted students graduated from high school, whereas only 24% of the retained students did the same (Jimerson & Schuder, 1996).

Chicago Longitudinal Study

Another series of studies is related to the Chicago Longitudinal Study, which followed 1,164 low-income children who had attended a preschool program from their entrance in kindergarten through age 14. Of these children, 296 had been retained once and 19 had multiple retentions. Besides analyzing data for predictors and demographics as discussed earlier, the researchers focused on academic outcomes, especially reading and mathematics, as measured by the *Iowa Test of Basic Skills,* a norm-referenced test with internal consistency coefficients of .92 and .95, respectively (McCoy & Reynolds, 1999). Regression analysis and matched comparison samples were used to control for differences between the groups. . . .

[T]he difference in scores between retained and nonretained students was 9.5 points ($p < .001$). By extension, early retention (Grades 1–3) had a greater effect on reading achievement than later retention (Grades 4–7). Similar results were obtained for mathematics achievement, with a difference of 8.9 points after multiple regression ($p < .001$).

The results of the Minnesota and Chicago studies have contributed to the knowledge base first analyzed by Jackson (1975) and Holmes and colleagues (Holmes, 1989; Holmes & Matthews, 1984). The use of a longitudinal approach has provided insight into the effects of retention across the years. These outcomes are useful as a lens to discuss other, more limited studies that nonetheless have yielded similar results, especially as they apply to nonacademic effects, high school dropout data, and adult outcomes.

Nonacademic Effects

In addition to academic achievement, grade retention apparently can be damaging to the social and emotional development of children, especially as it relates to personal adjustment. For example, the perception of school self-concept, as measured by a survey of 12 items, was more positive among retained students in the 1992 Chicago study (Reynolds, 1992), although this effect had vanished by the time the students reached age 14 (McCoy & Reynolds, 1999). However, delinquency, as measured by school discipline reports, was not associated with retention (McCoy & Reynolds, 1999).

In contrast, the retained children in the Minnesota project demonstrated significantly more behavior problems and lower peer acceptance than nonretainees. Other studies have examined the opinions held by students, teachers, and peers. In a study of third- through sixth-grade students in an urban center in New York, retained students scored lower than their peers on cognitive competence, defined as "beliefs that they can control academic outcomes, . . . that they have what it takes to do well in school, . . . and what it takes to execute those strategies" (Pierson & Connell, 1992, p. 301). These beliefs may persist in high school as well. An inquiry of secondary students in a rural New York community found that those who had been retained showed lower educational expectations for themselves, more disruptive behavior, less impulse control, and an external locus of control when compared to a group of matched-ability peers who had not been retained (Hagborg, Masella, Palladino, & Shepardson, 1991). . . .

High School Dropout Rates

A frequently quoted finding about retention concerns its association with dropping out of school. Indeed, retention and high school dropout are correlated (Rumberger, 1987; Rush & Vitale, 1994). Much of the evidence for this relationship has been documented in longitudinal studies like the ones discussed earlier. Another notable study is the federal High School and Beyond (HS&B) study, a project that was conducted as part of the larger NELS '88 research. HS&B followed a nationally stratified cohort of 30,030 students from 1,015 schools who were sophomores in 1980 through the end of the study in 1992. One aspect of the study included the examination of dropout rates. Among the cohort, researchers found that whereas the overall rate of dropout was 12.4%, the dropout rate jumped to 27.2% for retainees—leading the researchers to assert that retainees were twice as likely to drop out as students who were never retained (Barro & Kolstad, 1987). They also evaluated age in grade level and its correlation to dropping out. The modal age for entering ninth graders is 14.5 years, and, in this study, students entering at age 15 to 15.25 were twice as likely to subsequently drop out of high school. The figures are even more striking for those students entering at age 15.5 or above—the expected age for those who have been retained once in their educational career. These students were found to be three times as likely to drop out before completing high school (Barro & Kolstad, 1987), and these calculations remained consistent across gender and ethnicity groups.

Adult Outcomes

The groups from the Minnesota Mother–Child Interaction Project were again examined at the age of 21 (Jimerson, 1999). In addition to the continuation of academic and adjustment paths identified in the 1997 study, education and employment outcomes were also studied. Retainees were most likely to drop out of school (69%) compared to the low-achieving, nonretained group (46%) and the control group (29%) and were the least likely of the three groups to pursue postsecondary schooling. Furthermore, their average hourly pay at the age of 20 was adversely affected: Retainees averaged $6.59, versus $8.42 and $8.57 for the low-achieving and control groups, respectively, and these differences were statistically significant. Indeed, the comparison (low-achieving nonretained) group was found to be statistically similar to the control group on measures of postsecondary enrollment and employment, including "employment competence (stability, quality, commitment, and status of employment)" (Jimerson, 1999, p. 262).

The postschool outcomes for the retained students should be considered cautionary. An older study of adults who had been retained in school revealed that they were more likely to be incarcerated, abuse drugs and alcohol, and receive welfare than those that were never retained (Royce, Darlington, & Murray, 1983). Jimerson (1999) suggested that when students are retained in the early grades, a trajectory of likely negative outcomes is triggered, and that "numerous factors conspire toward its continuation" (p. 248). Nevertheless, other factors, such as the behavioral and social adjustment differences noted early in the lives of the Minnesota children, could also contribute to this trajectory.

The evidence gathered in the last 30 years on the practice of retention suggests that it is academically ineffective and is potentially detrimental to children's social and emotional health. The seeds of failure may be sown early for students who are retained, as they are significantly more likely to drop out of high school. Furthermore, the trajectory of adverse outcomes appears to continue into young adulthood, when wages and postsecondary educational opportunities are depressed.

Is Social Promotion the Answer?

In 1983, the National Commission on Excellence in Education released its report, *A Nation at Risk,* which reported on the quality of teaching and learning in America's schools. The report described a "rising tide of mediocrity" (p. 2) and charged educators and legislators with improving America's schools through the establishment of standards of learning.

No other educational reform in the last decade has changed the face of education like the standards movement. Forty-nine of the nation's 50 states have adopted academic content and performance standards in an effort to articulate exactly what is expected of public school students (Iowa remains the only state without a standards document). The algorithm of establishing standards in education is so deeply ingrained that in recent years, standards have also emerged for teachers (National Board for Professional Teaching Standards), administrators (Principal Leadership Standards of Excellence), paraprofessionals (Paraprofessional and School-Related Personnel Standards), and parent involvement (National Parent–Teacher Association). Clearly, the use of standards as a vehicle to communicate expectations to educators has become a standard itself.

The practice of *social promotion*—advancing a student to the next grade level when she or he has not mastered all of the content for the previous grade—has come under attack as a practice that dilutes the excellence of learning available in the public school system. Social promotion had been a popular practice through the 1970s (Kelly, 1999) and was now reconstrued as a by-product of the "soft-headed, open education, child-centered curriculum" of the era (Shepard & Smith, 1989, p. 1). By the mid-1980s, public opinion polls indicated that the general public felt strongly (72%) that promotion to the next grade level should be contingent on mastery of grade-level requirements (Shepard & Smith, 1989).

States and districts quickly responded and began instituting strict retention policies to make social promotion much more unlikely. The widely touted Promotional Gates Program was created in New York City in the 1980s as a mandatory end to social promotion. Competency levels were established, and students who did not pass were sent to special classes with an enrollment cap of 20, specially trained teachers, and new materials (House, 1989). The program was disbanded after 2 years because the $40 million dollar cost yielded no appreciable achievement gains (House, 1989). Despite the failure of this program, modified versions of it have been recreated in Chicago (Chicago Panel on School Policy, 2001); Washington, DC; Milwaukee; Denver; Long Beach (Kelly, 1999); and San Diego (San Diego Unified School District, 2001). Programs such as these have been criticized as being more about public relations than about scholarship (House, 1989). Meanwhile, the political rhetoric surrounding social promotion increased in the 1990s, and social promotion was even mentioned in the 1998 State of the Union Address: "When we promote a child from grade to grade who hasn't mastered the work, we don't do that child any favors. It is time to end social promotion" (Clinton, 1998). This renewed attention to social promotion prompted 17 states to create specific policies banning social promotion as an option (Thomas, 2000).

Although the practice of social promotion has been the subject of debate in and out of educational circles, the research on low-achieving children who are socially promoted to the next grade level is sparse. No data on social promotion are kept by states, and the U.S. Department of Education (1999) has described social promotion as "a hidden problem" (p. 6). Social promotion is commonly viewed as half of a bimodal choice, with retention being the only other option. Therefore, much of the research on social promotion is indirect and confined to the comparison groups of large studies on retention. The results of achievement measures by the comparison groups can be extrapolated to provide some evidence of the effect of social promotion. For example, Holmes (1989) performed a meta-analysis of 63 studies that included a low-achieving, nonretained subgroup in the research design. He reported that retained students averaged 0.33 standard deviations below their socially promoted peers on measures of academic achievement and personal adjustment. Furthermore, he asserted that these findings were limited because, in these studies, the socially promoted groups did not receive any remediation. Similarly, Reynolds (1992) found that at the end of fourth grade, a socially promoted subgroup had gains of 8 months in reading and 7 months in math over their similarly achieving but retained peers, despite receiving no additional intervention. Important to note, the retained students performed below the socially promoted group even though they had an extra year of schooling. These findings have not been supported by other, smaller studies that reported no achievement differences between retained and socially promoted students (Johnson et al., 1990; Westbury, 1994). It is important to note that the Johnson et al. study employed a research design that favored social promotion because it did not use a matched sample but, rather, compared retained and nonretained students. In a study of 74 third through sixth graders, Pierson and Connell (1992) found no differences between retained and socially promoted students in self-worth, cognitive competence, and effort, although they did find that retained students outperformed their promoted peers in academic performance. . . .

The research on the effectiveness of social promotion has been thin, and the extrapolated results show limited benefits to the practice. A phase of high accountability coupled with content and performance standards has made social promotion a thorn in the side of administrators and educators who are attempting to raise achievement through higher expectations for all learners. Therefore, the practice and policy of retaining low-performing children has been used as an alternative to promoting students who have not met competency standards.

Voluntary Retention— "Academic Redshirting"

Prevalence

Whereas social promotion and retention continue to occur at alarming levels nationally, late kindergarten enrollment has emerged among parents and educators seeking to mitigate the harmful effects of either practice. Over the last decade, many young children have been enrolled a year or more after their fifth birthday in the hope of giving them an opportunity to develop early literacy behaviors. In 1995, 9% of all first and second graders had experienced delayed entry into kindergarten, according to the National Household Education Survey (Zill, Loomis, & West, 1997). The parents of these children typically cite one of two reasons for doing so—either the child's birthday occurs late in the year (July through December), making him or her younger than peers, or the child has exhibited less mature behavior (academic or social) than others of the same age. In both cases, the parents hope that their child will benefit from another year of growth and development before entering school. In some instances, the parents may be reluctant to admit that there may be a competitive component to the decision—a hope that their child's physical, emotional, and academic growth may give him or her a comparative advantage over classmates who may be up

to a year younger (Kagan, 1990). For this reason, the purposeful delay of entry into kindergarten to improve future performance is sometimes called "academic redshirting," after the practice of benching college athletes for a year to allow them additional time to refine their skills and build physical prowess. The use of delayed kindergarten entry is so popular that a survey of state education officials estimated that between 10% and 50% of children experience delayed kindergarten enrollment (Gnezda, Garduque, & Schultz, 1991). Although the 50% figure represents an extreme, it is notable as an example of the "groupthink" that can emerge in a community.

The prevalence of academic redshirting is often ascribed to predominantly middle-class, White, suburban communities. Indeed, there is some evidence that children from higher income households are more likely to experience delayed kindergarten entry (Cosden, Zimmer, & Tuss, 1993). Delaying enrollment in school can be burdensome for many families, for school attendance represents childcare as well as education. For some families, this means that the primary caregiver can return to paid employment. The economic impact of keeping a child and the caregiver home an additional year may be prohibitive, and, therefore, lower income families are less likely to delay enrollment (Gredler, 1992).

The socioeconomic status of the family can also play a subtle role in determining whether the child has had preschool experience. A study of a school readiness instrument in Georgia revealed that students who had attended a preschool had higher scores on the instrument, regardless of the type of preschool program (Taylor, Gibbs, & Slate, 2000). Studies over the past 3 decades have found that preschool experience is positively correlated to kindergarten readiness (Gullo & Burton, 1992; Osterlind, 1980–1981). Access to high-quality preschool education has been identified as critical for later school success among children from low-income households (Bruner, 1960; Snow, Burns, & Griffin, 1998). Despite nearly 40 years of research on the importance of affordable preschool education for children of low-income families, the availability of preschool education is variable. Dickinson and Sprague (2001) quoted a Children's Defense Fund study reporting that only 42% of children from households with incomes under $15,000 annually were enrolled in preschool, compared with 65% of children whose parents earned more than $50,000.

However, other studies have found a stronger correlation of delayed enrollment with gender and ethnicity than with wealth or parent educational levels. The National Household Education Survey in both 1993 and 1995 found no correlation with income or education level, although the 1991 survey did (Zill et al., 1997). They found a far stronger correlation to gender—11% of all boys experienced delayed enrollment, compared to 6% of girls, $\beta = .57$, $p < .01$. Furthermore, the child's ethnicity was also a predictor, with White, non-Hispanic children more likely to be academically redshirted than African

American children, β = .50, p < .05. However, Graue and DiPerna's (2000) study of the enrollment data of 8,000 Wisconsin students found somewhat different results. As in Zill et al.'s study, boys constituted the majority of kindergarten redshirts; however, the likelihood of delaying entry for these students seemed more closely tied to summer birthdays that fell just before the cutoff date for enrollment (Graue & DiPerna, 2000).

The data yielded by these surveys are valuable for describing the characteristics of children who experience delayed entry into kindergarten across the nation. However, other researchers studying the impact of readiness tests for kindergarten enrollment have presented different results regarding ethnicity. In many communities, these developmental screenings are administered to all incoming kindergartners, and the parents of those children not scoring high enough are counseled into forgoing enrollment for a year (Meisels, 1999). Many of these "less ready" children come from low-income African American and Hispanic households (Bredekamp & Shepard, 1989; Kagan, 1990). . . .

Kindergarten Readiness Tests

Most of the instruments used for kindergarten readiness are developmental inventories that assess an array of academic, social, and motor behaviors. Skills that are frequently targeted for measurement include the ability to recite one's own name, point to shapes and colors, count, stand on one foot, and tell a story (Lamberty & Crnic, 1994). These developmental screenings are often administered during so-called "kindergarten round-ups"—large meetings where parents have their children tested and registered for the upcoming school year. The predictive validity of such instruments has been called into question (Dever & Barta, 2001; Ellwein, Walsh, & Eads, 1991). Despite position statements from the American Academy of Pediatrics (1995) and the National Association for the Education of Young Children (1990) against the practice of using screening tests to make decisions about kindergarten entrance, it is estimated that one third of all states require such screenings (Cannella & Reiff, 1989). One of the most widely used instruments, the *Gesell Preschool Test,* has been found to be unreliable (Meisels, 1987). A meta-analysis of 60 studies of preschool screening results and their correlation to later student performance found only a small effect size (r = .27, or 10% of the variance) on social and behavioral domains, and a moderate effect size (r = .49, or 25% of the variance) for academic outcomes (La Paro & Pianta, 2000). The authors noted that "factors other than the child's skills (even in the same domain) account for the majority of the variability in academic/cognitive and social/behavioral performance in the early grades" (p. 475). Despite evidence of questionable results from these screenings and their impact on enrollment for African American and Hispanic children, they remain in wide use across the country.

It does not appear that what the Gesell Institute has called "the gift of time"—delayed enrollment—has meaningful positive effects. A comparison study of 314 second graders who had either been retained or experienced delayed enrollment found no significant differences in academic performance (Kundert, May, & Brent, 1995). It is because of results such as these that some critics have described academic redshirting as another form of retention.

A disturbing trend in the growing prevalence of delayed enrollment is its impact on the classroom environment. Undeniably, kindergarten expectations have altered considerably from the days when this first school experience was built around socialization and play experiences. Today's kindergartner encounters a far more academically rigorous experience than his or her parents did (Bracey, 2000). But the presence of older students may be influencing this trend as well. Some educators have charged that the "graying of the kindergarten" has resulted in higher teacher expectations for *all* students, including those who enrolled when first eligible (Meisels, 1992; Shepard & Smith, 1988). Graue and DiPerna (2000) reported that one of the Wisconsin school districts they studied had a redshirt rate of 94%—admittedly an extreme example, but a telling example of how a community can shift expectations for kindergarten without ever enacting a policy. Another concern is the de facto elimination of the natural diversity of the classroom. A homogenization occurs when certain groups of children—predominantly boys, children with later birthdays, or children with low readiness scores—are held out of kindergarten. Savvy parents understand this trend toward increasingly higher academic demands. Evelyn Vuko, education columnist for the *Washington Post,* held an online chat in February 2002 with parents of young children. Nearly 45% of the questions concerned kindergarten enrollment age (Vuko, 2002). Puzzled parents have begun to describe these conversations as the "begindergarten dilemma."

Recommendations: A Call for New Research

The failure of children in the primary grades has caused widespread concern among parents, educators, and researchers, even as enormous financial resources are allocated each year to educating these children. Social promotion—the practice of advancing a low-achieving child to the next grade in the hope he or she will "catch up"—has grown less acceptable to policymakers, even as the few studies conducted have shown little harm resulting from the practice. The growing disdain for social promotion seems to be fueled by political rhetoric rather than by documented student outcomes. Although research on in-grade retention of students who have failed academically (and often socially) is more prevalent, unanswered questions remain. What is clear is that students who have been retained are more likely to be boys, African American, and poor. Retainees are more likely to drop out of school, work at lower paying jobs, suffer from substance abuse problems, and spend time in jail. Despite these dire outcomes, the rates of retention have continued to rise the past decade.

Given the elimination of social promotion policies in many states and the negative outcomes of retention, parents of young children are increasingly opting for a third choice—delayed entry into kindergarten. This practice is associated with more affluent parents, who are not dependent on public school enrollment for childcare. However, as with retention, boys are more likely to be academically redshirted, as are children with late birthdays. It appears that kindergarten screening tests may be a factor in delayed enrollment. These screening instruments, which have been criticized by some researchers as lacking in predictive validity, do not favor students from low-income families. The practice of voluntary retention has resulted in a demographic aging of the kindergarten classroom. In some communities, nearly 50% of entering kindergarten students may be 6 years old on the first day of school (Vuko, 2002), causing some researchers to speculate about the effect on teacher expectations for kindergarten students.

Given the rapid increase in mandatory retention policies and the rising incidence of voluntary retention by parents, the field is in need of a new generation of studies that focus on the effectiveness of these practices. Educators are asking the following questions about effective interventions:

- Which students are best served by retention? Are there students for whom retention should not be considered?
- What are the long-term effects of retention and social promotion over the course of a child's academic career?
- Is social promotion effective for students? Under what circumstances might it be effective?
- Is delayed kindergarten enrollment changing the composition of the kindergarten classroom? Is this resulting in a change in expectations?
- Do children benefit from voluntary retention to delay kindergarten enrollment?
- How do children with disabilities respond to retention, social promotion, and delayed enrollment?
- Which early and ongoing interventions must accompany any of these practices?

These questions are perhaps best answered by the use of some of the methods employed in the Chicago and Minnesota studies. Large-scale, well-matched studies of children possessing a variety of skills and challenges could answer these questions. The aforementioned studies have contributed greatly to our knowledge of these practices. However, children with disabilities and students from a variety of socioeconomic backgrounds have not been studied as closely.

A limitation of this review is that it has not discussed early reading achievement. The body of research on reading acquisition and intervention is sufficiently large to warrant a separate review. It would be useful to the knowledge base to examine factors related to reading and intervention for students who fail to achieve using the lens of retention and promotion. For example, the work of Vellutino and Scanlon (2001) is promising in its emphasis on early intervention to prevent retention.

Retention, social promotion, and academic redshirting have, at one time or another, been called "the gift of time." Perhaps it is time to redefine this cliché. Perhaps the true "gift of time" is in the work of the educational researchers who can answer the questions of teachers, administrators, and parents.

References

Abidin, R. R., Golladay, W. M., & Howerton, A. L. (1971). Elementary school retention: An unjustifiable, discriminatory, and noxious policy. *Journal of School Psychology, 9*, 410–414.

Alexander, K. L., Entwisle, D. R., & Dauber, S. L. (1994). *On the success of failure: A reassessment of the effects of retention in the primary grades.* New York: Cambridge University Press.

American Academy of Pediatrics. (1995). The inappropriate use of school "readiness" tests. *Pediatrics, 95*, 437–438.

Ayres, L. P. (1909). *Laggards in our schools: A study of retardation and elimination in city school systems.* Philadelphia: Russell Sage.

Barro, S. M., & Kolstad, A. J. (1987). *Who drops out of high school? Findings from high school and beyond* (Technical Report no. CS 87–397c). . . .

Binet, A. (1969). *The experimental psychology of Alfred Binet: Selected papers* (R. H. Pollack & M. J. Brenner, Trans.). New York: Springer.

Binet, A., & Simon, T. (1916). *The development of intelligence in children: The Binet-Simon scale.* Baltimore: Williams and Wilkins.

Bracey, G. W. (2000). A children's garden no more. *Phi Delta Kappan, 81*, 712–713.

Bredekamp, S., & Shepard, L. (1989). How best to protect children from inappropriate school expectations, practices, and policies. *Young Children, 44*(3), 14–24.

Bruner, J. (1960). *The process of education.* Cambridge, MA: Harvard University Press.

Bureau of the Census. (1995). *Current population survey.* Washington, DC: Author.

Byrnes, D. A. (1989). Attitudes of students, parents, and educators toward repeating a grade. In L. A. Shepard & M. L. Smith (Eds.), *Flunking grades: Research and policies on retention* (pp. 108–131). New York: Falmer Press.

Byrnes, D., & Yamamoto, K. (1985). Academic retention: A look inside. *Education, 106*, 208–214.

Cannella, G. S., & Reiff, J. C. (1989). Mandating early childhood entrance/retention assessment: Practices in the United States. *Child Study Journal, 19*(2), 83–99.

Chicago Panel on School Policy. (2001). *Initiatives status report: Transition centers.* . . .

Children's Defense Fund. (2003). *Prekindergarten initiatives: Efforts to help children enter school ready to succeed.* . . .

Clinton, W. (1998). *1998 State of the union address: Full text.* . . .

Cosden, M., Zimmer, J., & Tuss, P. (1993). The impact of age, sex, and ethnicity on kindergarten entry and retention decisions. *Educational Evaluation and Policy Analysis, 15,* 209–222.

Cunningham, P. M., Hall, D. P., & Defee, M. (1998). Nonability-grouped, multilevel instruction: Eight years later. *The Reading Teacher, 51,* 652–664.

Dauber, S. L., Alexander, K. L., & Entwisle, D. R. (1993). Characteristics of retainees and early precursors of retention in grade: Who is held back? *Merrill-Palmer Quarterly, 39,* 426–433.

Dawson, P. (1998). A primer on student retention: What the research says. *Communique (Milwaukee, WI), 26*(8), 28–30.

Dever, M. T., & Barta, J. (2001). Standardized entrance assessment in kindergarten: A qualitative analysis of the experiences of teachers, administrators, and parents. *Journal of Research in Childhood Education, 15,* 220–233.

Dewey, J. (1998). Experience, knowledge, and value: A rejoinder. In J. A. Boydston (Ed.), *John Dewey: The later works, 1925–1953* (Vol. 15, pp. 3–90). Carbondale: Southern Illinois University Press (Original work published 1939).

Dickinson, D. K., & Sprague, K. E. (2001). The nature and impact of early childhood care environments on the language and literacy development of children from low-income families. In S. B. Neuman & D. K. Dickinson (Eds.), *Handbook of early literacy research* (pp. 263–280). New York: Guilford.

Ellwein, M. C., Walsh, D. J., & Eads, G. M., II. (1991). Using readiness tests to rout kindergarten students: The snarled intersection of psychometrics, policy, and practice. *Educational Evaluation and Policy Analysis, 13,* 159–175.

Gates, A. I., & Pritchard, M. C. (1942). *Teaching reading to slow-learning pupils: A report on an experiment in New York City public school 500 (Speyer School).* New York: Columbia University.

Gastright, J. F. (1989, March). *The nation reacts: A survey of promotion/retention rates in 40 urban school districts.* Paper presented at the annual meeting of the American Educational Research Association, San Francisco, CA. (ERIC Document Reproduction Service No. ED307-714)

Gnezda, M. T., Garduque, L., & Schultz, T. (1991). *Improving instruction and assessment in early childhood education.* Washington, DC: National Academy Press.

Gould, S. J. (1996). *The mismeasure of man.* New York: Norton.

Graue, M. E., & DiPerna, J. (2000). Redshirting and early retention: Who gets the "gift of time" and what are its outcomes? *American Educational Research Journal, 37,* 509–534.

Gredler, G. (1992). *School readiness: Assessment and educational issues.* Brandon, VT: Clinical Psychology.

Gullo, D. F., & Burton, C. B. (1992). Age of entry, preschool experience, and sex as antecedents of academic readiness in kindergarten. *Early Childhood Research Quarterly, 7,* 175–186.

Gurewitz, S., & Kramer, J. (1995). Retention across elementary schools in a midwestern school district. *Research in the Schools, 2*(2), 15–21.

Hagborg, W. J., Masella, G., Palladino, P., & Shepardson, J. (1991). A follow-up study of high school students with a history of grade retention. *Psychology in the Schools, 28,* 310–317.

Haney, W. (2001, January). *Revisiting the myth of the Texas miracle in education: Lessons about dropout research and dropout prevention.* Paper presented at the Dropout Research Conference, Cambridge, MA.

Hofstadter, R. (1955). *Social Darwinism in American thought* (rev. ed.). Boston: Beacon Press.

Holmes, C. T. (1989). Grade level retention effects: A meta-analysis of research studies. In L. A. Shepard & M. L. Smith (Eds.), *Flunking grades: Research and policies on retention* (pp. 16–33). New York: Falmer Press.

Holmes, C. T., & Matthews, K. M. (1984). The effects of nonpromotion on elementary and junior high school pupils: A meta-analysis. *Review of Educational Research, 54,* 225–236.

Holmes, C. T., & Saturday, J. (2000). Promoting the end to retention. *Journal of Curriculum and Supervision, 15,* 300–314.

House, E. R. (1989). Policy implications of retention research. In L. A. Shepard & M. L. Smith (Eds.), *Flunking grades: Research and policies on retention* (pp. 202–213). New York: Falmer Press.

Jackson, G. B. (1975). The research evidence on the effect of grade retention. *Review of Educational Research, 45,* 438–460.

James, W. (1899). *Talks to teachers on psychology: And to students on some of life's ideals.* New York: Henry Holt.

Jimerson, S. R. (1999). On the failure of failure: Examining the association between early grade retention and education and employment outcomes during late adolescence. *Journal of School Psychology, 37,* 243–272.

Jimerson, S., Carlson, E., Rotert, M., Egeland, B., & Sroufe, L. A. (1997). A prospective, longitudinal study of the correlates and consequences of early grade retention. *Journal of School Psychology, 35,* 3–25.

Jimerson, S. R., & Schuder, M. R. (1996). *Is grade retention an appropriate academic intervention? Longitudinal data provide further insights.* Paper presented at the Head Start National Research Conference, Washington, DC.

Johnson, E. R., Merrell, K. W., & Stover, L. (1990). The effects of early grade retention on the academic achievement of fourth-grade students. *Psychology in the Schools, 27,* 333–338.

Kagan, S. L. (1990). Readiness 2000: Rethinking rhetoric and responsibility. *Phi Delta Kappan, 72,* 272–279.

Karweit, N. L. (1999). *Grade retention: Prevalence, timing, and effects.* Technical Report, Center for Research on the Education of Students Placed at Risk. Baltimore: Johns Hopkins University.

Kelly, K. (1999, January–February). Retention vs. promotion: Schools search for alternatives. *Harvard Education Letter Research Online. . . .*

Kundert, D. K., May, D. C., & Brent, R. (1995). A comparison of students who delay kindergarten entry and those who are retained in grades K–5. *Psychology in the Schools, 32,* 202–209.

Lamberty, G., & Crnic, K. (1994). School readiness conference: Recommendations. *Early Education and Development, 5,* 165–176.

La Paro, K. M., & Pianta, R. C. (2000). Predicting children's competence in the early school years: A meta-analytic review. *Review of Educational Research, 70,* 443–484.

Lapp, D., Fisher, D., Flood, J., & Moore, K. (2002). "I don't want to teach it wrong": An investigation of the role families believe they should play in the early literacy development of their children. In D. L. Schallert, C. M. Fairbanks, J. Worthy, & B. Maloch, & J. V. Hoffman, (Eds.), *National Reading Conference Yearbook, 51* (pp. 275–286). Oak Creek, WI: National Reading Conference.

McCoy, A. R., & Reynolds, A. J. (1999). Grade retention and performance: An extended investigation. *Journal of School Psychology, 37,* 273–298.

McMillen, M., & Kaufman, P. (1993). *Dropout rates in the United States: 1993* (NCES Rep. No. 90-659). Washington, DC: U.S. Department of Education, National Center for Education Statistics.

Meisels, S. J. (1987). Uses and abuses of developmental screening and school readiness testing. *Young Children, 42*(2), 4–6.

Meisels, S. J. (1992). Doing harm by doing good: Iatrogenic effects of early childhood enrollment and promotion policies. *Early Childhood Research Quarterly, 7,* 155–174.

Meisels, S. J. (1999). Assessing readiness. In R. C. Pianta & M. Cox (Eds.), *The transition to kindergarten: Research, policy, training, and practice* (pp. 39–66). Baltimore: Brookes.

Meisels, S. J., & Liaw, F. (1993). Failure in grade: Do retained students catch up? *The Journal of Educational Research, 87,* 69–77.

Miedel, W. T., & Reynolds, A. J. (1998). Parent involvement in early intervention for disadvantaged children: Does it matter? *Journal of School Psychology, 37,* 379–402.

Monaghan, E. J., & Barry, A. L. (1999). *Writing the past: Teaching reading in colonial America and the United States 1640–1940.* Newark, DE: International Reading Association.

Mondale, S., & Patton, S. B. (2001). *School: The story of American public education.* Boston: Beacon Press.

Morris, D. R. (2001). Assessing the implementation of high-stakes reform: Aggregate relationships between retention rates and test results. *NASSP Bulletin, 85,* 18–34.

National Association for the Education of Young Children. (1990). *Guidelines for appropriate curriculum content and assessment in programs serving children ages 3 through 8. . . .*

National Commission on Excellence in Education. (1983). *A nation at risk: The imperative for educational reform.* Washington, DC: Author.

Osterlind, S. J. (1980–1981). Preschool impact on children: Its sustaining effects into kindergarten. *Educational Research Quarterly, 5*(4), 21–30.

Pierson, L. H., & Connell, J. P. (1992). Effect of grade retention on self-system processes, school engagement, and academic performance. *Journal of Educational Psychology, 84,* 300–307.

Pulliam, J. D., & Van Patten, J. (1995). *History of education in America* (6th ed.). Englewood Cliffs, NJ: Merrill.

Resnick, M. D., Bearman, P. S., Blum, R. W., Bauman, K. E., Harris, K. M., Jones, J., et al. (1997). Protecting adolescents from harm: Findings from the national longitudinal study on adolescent health. *Journal of the American Medical Association, 278,* 823–832.

Reynolds, A. J. (1992). Mediated effects of preschool intervention. *Early Education and Development, 3,* 139–164.

Roderick, M. R. (1995). Grade retention and school dropouts: Investigating the association. *American Educational Research Journal, 31,* 729–759.

Royce, J., Darlington, R., & Murray, H. (1983). Pooled analyses: Findings across studies. In the Consortium for Longitudinal Studies (Eds.), *As the twig is bent: Lasting effects of preschool programs* (pp. 411–459). Hillsdale, NJ: Erlbaum.

Rumberger, R. W. (1987). High school dropouts: A review of issues and evidence. *American Educational Research Journal, 32,* 101–121.

Rumberger, R. (1995). Dropping out of middle school: A multilevel analysis of students and schools. *American Educational Research Journal, 32,* 583–625.

Rush, S., & Vitale, P. A. (1994). Analysis for determining factors that place elementary students at risk. *The Journal of Educational Research, 87,* 325–333.

San Diego Unified School District. (2001, March). *The blueprint for student success: Expanded strategies for prevention, intervention, and retention.* San Diego, CA: Author.

Shepard, L. A., & Smith, M. L. (1988). Escalating academic demand in kindergarten: Counterproductive policies. *Elementary School Journal, 89,* 135–145.

Shepard, L. A., & Smith, M. L. (1989). *Flunking grades: Research and policies on retention.* London: Falmer Press.

Snow, C. E., Burns, S. M., & Griffin, P. (1998). *Preventing reading difficulties in young children.* Washington, DC: National Academy Press.

Southern Regional Education Board. (2001). *Finding alternatives to failure: Can states end social promotion and reduce retention rates?* (SREB Rep. No. 00H03). Atlanta, GA: Author.

Taylor, K. K., Gibbs, A. S., & Slate, J. R. (2000). Preschool attendance and kindergarten readiness. *Early Childhood Education Journal, 27,* 191–195.

Thomas, V. G. (2000). Ending social promotion: Help or hindrance? *Kappa Delta Pi Record, 37*(1), 30–32.

U.S. Department of Education. (1999). *Taking responsibility for ending social promotion: A guide for educators and state and local leaders.* Washington, DC: Author.

Vellutino, F. R., & Scanlon, D. M. (2001). Emergent literacy skills, early instruction, and individual differences as determinants of difficulties in learning to read: The case for early intervention. In S. B. Neuman & D. K. Dickinson (Eds.), *Handbook of early literacy research* (pp. 295–321). New York: Guilford.

Vuko, E. (2002, February 12). *Teachers say. . . .*

Wechsler, D. (1997). *Wechsler adult intelligence scale* (3rd ed.). San Antonio, TX: Harcourt Assessment.

Westbury, M. (1994). The effect of elementary grade retention on subsequent school achievement and ability. *Canadian Journal of Education, 19,* 241–250.

Wheat, H. G. (1923). *The teaching of reading: A textbook of principles and methods.* Boston: Ginn.

Zill, N., Loomis, L. S., & West, J. (1997). *The elementary school performance and adjustment of children who enter kindergarten late or repeat kindergarten: Findings from the National Surveys.* Washington, DC: Office of Educational Research and Improvement.

NANCY FREY, PH.D., is a Professor of Literacy in the School of Teacher Education at San Diego State University. She is the recipient of the 2008 Early Career Achievement Award from the National Reading Conference, as well as a co-recipient of the Christa McAuliffe award for excellence in teacher education from the American Association of State Colleges and Universities. In addition to publishing with her colleague, Doug Fisher, she teaches a variety of courses in SDSU's teacher-credentialing and reading specialist programs on elementary and secondary reading instruction, literacy in content areas, and supporting students with diverse learning needs. Nancy is a credentialed special educator and reading specialist in California.

EXPLORING THE ISSUE

Should Struggling Students Be Retained?

Critical Thinking and Reflection

1. For some, grade retention is a socio-political problem with racial and ethnic minority students from lower socioeconomic backgrounds disproportionately retained in addition to apparent gender biases with more males than females retained. Based on the readings, summarize briefly the role minority status or gender appears to play in retention decisions and outcomes. What position do Lorence and Dworkin take on this issue to support their research? Do you agree with their rationale? Why or why not?
2. Imagine you are a second-grade teacher. What factors would influence your decision about whether or not to retain a student? How would you weigh these different factors in making your decision? How would you include the family in making your decision? Explain the steps in your reasoning.
3. Lorence and Dworkin argue that despite conventional wisdom based, in part, on the results of meta-analyses, there really is no evidence overwhelmingly showing that grade retention is ineffective. Do you agree with their conclusion? Why or why not? How do you think they arrived at a different conclusion than Frey?

Is There Common Ground?

In the first selection, Jon Lorence and Anthony Gary Dworkin reach a conclusion, suggesting that the findings from the research literature have serious shortcomings and that under some circumstances repeating a grade can benefit academically struggling students. In the second selection, Nancy Frey, after reviewing the available evidence in relation to aims of teachers and the needs of students, concludes that retention is academically ineffective and possibly detrimental. With the demand for increased accountability, state and local district policymakers are mandating retention if required promotion benchmarks are not met. At the same time, professional opinion informed by research studies warn that the consequences of retention are not benign but can be detrimental. Discerning who is "right" or what the most effective course of action should be from a policy perspective but also for an individual struggling student remains a challenge with no clear or definitive answer. What inferences can be reasonably made when summaries of the same research findings reach different conclusions?

For starters, there are critical voices of the research by educational researchers themselves pointing out some of the shortcomings. One important observation made by Lorence and Dworkin, for example, highlights that almost all of the retention research is based on teacher-initiated judgment but contemporary criteria are largely based on standardized test scores. How this difference in decision making will affect outcomes is not well understood. Another important caveat, often ignored, is that retention impact may be very grade specific. There likely are very real differences between primary and secondary retention policy outcomes. Another issue concerns the possible reasons for retention in the first place. Educational improvement (or lack thereof) during a retained year will likely vary in relation to the reason the student was retained (academic failure, learning disability, emotional immaturity, behavioral problems) and, in each case, these reasons are likely prognostic. Finally, the nature of the instructional experience that occurs in the repeated year is likely a major explanation for the effect of retention, positive or negative. Repeated exposure to ineffective instruction is unlikely to be beneficial. Or, if a student is in need of enhanced educational assistance but does not receive the necessary support during the repeated grade, there is little reason to expect reasonable gains. It is especially worth noting that lost in much of the debate and discussion are the needs of children with disabilities. How children with learning and behavioral disabilities respond to retention or social promotion has not been studied extensively. Considering broad policies of accountability with respect to achievement based on standardized testing, there are myriad concerns related to retention and the unique learning needs of student with special education requirements.

Given the potential costs to the student (e.g., negative self-esteem) and society (e.g., dropping out) associated with retention, as reviewed by Lisa Bowman, "Grade Retention: Is It a Help or Hindrance to Student Academic Success" in *Preventing School Failure* (Spring 2005), there should be considerable effort made at the individual but also the policy level to consider the consequences, not the least of which should focus on pre- and in-service teacher education and preparation with respect to retention policy and practices. There needs to be additional focus on high quality instruction and the value of progress monitoring to regularly evaluate student progress to help identify early students in need of additional academic support. For educational researchers the focus needs to shift away from the dichotomy (yes versus no) but, as suggested by Frey, to the range of possible factors that influence outcomes both positive and negative.

Create Central

www.mhhe.com/createcentral

Additional Resources

K. L. Alexander, D. R. Entwhisle, and S. L. Dauber provide an accessible book, *On the Success of Failure: A Reassessment of the Effects of Retention in the Primary Grades* (Cambridge University Press 2003).

For a very readable collection of research reports and essays on reviewing alternatives to retention and social promotion, see *Moving Beyond Retention and Social Promotion,* edited by E. McCay in *Phi Delta Kappa* Hot Topic Series (January 2001).

S. Jimerson provides an insightful series of observations in his chapter "Is Grade Retention Educational Malpractice? Empirical Evidence from Meta-Analyses Examining the Efficacy of Grade Retention," found in *Can Unlike Students Learn Together,* edited by H. Walberg, A. J. Reynolds, and M. C. Wang (Information Age Publishing 2004).

An important early account of policy recommendation against retention can be found in "Elementary School Retention: An Unjustifiable, Discriminatory, and Noxious Educational Policy," by R. P. Abidin, W. M. Golladay, and A. L. Howerton, in the *Journal of School Psychology* (vol. 9, 1971).

Internet References . . .

National Association of School Psychologists Grade Retention and Social Promotion White Paper

http://www.nasponline.org/about_nasp
/positionpapers/WhitePaper
_GradeRetentionandSocialPromotion.pdf

National Association of School Psychologists Grade Retention and Social Promotion Position Statement

http://www.nasponline.org/about_nasp
/positionpapers/GradeRetentionandSocialPromotion
.pdf

National Dropout Prevention Center Policy Statement on Student Grade Retention

http://www.dropoutprevention.org/retention-policya

Selected, Edited, and with Issue Framing Material by:
Leonard Abbeduto, *University of California, Davis*
and
Frank Symons, *University of Minnesota*

ISSUE

Is Full Inclusion Always the Best Option for Children with Disabilities?

YES: **Michael F. Giangreco,** from "Extending Inclusive Opportunities," *Educational Leadership* (February 2007)

NO: **James M. Kauffman, Kathleen McGee, and Michele Brigham,** from "Enabling or Disabling? Observation on Changes in Special Education," *Phi Delta Kappan* (April 2004)

Learning Outcomes

After reading this issue, you will be able to:

- Define the term "full inclusion."
- Understand the intent of full inclusion.
- Discuss the potential advantages and disadvantages of full inclusion for an individual student with a disability.
- Discuss the potential advantages and disadvantages of full inclusion for an individual student without a disability.

ISSUE SUMMARY

YES: Michael F. Giangreco, who is a professor of education at the University of Vermont, argues that even students with severe disabilities are best served within the "regular" education classroom along with their typically developing peers. He also outlines strategies for achieving inclusion and shows how it creates a classroom that benefits all students, regardless of ability level.

NO: James M. Kauffman, who is a professor at the University of Virginia at Charlottesville, and Kathleen McGee and Michele Brigham, who are both special education teachers, argue that the goal of education for students with disabilities should be to increase their level of competence and independence. They conclude that full inclusion involves "excessive" accommodations that actually become barriers to achieving this goal.

Public Law (P.L.) 94-142, the Education for All Handicapped Children Act (1975), required that all children with disabilities, whatever the nature or severity of their disability, be provided a free and appropriate education within the least restrictive environment possible. Later laws—P.L. 99-457, the 1986 Education of the Handicapped Act, and P.L. 101-476, the 1990 Individuals with Disabilities Education Act (IDEA)—clarified, strengthened, and expanded the 1975 legislation. Before the enactment of these laws, many children with disabilities, especially those with more severe or challenging disabilities, were segregated from their more typically developing peers. Students with disabilities attended special classes in their neighborhood schools, or they attended special schools for those with disabilities. In either case, they had minimal contact with their typically developing peers. Advocates for people

with disabilities argued that a separate education denies children with disabilities the same opportunities afforded everyone else.

Rather than being segregated, many children with disabilities are now placed ("mainstreamed") into the regular classroom on at least a part-time basis. Mainstreaming ensures that students with disabilities have contact with their typically developing peers and the regular education curriculum. In recent years, advocates for people with disabilities have successfully argued that simple physical presence in the regular classroom may not lead to full participation in the classroom's intellectual or social life. Advocates, therefore, have argued that schools must move beyond mainstreaming to full inclusion. Full inclusion refers to placement in the regular classroom with appropriate supports and services—such as an interpreter who signs the teacher's talk for a student with impaired hearing—and includes active efforts to ensure participation in the life of the class. Moreover, it is argued that these supports and services must be tailored to the unique needs of each individual as set forth in the Individual Educational Plan (IEP). The IEP is prepared annually by a multidisciplinary team composed of, for example, the school psychologist, a special education teacher, the regular classroom teacher, and a speech-language clinician, all of whom assess the student's current level of functioning and set short- and long-term goals for his or her educational progress.

Although full inclusion may be the ideal, school districts have been granted considerable latitude by the courts to make educational placements. For example, the courts have allowed less than full inclusion if a student is unlikely to derive sufficient academic or nonacademic benefit from inclusion, if a student's placement in the regular classroom is likely to be disruptive, or if the cost of inclusion would be prohibitive for the district. As a result of these constraints, many students experience less than full inclusion—some may have "pull-out" classes, which segregate them from their more typically developing peers for part of the school day; others may be segregated for almost their entire school experience.

Often, the issue of inclusion is most heated in the case of students with severe disabilities, and both of the accompanying selections focus largely on such students. In the first selection, Michael F. Giangreco argues that inclusion of students with even severe disabilities is possible and desirable, and he outlines strategies for accomplishing this. These strategies, which he terms the *multilevel curriculum and curriculum overlapping,* entail adapting the content of the curriculum or level of support provided to the student, but doing so within the shared activities of the classroom. In the second selection, James M. Kauffman and his colleagues argue, first, that the goal of education for students with disabilities is to provide them with the skills needed to increase their independence and bring them as close as possible in terms of functioning to their "mainstream" peers. They then argue that inclusion, with its emphasis on accommodation, thwarts this goal by actually increasing dependence on special assistance, reinforcing maladaptive behaviors, and failing to "push" students to acquire new skills.

YES

Michael F. Giangreco

Extending Inclusive Opportunities

Ms. Santos,[1] a 5th grade teacher, had successfully included students with learning disabilities or physical limitations in her classroom for years. Even in years when none of her students had been identified as having disabilities, her students' abilities and needs had varied, sometimes substantially. She regularly taught students whose native languages were not English and students who displayed challenging behaviors or fragile emotional health. The range of her students' reading abilities typically spanned several years.

Ms. Santos had confidently made *instructional* accommodations for all her students, for example, by modifying materials and giving individualized cues—but she had rarely needed to modify her curriculum. Students with and without disabilities in her class worked on the same topics, although sometimes at differing levels and paces. But when a boy who worked far below 5th grade level was assigned to her class, Ms. Santos faced a question that looms large for teachers trying to make inclusion work: How can we achieve true curricular inclusion for students who function substantially below grade level?

Facing a New Challenge

Last school year, Ms. Santos welcomed Chris into her 5th grade class. A boy new to the school, Chris had a good sense of humor, liked many kinds of music, and had a history of making friends and liking school. Unfortunately, in the eyes of most people, these qualities were overshadowed by the severity of his intellectual, behavioral, sensory, and physical disabilities. Because Chris came to her class functioning at a kindergarten or prekindergarten level in all academic areas, Ms. Santos had trouble conceiving of how he could learn well in a 5th grade class, and she worried about what Chris's parents and her colleagues would expect. By suggesting how a teacher might handle this kind of situation, I hope to assist teachers and other professionals who are attempting to successfully include students with significant disabilities within mainstream classrooms.

Extending Student Participation

The Individuals with Disabilities Education Improvement Act of 2004 presumes that the first placement option a school system must consider for each student with a disability, regardless of disability category or severity, is the regular classroom. Students with disabilities are entitled to supplemental supports that enable them to meaningfully pursue individually determined learning outcomes—including those from the general education curriculum. The question to be asked is not whether a student is able to pursue the same learning outcomes as his or her age-level peers, but whether that student's needs can be appropriately addressed in the general education setting.

The participation of students with disabilities within general education classes can be broadly characterized along two dimensions: each student's *program* (such as the goals of the student's individualized education program) and each student's *supports*. Supports are anything that the school provides to help the student pursue education goals—for example materials, adaptations, or a classroom aide (Giangreco, 2006).

Within a school day, or even within a single activity, an individual student will sometimes require modifications to the general education program and at other times be able to work within the standard program. Likewise, the number of supports teachers will need to provide for students will fluctuate greatly. In some scenarios, a student with a disability can do the same academic work his or her classmates are doing. These kinds of opportunities help teachers and students interact in a natural way, show classmates that students with learning needs don't always need special help, and allow students to avoid unnecessary supports.

Setting the Stage for Curricular Modifications

Chris was fortunate that he was assigned a teacher who already had good practices in place for including students with IEPs. Ms. Santos created opportunities for many types of instructional interactions through a busy classroom schedule of inquiry-based activities. Her ability to teach students with disabilities grew out of her belief that the core of teaching and learning was the same, regardless of whether a student had a disability label.

Although Ms. Santos was not sure how to meet the challenge of including Chris in her classroom, she asked important questions to clarify her own role as a team member, understand the curricular expectations for Chris, and get a vision for how to teach a class with a wider mix of abilities than she had encountered before. As part of that vision, she drew on the power of relationships, both in drawing Chris into her plans for students and in building a collaborative team of special educators, parents, and others. In her classroom community, she expected students to help one another learn and be responsible for helping the classroom run smoothly. As much as possible, she also planned for Chris to have an active voice in telling his teachers which supports helped him and which did not.

For Chris to be a viable social member of the classroom, he would have to participate in the academic work, not just be physically present or socially accepted. Ms. Santos knew how frustrating and embarrassing it can be for students when curriculum content is over their heads, and she also knew the hazards of underestimating students. She sought ways to adjust the curriculum to an appropriate level of difficulty for Chris, while leaving opportunities for him to surprise her with his capabilities.

When Curriculum Modifications Are Essential

In many inclusion scenarios, such as the one Ms. Santos faced, modifications to the general education program will be essential. Sometimes the student will need individualized content but will not require specialized supports to work with that content. For example, the teacher might assign a student five new vocabulary words instead of 10, or assign that learner single-digit computation instead of decimals.

In some situations, the classroom teacher will need to both modify the general education program and provide individualized supports. Although students with more severe disabilities may often need both program and support accommodation to succeed in a mainstream class, teachers may not need to alter both the curriculum and the types of support available for all classroom work a student with a disability undertakes. Even a student with significant disabilities, like Chris, rarely needs both an individualized education program and individualized supports all the time.

Multilevel Curriculum and Curriculum Overlapping

Multilevel curriculum and *curriculum overlapping* are two approaches to adapting curriculum that facilitate participation of students with significant disabilities. In the multilevel curriculum approach, students with disabilities and their peers participate in a shared activity. Each student has individually appropriate learning outcomes that are within the same curriculum area but that may be at grade level or below (or above) grade level (Campbell, Campbell, Collicott, Perner, & Stone, 1988; Peterson & Hittie, 2003). Students of different ability levels may be working on the same or different subject matter within the same academic area. In curriculum overlapping, students with disabilities and nondisabled peers participate together in an activity, but they pursue learning outcomes from different curriculum areas, including such broadly defined curriculum areas as social skills.

Multilevel Curriculum in Action

Let's go back to Ms. Santos's challenge of including Chris as an academic member of her class and see how she used multilevel curriculum. In class work for a social studies unit, Chris and his classmates studied the Revolutionary War. But Ms. Santos adapted Chris's level of learning outcomes to suit him: His goals were to become familiar with historical people, places, and events, whereas his classmates' goals were to demonstrate knowledge of political and economic factors that led to the war.

To reinforce students' learning, Ms. Santos created a Revolutionary War board game that drew on both the class's grade-appropriate learning goals and Chris's lower-level goals to advance in the game. The game board had colored spaces, and each color a student landed on corresponded to a stack of question cards related to the desired content, with blue cards for historical people, green cards for historical places, and so on. Ms. Santos and a special educator had set aside specially prepared cards for Chris with questions matched to his learning outcomes. The rest of the class drew cards matched to their goals.

Another player read aloud for Chris each question and the multiple-choice answers, which were given both verbally and with images. For example, the question, "What American Revolutionary War hero became the first president of the United States?" might be followed by the labeled images of George Washington and two other famous people. When Chris was learning new content, Ms. Santos made the distracter choices substantially different and included at least one absurd choice (such as George Washington, Abraham Lincoln, and LeBron James). As Chris became more proficient, she used distracter choices that were more difficult to spot. When Chris answered a question correctly, he rolled dice and moved forward. Although this activity focused on social studies, Chris also learned the social skill of taking turns and such math skills as counting.

Curriculum Overlapping in Action

Curriculum overlapping is a vital strategy for classrooms in which there are substantial differences between the learning outcomes most of the students are pursuing and the outcomes a student with a disability is pursuing.

For example, in a human biology unit, a group of four students might assemble a model of the human cardiovascular system. The primary goal of three students is to learn anatomical structures and their functions. The fourth student, who has significant disabilities, shares the activity, but has learning goals within the curriculum area of communications and social skills, such as learning to follow directions, taking turns, or making requests using a communication device.

One way to start planning for curriculum overlapping with a student who has significant disabilities is to make a simple matrix with the student's individually determined learning outcomes down the side and a list of regularly occurring classes or activities across the top. Team members can then identify where they should focus additional energy to ensure meaningful participation.

Ms. Santos and her team did this. They established cross-lesson routines through which Chris's individual learning outcomes could be embedded within many class activities. For example, Chris had a series of learning objectives involving communication and social skills, including matching to a sample; discriminating between different symbols and photos; following one- and two-step instructions; responding to questions; and describing events, objects, or emotions. Ms. Santos routinely embedded these skills in activities and lessons Chris participated in across different content areas as a form of curriculum overlapping.

While pursuing these learning outcomes, Chris might also work with the actual curricular content. For example, in a geography activity Chris might distinguish between maps of European countries, first discriminating between highly different pairs (a map of Italy paired with an image that is not a map); followed by slightly more similar pairs (a map of Greece and a map of China); followed by even more similar pairs (maps of France and Germany).

When first using multilevel curriculum and curriculum overlapping, teams often feel that they don't have enough for their student with a significant disability to do within the typical classroom activities. But as they persist in collaborative planning, seek input directly from the student, and involve classmates in problem solving, they find new opportunities for the student's meaningful participation and learning.

Although multilevel curriculum and curriculum overlapping are primarily ways to include students with disabilities, they also enable more meaningful participation for students functioning above grade level. Applying multilevel curriculum allows teachers to stretch their curriculum away from a "middle zone" in which all students share the same curricular content, level, and amount of work. The practices many people associate with differentiated instruction (Tomlinson, 2001) occur within the boundaries of this middle zone. Multilevel curriculum stretches the concept of differentiated instruction. With curriculum overlapping, the boundaries of curriculum planning expand even further to create effective learning situations for students working both far above and far below their peers.

In the interest of access to the general education curriculum, teachers and teams working with students with disabilities should first consider whether the student can pursue the same learning outcomes as classmates or whether multilevel curriculum and instruction will provide enough accommodation before using curriculum overlapping.

Making It Happen

Implementing either multilevel curriculum and instruction or curriculum overlapping requires time, collaboration, and creativity. But the reward is the authentic inclusion of students who function substantially below grade level. Approaching inclusive education this way contributes to a positive classroom culture, acknowledges differences, promotes acceptance, and provides opportunities for real-life problem solving.

Some claim that inclusion of students with certain disabilities is impossible because in many schools the curriculum is one-size-fits-all and differentiation is minimal or nonexistent. Although it is difficult to include a student with significant disabilities in such classes, this begs the question of whether one-size-fits-all classes are what we want for anyone. Instructional practices such as cooperative learning and differentiated instruction are often beneficial for general education students, too.

Students with disabilities bring educators a challenge to make our teaching practices more inclusive. Meeting the challenge invariably improves the way we teach the broader range of students who don't have disabilities.

References

Campbell, C., Campbell, S., Collicott, J., Perner, D., & Stone, J. (1988). Individualized instruction. *Education New Brunswick, 3,* 17–20.

Giangreco, M. F. (2006). Foundational concepts and practices for educating students with severe disabilities. In M. E. Snell & F. Brown (Eds.), *Instruction of students with severe disabilities* (6th ed., pp. 1–27). Upper Saddle River, NJ: Pearson Education/Prentice-Hall.

Peterson, J. M., & Hittie, M. M. (2003). *Inclusive teaching: Creating effective schools for all learners.* Boston: Allyn and Bacon.

Tomlinson, C. A. (2001). *How to differentiate instruction in mixed-ability classrooms* (2nd ed.). Alexandria, VA: ASCD.

Note

1. Ms. Santos is a composite of teachers I have observed who work with students with severe disabilities.

MICHAEL F. GIANGRECO is professor of education at the University of Vermont.

James M. Kauffman, Kathleen McGee,
and Michele Brigham

 **NO**

Enabling or Disabling? Observations on Changes in Special Education

Schools need demanding and distinctive special education that is clearly focused on instruction and habilitation.[1] Abandoning such a conception of special education is a prescription for disaster. But special education has increasingly been losing its way in the single-minded pursuit of full inclusion.

Once, special education's purpose was to bring the performance of students with disabilities closer to that of their nondisabled peers in regular classrooms, to move as many students as possible into the mainstream with appropriate support.[2] For students not in regular education, the goal was to move them toward a more typical setting in a cascade of placement options.[3] But as any good thing can be overdone and ruined by the pursuit of extremes, we see special education suffering from the extremes of inclusion and accommodation.

Aiming for as much normalization as possible gave special education a clear purpose. Some disabilities were seen as easier to remediate than others. Most speech and language disorders, for example, were considered eminently remediable. Other disabilities, such as mental retardation and many physical disabilities, were assumed to be permanent or long-term and so less remediable, but movement *toward* the mainstream and increasing independence from special educators were clear goals.

The emphasis in special education has shifted away from normalization, independence, and competence. The result has been students' dependence on whatever special programs, modifications, and accommodations are possible, particularly in general education settings. The goal seems to have become the *appearance* of normalization without the *expectation* of competence.

Many parents and students seem to want more services as they learn what is available. Some have lost sight of the goal of limiting accommodations in order to challenge students to achieve more independence. At the same time, many special education advocates want all services to be available in mainstream settings, with little or no acknowledgment that the services are atypical. Although teachers, administrators, and guidance counselors are often willing and able to make accommodations, doing so is not always in students' best long-term interests. It gives students with disabilities what anthropologist Robert Edgerton called a cloak—a pretense, a cover, which actually fools no one—rather than actual competence.[4]

In this article, we discuss how changes in attitudes toward disability and special education, placement, and accommodations can perpetuate disability. We also explore the problems of ignoring or perpetuating disability rather than helping students lead fuller, more independent lives. Two examples illustrate how we believe good intentions can go awry—how attempts to accommodate students with disabilities can undermine achievement.

"But he needs resource. . . ." Thomas, a high school sophomore identified as emotionally disturbed, was assigned to a resource class created to help students who had problems with organization or needed extra help with academic skills. One of the requirements in the class was for students to keep a daily planner in which they entered all assignments; they shared their planner with the resource teacher at the beginning of class and discussed what academic subjects would be worked on during that period.

Thomas consistently refused to keep a planner or do any work in resource (he slept instead). So a meeting was set up with the assistant principal, the guidance counselor, Thomas, and the resource teacher. As the meeting was about to begin, the principal announced that he would not stay because Thomas felt intimidated by so many adults. After listening to Thomas' complaints, the guidance counselor decided that Thomas would not have to keep a planner or show it to the resource teacher and that the resource teacher should not talk to him unless Thomas addressed her first. In short, Thomas would not be required to do any work in the class! When the resource teacher suggested that, under those circumstances, Thomas should perhaps be placed in a study hall, because telling the parents that he was in a resource class would be a misrepresentation, the counselor replied, "But he *needs* the resource class."

"He's too bright. . . ." Bob, a high school freshman with Asperger's Syndrome, was scheduled for three honors classes and two Advanced Placement classes. Bob's IEP (individualized education program) included a two-page list of accommodations. In spite of his having achieved A's and B's, with just a single C in math, his mother did not feel that his teachers were accommodating him appropriately. Almost every evening, she e-mailed his teachers and his

case manager to request more information or more help for Bob, and she angrily phoned his guidance counselor if she didn't receive a reply by the end of the first hour of the next school day.

A meeting was scheduled with the IEP team, including five of Bob's seven teachers, the county special education supervisor, the guidance counselor, the case manager, the principal, and the county autism specialist. When the accommodations were reviewed, Bob's mother agreed that all of them were being made. However, she explained that Bob had been removed from all outside social activities because he spent all night, every night, working on homework. The accommodation she demanded was that Bob have *no* homework assignments. The autism specialist agreed that this was a reasonable accommodation for a child with Asperger's Syndrome.

The teachers of the honors classes explained that the homework in their classes, which involved elaboration and extension of concepts, was even more essential than the homework assigned in AP classes. In AP classes, by contrast, homework consisted primarily of practice of concepts learned in class. The honors teachers explained that they had carefully broken their long assignments into segments, each having a separate due date before the final project, and they gave illustrations of their expectations. The director of special education explained the legal definition of accommodations (the mother said she'd never before heard that accommodations could not change the nature of the curriculum). The director also suggested that, instead of Bob's sacrificing his social life, perhaps it would be more appropriate for him to take standard classes. What Bob's mother was asking, he concluded, was not legal. She grew angry, but she did agree to give the team a "little more time" to serve Bob appropriately. She said she would "be back with her claws and broomstick" if anyone ever suggested that he be moved from honors classes without being given the no-homework accommodation. "He's too bright to take anything less than honors classes, and if you people would provide this simple accommodation, he would do just fine," she argued. In the end, she got her way.

Attitudes Toward Disability and Special Education

Not that many decades ago, a disability was considered a misfortune—not something to be ashamed of but a generally undesirable, unwelcome condition to be overcome to the greatest extent possible. Ability was considered more desirable than disability, and anything—whether a device or a service—that helped people with disabilities to do what those without disabilities could do was considered generally valuable, desirable, and worth the effort, cost, and possible stigma associated with using it.

The disability rights movement arose in response to the widespread negative attitudes toward disabilities, and it had a number of desirable outcomes. It helped overcome some of the discrimination against people with disabilities. And overcoming such bias and unfairness in everyday life is a great accomplishment. But the movement has also had some unintended negative consequences. One of these is the outright denial of disability in some cases, illustrated by the contention that disability exists only in attitudes or as a function of the social power to coerce.[5]

The argument that disability is merely a "social construction" is particularly vicious in its effects on social justice. Even if we assume that disabilities are socially constructed, what should that mean? Should we assume that socially constructed phenomena are not "real," are not important, or should be discredited? If so, then consider that dignity, civil rights, childhood, social justice, and nearly every other phenomenon that we hold dear are social constructions. Many social constructions are not merely near and dear to us, they are real and useful in benevolent societies. The important question is whether the idea of disability is useful in helping people attain dignity or whether it is more useful to assume that disabilities are not real (i.e., that, like social justice, civil rights, and other social constructions, they are fabrications that can be ignored when convenient). The denial of disability is sometimes expressed as an aversion to labels, so that we are cautioned not to communicate openly and clearly about disabilities but to rely on euphemisms. But this approach is counterproductive. When we are able only to whisper or mime the undesirable difference called disability, then we inadvertently increase its stigma and thwart prevention efforts.[6]

The specious argument that "normal" does not exist—because abilities of every kind are varied and because the point at which normal becomes abnormal is arbitrary—leads to the conclusion that no one actually has a disability or, alternatively, that everyone has a disability. Then, some argue, either no one or everyone is due an accommodation so that no one or everyone is identified as disabled. This unwillingness to draw a line defining something (such as disability, poverty, or childhood) is based either on ignorance regarding the nature of continuous distributions or on a rejection of the unavoidably arbitrary decisions necessary to provide special services to those who need them and, in so doing, to foster social justice.[7]

Another unintended negative consequence of the disability rights movement is that, for some people, disability has become either something that does not matter or something to love, to take pride in, to flaunt, to adopt as a positive aspect of one's identity, or to cherish as something desirable or as a badge of honor. When disability makes no difference to us one way or the other, then we are not going to work to attenuate it, much less prevent it. At best, we will try to accommodate it. When we view disability as a desirable difference, then we are very likely to try to make it more pronounced, not to ameliorate it.

Several decades ago, special education was seen as a good thing—a helpful way of responding to disability, not something everyone needed or should have, but a useful and necessary response to the atypical needs of students with disabilities. This is why the Education for All Handicapped Children Act (now the Individuals with Disabilities Education Act) was written. But in the minds of many people, special education has been transformed from something helpful to something awful.[8]

The full-inclusion movement did have some desirable outcomes. It helped overcome some of the unnecessary removal of students with disabilities from general education. However, the movement also has had some unintended negative consequences. One of these is that special education has come to be viewed in very negative terms, to be seen as a second-class and discriminatory system that does more harm than good. Rather than being seen as helpful, as a way of creating opportunity, special education is often portrayed as a means of shunting students into dead-end programs and killing opportunity.[9]

Another unintended negative consequence of full inclusion is that general education is now seen by many as the *only* place where fair and equitable treatment is possible and where the opportunity to learn is extended to all equally.[10] The argument has become that special education is good only as long as it is invisible (or nearly so), an indistinguishable part of a general education system that accommodates all students, regardless of their abilities or disabilities. Usually, this is described as a "unified" (as opposed to "separate") system of education.[11] Special education is thus something to be avoided altogether or attenuated to the greatest extent possible, regardless of a student's inability to perform in a general setting. When special education is seen as discriminatory, unfair, an opportunity-killing system, or, as one writer put it, "the gold-plated garbage can of American schooling,"[12] then it is understandable that people will loathe it. But this way of looking at special education is like seeing the recognition and treatment of cancer as the cause of the problem.

The reversal in attitudes toward disability and special education—disability from undesirable to inconsequential, special education from desirable to awful—has clouded the picture of what special education is and what it should do for students with disabilities. Little wonder that special education stands accused of failure, that calls for its demise have become vociferous, and that contemporary practices are often more disabling than enabling. An unfortunate outcome of the changing attitudes toward disability and special education is that the benefit of special education is now sometimes seen as freedom from expectations of performance. It is as if we believed that, if a student has to endure the stigma of special education, then the compensation should include an exemption from work.

Placement Issues

Placing all students, regardless of their abilities, in regular classes has exacerbated the tendency to see disability as something existing only in people's minds. It fosters the impression that students are fitting in when they are not able to perform at anywhere near the normal level. It perpetuates disabilities; it does not compensate for them.

Administrators and guidance counselors sometimes place students in programs for which they do not qualify, even as graduation requirements are increasing and tests are mandated. Often, these students' *testing* is modified although their *curriculum* is not. The students may then feel that they have beaten the system. They are taught that the system is unfair and that the only way to win is by gaming it. Hard work and individual responsibility for one's education are often overlooked—or at least undervalued.

Students who consistently fail in a particular curriculum must be given the opportunity to deal with the natural consequences of that fact as a means of learning individual responsibility. For example, social promotion in elementary and middle school teaches students that they really don't have to be able to do the work to pass. Students who have been conditioned to rely on social promotion do not believe that the cycle will end until it does so—usually very abruptly in high school. Suddenly, no one passes them on, and no one gives them undeserved credit. Many of these students do not graduate in four years. Some never recover, while other find themselves forced to deal with a very distasteful situation.

No one wants to see a student fail, but to alter any standard without good reason is to set that same student up for failure later in life. Passing along a student with disabilities in regular classes, pretending that he or she is performing at the same level as most of the class or that it doesn't really matter (arguing that the student has a legal "right" to be in the class) is another prescription for disappointment and failure in later life. Indeed, this failure often comes in college or on the job.

Some people with disabilities do need assistance. Others do not. Consider Deborah Groeber, who struggled through degenerative deafness and blindness. The Office of Affirmative Action at the University of Pennsylvania offered to intercede at the Wharton School, but Groeber knew that she had more influence if she spoke for herself. Today, she is a lawyer with three Ivy League degrees.[13] But not every student with disabilities can do or should be expected to do what Groeber did. Our concern is that too many students with disabilities are given encouragement based on pretense when they could do much more with appropriate special education.

Types of Accommodations

Two popular modifications in IEPs are allowing for the use of calculators and granting extended time on tests and assignments. Calculators can be a great asset, but they should be used when calculating complex problems or when doing word problems. Indiscriminate use of a calculator renders many math tests invalid, as they become a contest to see if buttons can be pushed successfully and in the correct order, rather than an evaluation of ability to do arithmetic or use mathematical knowledge.

Extended time on assignments and tests can also be a useful modification, but it can easily be misused or abused. Extended time on tests should mean *continuous* time so that a test is not studied for first and taken later. Sometimes a test must be broken into smaller segments that can be completed independently. However, this could put students with disabilities at a disadvantage, as one part of a test might help with remembering another part. Extensions on assignments need to be evaluated each time they are given, not simply handed out automatically because they are written into an IEP. If a student is clearly working hard, then extensions may be appropriate. If a student has not even been attempting assignments, then more time might be an avoidance tactic. Sometimes extended time means that assignments pile up and the student gets further and further behind. The result can then be overwhelming stress and the inability to comprehend discussions because many concepts must be acquired in sequence (e.g., in math, science, history, and foreign languages).

Reading tests and quizzes aloud to students can be beneficial for many, but great caution is required. Some students and teachers want to do more than simply read a test. Reading a test aloud means simply reading the printed words on the page *without* inflections that can reveal correct answers and without explaining vocabulary. Changing a test to open-notes or open-book, without the knowledge and consent of the classroom teacher, breaches good-faith test proctoring. It also teaches students dependence rather than independence and accomplishment. Similarly, scribing for a student can be beneficial for those who truly need it, but the teacher must be careful not to add details and to write only what the student dictates, including any run-on sentences or fragments. After scribing, if the assignment is not a test, the teacher should edit and correct the paper with the student, as she might do with any written work. But this must take place *after* the scribing.

How Misguided Accommodations Can Be Disabling

"Saving" a child from his or her own negative behavior reinforces that behavior and makes it a self-fulfilling prophecy. Well-intentioned guidance counselors often feel more responsibility for their students' success or failure than the students themselves feel. Sometimes students are not held accountable for their effort or work. They seem not to understand that true independence comes from *what* you know, not *whom* you know. Students who are consistently enabled and not challenged are never given the opportunity to become independent. Ann Bancroft, the polar explorer and dyslexic, claims that, although school was a torment, it was disability that forged her iron will.[14] Stephen Cannell's fear for other dyslexics is that they will quit trying rather than struggle and learn to compensate for their disability.[15]

Most parents want to help their children. However, some parents confuse making life *easier* with making life *better* for their children. Too often, parents feel that protecting their child from the rigors of academic demands is in his or her best interest. They may protect their child by insisting on curricular modifications and accommodations in assignments, time, and testing. But children learn by doing, and not allowing them to do something because they might fail is denying them the opportunity to succeed. These students eventually believe that they are not capable of doing what typical students can do, even if they are. Sometimes it is difficult for teachers to discern what a student actually can do and what a parent has done until an in-class assignment is given or a test is taken. At that point, it is often too late for the teacher to do much remediation. The teacher may erroneously conclude that the student is simply a poor test-taker.

In reality, the student may have been "protected" from learning, which will eventually catch up with him or her. Unfortunately, students may not face reality until they take a college entrance exam, go away to college, or apply for a job. Students who "get through" high school in programs of this type often go on to flunk out of college. Unfortunately, the parents of these students frequently blame the college for the student's failure, criticizing the postsecondary institution for not doing enough to help. Instead, they should be upset both with the secondary institution for not preparing the child adequately for the tasks to come and with themselves for their own overprotection.

The Benefits of Demands

Many successful adults with disabilities sound common themes when asked about their ability to succeed in the face of a disability. Tom Gray, a Rhodes Scholar who has a severe learning disability, claims that having to deal with the hardest experiences gave him the greatest strength.[16] Stephen Cannell believes that, if he had known there was a reason beyond his control to explain his low achievement, he might not have worked as hard as he did. Today, he knows he has a learning disability, but he is also an Emmy Award-winning television writer and producer.[17] Paul Orlalea, the dyslexic founder of Kinko's, believes God gave him an advantage in the challenge presented by his disability and that others should work with their strengths. Charles Schwab, the learning-disabled founder of Charles Schwab, Inc., cites his ability to think differently and to make creative leaps that more sequential thinkers don't make as chief reasons for his success. Fannie Flagg, the learning-disabled author, concurs and insists that learning disabilities become a blessing *only if you can overcome them*.[18] Not every student with a disability can be a star performer, of course, but all should be expected to achieve all that they can.

Two decades ago, special educators thought it was their job to assess a student's achievement, to understand what the student wanted to do and what an average peer could do, and then to develop plans to bridge the gap, if possible. Most special educators wanted to see that each student had the tools and knowledge to succeed as independently as possible. Helping students enter the typical world was the mark of success for special educators.

The full-inclusion movement now insists that *every* student will benefit from placement in the mainstream. However, some of the modifications and accommodations now being demanded are so radical that we are doing an injustice to the entire education system.[19] Special education must not be associated in any way with "dumbing down" the curriculum for students presumed to be at a given grade level, whether disabled or not.

Counselors and administrators who want to enable students must focus the discussion on realistic goals and plans for each student. An objective, in-depth discussion and evaluation must take place to determine how far along the continuum of successfully completing these goals the student has moved. If the student is making adequate progress independently, or with minimal help, special education services might not be necessary. If assistance is required to make adequate progress on realistic goals, then special education may be needed. Every modification and every accommodation should be held to the same standard: whether it will help the student attain these goals—*not* whether it will make life easier for the student. Knowing where a student is aiming can help a team guide that student toward success.

And the student must be part of this planning. A student who claims to want to be a brain surgeon but refuses to take science courses needs a reality check. If a student is unwilling to attempt to reach intermediate goals or does not succeed in meeting them, then special education cannot "save" that student. At that point, the team must help the student revisit his or her goals. Goals should be explained in terms of the amount of work required to complete them, not whether or not the teacher or parent feels they are attainable. When goals are presented in this way, students can often make informed decisions regarding their attainability and desirability. Troy Brown, a university dean and politician who has both a doctorate and a learning disability, studied at home with his mother. He estimates that it took him more than twice as long as the average person to complete assignments. Every night, he would go to bed with stacks of books and read until he fell asleep, because he had a dream of attending college.[20]

General educators and special educators need to encourage all students to be responsible and independent and to set realistic expectations for themselves. Then teachers must help students to meet these expectations in a more and more independent manner. Special educators do not serve students well when they enable students with disabilities to become increasingly dependent on their parents, counselors, administrators, or teachers—or even when they fail to increase students' independence and competence.

Where We Stand

We want to make it clear that we think disabilities are real and that they make doing certain things either impossible or very difficult for the people who have them. We cannot expect people with disabilities to be "just like everyone else" in what they can do. . . .

In our view, students with disabilities *do* have specific shortcomings and *do* need the services of specially trained professionals to achieve their potential. They *do* sometimes need altered curricula or adaptations to make their learning possible. If students with disabilities were just like "regular" students, then there would be no need whatever for special education. But the school experiences of students with disabilities obviously will not be—*cannot* be—just like those of students without disabilities. We sell students with disabilities short when we pretend that they are no different from typical students. We make the same error when we pretend that they must *not* be expected to put forth extra effort if they are to learn to do some things—or learn to do something in a different way. We sell them short when we pretend that they have competencies that they do not have or pretend that the competencies we expect of most students are not important for them.

Like general education, special education must push students to become all they can be. Special education must countenance neither the pretense of learning nor the avoidance of reasonable demands.

Notes

1. James M. Kauffman and Daniel P. Hallahan, *Special Education: What It Is and Why We Need It* (Boston: Allyn & Bacon, forthcoming).
2. Doug Fuchs et al., "Toward a Responsible Reintegration of Behaviorally Disordered Students," *Behavioral Disorders*, February 1991, pp. 133–47.
3. Evelyn Deno, "Special Education as Developmental Capital," *Exceptional Children*, November 1970, pp. 229–37; and Dixie Snow Huefner, "The Mainstreaming Cases: Tensions and Trends for School Administrators," *Educational Administration Quarterly*, February 1994, pp. 27–55.
4. Robert B. Edgerton, *The Cloak of Competence: Stigma in the Lives of the Mentally Retarded* (Berkeley, Calif.: University of California Press, 1967); idem, *The Cloak of Competence*, rev. ed. (Berkeley, Calif.: University of California Press, 1993); and James M. Kauffman, "Appearances, Stigma, and Prevention," *Remedial and Special Education*, vol. 24, 2003, pp. 195–98.
5. See, for example, Scot Danforth and William C. Rhodes, "Deconstructing Disability: A Philosophy for Education," *Remedial and Special Education*, November/December 1997, pp. 357–66; and Phil Smith, "Drawing New Maps: A Radical Cartography of Developmental Disabilities," *Review of Educational Research*, Summer 1999, pp. 117–44.

6. James M. Kauffman, *Education Deform: Bright People Sometimes Say Stupid Things about Education* (Lanham, Md.: Scarecrow Education, 2002).

7. Ibid.

8. James M. Kauffman, "Reflections on the Field," *Behavioral Disorders,* vol. 28, 2003, pp. 205–8.

9. See, for example, Clint Bolick, "A Bad IDEA Is Disabling Public Schools," *Education Week,* 5 September 2001, pp. 56, 63; and Michelle Cottle, "Jeffords Kills Special Ed. Reform School," *New Republic,* 18 June 2001, pp. 14–15.

10. See, for example, Dorothy K. Lipsky and Alan Gartner, "Equity Requires Inclusion: The Future for All Students with Disabilities," in Carol Christensen and Fazal Rizvi, eds., *Disability and the Dilemmas of Education and Justice* (Philadelphia: Open University Press, 1996), pp. 144–55; and William Stainback and Susan Stainback, "A Rationale for Integration and Restructuring: A Synopsis," in John W. Lloyd, Nirbhay N. Singh, and Alan C. Repp, eds., *The Regular Education Initiative: Alternative Perspectives on Concepts, Issues, and Models* (Sycamore, Ill.: Sycamore, 1991), pp. 225–39.

11. See, for example, Alan Gartner and Dorothy K. Lipsky, *The Yoke of Special Education: How to Break It* (Rochester, N.Y.: National Center on Education and the Economy, 1989). For an alternative view, see James M. Kauffman and Daniel P. Hallahan, "Toward a Comprehensive Delivery System for Special Education," in John I. Goodlad and Thomas C. Lovitt, eds., *Integrating General and Special Education* (Columbus, Ohio: Merrill, 1993), pp. 73–102.

12. Marc Fisher, "Students Still Taking the Fall for D.C. Schools," *Washington Post,* 13 December 2001, p. B–1.

13. Elizabeth Tener, "Blind, Deaf, and Very Successful," *McCall's,* December 1995, pp. 42–46.

14. Christina Cheakalos et al., "Heavy Mettle: They May Have Trouble Reading and Spelling, but Those with the Grit to Overcome Learning Disabilities Like Dyslexia Emerge Fortified for Life," *People,* 30 October 2001, pp. 18, 58.

15. Ibid.

16. Ibid.

17. Stephen Cannell, "How to Spell Success," *Reader's Digest,* August 2000, pp. 63–66.

18. Cheakalos et al., op cit.

19. Anne Proffit Dupre, "Disability, Deference, and the Integrity of the Academic Enterprise," *Georgia Law Review,* Winter 1998, pp. 393–473.

20. Cheakalos et al., op cit.

JAMES M. KAUFFMAN is a professor emeritus of education at the University of Virginia in Charlottesville.

KATHLEEN MCGEE AND MICHELE BRIGHAM are special education teachers.

EXPLORING THE ISSUE

Is Full Inclusion Always the Best Option for Children with Disabilities?

Critical Thinking and Reflection

1. What are some of the challenges to implementing the multilevel curriculum and curriculum overlapping strategies described by Giangreco?
2. Kauffman and colleagues argue that the goal of education for students with disabilities should be "normalization." Do you agree? Why or why not?
3. Some scholars have argued that the need for inclusion cannot be assessed by research or empirical data. These scholars believe that inclusion hinges on ethical and ideological issues. Do you agree or disagree? Why?

Is There Common Ground?

It is possible that research on inclusion to date has been inconclusive because researchers have focused on the wrong question. Much of the research in this area seems to have been designed to determine "once and for all" whether students with disabilities have better outcomes in segregated or inclusive educational programs. It is unlikely, however, that inclusion in all its forms will lead to better outcomes for all students and under all conditions. This has led some scholars to encourage researchers to ask more focused questions, such as, what types of students benefit from inclusion? What types of strategies are needed for inclusion to be effective? What types of training and belief systems do teachers need for inclusion to work? What resources are associated with effective inclusive programs? Addressing these questions may help educators to learn more about when and why inclusion is effective or ineffective.

Some scholars have argued that deciding whether or not inclusion is the best option for students with disabilities is an ethical question and, therefore, not answerable by research. See, for example, "Inclusion Paradigms in Conflict," by Peter V. Paul and Marjorie E. Ward, *Theory Into Practice* (vol. 35, no. 1, 1996). These scholars argue that segregated education is by its very nature discriminatory because it denies students with disabilities access to the same experiences and opportunities afforded everyone else. Although these scholars see a role for empirical research, that role is not to learn whether inclusion should occur but rather how it should occur.

Create Central

www.mhhe.com/createcentral

Additional Resources

Wayne Sailor and Blair Roger, "Rethinking Inclusion: Schoolwide Applications," *Phi Delta Kappan* (March 2005).

Cindy L. Praisner, "Attitudes of Elementary School Principals toward the Inclusion of Students with Disabilities," *Exceptional Children* (Winter 2003).

Susan Unok Marks, "Self-Determination for Students with Intellectual Disabilities and Why I Want Educators to Know What It Means," *Phi Delta Kappan* (September 2008).

Maury Miller, "What Do Students Think about Inclusion," *Phi Delta Kappan* (January 2008).

Internet References . . .

Maryland Coalition for Inclusive Education

http://www.mcie.org/

National Dissemination Center for Children with Disabilities

http://nichcy.org/

The Association for Persons with Severe Handicaps

http://tash.org/

Are Schools Closing the Achievement Gap between Students from Different Ethnic and Racial Backgrounds? by Abbeduto and Symons

61

Selected, Edited, and with Issue Framing Material by:
Leonard Abbeduto, *University of California, Davis*
and
Frank Symons, *University of Minnesota*

ISSUE

Are Schools Closing the Achievement Gap between Students from Different Ethnic and Racial Backgrounds?

YES: Carol Corbett Burris and Kevin G. Welner, from "Closing the Achievement Gap by Detracking," *Phi Delta Kappan* (April 2005)

NO: William H. Schmidt, Leland S. Cogan, and Curtis C. McKnight, from "Equality of Educational Opportunity: Myth or Reality in U.S. Schooling?" *American Educator* (Winter 2010–2011)

Learning Outcomes

After reading this issue, you will be able to:

- Discuss the data regarding racial and ethnic differences in academic achievement in the United States.
- Understand the differences in school experiences of students from different ethnic and racial groups and different economic circumstances.
- Define ability-level tracking and understand its uses and misuses.
- Understand some of the factors that can maintain or close the achievement gap.

ISSUE SUMMARY

YES: Carol Corbett Burris and Kevin G. Welner argue that the achievement gap between white students and African American and Hispanic students can be closed by "detracking" and having similarly high expectations and similar curricular demands on all students. Burris and Weiner provide an example of the positive effects on the achievement gap of such changes in one school district, Rockville Centre in New York State.

NO: William H. Schmidt, Leland S. Cogan, and Curtis C. McKnight argue that students are exposed to different academic content, with that content depending on the demographics of the neighborhood in which they live. Students in economically disadvantaged neighborhoods, which include an overrepresentation of ethnic and racial minorities, are exposed to less demanding content and thus achieve less. Moreover, this economic variation in exposure to learning opportunities is pervasive and persistent in the United States.

In 2014, the nation will witness the sixtieth anniversary of the U.S. Supreme Court's decision in *Brown v. the Board of Education*, which declared that the segregation of public schools according to race denied African American children the same educational opportunities as white children. Many educators and policymakers, however, do not view this anniversary as an occasion to celebrate, pointing to the continuing gap between the academic achievement of white students, on the one hand, and African American and Hispanic students, on the other hand. Put simply, compared to white students, African American and Hispanic students, on average, score lower on standardized achievement tests and tests of basic skills in mathematics and science, are more likely to leave school before graduating from high school, and are less likely to attend college.

What role do schools play in creating or maintaining this achievement gap? Some critics of public education suggest that schools have created the gap through discriminatory practices and subtle forms of racism perpetrated by teachers, administrators, and support staff, such as having lower expectations for African American and Hispanic students and assigning them to low achieving-track or special education classes at substantially higher rates than their white peers. These critics also point out that the achievement gap actually widens over the school years, with African American and Hispanic students falling further and further behind their white peers as they move through the elementary to the middle and, eventually, the high school years. Critics suggest that this increasing gap is evidence that schools are causing, or at least contributing to, the problem. Indeed, in keeping with this notion, President George W. Bush's controversial No Child Left Behind policy was based on the assumption that any student can succeed if given appropriate educational opportunities.

Many defenders of public education argue that it is not schools that are to blame for the existence of the achievement gap, but rather the broader social and economic conditions that create a wide array of disparities among different ethnic and racial groups. Years of pervasive societal discrimination, it is argued, have led to high rates of poverty among African American and Hispanic families, and thereby to less adequate material resources in homes, including books and other materials, that support academic growth; more limited access to the health care and nutrition necessary to ensure optimal development; and exposure to a variety of hazardous conditions, from lead in paint used in homes to crime and violence, all of which interfere with learning. These defenders of public education point out that children who live in poverty begin school less well prepared (e.g., with fewer preliteracy skills, such as the recognition that print encodes language) than their more affluent peers and thus, wider social forces

rather than schooling are to blame for the achievement gap. Thus, it is unreasonable, according to these defenders of public schools, to expect that schools can overcome the pervasive social and economic barriers that exist before an African American or Hispanic child begins school and continue in his or her out-of-school hours.

In the first of the following selections, Carol Corbett Burris and Kevin G. Welner argue that the achievement gap between white students and African American and Hispanic students is a consequence of the overrepresentation of minority students in low achieving-track classes. Thus, for Burris and Weiner, the answer is to detrack schools, and they provide a successful example from a suburban school district in New York State. In the second selection, William H. Schmidt, Leland S. Cogan, and Curtis C. McKnight argue that students in economically disadvantaged neighborhoods, which include an overrepresentation of ethnic and racial minorities, are exposed to less demanding content and thus achieve less. Moreover, Schmidt and colleagues argue that this economic variation in exposure to learning opportunities is pervasive and persistent in the United States.

Are Schools Closing the Achievement Gap between Students from Different Ethnic and Racial Backgrounds? by Abbeduto and Symons

63

YES

Carol Corbett Burris and Kevin G. Welner

Closing the Achievement Gap by Detracking

The most recent Phi Delta Kappa/Gallup Poll of the Public's Attitudes Toward the Public Schools found that 74% of Americans believe that the achievement gap between white students and African American and Hispanic students is primarily due to factors unrelated to the quality of schooling that children receive.[1] This assumption is supported by research dating back four decades to the Coleman Report and its conclusion that schools have little impact on the problem.[2] But is the pessimism of that report justified? Or is it possible for schools to change their practices and thereby have a strongly positive effect on student achievement? We have found that when all students—those at the bottom as well as the top of the "gap"—have access to first-class learning opportunities, all students' achievement can rise.

Because African American and Hispanic students are consistently overrepresented in low-track classes, the effects of tracking greatly concern educators who are interested in closing the achievement gap.[3] Detracking reforms are grounded in the established ideas that higher achievement follows from a more rigorous curriculum and that low-track classes with unchallenging curricula result in lower student achievement.[4] Yet, notwithstanding the wide acceptance of these ideas, we lack concrete case studies of mature detracking reforms and their effects. This article responds to that shortage, describing how the school district in which Carol Burris serves as a high school principal was able to close the gap by offering its high-track curriculum to all students, in detracked classes.

Tracking and the Achievement Gap

Despite overwhelming research demonstrating the ineffectiveness of low-track classes and of tracking in general, schools continue the practice.[5] Earlier studies have argued that this persistence stems from the fact that tracking is grounded in values, beliefs, and politics as much as it is in technical, structural, or organizational needs.[6] Further, despite inconsistent research findings,[7] many parents and educators assume that the practice benefits high achievers. This is partly because parents of high achievers fear that detracking and heterogeneous grouping will result in a "watered-down" curriculum and lowered learning standards for their children.

And so, despite the evidence that low-track classes cause harm, they continue to exist. Worse still, the negative achievement effects of such classes fall disproportionately on minority students, since, as noted above, African American and Hispanic students are overrepresented in low-track classes and underrepresented in high-track classes, even after controlling for prior measured achievement.[8] Socioeconomic status (SES) has been found to affect track assignment as well.[9] A highly proficient student from a low socioeconomic background has only a 50-50 chance of being placed in a high-track class.[10]

Researchers who study the relationship between tracking, race/ethnicity, and academic performance suggest different strategies for closing the achievement gap. Some believe that the solution is to encourage more minority students to take high-track classes.[11] Others believe that if all students are given the enriched curriculum that high-achieving students receive, achievement will rise.[12] They believe that no students—whatever their race, SES, or prior achievement—should be placed in classes that have a watered-down or remedial academic curriculum and that the tracking system should be dismantled entirely.[13] In this article, we provide evidence for the success of this latter approach. By dismantling tracking and providing the high-track curriculum to all, we can succeed in closing the achievement gap on important measures of learning.

Providing "High-Track" Curriculum to All Students

The Rockville Centre School District is a diverse suburban school district located on Long Island. In the late 1990s, it embarked on a multiyear detracking reform that increased learning expectations for all students. The district began replacing its tracked classes with heterogeneously grouped classes in which the curriculum formerly reserved for the district's high-track students was taught.

This reform began as a response to an ambitious goal set by the district's superintendent, William Johnson, and the Rockville Centre Board of Education in 1993: *By the year 2000, 75% of all graduates will earn a New York State Regents diploma.* At that time, the district and state rates of earning Regents diplomas were 58% and 38% respectively.

To qualify for a New York State Regents diploma, students must pass, at a minimum, eight end-of-course

From *Phi Delta Kappan*, April 2005, pp. 594–598. Copyright © 2005 by Phi Delta Kappan. Reprinted by permission of Phi Delta Kappan and Carol Corbett Burris/The Liberty Partnership Program and Kevin G. Welner.

Regents examinations, including two in mathematics, two in laboratory sciences, two in social studies, one in English language arts, and one in a foreign language. Rockville Centre's goal reflected the superintendent's strong belief in the external evaluation of student learning as well as the district's commitment to academic rigor.

Regents exams are linked with coursework; therefore, the district gradually eliminated low-track courses. The high school eased the transition by offering students instructional support classes and carefully monitoring the progress of struggling students.

While the overall number of Regents diplomas increased, a disturbing profile of students who were not earning the diploma emerged. These students were more likely to be African American or Hispanic, to receive free or reduced-price lunch, or to have a learning disability. At the district's high school, 20% of all students were African American or Hispanic, 13% received free and reduced-price lunch, and 10% were special education students. If these graduates were to earn the Regents diploma, systemic change would need to take place to close the gaps for each of these groups.

Accelerated Mathematics in Heterogeneous Classes

On closer inspection of the data, educators noticed that the second math Regents exam presented a stumbling block to earning the diploma. While high-track students enrolled in trigonometry and advanced algebra in the 10th grade, low-track students did not even begin first-year algebra until grade 10.

In order to provide all students with ample opportunity to pass the needed courses and to study calculus prior to graduation, Superintendent Johnson decided that all students would study the accelerated math curriculum formerly reserved for the district's highest achievers. Under the leadership of the assistant principal, Delia Garrity, middle school math teachers revised and condensed the curriculum. The new curriculum was taught to all students, in heterogeneously grouped classes. To support struggling learners, the school initiated support classes called math workshops and provided after-school help four afternoons a week.

The results were remarkable. Over 90% of incoming freshmen entered the high school having passed the first Regents math examination. The achievement gap dramatically narrowed. Between the years of 1995 and 1997, only 23% of regular education African American or Hispanic students had passed this algebra-based Regents exam before entering high school. After universally accelerating all students in heterogeneously grouped classes, the percentage more than tripled—up to 75%. The percentage of white or Asian American regular education students who passed the exam also greatly increased—from 54% to 98%.

Detracking the High School

The district approached universal acceleration with caution. Some special education students, while included in the accelerated classes, were graded using alternative assessments. This 1998 cohort of special education students would not take the first ("Sequential I") Regents math exam until they had completed ninth grade. (We use year of entry into ninth grade to determine cohort. So the 1998 cohort began ninth grade in the fall of 1998.) On entering high school, these students with special needs were placed in a double-period, low-track, "Sequential I" ninth-grade math class, along with low-achieving new entrants. Consistent with the recommendations of researchers who have defended tracking,[14] this class was rich in resources (a math teacher, special education inclusion teacher, and teaching assistant). Yet the low-track culture of the class remained unconducive to learning. Students were disruptive, and teachers spent considerable class time addressing behavior management issues. All students were acutely aware that the class carried the "low-track" label.

District and school leaders decided that this low-track class failed its purpose, and the district boldly moved forward with several new reforms the following year. All special education students in the 1999 cohort took the exam in the eighth grade. The entire 1999 cohort also studied science in heterogeneous classes throughout middle school, and it became the first cohort to be heterogeneously grouped in ninth-grade English and social studies classes.

Ninth-grade teachers were pleased with the results. The tone, activities, and discussions in the heterogeneously grouped classes were academic, focused, and enriched. Science teachers reported that the heterogeneously grouped middle school science program prepared students well for ninth-grade biology.

Detracking at the high school level continued, paralleling the introduction of revised New York State curricula. Students in the 2000 cohort studied the state's new biology curriculum, "The Living Environment," in heterogeneously grouped classes. This combination of new curriculum and heterogeneous grouping resulted in a dramatic increase in the passing rate on the first science Regents exam, especially for minority students who were previously overrepresented in the low-track biology class. After just one year of heterogeneous grouping, the passing rate for African American and Hispanic students increased from 48% to 77%, while the passing rate for white and Asian American students increased from 85% to 94%.

The following September, the 2001 cohort became the first class to be heterogeneously grouped *in all subjects* in the ninth grade. The state's new multiyear "Math A" curriculum was taught to this cohort in heterogeneously grouped classes in both the eighth and ninth grades.

In 2003, some 10th-grade classes detracked. Students in the 2002 cohort became the first to study a heterogeneously grouped pre-International Baccalaureate (IB)

Are Schools Closing the Achievement Gap between Students from Different Ethnic and Racial Backgrounds? by Abbeduto and Symons

65

10th-grade curriculum in English and social studies. To help all students meet the demands of an advanced curriculum, the district provides every-other-day support classes in math, science, and English language arts. These classes are linked to the curriculum and allow teachers to pre- and post-teach topics to students needing additional reinforcement.

Closing the Gap on Other Measures That Matter

New York's statewide achievement gap in the earning of Regents diplomas has persisted. In 2000, only 19.3% of all African American or Hispanic 12th-graders and 58.7% of all white or Asian American 12th-graders graduated with Regents diplomas. By 2003, while the percentage of students in both groups earning the Regents diploma increased (26.4% of African American or Hispanic students, 66.3% of white or Asian American students), the gap did not close.

In contrast, Rockville Centre has seen both an increase in students' rates of earning Regents diplomas and a decrease in the gap between groups. . . . For those students who began South Side High School in 1996 (the graduating class of 2000), 32% of all African American or Hispanic and 88% of all white or Asian American graduates earned Regents diplomas. By the time the cohort of 1999 graduated in 2003, the gap had closed dramatically—82% of all African American or Hispanic and 97% of all white or Asian American graduates earned Regents diplomas. In fact, . . . for this 1999 cohort (the first to experience detracking in all middle school and most ninth-grade subjects), the Regents diploma rate for the district's minority students surpassed New York State's rate for white or Asian American students.

In order to ensure that the narrowing of the gap was not attributable to a changing population, we used binary logistic regression analyses to compare the probability of earning a Regents diploma before and after detracking. In addition to membership in a detracked cohort, the model included socioeconomic and special education status as covariates. Those students who were members of the 1996 and 1997 cohorts were compared with members of the 1998–2000 cohorts. We found that membership in a cohort subsequent to the detracking of middle school math was a significant contributor to earning a Regents diploma. . . . In addition, low-SES students and special education students in the 2001 cohort also showed sharp improvement.

These same three cohorts (1998–2000) showed significant increases in the probability of minority students' studying advanced math courses. Controlling for prior achievement and SES, minority students' enrollment in trigonometry, precalculus, and Advanced Placement calculus all grew.[15] And as more students from those cohorts studied AP calculus, the enrollment gap decreased from

38% to 18% in five years, and the AP calculus scores significantly increased. . . .

Finally, detracking in the 10th grade, combined with teaching all students the pre-IB curriculum, appears to be closing the gap in the study of the IB curriculum. This year 50% of all minority students will study IB English and "History of the Americas" in the 11th grade. In the fall of 2003, only 31% chose to do so.

✦

Achievement follows from opportunities—opportunities that tracking denies. The results of detracking in Rockville Centre are clear and compelling. When all students were taught the high-track curriculum, achievement rose for all groups of students—majority, minority, special education, low-SES, and high-SES. This evidence can now be added to the larger body of tracking research that has convinced the Carnegie Council for Adolescent Development, the National Governors' Association, and most recently the National Research Council to call for the reduction or elimination of tracking.[16] The Rockville Centre reform confirms common sense: closing the "curriculum gap" is an effective way to close the "achievement gap."

Notes

1. Lowell C. Rose and Alec M. Gallup, "The 36th Annual Phi Delta Kappa/Gallup Poll of the Public's Attitudes Toward the Public Schools," *Phi Delta Kappan,* September 2004, p. 49.
2. James Coleman et al., *Equality of Educational Opportunity* (Washington, D.C.: U.S. Government Printing Office, 1966).
3. Kevin G. Welner, *Legal Rights, Local Wrongs: When Community Control Collides with Educational Equity* (Albany: SUNY Press, 2001).
4. Clifford Adelman, *Answers in the Tool Box: Academic Intensity, Attendance Patterns, and Bachelor's Degree Attainment* (Washington, D.C.: Office of Educational Research, U.S. Department of Education, 1999); . . . Henry Levin, *Accelerated Schools for At-Risk Students* (New Brunswick, N.J.: Rutgers University, Center for Policy Research in Education, Report No. 142, 1988); Mano Singham, "The Achievement Gap: Myths and Realities," *Phi Delta Kappan,* April 2003, pp. 586–91; and Jay P. Heubert and Robert M. Hauser, *High Stakes: Testing for Tracking, Promotion, and Graduation* (Washington, D.C.: National Research Council, 1999).
5. Jeannie Oakes, Adam Gamoran, and Reba Page, "Curriculum Differentiation: Opportunities, Outcomes, and Meanings," in Philip Jackson, ed., *Handbook of Research on Curriculum* (New York: Macmillan, 1992), pp. 570–608.
6. Welner, op. cit.

7. Frederick Mosteller, Richard Light, and Jason Sachs, "Sustained Inquiry in Education: Lessons from Skill Grouping and Class Size," *Harvard Educational Review,* vol. 66, 1996, pp. 797–843; Robert Slavin, "Achievement Effects of Ability Grouping in Secondary Schools: A Best-Evidence Synthesis," *Review of Educational Research,* vol. 60, 1990, pp. 471–500; and James Kulik, *An Analysis of the Research on Ability Grouping: Historical and Contemporary Perspectives* (Storrs, Conn.: National Research Center on the Gifted and Talented, University of Connecticut, 1992).

8. Roslyn Mickelson, "Subverting Swann: First- and Second-Generation Segregation in Charlotte-Mecklenburg Schools," *American Educational Research Journal,* vol. 38, 2001, pp. 215–52; Robert Slavin and Jomills Braddock II, "Ability Grouping: On the Wrong Track," *College Board Review,* Summer 1993, pp. 11–17; and Welner, op. cit.

9. Samuel Lucas, *Tracking Inequality: Stratification and Mobility in American High Schools* (New York: Teachers College Press, 1999).

10. Beth E. Vanfossen, James D. Jones, and Joan Z. Spade, "Curriculum Tracking and Status Maintenance," *Sociology of Education,* vol. 60, 1987, pp. 104–22.

11. John Ogbu, *Black American Students in an Affluent Suburb* (Mahwah, N.J.: Erlbaum, 2003).

12. Levin, op. cit.; and Slavin and Braddock, op. cit.

13. Jeannie Oakes and Amy Stuart Wells, "Detracking for High Student Achievement," *Educational Leadership,* March 1998, pp. 38–41; and Susan Yonezawa, Amy Stuart Wells, and Irene Sema, "Choosing Tracks: 'Freedom of Choice' in Detracking Schools," *American Educational Research Journal,* vol. 39, 2002, pp. 37–67.

14. Maureen Hallinan, "Tracking: From Theory to Practice," *Sociology of Education,* vol. 67, 1994, pp. 79–91; and Tom Loveless, *The Tracking Wars: State Reform Meets School Policy* (Washington, D.C.: Brookings Institution Press, 1999).

15. Carol Corbett Burris, Jay P. Heubert, and Henry M. Levin, "Math Acceleration for All," *Educational Leadership,* February 2004, pp. 68–71.

16. Carnegie Council on Adolescent Development, *Turning Points: Preparing American Youth for the 21st Century* (New York: Carnegie Corporation, 1989); *Ability Grouping and Tracking: Current Issues and Concerns* (Washington, D.C.: National Governors Association, 1993); and National Research Council, *Engaging Schools: Fostering High School Students' Motivation to Learn* (Washington, D.C.: National Academies Press, 2004).

Carol Corbett Burris is the principal of South Side High School in Rockville Centre, New York.

Kevin G. Welner is a professor and director of the National Education Policy Center at the University of Colorado at Boulder.

Are Schools Closing the Achievement Gap between Students from Different Ethnic and Racial Backgrounds? by Abbeduto and Symons

67

William H. Schmidt, Leland S. Cogan, and Curtis C. McKnight

 **NO**

Equality of Educational Opportunity: Myth or Reality in U.S. Schooling?

Public schooling is often regarded as "the great equalizer" in American society. For more than 100 years, so the story goes, children all across the country have had an equal opportunity to master the three Rs: reading, writing, and arithmetic. As a result, any student willing to work hard has the chance to go as far as his or her talent allows, regardless of family origin or socioeconomic status.

This assumption regarding opportunity and emphasis on individual talent and effort seems to be a natural offshoot of the rugged individualism and self-reliance that are so much a part of the fabled American character. We have long celebrated our cowboys, entrepreneurs, and standout athletes—but we have also long ignored those who have not succeeded. When success is individual, so is failure. It must result from a lack of effort, talent, motivation, application, or perseverance, not a lack of opportunity. Right?

Not according to our research. Defining educational equality in the most basic, foundational way imaginable—equal coverage of core academic content—we've found that America's schools are far from being the equalizers we, as a nation, want them to be.

So what? Does it really matter that "the great equalizer" is a myth? To our way of thinking, it does. First, as researchers, we believe it is always important to question our assumptions—and that goes for our national assumptions about equality and individualism as well as our personal assumptions. Second, the more we study schools, the more inequity we see. While other researchers have tackled important issues like disparities in teachers' qualifications and in classroom resources, we have focused on the basic question of what mathematics topics are taught. We have been disturbed to see that whether a student is even exposed to a topic depends on where he or she lives. Third, we find that those who don't question basic assumptions draw tragic, unsupportable conclusions. Take, for example, the controversial book *The Bell Curve,*[1] in which Richard J. Herrnstein and Charles Murray wrongly argued that unequal educational outcomes can *only* be explained by the unfortunate but unavoidable distribution of inherited abilities that relegate some students to the low end of the intelligence distribution. As we will show, unequal educational outcomes are clearly related to unequal educational opportunities.

In this article, we explore the extent to which students in different schools and districts have an equal opportunity to learn mathematics. Specifically, we discuss research on (1) the amount of variability in content coverage in eighth grade across 13 districts (or consortia of districts) and 9 states, and (2) the variation in mathematics courses offered by high schools in 18 districts spread across 2 states. We knew we would find some variability in terms of content coverage and course offerings, so our real question had to do with the nature and extent of the differences and whether they seemed to matter in terms of student achievement. Simply put, sometimes differences yield equivalent results, but sometimes differences make a difference.

In the United States, research like this is necessary because our educational system is not one system, but a disparate set of roughly 15,000 school districts distributed among 50 states and the District of Columbia. While states, with varying degrees of focus, rigor, and coherence,[2] have developed academic standards, local districts still maintain *de facto* control of their curriculum—some have written their own standards, some have written their own curriculum, some mandate the use of selected textbooks, and some leave all such decisions up to the schools. Even in states that control the range of textbooks that may be adopted by districts, the districts themselves always control (or choose to allow schools to control) which content within those textbooks will be covered or emphasized.

Leaving the choice of content coverage to individual districts and schools (with very few state controls) makes it possible and even *probable* that schools cannot be the equalizers we would like them to be. With roughly 15,000 school systems, American children simply are not likely to have equal educational opportunities as defined at the most basic level of equivalent content coverage. It is therefore highly questionable and even unfair to assume that differences in student achievement and learning are the sole result of differences in individual students' efforts and abilities. To assert that those who do not achieve at prescribed levels fail to do so because they cannot, or do not, take advantage of the opportunities afforded them is, at best, to mistake part of the story for the whole. The whole story also must consider the radically different opportunities provided by different schools, districts, and states, and acknowledge that which opportunities are

Reprinted with permission from the Winter 2010–2011 issue of *American Educator,* the quarterly journal of the American Federation of Teachers, AFL-CIO.

provided is determined by socioeconomic factors, housing patterns, community structures, parental decisions, and many other factors that have one thing in common—they are all beyond the control of individual students.

In the research literature, the concept we are exploring is called the "opportunity to learn" (OTL). While it has been defined in many ways, to our way of thinking the specific mathematics content is the defining element of an educational opportunity in mathematics. Of course, many things can and do affect how that content is delivered. But our research focuses on equivalent content coverage because this allows a more precise definition of "equal educational opportunity" as it relates to learning. Without equality in content coverage, there can be no equality in opportunity related to that content, no matter the equality of other resources provided. Ultimately, learning specific content is the goal. The mathematics itself is at the heart of the opportunity to learn and thus is a very salient component in examining equality of educational opportunity. In addition, it is a factor that policymakers can address.

In all, our research aims to answer one question: do all the different mathematics content roads fairly and equally lead to the same high-quality educational outcomes? As we will explain below, they do not.

Inequality in Eighth Grade

For our research on eighth-grade mathematics, we examined the extent to which students in different districts and states had the same opportunity to learn specific mathematics topics and how that was related to their academic achievement. To do this, we analyzed a unique set of data from a study that replicated the 1995 Third International Mathematics and Science Study (TIMSS)—the most extensive multinational comparative study ever attempted. In addition to assessing student achievement in over 40 countries, the 1995 TIMSS collected a great deal of other data, including detailed information on the mathematics curricula and classroom content coverage.

The replica study had many components or substudies. The part we are concerned with here is the TIMSS 1999 Benchmarking Study, which was designed to compare—or benchmark—U.S. states and districts against the countries that participated in the 1999 TIMSS. For the benchmarking study we worked with 13 school districts (or consortia of districts) and 9 states, all of which chose (and paid) to participate as we gathered extensive data on their eighth-grade mathematics content coverage and student achievement. A total of 36,654 students in these states and districts took the 1999 TIMSS test and provided a wide array of demographic and socioeconomic data, including age, gender, racial/ethnic group, whether English was spoken in the home, what education-related possessions were in the home (e.g., computer, dictionary, and number of books), parental education level, number of adults in the home, etc. In addition, the students' 1,861 mathematics

teachers filled out a questionnaire on the topics they had covered during the school year.

The mathematics topics listed in the teacher questionnaire were based on the mathematics content framework[3] developed for the 1995 TIMSS; it consists of 44 specific mathematics topics (e.g., common fractions, percentages, 3-D geometry, etc.) that cover the full range of K-12 mathematics. On the questionnaire, teachers indicated whether they had taught each topic for 1 to 5 periods, more than 5 periods, or not at all.

Gathering all these data was simply the first step. We didn't just want to know what was being taught in our states and districts; we wanted some sense of how each topic fit into the scope and sequence of mathematics schooling across the grades from an international perspective (hence the benchmarking idea). Using the 1995 TIMSS multinational mathematics curriculum data, we developed an International Grade Placement (IGP) topic index to indicate the grade in which the most countries typically emphasized each topic. We say "emphasized" each topic because we realize that topics are often taught in multiple grades. Nonetheless, we were able to identify the grade in which each topic typically received its greatest instructional focus. Each topic was assigned a value between 1 and 12 indicating an international consensus regarding the grade in which the topic should be emphasized. For example, the first topic, whole numbers, has an IGP value of 1.7. This means that most countries give whole numbers their greatest instructional focus toward the end of first grade.

Given the hierarchical nature of school mathematics (in which addition must come before multiplication, fractions before exponents, etc.), we think it is reasonable to assume that topics receiving their main instructional focus in later grades in most countries are more difficult than those receiving their main focus in earlier grades. Thus, our IGP topic values provide an indication of some international consensus regarding the rigor and appropriate grade level of each topic.

With this IGP topic index and the teacher questionnaire, we developed a measure of students' opportunity to learn mathematics in each of the 1,861 eighth-grade classrooms we were studying. Our opportunity-to-learn measure took into account which topics were taught, how much time was devoted to each topic, and what the IGP value was for each topic. Using this measure, we assigned each classroom a value between 1 and 12 to indicate the average international grade level of all the topics taught (weighted by instructional time). In effect, our opportunity-to-learn measure assigns an International Grade Placement value to each classroom. Averaging all the IGP values for the classrooms in a district, we can then determine each district's IGP value. And, we can do the same for each state.

A classroom that spent a lot of time on fractions (a fourth-grade topic, according to our IGP topic index), and very little time on algebraic expressions or formulas (seventh-grade topics), might have an IGP classroom value of a little more than 5, indicating a content mix that in most TIMSS countries is taught during the fifth grade. In contrast, a classroom that spent the vast majority of its time on geometry and algebra topics would have a value of about 7 to 8, because almost all time was spent on seventh- and eighth-grade topics.

Students' Opportunity to Learn Mathematics

As we briefly explained in the introduction, school districts have far more influence than states over what content gets taught. So, our discussion focuses on our district-level findings. As for the state-level findings, suffice it to say that we did all the same analyses with our state-level data as with our district-level data, and the findings were very similar. Although variation among states on all opportunity-to-learn indicators was less than that among the districts, this did not alter the pattern or significance of the observed relationships and did not change our conclusions. (The lesser variation at the state level is to be expected as states represent a broader combination of many districts.)

Internationally, the focus of eighth grade for all students in virtually all of the TIMSS countries—except the United States—is algebra and geometry. In our study, not a single district had all of its students focusing mainly on algebra and geometry. This is reflected in the districts' IGP values, which ranged from 6.0 to 6.9. This means that in some districts, eighth-grade teachers (on average) were teaching content typically found at the end of fifth or the beginning of sixth grade internationally, while in other districts, the content came closer to that found at the end of sixth or the beginning of seventh grade. Not only is this a lot of variation in students' opportunity to learn mathematics, it indicates that *all students* were being shortchanged since none of the districts were focusing on eighth-grade (or even seventh-grade) content.

Of course the real question is, does any of this variation in mathematics learning opportunities make any difference in students' achievement? We addressed this issue through a set of analyses that we briefly describe here.

On the basis of decades of findings that students with higher socioeconomic status typically have higher scores on achievement tests,[4] some researchers and policymakers have hypothesized that socioeconomic status has a *greater* impact on achievement than does schooling itself. Some have even gone so far as to conclude that schooling doesn't really matter. Indeed, among our districts, we found a strong relationship between students' mathematics achievement as measured by their TIMSS scores, and the percentage of students' parents who had a college or university degree (a common indicator of socioeconomic status).

Does this mean that all the differences we found in students' opportunity to learn mathematics are not important? Not at all. As IGP value—and, therefore, a more demanding opportunity to learn mathematics—increased, so did achievement. The relationship between students' opportunity to learn and achievement was every bit as strong as the relationship between their socioeconomic status and achievement.

Nonetheless, we still do not have the whole story. Sadly, in our "land of opportunity," students' socioeconomic status is related not only to their achievement, but also to their opportunity to learn. Across the districts we found a strong relationship between the percentage of students' parents with a college or university degree and the district IGP value. This means that the more parents with a college or university degree in a district, the higher the IGP value and the higher the average mathematics achievement. The estimated increase in opportunity to learn was not trivial: the mathematics content coverage in districts in which around 60 percent of students' parents had a college or university degree was about one-half of a grade level ahead of districts in which less than 30 percent of students' parents had a college or university degree.

These results have profound policy implications. The realization of the fundamental vision of public schools as the great equalizers rests on the assumption that content coverage is essentially the same for all children. If some are not taught essential mathematics topics in their schooling, why would we believe they will learn mathematics as well as those who are exposed to all essential content? . . .

Finding that socioeconomic status and opportunity to learn are both independently related to achievement is not surprising; these relationships have been studied previously in various ways with various types of data—both national and international, but not at the district level. In fact, we found such relationships when we analyzed the international TIMSS data.[5] However, what is unique to the United States is the strong estimated relationship between socioeconomic status and opportunity to learn. When high-quality national or regional standards (and/or curricula are in place, as they typically are in other countries, that linkage is essentially minimized if not eliminated.[6]

As a result of its strong correlation between socioeconomic status and opportunity to learn, *the United States has a particularly strong relationship between socioeconomic status and achievement.* Using the 1995 TIMSS data, we found that the correlation between socioeconomic status and achievement was stronger in the United States than in 32 (out of 40) other countries. This raises the issue of equality, given that the lower the income-level composition of a district, the more likely it is that content coverage will be less demanding and that the average mathematics achievement of eighth-graders will be lower. Most other countries have clear, detailed national or regional academic standards and/or curricula that define content coverage and therefore minimize the influence of socioeconomic status on opportunity to learn.[7]

The implication of our conceptual model is that by adopting focused, rigorous, coherent, and common content-coverage frameworks, the United States could minimize the impact of socioeconomic status on content coverage—a goal toward which virtually all our international economic peers are making progress.

Hopefully, the recently developed Common Core State Standards (see www.corestandards.org) will help the United States offer students greater equity in their opportunity to learn. But for now, a burning question remains: which is more important to student learning, socioeconomic status or opportunity to learn? An easy question to pose, but not a simple one to answer due to the complex nature of our U.S. education system. To disentangle these relationships, we analyzed the relationship between socioeconomic status, IGP value, and achievement at the classroom and district levels.

At the classroom level, controlling for socioeconomic status and students' prior achievement, the IGP value was statistically significantly related to achievement (actually, residual gain in achievement), as were our measures of socioeconomic status. For a one grade-level increase in IGP value, the increase in mean achievement at the classroom level was .15 of a standard deviation. That's like a student in the 50th percentile moving to the 56th percentile.

The impact of district-level opportunity to learn on student achievement (controlling for student- and classroom-level variables) was approximately one-third of a standard deviation. So, our best estimate indicates that an increase of one grade-level in IGP value at the district level would move a student from the 50th percentile to roughly the 65th percentile on mathematics achievement. Thus, the answer to our question is that student achievement is significantly related to socioeconomic status, but, *having controlled for this at all three levels (student, classroom, and district), both classroom- and district-level opportunity to learn is also significantly related to student achievement.* Variation in students' opportunity to learn comes from both the classroom and the district. This is both good and bad news. It is good news because opportunity to learn is something districts and teachers can change. The bad news is that districts seem to persist in providing less rigorous content to students with lower socioeconomic status.

The bottom line is that equality of educational opportunity, where opportunity is defined in terms of content coverage, does not exist within or across districts. Just as problematic is our initial finding: for these districts, the typical content covered in these eighth-grade classrooms is considered sixth-grade content internationally. *Other TIMSS countries are typically two grade levels ahead of the United States in terms of the rigor of their curricula.* Fortunately, our research suggests that the achievement of U.S. students would likely increase substantially if we would make our mathematics content more demanding.

Up to this point, we've dealt with the consequences of content variation at the middle school (eighth-grade) level. Do these differences in opportunity to learn persist once students move to high school? We address this in the next section.

Inequality in High School

As part of a research and development project called Promoting Rigorous Outcomes in Mathematics and Science Education (PROM/SE), we have worked with nearly 60 school districts in two states, Michigan and Ohio (because the work is ongoing, we will not identify the districts). To explore the extent to which high school students have an equal opportunity to learn mathematics, we examined the transcripts of 14,000 seniors in 30 high schools in 18 of our PROM/SE districts. As we explain below, we found a shocking number of mathematics courses and dramatic differences in students' course taking.

Much of the variation we found is the result of the pervasive use of high school tracking (i.e., offering different levels of the same course, such as Basic Algebra, Algebra, and Honors Algebra). While tracking today is typically not as rigid as it used to be (with students in the college, general, or vocational track for all their courses), it still has an impact on students' opportunity to learn.

Most schools and districts in the United States track students because they believe it optimizes students' achievement. Advocates of tracking argue that this type of curricular differentiation facilitates teaching and learning, as it matches students' current knowledge and ability levels to the most suitable curriculum. Tracking theory contends that some students would struggle immensely in a high-level curriculum, while a low-level curriculum would confine others.

Most research on secondary school mathematics tracking, however, has found that it tends to adversely impact students in low-level courses compared with their peers in high-level courses. Students in low-tracked mathematics courses are less likely to expect to go to college, less likely to actually attend college (even after controlling for students' postsecondary expectations), and have lower self-images.[8] Perhaps most salient, though, is that many studies have found that mathematics tracking tends to exacerbate achievement inequalities between high- and low-tracked students.[9]

In order for multiple mathematics tracks to exist, the school must offer multiple mathematics courses. A school that offers four mathematics courses—one corresponding to each grade level—and requires all of its students to take these courses, only offers one possible sequence of courses and thus one track. However, this is highly uncommon. Schools typically offer more than four mathematics courses—often many more—and allow students to choose from numerous possible sequences of courses. These sequences can, and often do, vary by the number of courses taken, the order in which courses are taken, and the types of courses taken.

To find out just how much variability there was in our 30 high schools and 18 districts, we began by counting the number of distinct mathematics courses offered. We treated each new course title as a different course, even in cases like "Formal Geometry" and "Geometry," or "Applied Algebra" and "Algebra I." Previous research has shown that the covered content in two courses with a similar title can vary wildly.[10] We therefore find it more prudent to assume that if schools choose to give courses different titles, then it is most likely that the content is different, at least to some extent.

In all, we found 270 different mathematics course titles, including 39 focused on mathematics below algebra, 11 on beginning algebra, 9 on geometry, and 9 on advanced algebra. . . .

Of course, what really matters is not all 270 courses, but which courses are offered in each of the 18 districts. We focus on the district rather than the school because the district sets curriculum policies. Of course, high schools in the same district may not offer the exact same number or types of mathematics courses, but we found the variation among schools in the same district to be quite small. In contrast, we found that the number of mathematics courses offered by each district varied considerably. If a district were to offer only one course for each mathematics content category (e.g., beginning algebra, geometry, precalculus, etc.), then there would be fewer than 10 courses offered. Looking across our 18 districts, the number of courses ranges from a low of 10 to a high of 58, with most districts offering close to 30 mathematics courses.

All these courses means that students in each school can arrange the type, number, and order of their courses, and thus vary their exposure to mathematics, in numerous ways. For example, two students in the same school may take substantively different sequences of courses—such as Basic Math, then Algebra, then Geometry; versus Geometry, then Advanced Algebra, then Precalculus—*and* take different versions of these courses—such as Elementary Geometry versus Honors Geometry.

We have, until this point, focused on the total number of courses offered, seeing large variation in both the number and the types of courses. The variation in actual courses taken, however, is not as large as it could be. Many students take similar courses. About 40 percent of the students in our study took Algebra I, Geometry, and Algebra II. Nevertheless, variation in course taking remains significant.

One particular way that students' mathematics course taking varies is in the number of courses they take. We examined the number of mathematics courses taken by each of the 14,000 seniors in our 18 districts. We were dismayed to find that in half the districts, anywhere from 10 to 27 percent of students took just one mathematics course in high school. (In the other districts, anywhere from 0 to 7 percent took just one course.) At the other extreme, in four districts the vast majority of students took four or more mathematics courses. Across districts, variation was common. Most districts had students who took anywhere from one to four or more courses.

Although we began this study well aware that high school students have options in selecting their mathematics courses, we were startled by the differences across

districts. Students may attend high school in the same district, but as they graduate there is little commonality in the type or amount of mathematics to which they have been exposed. We do not believe all high school students should take the same courses, but we do believe there should be a high degree of overlap across programs for most students. We certainly do not see any reason for 270 mathematics courses, or for 25 percent of students in one district to take just one mathematics course while more than 90 percent of students in another district take more than four courses.

Most nations endorse the idea that, as public policy, *all* their children should have equal educational opportunities. For the vast majority of 1995 TIMSS countries, intended mathematics content coverage was indeed the same for all their students through what we would call middle school. Even in countries that appear to be creating different tracks, the reality is that basic content is covered by all, with advanced students studying the same topics more deeply.[11] The associated differences among student performance on the TIMSS achievement test were thus far more a matter of individual student ability and effort, combined with differences in teacher quality, than a matter of public policy that supported or even encouraged regional or local differences in students' opportunity to learn.

Sadly, this is not the case in the United States. Not only do we have great variability across districts in eighth grade and high school, but by international standards, our eighth-grade students are exposed to sixth-grade mathematics content. Differences in mathematics achievement are *not* simply the result of differences in student ability and effort, but also matters of chance or social factors such as poverty and housing patterns that influence where a student happens to attend school. There's just no escaping that less opportunity to learn challenging mathematics corresponds to lower achievement.

Though we wish it weren't so, the United States *cannot* be considered a country of educational equality, providing equal educational opportunities to *all* students. This lack of equality in content coverage is not merely an issue for the poor or minorities. Rather, any student in the United States can be disadvantaged simply because of where he or she attends school. In school mathematics at least, the playing field for students is not level. For all students—the lucky few and the unlucky many—educational opportunity depends on factors that cannot be wholly overcome by student ability and effort.

As a nation, we must act to correct these inequities. The solution is not as easy as simply making sweeping changes in course content, but improvement is possible. Although the research we presented here is limited to eighth grade and high school, we suspect changes would need to be made from preschool through high school in mathematics content coverage, textbooks, teacher training, and professional development. Without such changes, the inequality in opportunity to learn mathematics will continue to epitomize the worst sort of playing field: how it tilts depends on where one stands.

References

1. Richard J. Herrnstein and Charles Murray, *The Bell Curve: Intelligence and Class Structure in American Life* (New York: Free Press, 1994).

2. William H. Schmidt, "What's Missing from Math Standards? Focus, Rigor, and Coherence," *American Educator* 32, no. 1 (Spring 2008): 22–24.

3. David F. Robitaille, William H. Schmidt, Senta Raizen, Curtis McKnight, Edward Britton, and Cynthia Nicol, *Curriculum Frameworks for Mathematics and Science* (Vancouver: Pacific Educational Press, 1993).

4. James S. Coleman, Ernest Q. Campbell, Carol J. Hobson, James McPartland, Alexander M. Mood, Frederic D. Weinfeld, and Robert L. York, *Equality of Educational Opportunity* (Washington, DC: National Center for Educational Statistics, 1966).

5. William H. Schmidt, Curtis C. McKnight, Richard T. Houang, HsingChi Wang, David E. Wiley, Leland S. Cogan, and Richard G. Wolfe, *Why Schools Matter: A Cross-National Comparison of Curriculum and Learning* (San Francisco: Jossey-Bass, 2001).

6. Schmidt et al., *Why Schools Matter,* chapter 4.

7. Schmidt et al., *Why Schools Matter,* chapter 4.

8. Karl L. Alexander, Martha Cook, and Edward L. McDill, "Curriculum Tracking and Educational Stratification: Some Further Evidence," *American Sociological Review* 43, no. 1 (1978): 47–66; Karl L. Alexander and Martha A. Cook, "Curricula and Coursework: A Surprise Ending to a Familiar Story," *American Sociological Review* 47, no. 5 (1982): 626–640; Karl L. Alexander and Bruce K. Eckland, "School Experience and Status Attainment," in *Adolescence in the Life Cycle: Psychological Change and Social Context,* ed. Sigmund D. Dragastin and Glen H. Elder Jr. (Washington, DC: Hemisphere, 1975), 171–210; Karl L. Alexander and Edward L. McDill, "Selection and Allocation within Schools: Some Causes and Consequences of Curriculum Placement," *American Sociological Review* 41, no. 6 (1976): 963–980; Jeannie Oakes, *Keeping Track: How Schools Structure Inequality* (New Haven, CT: Yale University Press, 1985); James E. Rosenbaum, "Track Misperceptions and Frustrated College Plans: An Analysis of the Effects of Tracks and Track Perceptions in the National Longitudinal Survey," *Sociology of Education* 53, no. 2 (1980): 74–88; and Beth E. Vanfossen, James D. Jones, and Joan Z. Spade, "Curriculum Tracking and Status Maintenance," *Sociology of Education* 60, no. 2 (1987): 104–122.

9. Adam Gamoran, "The Stratification of High School Learning Opportunities," *Sociology of Education* 60, no. 3 (1987): 135–155; Adam Gamoran and Robert D. Mare, "Secondary School Tracking and Educational Inequality: Compensation, Reinforcement, or Neutrality?" *American Journal of Sociology* 94 (1989): 1146–1183; Adam Gamoran, Andrew C. Porter, John Smithson, and Paula A. White, "Upgrading High School Mathematics Instruction: Improving Learning Opportunities for Low-Achieving, Low-Income Youth," *Educational Evaluation and Policy Analysis* 19, no. 4 (1997): 325–338; Maureen T. Hallinan and Warren Kubitschek, "Curriculum Differentiation and High School Achievement," *Social Psychology of Education* 3(1999): 41–62; Thomas B. Hoffer, "Middle School Ability Grouping and Student Achievement in Science and Mathematics," *Educational Evaluation and Policy Analysis* 14, no. 3 (1992): 205–227; Xin Ma, "A Longitudinal Assessment of Antecedent Course Work in Mathematics and Subsequent Mathematical Attainment," *Journal of Educational Research* 94, no. 1 (2000): 16–28; Barbara Schneider, Christopher B. Swanson, and Catherine Riegle-Crumb, "Opportunities for Learning: Course Sequences and Positional Advantages," *Social Psychology of Education* 2 (1998): 25–53; and David Lee Stevenson, Kathryn S. Schiller, and Barbara Schneider, "Sequences of Opportunities for Learning," *Sociology of Education* 67 (1994): 187–198.

10. Leland S. Cogan, William H. Schmidt, and David E. Wiley, "Who Takes What Math and in Which Track? Using TIMSS to Characterize U.S. Students' Eighth-Grade Mathematics Learning Opportunities," *Educational Evaluation and Policy Analysis* 23, no. 4 (2001): 323–341.

11. Schmidt et al., *Why Schools Matter,* chapter 4.

WILLIAM H. SCHMIDT is a university distinguished professor and codirector of the Education Policy Center at Michigan State University.

LELAND S. COGAN is a research associate at the Center for the Study of Curriculum at Michigan State University.

CURTIS C. MCKNIGHT is a professor emeritus of the University of Oklahoma.

Are Schools Closing the Achievement Gap between Students from Different Ethnic and Racial Backgrounds? by Abbeduto and Symons

73

EXPLORING THE ISSUE

Are Schools Closing the Achievement Gap between Students from Different Ethnic and Racial Backgrounds?

Critical Thinking and Reflection

1. Reflect on your experiences in elementary through high school. Can you generate examples of ways in which your racial and ethnic identity (or that of a peer) affected treatment by teachers or other school personnel?
2. Do you think that the detracking discussed by Burris and Welner and the types of curricular changes suggested by Schmidt and colleagues would close the achievement gap? Why or why not?
3. Do you think that schools should have "closing the achievement gap" as a goal?

Is There Common Ground?

It would appear from the results described by Burris and Welner that the answer to our question should be a resounding "yes." After all, Burris and Welner describe what seem to be substantial improvements in several indicators of the academic achievement of the participating students in the Rockville Centre School District. It is important to recognize, however, that before we fully understand the effects of any educational intervention or curricular change, we must evaluate both the long-term effects and their generalizability. Maintaining the momentum of these curricular changes may be especially difficult because so many of the students may still experience the pernicious effects of ethnic and racial discrimination outside of school. So it will be important to continue to follow the achievement of the students experiencing the curricular change as well as cohorts of students who experience the curriculum in later years to determine the long-term effects of the change. Even if the effects last, we must still be concerned with whether the changes will lead to similar positive results if implemented in other school districts enrolling different types of students, with different resources, and different levels of support from administrators.

It is also important to point out that even if current school-based approaches turn out not to have lasting, transportable effects on the achievement gap, it is possible that more dramatic (i.e., far-reaching) changes could be successful. So, for example, perhaps extending the school year through the summer would help to reduce the achievement gap when coupled with the sorts of curricular changes described by Burris and Welner. In fact, there is considerable evidence that many of the benefits accrued during the school year by economically disadvantaged African American and Hispanic students are "lost" during the summer, presumably because the pernicious effects of poverty overwhelm the benefits of schooling. Other changes might include having schools provide after-school care for students.

The selection by Schmidt and colleagues identifies many of the same factors as at the root of the achievement gap as does the Burris and Welner selection. Nevertheless, the tone of the former selection is decidedly more pessimistic; hence, our categorization as providing a "no" response to the question: Are Schools Closing the Achievement Gap between Students from Different Ethnic and Racial Backgrounds? The difference between the selections lies in part in the fact that whereas Burris and Welner focus on what can be done at the level of an individual school, Schmidt and colleagues take a broader perspective, summarizing the state of affairs in U.S. schools as a whole or at a somewhat more granular level, at the level of the city or school district. This difference in perspective between the selections also provides a valuable lesson: changing a single class or a single school may by possible, but changing the educational system is far more daunting and, more importantly, will probably require different forms of intervention including, perhaps, changes in law.

Create Central

www.mhhe.com/createcentral

Additional Resources

James Gallagher, "Education, Alone, Is a Weak Treatment," *Education Weekly* (July 1998).

Jonathon Kozol, *Savage Inequalities: Children in America's* Schools (Crown, 1991).

Richard Rothstein, "Class and the Classroom," *American School Board Journal* (October 2004).

Internet References . . .

National Education Association

http://www.nea.org

Achievement First: Public Charter Schools

http://www.achievementfirst.org/

The Achievement Gap Initaitive at Harvard University

http://www.agi.harvard.edu/

Selected, Edited, and with Issue Framing Material by:
Leonard Abbeduto, *University of California, Davis*
and
Frank Symons, *University of Minnesota*

ISSUE

Does the Current Generation of Students Require Digital Tools for Learning?

YES: Marc Prensky, from "Listen to the Natives," *Educational Leadership* (December 2005/January 2006)

NO: Sue Bennett, Karl Maton, and Lisa Kervin, from "The 'Digital Natives' Debate: A Critical Review of the Evidence" *British Journal of Educational Technology* (vol. 39, no. 5, September 2008)

Learning Outcomes

After reading this issue, you will be able to:

- Define "digital native" and "digital immigrant."
- Describe what the differences are with respect to underlying issues concerning knowledge access.
- Compare the levels of evidence for and against the position that schools much change to support a new generation of students with different learning needs/styles.

ISSUE SUMMARY

YES: Marc Prensky, speaker, writer, consultant, and game designer in education and learning areas, argues that there is a generational shift and that today's students, having spent their lifetimes immersed in technology, learn differently and have unique educational needs reflecting their digital preferences.

NO: Sue Bennett, senior lecturer, Faculty of Education, University of Wollongong; Karl Maton, lecturer, Department of Sociology and Social Policy, University of Sydney; Lisa Kervin, lecturer, Faculty of Education, University of Wollongong argue that there is little compelling empirical evidence supporting the contention of a "digital divide" in terms of fundamentally different learning styles and educational needs.

The notion of a "digital divide" between students and educators resonates; one only has to stroll through a college campus, walk into a high-school cafeteria, sit on a school bus with middle school students, or attend an elementary school after-school event to be impressed by the ever-present digital technology in the lives of children and youth. The popular press and commentators on education argue that a new generation of students exists, those born into a digital world (digital natives) different than all of those before them (so called digital immigrants). That the world they were born into is different is not in dispute; what is less clear, however, is that there is something fundamentally different about the children and students themselves. The claims are that they—digital natives—learn (process information) differently and therefore the way they need to be educated needs to change. As with other *Taking Sides* issues, a good starting point is to consider what specifically is being claimed and what the nature of the evidence is in relation to the claim. Additionally, particularly for the two selected articles for this issue, it is worth a short discussion on the types of articles and their approach to the issue.

The style of the selections differs dramatically. One (Prensky) is an opinion piece filled with ideas and a sense of urgency about what is wrong with the current situation and suggestions for improving practice; the other (Bennett) provides a more scholarly review of the argument, assumptions, and research evidence. Regardless of style, both are trying to persuade the reader in the sense of arguing for a particular conclusion. Prensky utilizes rhetorical techniques and an appeal to emotion by relying on common sense and anecdotes with assertions focused on action before it is too late. Bennett relies on trying to isolate assumptions underlying the "digital native" concept and then articulates what the nature of the scientific evidence is for (or against) the claim. The net effect, I think, of the two selections is that the issue is probably not as simple a dichotomy as it would seem; there are clear issues regarding the "digital world" and its effects on school-age students. Although some of the arguments seem like "old wine in a new bottle" (similar concerns/issues surfaced with the widespread adoption of televisions in people's homes, computers in classrooms, etc.), there is little doubt that the effect of the Internet and all of the corresponding digital technologies is changing the educational landscape.

One of the most comprehensive evaluations of secondary students and the Internet was completed through the Pew Internet and American Life Project, an ongoing project of the Pew Research Center (http://www.pewinternet.org/~/media//Files/Reports/2012/PIP_TeacherSurveyReportWithMethodology110112.pdf). The project was a large-scale survey of advanced placement (AP) and national writing project (NWP) teachers about their perspectives on their teenaged students with regard to research abilities in the "digital world." The results were—perhaps not surprisingly—mixed. The majority (3/4) of the teachers reported "mostly positive" effects for the Internet and digital search tools on their students' research abilities, but an even larger majority (87 percent) reported that digital technologies were creating an "easily distracted generation with short attention spans," with 64 percent suggesting that current digital technologies (search engines, etc.) "do more to distract students than to help them academically." Research for the teens they were responsible for teaching was synonymous with "Googling." A deep concern expressed by the teachers surveyed related to "critical engagement"—both in terms of discerning among sources of information as well as the depth with which Internet-obtained information was critically evaluated. This concern has been noted by others. When examining middle-school students interacting with Internet-search obtained material, Eagleton, Guinee, and Langlais observed students engaged in what they called "hasty, random choices with little thought and evaluation" (from "Teaching Internet Literacy Strategies: The Hero Inquiry Project," *Voices from the Middle* [vol. 10, no. 3, pp. 28–35]).

As with almost all issues framed as dichotomies, the truth of the matter probably lies somewhere in the middle; there is little doubt that we are fully immersed in a digital information age. It is clear, too, that schools and educators have important roles to play. Less clear, however, is whether the way students fundamentally learn is different. Opportunities to access information has certainly changed, but the need for high quality teachers, engaging instruction, student opportunities to respond, efficient lesson pacing, self-directed learning, and interactivity remains paramount; but these are some of the already recognized cardinal features of effective instruction. In the end, as Bennett and colleagues suggest, education (and educators) have a critical role in developing and fostering information literary necessary to support learning. How the digital tools of today can most effectively be leveraged for our students of today (and tomorrow) is of critical importance.

YES

Marc Prensky

Listen to the Natives

Schools are stuck in the 20th century. Students have rushed into the 21st. How can schools catch up and provide students with a relevant education?

School didn't teach me to read—I learned from my games.

—A student

Educators have slid into the 21st century—and into the digital age—still doing a great many things the old way. It's time for education leaders to raise their heads above the daily grind and observe the new landscape that's emerging. Recognizing and analyzing its characteristics will help define the education leadership with which we should be providing our students, both now and in the coming decades.

Times have changed. So, too, have the students, the tools, and the requisite skills and knowledge. Let's take a look at some of the features of our 21st century landscape that will be of utmost importance to those entrusted with the stewardship of our children's 21st century education.

Digital Natives

Our students are no longer "little versions of us," as they may have been in the past. In fact, they are so different from us that we can no longer use either our 20th century knowledge or our training as a guide to what is best for them educationally.

I've coined the term *[digital] native* to refer to today's students (2001). They are native speakers of technology, fluent in the digital language of computers, video games, and the Internet. I refer to those of us who were not born into the digital world as *[digital] immigrants*. We have adopted many aspects of the technology, but just like those who learn another language later in life, we retain an "accent" because we still have one foot in the past. We will read a manual, for example, to understand a program before we think to let the program teach itself. Our accent from the predigital world often makes it difficult for us to effectively communicate with our students.

Our students, as digital natives, will continue to evolve and change so rapidly that we won't be able to keep up. This phenomenon renders traditional catch-up methods, such as inservice training, essentially useless. We need more radical solutions. For example, students could learn algebra far more quickly and effectively if instruction were

available in game format. Students would need to beat the game to pass the course. They would be invested and engaged in the process.

We also need to select our teachers for their empathy and guidance abilities rather than exclusively for their subject-matter knowledge. We all remember best those teachers who cared about us as individuals and who cut us some slack when necessary. In today's rush to find teachers qualified in the curriculum, we rarely make empathy a priority.

Shifting Gears

As educators, we must take our cues from our students' 21st century innovations and behaviors, abandoning, in many cases, our own predigital instincts and comfort zones. Teachers must practice putting engagement before content when teaching. They need to laugh at their own digital immigrant accents, pay attention to how their students learn, and value and honor what their students know. They must remember that they are teaching in the 21st century. This means encouraging decision making among students, involving students in designing instruction, and getting input from students about how *they* would teach. Teachers needn't master all the new technologies. They should continue doing what they do best: leading discussion in the classroom. But they must find ways to incorporate into those discussions the information and knowledge that their students acquire outside class in their digital lives.

Our young people generally have a much better idea of what the future is bringing than we do. They're already busy adopting new systems for communicating (instant messaging), sharing (blogs), buying and selling (eBay), exchanging (peer-to-peer technology), creating (Flash), meeting (3D worlds), collecting (downloads), coordinating (wikis), evaluating (reputation systems), searching (Google), analyzing (SETI), reporting (camera phones), programming (modding), socializing (chat rooms), and even learning (Web surfing).

We need to help all our students take advantage of these new tools and systems to educate themselves. I know this is especially hard when we're the ones floundering, but teachers can certainly ask students, "Does anyone do anything on the Web that is relevant to what we're discussing?" or "Can you think of any examples of this problem in your computer games?" Teachers can also help students figure out who bas the best access to technology outside school and encourage students to form study groups so that more students benefit from this access. Teachers can learn what technological equipment they need in their classrooms simply by asking students, and they can lobby to get these items installed in school computer labs and libraries.

Student Engagement

More and more of our students lack the true prerequisites for learning—engagement and motivation—at least in terms of what we offer them in our schools. Our kids *do* know what engagement is: Outside school, they are fully engaged by their 21st century digital lives.

If educators want to have relevance in this century, it is crucial that we find ways to engage students in school. Because common sense tells us that we will never have enough truly great teachers to engage these students in the old ways—through compelling lectures from those rare, charismatic teachers, for example—we must engage them in the 21st century way: electronically. Not through expensive graphics or multimedia, but through what the kids call "gameplay." We need to incorporate into our classrooms the same combination of desirable goals, interesting choices, immediate and useful feedback, and opportunities to "level up" (that is, to see yourself improve) that engage kids in their favorite complex computer games. One elementary school in Colorado, for example, takes its students on a virtual journey to a distant planet in a spaceship powered by knowledge. If the students don't have enough knowledge to move the ship, they need to find it—in one another.

Collaborating with Students

As 21st century educators, we can no longer decide for our students; we must decide *with* them, as strange as that may feel to many of us. We need to include our students in everything we do in the classroom, involving them in discussions about curriculum development, teaching methods, school organization, discipline, and assignments. Faculty or administration meetings can no longer be effective without student representation in equal numbers. Our brightest students, trusted with responsibility, will surprise us all with their contributions.

This may sound like the inmates are running the asylum. But it's only by listening to and valuing the ideas of our 21st century students that we will find solutions to many of our thorniest education problems. For example, putting a Webcam in every classroom is a digital native way to show administrators and parents what really goes on. Teachers could also volunteer for this activity to document and share best practices.

Students could quite feasibly invent technological solutions to streamline homework submission and correction, freeing up teachers for more meaningful work. Encouraged to share their expertise, students can be a teacher's best resource for suggesting better access to technology, defining the kinds of technology that teachers should be using in the classroom, and showing teachers bow they can use specific hardware and software tools to teach more effectively.

Flexible Organization

In this century, we *must* find alternatives to our primary method of education organization—what I call *herding*. Herding is students' involuntary assignment to specific classes or groups, not for their benefit but for ours. Nobody likes to be herded, and nobody learns best in that environment. As educators become "teacherds" rather than teachers, we all lose. And creating smaller schools or classrooms is no solution if the result is simply moving around smaller herds.

There are two effective 21st century alternatives to herding. The first is one-to-one personalized instruction, continually adapted to each student as he or she learns. This practice has become next to impossible with growing class sizes, but it is still doable. Modem computer and video games have already figured out bow to adapt every moment of an experience to a player's precise capabilities and skills. So has computerized adaptive testing. Classrooms need to capitalize on students' individual capabilities and skills in the same way.

How can we make our instruction more adaptive and, as a result, far more effective? Just ask the students; they'll know. Adaptivity, along with connectivity, is where digital technology will have its greatest impact on education.

The second alternative to herding is having all learning groups self-select. Kids love working with their friends, especially virtually. I'm not saying, of course, that students should join *any* group in this context, but that they should be able to choose their own learning partners rather than having teachers assign them. Optimally and under proper supervision, a 4th grader in one school could choose a learning partner in any 4th grade class in the world. Teachers could also guide students in selecting an approved adult expert to partner with.

If we let our students choose all the groups they want to be part of—without forcing them into any one group— we will all be better off. One great advantage of virtual groups over herds is that nobody gets left out. Everybody can find *someone* in the world to work with. Teachers and administrators must be willing to set this up, provide the necessary vetting, and let it happen.

Digital Tools

Today's students have mastered a large variety of tools that we will never master with the same level of skill. From computers to calculators to MP3 players to camera phones, these tools are like extensions of their brains. Educating or evaluating students without these tools makes no more sense to them than educating or evaluating a plumber without his or her wrench.

One of the most important tools for 21st century students is not the computer that we educators are trying so hard to integrate, but the cell phone that so many of our schools currently ban. "Cell Phones Catapult Rural Africa to 21st Century," blared a recent front-page *New York Times* headline (LaFraniere, 2005). They can catapult our students into the future as well.

Cell phones have enormous capabilities these days: voice, short messaging service (SMS), graphics, user-controlled operating systems, down-loadables, browsers, camera functions (still and video), and geopositioning. Some have sensors, fingerprint readers, and voice recognition. Thumb keyboards and styluses as well as plugin screens and headphones turn cell phones into both input and output mechanisms.

The voice capabilities of the cell phone can help users access language or vocabulary training or narrate a guided tour. Teachers could deliver interactive lessons over a cell phone and use short messaging service to quiz or tutor students. Students could access animations in such subjects as anatomy and forensics. Students will soon be able to download programs into their cell phones, opening up new worlds of learning.

In Europe, China, Japan, and the Philippines, the public is already using mobile phones as learning tools. We in the United States need to join them and overcome objections that students are "using them for cheating" (so make the tests open book!) or for "inappropriate picture taking" (so instill some responsibility!). In the United Kingdom, teachers are evaluating student projects over mobile phones. The student describes the project, and the teacher analyzes the student's voiceprint for authentication.

Let's admit that the *real* reason we ban cell phones is that, given the opportunity to use them, students would "vote with their attention," just as adults "vote with their feet" by leaving the room when a presentation is not compelling. Why shouldn't our students have the same option with their education when educators fail to deliver compelling content?

Programming

The single most important differentiator between 20th century analog and 21st century digital technology is programmability Programming is perhaps *the* key skill necessary for 21st century literacy in this arena, teachers and schools are stuck in ancient times. If you wanted to get something written back then, you had to find a scribe; today, you need a programmer.

All 21st century kids are programmers to some degree. Every time they download a song or ring tone, conduct a Google search, or use any software, they are, in fact, programming. To prepare kids for their 21st century lives, we must help them maximize their tools by extending their programming abilities. Many students are already proficient enough in programs like Flash to submit their assignments in this medium. Schools should actively teach students this technology and encourage them to use it.

Of course, extending this literacy with our current teaching corps is problematic. A number of teachers I know have taken matters into their own hands, creating programming courses—especially in popular game programming—for students during the summer months, after school, and even in class. We need to capture these approaches and curriculums and make them available over the Web for all to use. Teachers can also arrange for certain students to teach these classes to their peers. In addition, outside experts are often willing to volunteer their services.

Legacy Versus Future Learning

Currently, the curriculums of the past—the "legacy" part of our kids' learning—are interfering with and cutting into the "future" curriculum—the skills and knowledge that students need for the 21st century. We need to consolidate and concentrate important legacy knowledge and make room in school for 21st century learning. Our schools should be teaching kids how to program, filter knowledge, and maximize the features and connectivity of their tools. Students should be learning 21st century subject matter, such as nanotechnology, bioethics, genetic medicine, and neuroscience.

This is a great place for involving guest teachers from professions doing cutting-edge work in these emerging fields. If every district or school found just one expert willing to contribute his or her expertise; set up and videotaped a meaningful series of Q&A exchanges with students; and put those videos on the Web, enhancing them with additional relevant materials, we'd soon have a 21st century curriculum.

Students want and deserve to receive this content through 21st century tools that are powerful, programmable, and customizable—through tools that belong to them. We could offer this content to them on their cell phones, for example. A big part of our problem is figuring out how to provide this before the end of the 21st century.

School Versus After School

Pragmatically, our 21st century kids' education is quickly bifurcating. The formal half, "school," is becoming an increasingly moribund and irrelevant institution. Its only function for many students is to provide them with a credential that their parents say they need. The informal, excit-

---

TECHNO-BYTE

U.S. teachers who say that computer technology has affected the way they teach:

- To some extent—86 percent.
- A great deal—55.6 percent.

—eSchool News, 2005

---

ing half of kids' education occurs "after school." This is the place where 21st century students learn about their world and prepare themselves for their 21st century lives. It is revealing that one of the most prevalent student demands regarding technology is to keep their schools' computer labs open until midnight (and for us to stay out of their way while they are there). It is equally telling that so many software and Web programs aimed at enhancing kids' education are designed for after-school rather than in-school use.

If our schools in the 21st century are to be anything more than holding pens for students while their parents work, we desperately need to find ways to help teachers integrate kids' technology-rich after-school lives with their lives in school. It doesn't help if, in the words of Henry Kelly, president of the Federation of American Scientists, "the cookies on my daughter's computer know more about her interests than her teachers do." It helps even less that a great many of our teachers and administrators have no idea what a *cookie* or a *blog* or a *wiki* even is.

Student Voice

Our students, who are empowered in so many ways outside their schools today, have no meaningful voice at all in their own education. Their parents' voices, which up until now have been their proxies, are no longer any more closely aligned with students' real education needs than their teachers' voices are. In the 21st century, this lack of any voice on the part of the customer will soon be unacceptable.

Some organizations are trying to change this. For example, NetDay (www.netday.org) conducts an annual online student survey of technology use through its Speak Up Days. All school districts should participate in this survey. Then, instead of hearing from just the 200,000 students who responded in the last survey, we would know what 50 million of them are thinking. Districts would receive valuable input from their students that they could apply to improving instruction.

As we educators stick our heads up and get the lay of the 21st century land, we would be wise to remember this: If we don't stop and listen to the kids we serve, value their opinions, and make major changes on the basis of the valid suggestions they offer, we will be left in the 21st century with school buildings to administer—but with students who are physically or mentally somewhere else.

References

LaFraniere, S. (2005, Aug, 25). Cell phones catapult rural Africa to 21st century. *New York Times on the Web.* Available: http://msn-cnet.com/Cell+phones+catapult+rural+Africa+to+21st+century/2100-1039_3-5842901.html

Prensky, M. (2001). Digital natives, digital immigrants. *On the Horizon,* 9(5), 1–2. Available: www.marcprensky.com/writing/Prensky%20-%20Digital%20Natives,%20Digital-%20Immigrants%20-%20Partl.pdf

---

Marc Prensky is speaker, writer, consultant, and game designer in education and learning areas.

Sue Bennett, Karl Maton,
and Lisa Kervin

 **NO**

The "Digital Natives" Debate: A Critical Review of the Evidence

Commentators on education are arguing that a new generation of learners is entering our educational institutions, one which has grown up with information and communication technology (ICT) as an integral part of their everyday lives. It is claimed these young people's use of ICTs differentiates them from previous generations of students and from their teachers, and that the differences are so significant that the nature of education itself must fundamentally change to accommodate the skills and interests of these "digital natives" (Prensky, 2001a). We shall argue that though such calls for major change in education are being widely propounded, they have been subjected to little critical scrutiny, are undertheorised, and lack a sound empirical basis. There is thus a pressing need for theoretically informed research.

In this paper, we bring together educational research and the sociology of knowledge to provide an analysis of the current state of play in the digital natives debate. We begin by setting out the main claims made in the debate. Second, we explore the assumptions underlying these claims and the consequent arguments for educational change, highlighting the limited nature of the research evidence on which they are based. Third, we consider why such poorly evidenced claims have gained widespread currency by analysing the nature of the debate itself. This highlights how principal positions have created the academic equivalent of a "moral panic" that restricts critical and rational debate. Lastly, we argue that the debate as currently formulated is at an impasse, and the way forward requires a research agenda capable of providing a sound basis on which future debate and policymaking can be founded.

Claims about "Digital Natives"

The generation born roughly between 1980 and 1994 has been characterised as the "digital natives" (Prensky, 2001a) or the "Net generation" (Tapscott, 1998) because of their familiarity with and reliance on ICT. They are described as living lives immersed in technology, "surrounded by and using computers, videogames, digital music players, video cams, cell phones, and all the other toys and tools

of the digital age" (Prensky, 2001a, p. 1). Social researchers Howe and Strauss (2000, 2003), labelled this generation the "millenials," ascribing to them distinct characteristics that set them apart from previous generations. They offer a positive view of this new generation as optimistic, team-oriented achievers who are talented with technology, and claim they will be America's next "great generation."

Immersion in this technology-rich culture is said to influence the skills and interests of digital natives in ways significant for education. It is asserted, for example, that digital natives learn differently compared with past generations of students. They are held to be active experiential learners, proficient in multitasking, and dependent on communications technologies for accessing information and for interacting with others (Frand, 2000; Oblinger & Oblinger, 2005; Prensky, 2001a, b; Tapscott, 1999). Commentators claim these characteristics raise fundamental questions about whether education is currently equipped to meet the needs of this new cohort of students. Tapscott (1998), for example, described education in developed countries as already in crisis with more challenges to come: "There is growing appreciation that the old approach [of didactic teaching] is ill-suited to the intellectual, social, motivational, and emotional needs of the new generation" (p. 131). This was echoed by Prensky's (2001a) claim that: *"Our students have changed radically. Today's students are no longer the people our educational system was designed to teach"* [emphasis in original] (p. 1).

For those born prior to 1980, Prensky (2001a) has coined the term "digital immigrants." He claims that this section of the population, which includes most teachers, lacks the technological fluency of the digital natives and finds the skills possessed by them almost completely foreign. The disparity between the technological skills and interests of new students and the limited and unsophisticated technology use by educators is claimed to be creating alienation and disaffection among students (Levin & Arafeh, 2002; Levin, Richardson & Arafeh, 2002; Prensky, 2005a). Prensky (2001a) characterises this as "the biggest single problem facing education today" (p. 3). To address this proclaimed challenge, some high-profile commentators are arguing for radical changes in curriculum, pedagogy, assessment and professional development in education.

The debate over digital natives is thus based on two key claims: (1) that a distinct generation of "digital natives" exists; and (2) that education must fundamentally change to meet the needs of these "digital natives." These in turn are based on fundamental assumptions with weak empirical and theoretical foundations, which we will explore in the next sections.

On the Distinctive Characteristics of "Digital Natives"

The claim made for the existence of a generation of "digital natives" is based on two main assumptions in the literature, which can be summarised as follows:

1. Young people of the digital native generation possess sophisticated knowledge of and skills with information technologies.
2. As a result of their upbringing and experiences with technology, digital natives have particular learning preferences or styles that differ from earlier generations of students.

In the seminal literature on digital natives, these assertions are put forward with limited empirical evidence (eg, Tapscott, 1998), or supported by anecdotes and appeals to common-sense beliefs (eg, Prensky, 2001a). Furthermore, this literature has been referenced, often uncritically, in a host of later publications (Gaston, 2006; Gros, 2003; Long, 2005; McHale, 2005; Skiba, 2005). There is, however, an emerging body of research that is beginning to reveal some of the complexity of young people's computer use and skills.

Information Technology Use and Skills Amongst Young People

One of the founding assumptions of claims for a generation of digital natives is that young people live their lives completely immersed in technology and are "fluent in the digital language of computers, video games and the Internet" (Prensky, 2005b, p. 8). Frand (2000) claims that this immersion is so complete that young people do not even consider computers "technology" anymore. Personal testimonials (eg, McNeely, 2005; Windham, 2005) depicting young people's online lives as constantly connected appear to confirm such generalisations.

Recent research into how young people in post-compulsory education access and use technology, however, offers a more diverse view of the role of technology in the lives of young people. For example, a survey of 4374 students across 13 institutions in the United States (Kvavik, Caruso & Morgan, 2004) found that the majority of respondents owned personal computers (93.4%) and mobile phones (82%), but a much smaller proportion owned handheld computers (11.9%). The most common technology uses were word processing (99.5%), emailing (99.5%) and surfing the Net for pleasure (99.5%). These results do demonstrate high levels of ownership of some technologies by the respondents and high levels of some academic and recreational activities, and their associated skills. The researchers found, however, that only a minority of the students (around 21%) were engaged in creating their own content and multimedia for the Web, and that a significant proportion of students had lower level skills than might be expected of digital natives.

The general thrust of these findings is supported by two recent studies of Australian university students (Kennedy, Krause, Judd, Churchward & Gray, 2006; Oliver & Goerke, 2007) showing similar patterns in access to ICTs. These studies also found that emerging technologies were not commonly used, with only 21% of respondents maintaining a blog, 24% using social-networking technologies (Kennedy *et al*, 2006), and 21.5% downloading podcasts (Oliver & Goerke, 2007). As observed by Kennedy *et al* (2006), although many of the students were using a wide range of technologies in their daily lives, "there are clearly areas where the use of and familiarity with technology-based tools is far from universal" (p. 8). Some of this research (Kennedy *et al*, 2006; Kvavik *et al*, 2005) has identified potential differences related to socio-economic status, cultural/ethnic background, gender and discipline specialisation, but these are yet to be comprehensively investigated. Also not yet explored is the relationship between technology access, use and skill, and the attitudinal characteristics and dispositions commonly ascribed to the digital native generation.

Large-scale surveys of teenagers' and children's use of the Internet (cf, Lenhart, Madden & Hitlin, 2005; Livingstone & Bober, 2004) reveal high levels of online activity by many school-aged children, particularly for helping with homework and for social communication. The results also suggest that the frequency and nature of children's Internet use differs between age groups and socio-economic background. For instance, Internet use by teenagers is far from uniform and depends on the contexts of use, with widely varying experiences according to children's school and home backgrounds (Lee, 2005). This is further supported by recent research showing family dynamics and the level of domestic affluence to be significant factors influencing the nature of children's home computer use (Downes, 2002). These findings suggest that technology skills and experience are far from universal among young people.

In summary, though limited in scope and focus, the research evidence to date indicates that a proportion of young people are highly adept with technology and rely on it for a range of information gathering and communication activities. However, there also appears to be a significant proportion of young people who do not have the levels of access or technology skills predicted by proponents of the digital native idea. Such generalisations about a whole generation of young people thereby focus attention on technically adept students. With this comes the danger that those less interested and less able will be neglected, and that the potential impact of socio-economic and cultural factors will be overlooked. It may be that there is as much variation *within* the digital native generation as *between* the generations.

Distinctive Digital Native Learning Styles and Preferences

The second assumption underpinning the claim for a generation of digital natives is that because of their immersion in technology young people *"think and process information fundamentally differently* from their predecessors" (Prensky, 2001a, p. 1, emphasis in the original). Brown (2000), for example, contends "today's kids are always "multiprocessing"— they do several things simultaneously—listen to music, talk on the cell phone, and use the computer, all at the same time" (p. 13). It is also argued that digital natives are accustomed to learning at high speed, making random connections, processing visual and dynamic information and learning through game-based activities (Prensky, 2001a). It is suggested that because of these factors, young people prefer discovery-based learning that allows them to explore and to actively test their ideas and create knowledge (Brown, 2000).

Although such claims may appeal to our common-sense perceptions of a rapidly changing world, there is no evidence that multitasking is a new phenomenon exclusive to digital natives. The oft-used example of a young person doing homework while engaged in other activities was also applied to earlier generations doing homework in front of the television. Such examples may resonate with our personal observations, but research in cognitive psychology reveals a more complex picture. For example, multitasking may not be as beneficial as it appears, and can result in a loss of concentration and cognitive "overload" as the brain shifts between competing stimuli (Rubinstein, Meyer & Evans, 2001; Sweller, 1988).

Nor is there clear evidence that the interactivity prevalent in most recreational computer games is applicable to learning. The enthusiasm for educational games among some commentators rests on the possibility of harnessing the high levels of engagement and motivation reported by many game players to motivate students to learn. Although the idea has excited interest for many years, and there is some evidence that highly modified game-based approaches can support effective learning (Dede, 2005), research into how to design games that foster deep learning is inadequate (Moreno & Mayer, 2005). Furthermore, the substantially greater popularity of games amongst males compared to females (Kennedy *et al*, 2006; Kvavik *et al*, 2005) may limit the appeal of games to all learners. This is not to say that educational games might not be effective, but simply questions the assumption that their apparent popularity in everyday life makes them directly and unproblematically applicable to education.

Generalisations about the ways in which digital natives learn also fail to recognise cognitive differences in young people of different ages and variation within age groups.

Cognitive psychologists have studied the level and range of skills exhibited at different ages (Berk, 2006; Carlson & Sohn, 2000; Mityata & Norman, 1986). The notable differences identified throughout the key stages of infancy, early childhood, middle childhood and adolescence are significant for the digital native debate. For example, research findings have identified the developing capacity of short-term memory (Cowan, Nugent, Elliott, Ponomarev & Saults, 1999). As this capacity increases with age, so too do children's abilities to scan information more quickly, apply strategies to transform it more rapidly, hold more information within memory and move between tasks more easily. Thus, differences across the developmental stages need to be considered when making claims about the level of skills "young people" have and their ability to successfully utilise these when interacting with ICTs.

Furthermore, the claim that there might be a particular learning style or set of learning preferences characteristic of a generation of young people is highly problematic. Learning style theories (cf, Jonassen & Grabowski, 1993; Kolb, 1984) do differentiate between different preferences learners might have and different approaches they might adopt, but these are not seen as static, nor are they generalisable to whole populations. Such theories acknowledge significant variability between individuals. Research also shows that students change their approach to learning depending on their perception of what a task requires and their previous success with a particular approach (Biggs, 2003; Ramsden, 1992). To attribute a particular learning style or even general preferences to a whole generation is thus questionable.

In this section, we have examined the key assumptions underlying the claim that the generation of young people born between 1980 and 1994 are "digital natives." It is apparent that there is scant evidence to support this idea, and that emerging research challenges notions of a homogenous generation with technical expertise and a distinctive learning style. Instead, it suggests variations and differences within this population, which may be more significant to educators than similarities.

Some commentators might still argue that regardless of whether the digital native phenomenon is a generational trait or whether it is more due to exposure to ICTs, the education of tech-savvy students is still a major issue for education. This second prominent claim in the debate, that education must fundamentally change to accommodate digital natives' interests, talents and preferences, therefore requires exploration.

On Arguments for Fundamental Changes in Education

The claim we will now examine is that current educational systems must change in response to a new generation of technically adept young people. Current students have been variously described as disappointed (Oblinger, 2003), dissatisfied (Levin & Arafeh, 2002) and disengaged

(Prensky, 2005a). It is also argued that educational institutions at all levels are rapidly becoming outdated and irrelevant, and that there is an urgent need to change what is taught and how (Prensky, 2001a; Tapscott, 1998). For example, Tapscott (1999) urges educators and authorities to "[g]ive students the tools, and they will be the single most important source of guidance on how to make their schools relevant and effective places to learn" (p. 11). Without such a transformation, commentators warn, we risk failing a generation of students and our institutions face imminent obsolescence.

However, there is little evidence of the serious disaffection and alienation among students claimed by commentators. Downes' (2002) study of primary school children (5–12 years old) found that home computer use was more varied than school use and enabled children greater freedom and opportunity to learn by doing. The participants did report feeling limited in the time they were allocated to use computers at school and in the way their use was constrained by teacher-directed learning activities. Similarly, Levin and Arafeh's (2002) study revealed students' frustrations at their school Internet use being restricted, but crucially also their recognition of the school's *in loco parentis* role in protecting them from inappropriate material. Selwyn's (2006) student participants were also frustrated that their freedom of use was curtailed at school and "were well aware of a digital disconnect but displayed a pragmatic acceptance rather than the outright alienation from the school that some commentators would suggest" (p. 5).

This evidence points to differences in the ways young people use technology inside and outside of school, and suggests that school use of the Internet can be frustrating, but there is little basis to conclude that these differences are causing widespread and profound disengagement in learning. Rather, they tell us that technology plays a different role in students' home and school lives. This view is supported by research in postcompulsory education, indicating that students are not clamouring for greater use of technology (Kvavik *et al*, 2004; Lohnes & Kinzer, 2007). These studies demonstrate the need to be much more careful about the views we ascribe to young people about technology.

Furthermore, questions must be asked about the relevance to education of the everyday ICTs skills possessed by technically adept young people. For example, it cannot be assumed that knowing how to look up "cheats" for computer games on the Internet bears any relation to the skills required to assess a website's relevance for a school project. Indeed, existing research suggests otherwise. When observing students interacting with text obtained from an Internet search, Sutherland-Smith (2002) reported that many were easily frustrated when not instantly gratified in their search for immediate answers and appeared to adopt a "snatch and grab philosophy" (p. 664). Similarly, Eagleton, Guinee and Langlais (2003) observed middle-school students often making "hasty, random choices with little thought and evaluation" (p. 30).

Such research observes shallow, random and often passive interactions with text, which raise significant questions about what digital natives can actually do as they engage with and make meaning from such technology. As noted by Lorenzo and Dziuban (2006), concerns over students' lack of critical thinking when using Internet-based information sources imply that "students aren't as net savvy as we might have assumed" (p. 2). This suggests that students' everyday technology practices may not be directly applicable to academic tasks, and so education has a vitally important role in fostering information literacies that will support learning.

In summary, calls for a dramatic shift from text-based to multimedia educational resources, the increased use of computer games and simulations, and a move to constructivist approaches that emphasise student knowledge creation, problem solving and authentic learning (Brown, 2000; Oblinger, 2004; Tapscott, 1999) based solely on the supposed demands and needs of a new generation of digital natives must be treated with caution. This is not to discount other arguments made for changes to education that are based on theory and supported by clear research evidence, but we suggest that the same standards must be met before radical change is made on the basis of the digital native idea.

Discussion

Our analysis of the digital native literature demonstrates a clear mismatch between the confidence with which claims are made and the evidence for such claims. So, why have these claims gained such currency? Put another way, why have these arguments repeatedly been reproduced as if they were supported by empirical evidence? An examination of the nature of the "debate" itself offers some clues.

Cohen's (1972) notion of a "moral panic" is helpful in understanding the form taken by the digital natives debate. In general, moral panics occur when a particular group in society, such as a youth subculture, is portrayed by the news media as embodying a threat to societal values and norms. The attitudes and practices of the group are subjected to intense media focus, which, couched in sensationalist language, amplifies the apparent threat. So, the term "moral panic" refers to the form the public discourse takes rather than to an actual panic among the [populace]. The concept of moral panic is widely used in the social sciences to explain how an issue of public concern can achieve a prominence that exceeds the evidence in support of the phenomenon (see Thompson, 1998).

In many ways, much of the current debate about digital natives represents an academic form of moral panic. Arguments are often couched in dramatic language, proclaim a profound change in the world, and pronounce stark generational differences. These characteristics are exemplified in the followed quote from Prensky (2001a), but are also evident throughout much of the digital natives literature:

> Today's students have not just changed incrementally from those of the past. . . . A really big

discontinuity has taken place. One might even call it a "singularity"—an event which changes things so fundamentally that there is absolutely no going back. (p. 1)

Such claims coupled with appeals to common sense and recognisable anecdotes are used to declare an emergency situation, and call for urgent and fundamental change.

Another feature of this "academic moral panic" is its structure as a series of strongly bounded divides: between a new generation and all previous generations; between the technically adept and those who are not; and between learners and teachers. A further divide is then created between those who believe in the digital native phenomenon and those who question it. Teachers who do not change their practices are labelled as "lazy" and "ineffective" (Prensky, 2001a). Those who refuse to recognise what is described as an inevitable change are said to be in denial, resistant and out of touch, and are portrayed as being without legitimate concerns (Downes, 2007; Tapscott, 1998).

Thus, the language of moral panic and the divides established by commentators serve to close down debate, and in doing so allow unevidenced claims to proliferate. Not only does this limit the possibility for understanding the phenomenon, it may also alienate the very people being urged to change. Teachers, administrators and policymakers have every right to demand evidence and to expect that calls for change be based on well-founded and supported arguments. As is evident from the review in this paper, many of the arguments made to date about digital natives currently lack that support.

Without critical rational discussion, little progress can be made towards a genuine debate about digital natives. Sceptics can highlight the lack of empirical evidence to dismiss the notion of digital natives as hyperbole. Advocates making claims with little evidence are in danger of repeating a pattern seen throughout the history of educational technology in which new technologies promoted as vehicles for educational reform then fail to meet unrealistic expectations (Cuban, 2001).

Neither dismissive scepticism nor uncritical advocacy enable understanding of whether the phenomenon of digital natives is significant and in what ways education might need to change to accommodate it. As we have discussed in this paper, research is beginning to expose arguments about digital natives to critical enquiry, but much more needs to be done. Close scrutiny of the assumptions underlying the digital natives notion reveals avenues of inquiry that will inform the debate. Such understanding and evidence are necessary precursors to change.

Conclusion

The claim that there is a distinctive new generation of students in possession of sophisticated technology skills and with learning preferences for which education is not equipped to support has excited much recent attention.

Proponents arguing that education must change dramatically to cater for the needs of these digital natives have sparked an academic form of a "moral panic" using extreme arguments that have lacked empirical evidence.

The picture beginning to emerge from research on young people's relationships with technology is much more complex than the digital native characterisation suggests. While technology is embedded in their lives, young people's use and skills are not uniform. There is no evidence of widespread and universal disaffection, or of a distinctly different learning style the like of which has never been seen before. We may live in a highly technologised world, but it is conceivable that it has become so through evolution, rather than revolution. Young people may do things differently, but there are no grounds to consider them alien to us. Education may be under challenge to change, but it is not clear that it is being rejected.

The time has come for a considered and disinterested examination of the assumptions underpinning claims about digital natives such that researchable issues can be identified and dispassionately investigated. This is not to say that young people are not engaged and interested in technology and that technology might not support effective learning. It is to call for considered and rigorous investigation that includes the perspectives of young people and their teachers, and genuinely seeks to understand the situation before proclaiming the need for widespread change.

References

Berk, L. E. (2006). *Child development.* Boston, MA: Pearson.

Biggs, J. (2003). *Teaching for quality learning at university.* Buckingham, UK: OUP.

Brown, J. S. (2000). Growing up digital: how the Web changes work, education, and the ways people learn. *Change, March/April,* 10–20.

Carlson, R. A. & Sohn, M-Y. (2000). Cognitive control of multistep routines: information processing and conscious intentions. In S. Mondell and J. Driver (Eds), *Control of cognitive processes: attention and performance XVIII* (pp. 443–464). Cambridge, MA: The MIT Press.

Cohen, S. (1972). *Folk devils and moral panics.* London: MacGibbon & Kee.

Cowan, N., Nugent, L. D., Elliott, E. M., Ponomarev, I. & Saults, J. S. (1999). The role of attention in the development of short-term memory: age differences in the verbal span of apprehension. *Child Development, 70,* 1082–1097.

Cuban, L. (2001). *Oversold and underused: computers in the classroom.* Cambridge, MA: Harvard University.

Dede, C. (2005). Planning for neomillennial learning styles: implications for investments in faculty and technology. In D. Oblinger & J. Oblinger (Eds),

Educating the Net generation (pp. 15.1–15.22). Boulder, CO: EDUCAUSE. Retrieved March 31, 2006, from http://www.educause.edu/educatingthenetgen

Downes, S. (2007). Places to go: Google's search results for the "Net generation." *Innovate, 3,* 4. Retrieved June 27, 2007, from http://www.innovateonline.info /index.php?view=article&id=455

Downes, T. (2002). Blending play, practice and performance: children's use of computer at home. *Journal of Educational Enquiry, 3,* 2, 21–34.

Eagleton, M. B., Guinee, K. & Langlais, K. (2003). Teaching Internet literacy strategies: the hero inquiry project. *Voices from the Middle, 10,* 3, 28–35.

Frand, J. (2000). The information-age mindset: changes in students and implications for higher education. *EDUCAUSE Review, 35,* September-October, 14–24.

Gaston, J. (2006). Reaching and teaching the digital natives. *Library Hi Tech News, 23,* 3, 12–13.

Gros, B. (2003). The impact of digital games in education. *First Monday, 8, 7.* Retrieved February 21, 2007, from http://www.firstmonday.org/issues /issue8_7/xyzgros/index.html

Howe, N. & Strauss, W. (2000). *Millennials rising: the next great generation.* New York: Vintage.

Howe, N., & Strauss, W. (2003). *Millennials go to college.* Washington, DC: American Association of Collegiate Registrars and Admissions Officers.

Jonassen, D. & Grabowski, B. L. (1993). *Handbook of individual differences, learning and instruction.* Hillsdale, NJ: Lawrence Erlbaum.

Kennedy, G., Krause, K., Judd, T., Churchward, A. & Gray, K. (2006). *First year students' experiences with technology: are they really digital natives?* Melbourne, Australia: University of Melbourne. Retrieved April 10, 2007, from http://www.bmu.unimelb.edu.au /research/munatives/natives_report2006.rtf

Kolb, D. A. (1984). *Experiential learning: experience as the source of learning and development.* Englewood Cliffs, NJ: Prentice-Hall.

Kvavik, R. B., Caruso, J. B. & Morgan, G. (2004). *ECAR study of students and information technology 2004: convenience, connection, and control.* Boulder, CO: EDUCAUSE Center for Applied Research. Retrieved February 21, 2007, from http://www .educause.edu/ir/library/pdf/ers0405/rs/ers0405w.pdf

Kvavik, R. B. (2005). Convenience, communication, and control: how students use technology. In D. G. Oblinger & J. L. Oblinger (Eds.), *Educating the Net generation* (pp. 7.1–7.20). Boulder, CO: EDUCAUSE. Retrieved May 27, 2007, from http:// www.educause.edu/educatingthenetgen

Lee, L. (2005). Young people and the Internet: from theory to practice. *Nordic Journal of Youth Research, 13,* 4, 315–326.

Lenhart, A., Madden, M. & Hitlin, P. (2005).Teens and technology: Youth are leading the transition to a fully wired and mobile nation. Washington DC: Pew Internet & American Life Project.

Levin, D. & Arafeh, S. (2002). *The digital disconnect: the widening gap between Internet-savvy students and their schools.* Washington DC: Pew Internet & American Life Project. Retrieved April 10, 2007, from http://www.pewinternet.org/report_display. asp?r=67

Levin, D., Richardson, J., & Arafeh, S. (2002). Digital disconnect: students' perceptions and experiences with the Internet and education. In P. Baker & S. Rebelsky (Eds), *Proceedings of ED-MEDIA, World Conference On Educational Multimedia, Hypermedia and Telecommunications* (pp. 51–52). Norfolk, VA: Association for the Advancement of Computing in Education.

Livingstone, S. & Bober, M. (2004). Taking up online opportunities? Children's use of the Internet for education, communication and participation. *E-Learning, 1,* 3, 395–419.

Lohnes, S. & Kinzer, C. (2007). Questioning assumptions about students' expectations for technology in college classrooms. *Innovate, 3,* 5. Retrieved June 27, 2007, from http://www.innovateonline.info/ index.php?view=article&id=431

Long, S. A. (2005). What's new in libraries? Digital natives: if you aren't one, get to know one. *New Library World, 106,* 3/4, 187.

Lorenzo, G. & Dziuban, C. (2006). Ensuring the Net generation is Net savvy. EDUCAUSE Learning Initiative Paper 2. Boulder, CO: EDUCAUSE. Retrieved May 27, 2007, from http://www.educause .edu/ir/library/pdf/ELI3006.pdf

McHale, T. (2005). Portrait of a digital native. *Technology and Learning, 26,* 2, 33–34.

McNeely, B. (2005). Using technology as a learning tool, not just a cool new thing. In D. Oblinger & J. Oblinger (Eds), *Educating the Net generation* (pp. 4.1–4.10). Boulder, CO: EDUCAUSE. Retrieved March 31, 2006, from http://www.educause.edu /educatingthenetgen

Mityata, Y. & Norman, D. A. (1986). Psychological issues in support of multiple activities. In D. A. Norman & S. W. Draper (Eds), *User centred design* (pp. 265–284). New York: Lawrence Erlbaum.

Moreno, R. & Mayer, R. E. (2005). Role of guidance, reflection and interactivity in an agent-based multimedia game. *Journal of Educational Psychology, 97,* 1, 177–128.

Oblinger, D. (2003). Boomers, Gen-Xers and Millennials: understanding the new students. *EDUCAUSE Review, 38,* 4, July/August, 37–47.

Oblinger, D. (2004). The next generation of educational engagement. *Journal of Interactive Media in Education, 8.* Retrieved June 27, 2007, from http://www-jime.open.ac.uk/2004/8/oblinger-2004-8-disc-t.html

Oblinger, D. & Oblinger, J. (2005). Is it age or IT: first steps towards understanding the net generation. In D. Oblinger & J. Oblinger (Eds), *Educating the Net generation* (pp. 2.1–2.20). Boulder, CO: EDUCAUSE. Retrieved March 31, 2006, from http://www.educause.edu/educatingthenetgen

Oliver, B. and Goerke, V. (2007). Australian undergraduates' use and ownership of emerging technologies: implications and opportunities for creating engaging learning experiences for the Net generation. *Australasian Journal of Educational Technology, 23,* 2, 171–186. Retrieved June 27, 2007, from http://www.ascilite.org.au/ajet/ajet23/oliver.html

Prenksy, M. (2001a). Digital natives, digital immigrants. *On the Horizon, 9,* 5, 1–6.

Prenksy, M. (2001b). Digital natives, digital immigrants, part II. Do they really think differently? *On the Horizon, 9,* 6, 1–6.

Prensky, M. (2005a). Engage me or enrage me. *EDUCASE Review, 40,* 5, September/October, 61–64.

Prensky, M. (2005b). Listen to the natives. *Educational Leadership, 63,* 4, 8–13.

Ramsden, P. (1992). *Learning to teach in higher education.* London: Routledge.

Rubinstein, J., Meyer, D. E. & Evans, J. E. (2001). Executive control of cognitive processes in task switching. *Journal of Experimental Psychology: Human Perception and Performance, 27,* 4, 763–797.

Selwyn, N. (2006). Exploring the "digital disconnect" between net-savvy students and their schools. *Learning, Media and Technology, 31,* 1, 5–17.

Skiba, D. J. (2005). The millennials: have they arrived at your school of nursing? *Nursing Education Perspectives, 27,* 3, 370.

Sutherland-Smith, W. (2002). Weaving the literacy Web: changes in reading from page to screen. *The Reading Teacher, 55,* 7, 662–669.

Sweller, J. (1988). Cognitive load during problem solving: effects on learning. *Cognitive Science, 12,* 2, 257–285.

Tapscott, D. (1998). *Growing up digital: the rise of the Net generation.* New York: McGraw-Hill.

Tapscott, D. (1999). Educating the Net generation. *Educational Leadership, 56,* 5, 6–11.

Thompson, K. (1998). *Moral panics.* London: Routledge.

Windham, C. (2005). Father google & mother IM: confessions of a net gen learner. *EDUCAUSE Review, 40,* 5, 42–59.

SUE BENNETT is a senior lecturer, Faculty of Education, University of Wollongong.

KARL MATON is a lecturer, Department of Sociology and Social Policy, University of Sydney.

LISA KERVIN is a lecturer, Faculty of Education, University of Wollongong.

EXPLORING THE ISSUE

Does the Current Generation of Students Require Digital Tools for Learning?

Critical Thinking and Reflection

1. What distinguishes a digital native from a digital immigrant?
2. Do you think the distinction is valid from the perspective of schools/classrooms and what teachers are responsible for?
3. What kind of evidence should be generated to more clearly offset Bennett's primary concern?

Is There Common Ground?

From Prensky's point of view, the schools of today are really the schools of yesterday—they remain organized around old (if not failed) ideas of how children learn and their physical–social arrangements ("herding" by age into boxes called classrooms) belie this. Two key practice ideas underlying the "digital native" argument concern the effective use of one-to-one personalized instruction and self-selected learning groups. These approaches, in turn, are based on the concepts of adaptivity and connectivity—central to supporting learning and engagement in "digital natives." At the core is the notion that "digital natives" learn differently and schools must change to support the difference. An interesting component of the "digital native" perspective is a strong small "d" democratic and egalitarian theme. Prensky suggests that students ". . . have no meaningful voice at all in their own education" and advances a set of claims that "this lack of any voice on the part of the customer will soon be unacceptable." Embedded here is also the notion of schools as service organizations with students as customers and weight given to satisfaction (this is not trivial because it is relevant to issues of engagement and motivation).

Bennett takes issue with the generality (and finality) of the claims regarding learning differences among "digital natives." She and her colleagues are concerned and critical of the sweeping generalities leveled at a "generational cohort" and argue that there is insufficient evidence for validly doing so (there may be as many differences with regard to technology engagement and use within the generation defined as "digitally native" as between "natives" and "immigrants"). On the fundamental "digital native" claim that students of today learn differently, Bennett's review finds no compelling evidence supporting the claim. In fact, she and her colleagues cite scientific evidence that the popular claims about and common sense notion of the benefits of "multitasking," for example, may be overstated and misunderstood. Research from cognitive psychology has found evidence that there are disruptive effects from multitasking that can interfere with concentration (see J. Rubenstein, D. E. Meyers, and J. E. Evans [2001], "Executive Control of Cognitive Processes in Task Switching," *Journal of Experimental Psychology: Human Perception and Performance* [vol. 27, pp. 763–797]). Clearly, there is room for and need for more research in the area.

Create Central

www.mhhe.com/createcentral

Additional Resources

M. B. Eagleton, K. Guinee, and K. Langlais, "Teaching Internet Literacy Strategies: The Hero Inquiry Project," *Voices from the Middle* (vol. 10, no. 3, pp. 28–35, 2003).

L. Lee, "Young People and the Internet: From Theory to Practice," *Nordic Journal of Youth Research* (vol. 13, no. 4, pp. 315–326, 2005).

T. McHale, "Portrait of a Digital Native," *Technology and Learning* (vol. 26, no. 2, pp. 33–34, 2005).

Internet References . . .

First Year Students' Experiences with Technology: Are They Really Digital Natives? (Retrieved April 10, 2007)

http://www.bmu.unimelb.edu.au/research/munatives
/natives_report2006.rtf

Convenience, Communication, and Control: How Students Use Technology (Retrieved May 27, 2007)

http://www.educause.edu/educatingthenetgen

The Digital Disconnect: The Widening Gap Between Internet-Savvy Students and Their Schools (Retrieved April 10, 2007)

http://www.pewinternet.org/report_display.asp?r=67

Unit 2

Theories of Learning and Their Implications for Educational Practice

*S*ince the 1990s, there has been increasing dissatisfaction among politicians, parents, and educators with the performance of students in U.S. schools. Rightly or wrongly, the blame for failing students, the large number of students graduating with limited proficiency in key academic domains such as reading and mathematics, and a decline in rankings of overall student achievement relative to other nations has been placed squarely on the shoulders of teachers (and on the shoulders of those who train and supervise teachers). This has led to an increasing number of calls for reform of how and what teachers should teach. The criticisms and resulting proposals for reform have revolved around various theoretical controversies about teaching and learning that have characterized the field of educational psychology. Some of these controversies have been ongoing in the field for many years, such as the dispute about the educational value of constructivist approaches to learning. Other controversies have emerged more recently, such as the dispute about the pedagogical implications of research on brain structures and processes and the factors responsible for encouraging violent behavior among students. In the articles of this unit, we consider these and other controversies within the context of teaching and learning in the classroom.

Selected, Edited, and with Issue Framing Material by:
Leonard Abbeduto, *University of California, Davis*
and
Frank Symons, *University of Minnesota*

ISSUE

Is a Constructivist Approach to Teaching Effective?

YES: Kaya Yilmaz, from "Constructivism: Its Theoretical Underpinnings, Variations, and Implications for Classroom Instruction" *Educational Horizons* (Spring 2008)

NO: Richard E. Clark, Paul A. Kirschner, and John Sweller, from "Putting Students on the Path to Learning: The Case for Fully Guided Instruction" *American Educator* (Spring 2012)

Learning Outcomes

After reading this issue, you will be able to:

- Describe the basic principles of a constructivist approach to teaching and learning.
- Provide examples of a constructivist approach in the classroom.
- Summarize the differences, advantages, and disadvantages of a constructivist and a fully guided approach to teaching.

ISSUE SUMMARY

YES: Kaya Yilmaz argues in favor of constructivism, a child-centered approach to education that is defined by student participation in hands-on activities and extended projects that are allowed to "evolve" in accordance with the students' interests and initial beliefs. The student regulates his or her learning and discovers the "facts" or structure of a problem without being explicitly taught those facts or that structure.

NO: Richard E. Clark, Paul A. Kirschner, and John Sweller distinguish between the different learning needs of novices and experts. They also argue that constructivist approaches have failed and point to research demonstrating the superiority of teacher-centered fully guided approaches.

Observation of any school classroom in the United States at any point in history would reveal, to no one's surprise, a teacher (or teachers) and a varying number of students. In fact, although many other people, including administrators, parents, and even politicians, participate directly or indirectly in the educational process, most people view the teacher–student relationship as the primary determinant of what students accomplish in school. But the relationship between teachers and students has changed dramatically over the past few decades. In the 1950s, for example, the relationship was very much dominated by the teacher. He or she exerted a high degree of control over what students did at nearly every point throughout the day. In this teacher-centered approach, the teacher disseminated the "facts" to be learned to the students, typically within the context of a lecture. The teacher ensured that students would learn the facts by requiring that they listen carefully and engage in various highly structured, drill-and-practice activities. In recent years, however, students have come to exert considerably more control over

the educational process and the teacher–student relationship. In many classrooms today, students are much more likely to be "doing" rather than "listening." This doing is often in the form of participation in an extended project of some form, such as building a Civil War-era town or collecting and cataloging insects. The teacher may assign these projects, but it is the students who shape the projects to suit their own interests as well as the discoveries that they make along the way. Although labeled in different ways (e.g., project-based learning, discovery learning, hands-on learning), the hallmark of this constructivism approach is a high degree of self-directed student activity.

Concerns about student achievement, especially as compared to student achievement in other industrialized nations, have led some scholars and administrators to begin calling for a return to a more teacher-centered, fact-based approach to education. Critics have argued that the constructivist approach is inefficient; that is, because children "waste time" with incorrect "discoveries" before arriving at the correct one, there often is not enough time to teach them all of the content that should be mastered.

Other critics assert that some children never make the correct discoveries on their own and thus require greater teacher control and a more systematic introduction of the skills to be mastered. Finally, critics argue that acquisition of higher-order modes of thought applicable to a broad range of problems will not emerge without mastery of the rich networks of facts that constitute the domains of mathematics, physics, chemistry, and the like.

Supporters of the constructivist approach, however, are not without responses to these criticisms. They counter that a fact-based, teacher-centered approach is itself inefficient because of the sheer number of facts that compose any meaningful domain and because the "facts" change with new discoveries. This means, they argue, that the only lasting education is one that promotes higher modes of thought and action rather than storage of facts. Supporters also suggest that many attempts to implement a constructivist approach fail only because they do not go far enough; they merely insert a few student-initiated projects into an otherwise teacher-centered system. Finally,

supporters argue that the well-documented decline in student interest in academic tasks that occurs throughout the school years is the result of a teacher-centered orientation. They point to numerous examples of constructivist classrooms in which students appear to be highly engaged in the academic life of the classroom.

In the following selections, Kaya Ilmaz describes several different instantiations of constructivism, noting that they all share a focus on the child's attempt to construct meaning through a process of self-regulation. She also provides concrete examples of constructivism in the classroom. She also points out that constructivism is based on theories of how the child is "built" by its nature to learn. In their article, Richard E. Clark and colleagues argue that novices cannot be left to their own devices in the hopes that they will discover the meaning or structure of a problem or domain; instead, they argue that the learner's path must be highly structured and carefully controlled by the instructor. Thus, the two selections differ in the extent to which they put the onus of learning on the learner or the teacher.

Kaya Yilmaz

Constructivism: Its Theoretical Underpinnings, Variations, and Implications for Classroom Instruction

Constructivism

The philosophy of constructivism evolved from dissatisfaction with traditional Western theories of knowledge. As such, it contrasts sharply with objectivist epistemology and positivism (Crotty 1998; Hendry, Frommer, and Walker 1999; Glasersfeld 1995). In contrast to the objectivist notion of objective truth and meaning inherent in objects, independent of any consciousness, constructivism postulates that knowledge cannot exist outside our minds; truth is not absolute; and knowledge is not discovered but constructed by individuals based on experiences (Crotty 1998, 42; Fosnot 1996; Hendry, Frommer, and Walker 1999). Constructivism replaces the traditional conception of truth—as the correct representation of an external world—with the concept of viability, meaning that descriptions of states or events of the world are relative to the observer (Glasersfeld 1995, 8). The constructivist perspective, therefore, posits that knowledge is not passively received from the world or from authoritative sources but constructed by individuals or groups making sense of their experiential worlds (Maclellan and Soden 2004).

Constructivism advances meaning-making and knowledge construction as its foremost principles (Crotty 1998; Fosnot 1996; Phillips 1995). It views knowledge as temporary, nonobjective, internally constructed, developmental, and socially and culturally mediated (Fosnot 1996). Individuals are assumed to construct their own meanings and understandings, and this process is believed to involve interplay between existing knowledge and beliefs and new knowledge and experiences (Richardson 1997, 2003; Schunk 2004). This view of meaning-making through previously constructed knowledge implies that:

- Learners are intellectually generative individuals (with the capacity to pose questions, solve problems, and construct theories and knowledge) rather than empty vessels waiting to be filled.
- Instruction should be based primarily on developing learners' thinking.
- The locus of intellectual authority resides in neither the teacher nor the resources, but in the discourse facilitated by both teachers and learners (Maclellan and Soden 2004).

Domains of Constructivism

Constructivism is not a single or unified theory; rather, it is characterized by plurality and multiple perspectives. Varied theoretical orientations (Phillips 1995) explicate such different facets of constructivism as cognitive development, social aspects, and the role of context. According to Matthews (2000), the educational literature identifies eighteen different forms of constructivism in terms of methodological, radical, didactic, and dialectical considerations, yet many theorists and scholars place all forms of constructivism in three radically distinct categories: (1) sociological, (2) psychological, and (3) radical constructivism. All three categories share the epistemological assumption that knowledge or meaning is not discovered but constructed by the human mind (Richardson 2003).

Phillips (2000) has defined and explained the attributes of social and psychological constructivism:

> *Social constructionism* or *social constructivism:* A theory that bodies of knowledge or disciplines that have been built up are "human constructs, and that the form that knowledge has taken in these fields has been determined by such things as politics, ideologies, values, the exertion of power and the preservation of status, religious beliefs, and economic self-interest." This approach centers on the ways in which power, the economy, [and] political and social factors affect the ways in which groups of people form understandings and formal knowledge about their world. These bodies of knowledge are not considered to be objective representations of the external world.
>
> *Psychological constructivism:* This approach relates to a developmental or learning theory that suggests that individual learners actively construct the meaning around phenomena, and that these constructions are idiosyncratic, depending in part on the learners' background knowledge. The development of meaning may take place within a social group that affords its individual members the opportunity to share and provide warrant for these meanings. If the individuals within the group come to an agreement about the nature and warrant of a description of a phenomenon or its

relationship to others, these meanings become formal knowledge. (p. 6)

Radical constructivism, introduced by Ernst von Glasersfeld, assumes that external reality cannot be known and that the knowing subject constructs all knowledge, ranging from everyday observations to scientific knowledge; knowing thus inevitably reflects the perspective of the observer (Molebash 2002; Terhart 2003). According to radical constructivists, it is impossible to judge knowledge as an ontological or metaphysical reality (Terhart 2003). Knowing without metaphysics is possible; meaning exists in the realm of the experiential world and not ontologically, a view called postepistemology (Glasersfeld 1995, 6–7).

Gergen (1995) provides an explanation of radical constructivism by using esoteric terms borrowed from Moshman's (1982) classification of perspectives on constructivism as endogenous, exogenous, and dialectical. The first view emphasizes the individual's knowledge construction based on previous knowledge and experiences; the second, the role of environment or social context in knowledge construction; and the third, the relationship of various types of dynamic interactions between the individual and the environment.

Gergen (1995) distinguishes between two categories of knowledge: *exogenic* (or word centered) and *endogenic* (or mind centered). The exogenic tradition generally embraces a dualism: the existence of an external world (typically a material reality) is set against the existence of a psychological world (cognitive, subjective, symbolic, or phenomenological). Knowledge is achieved when the inner states of the individual reflect or accurately represent the existing states of the external world or when the mind serves as a "mirror of nature." The exogenic theorist views the external world or material world as a given. The endogenic thinker, however, is likely to view the mental world as self-evident. In contrast to the exogenic theorist's concentration on the environment, the endogenic theorist often emphasizes human beings' intrinsic capacities for reason, logic, and conceptual processing. Radical constructivism's endogenic view of knowledge emphasizes the mental processes of individuals and the ways in which they construct knowledge of the world from within. This perspective does not see knowledge as a reflection of the world as it is (p. 18).

Constructivist Pedagogy

Although constructivism is a recently emergent epistemological stance or theory of knowledge and knowing, it has come to inform different bodies of knowledge or disciplines ranging from philosophy to psychology, anthropology, and sociology. Constructivism has implications for pedagogical theory and research as well. Since its inception as an epistemology and philosophy, constructivist theory has prompted educators to build a constructivist pedagogy. Educational scholars have developed a range of definitions of constructivist learning and its attributes. Rooted in the field of cognitive science, constructivist pedagogy is especially informed by the ideas of John Dewey and William James; the later work of Jean Piaget; and the sociohistorical work of Lev Vygotsky, Jerome Bruner, and Ernst von Glasersfeld, to name a few (Fosnot 1996; Kivinen and Ristele 2003). Its genesis can be traced as far back as the eighteenth-century philosophers Vico and Kant.

Richardson (2003) calls constructivist pedagogy "the creation of classroom environments, activities, and methods that are grounded in a constructivist theory of learning, with goals that focus on individual students developing deep understandings in the subject matter of interest and habits of mind that aid in future learning." Fosnot (1996) offers this explanation of constructivist learning:

[A] self-regulatory process of struggling with the conflict between existing personal models of the world and discrepant new insights, constructing new representations and models of reality as human meaning-making venture with culturally developed tools and symbols, and further negotiating such meaning through cooperative social activity, discourse, and debate. (p. ix)

As a theory, constructivism proposes that learning is neither a stimulus-response phenomenon nor a passive process of receiving knowledge; instead, as an adaptive activity requiring building conceptual structures and self-regulation through reflection and abstraction, learning is an active process of knowledge construction influenced by how one interacts with and interprets new ideas and events (Lambert et al. 1995; Maclellan and Soden 2004; Glasersfeld 1995). "Individuals bring past experiences and beliefs, as well as their cultural histories and world views, into the process of learning" when they construct knowledge internally by interacting with environment (Kamii, Manning, and Manning 1991). This perspective views developmental stages as constructions of active learner reorganization. Likewise, it sets concept development and "deep" understanding, rather than behaviors or skills, through "authentic" tasks, as the goal of instruction (Fosnot 1996, 10–11).

Piaget's genetic epistemology or theory of cognitive development provides one of the building blocks of constructivist pedagogy. Drawing on biological concepts such as the concept of equilibrium-disequilibrium, Piaget attempted to explain how learning and the changes in cognitive structures occur (Fosnot 1996; Gillani 2003; Palincsar 1998). From his perspective, intellectual and cognitive development resembles a biological act that requires the organism's adaptation to environmental demands (Gillani 2003). Behavior and the organism stand as a whole system; thus any changes in one part of the system will cause other changes as behavior balances the structure of the organism against the characteristics of the environment (Fosnot 1996). Behaviors, Piaget believed, serve as the driving force of developing new cognitive structures.

Piaget believed that an individual encountering a new learning situation draws on prior knowledge to make the new experience understandable (Gillani 2003). A new event, situation, or learning environment can create contradictions with one's previous understandings; their insufficiency leads to perturbation and a state of disequilibration in the mental schemata, in which generic events and abstract concepts are stored and organized in terms of their common patterns (Fosnot 1996; Gillani 2003; Palincsar 1998). To form a state of equilibrium in the cognitive structure, the individual needs to modify or reorganize his or her schemata via adaptation.

The internal process of restructuring the schemata is accomplished through assimilation and accommodation (Gillani 2003). While assimilation integrates new information with existing knowledge, accommodation modifies or transforms existing cognitive structures in response to a new situation. According to Piaget, learners confronted with an imbalance may resort to three kinds of accommodations (Fosnot 1996): (1) disregarding the contradictions and adhering to their original scheme; (2) vacillating by maintaining the contradictory theories simultaneously and viewing each theory as separate or specific cases; or (3) forming a new, modified notion to explain and resolve the prior contradiction. In each type of response, the learner's internal and self-regulatory behavior leads to the compensations (p. 16).

Glasersfeld (1996) explains Piaget's theory in terms of its epistemological underpinnings. The application of the Piagetian notion of adaptation to cognitive structures implies that knowledge is not a representation of external reality but a map of actions and conceptual operations. Knowledge springs from (a) the person's "actions," which are grounded in and directed at objects in an environment, and (b) his or her "reflection" on objects, which embody the person's experiential world (pp. 3–4).

Apart from Piaget's genetic epistemology, learners can also be classified as absolute, transitional, independent, and contextual in terms of epistemological viewpoints (Baxter Magolda 1992). The absolute learner believes that (a) knowledge is fixed, absolute, and certain; (b) teachers and textbooks have the right answer; (c) the student has a duty to get it right; and (d) teachers should make it easier to find out what is expected. In contrast, a contextual learner (a) believes that knowledge is uncertain, tentative, and subject to change and revision; (b) is comfortable judging how personal knowledge and skills might apply to a situation; and (c) connects concepts to applied settings. Practicing constructivist teaching methods, teachers can transform students from absolute learners to contextual learners.

Vygotsky's theories come into play in shaping constructivist pedagogy. Slavin (2000) states:

> Four key principles derived from Vygotsky's ideas have played an important role [in modern constructivist thought]. Two of them are very important for cooperative learning. First is his emphasis on the social nature of learning. Children learn, he proposed, through joint interactions with adults and more capable peers. On cooperative projects children are exposed to their peers' thinking processes; this method not only makes the learning outcome available to all students, but also makes other students' thinking processes available to all. Vygotsky noted that successful problem solvers talk themselves through difficult problems. In cooperative groups, children can hear this inner speech out loud and can learn how successful problem solvers are thinking through their approaches. The second key concept is the idea that children learn best the concepts that are in their zone of proximal development. When children are working together, each child is likely to have a peer performing on a given task at a slightly higher cognitive level, exactly within the child's zone of proximal development. (p. 256)

Constructivist theory is descriptive rather than prescriptive; it does not prescribe rigid rules or procedures for designing a learning environment (Wasson 1996). Because the constructivist view of learning evolved from cognitivism, it shares several similarities with cognitive learning theories. What distinguishes constructivism from cognitivism is the notion that "knowledge does not and cannot have the purpose of producing an independent reality, but instead . . . has an adaptive function" (Glasersfeld 1995, 3).

The basic assumptions and principles of the constructivist view of learning can be summarized as follows:

- Learning is an active process.
- Learning is an adaptive activity.
- Learning is situated in the context in which it occurs.
- Knowledge is not innate, passively absorbed, or invented but constructed by the learner.
- All knowledge is personal and idiosyncratic.
- All knowledge is socially constructed.
- Learning is essentially a process of making sense of the world.
- Experience and prior understanding play a role in learning.
- Social interaction plays a role in learning.
- Effective learning requires meaningful, open-ended, challenging problems for the learner to solve. (Boethel and Dimock 2000; Fox 2001)

Fosnot (1996) suggests that several general principles of the constructivist view of learning can be applied to educational practices:

- *Learning is not the result of development; learning is development.* It requires invention and self-organization on the learner's part. Teachers should thus allow learners to raise their own questions, generate their own hypotheses and models as possibilities, and test them for viability.

- *Disequilibrium facilitates learning.* "Errors" should be perceived as a result of learners' conceptions and therefore not minimized or avoided. Challenging, open-ended investigations in realistic, meaningful contexts will allow learners to explore and generate many possibilities, whether affirming or contradictory. Contradictions, in particular, need to be illuminated, explored, and discussed.
- *Reflective abstraction is the driving force of learning.* As meaning-makers, humans seek to organize and generalize across experiences in representational form. Reflection through journals, representation in multisymbolic form, or connections made across experiences or strategies may facilitate reflective abstraction.
- *Dialogue within a community engenders further thinking.* The classroom should be a "community of discourse engaged in activity, reflection, and conversation." Learners (rather than teachers) are responsible for defending, proving, justifying, and communicating their ideas to the classroom community. Ideas are accepted as truth only as they make sense to the community and thus rise to the level of "taken-as-shared."
- *Learning proceeds toward developing structures.* As learners struggle to make meanings, they undertake progressive structural shifts in perspectives—in a sense, "big ideas." These learner-constructed, central-organizing ideas can be generalized across experiences, and they often require undoing or reorganizing earlier conceptions. This process continues throughout development. (pp. 29–30)

Implications of the Constructivist Framework for Classroom Teaching

Constructivism is a theory of learning, not a theory of teaching (Fosnot 1996; Richardson 2003). For this reason, although there is an enormous body of literature on constructivism, the elements of effective constructivist teaching are not known (Richardson 2003). Constructivist teaching theory, built on constructivist learning theory, is a set of prescriptions that challenge the transmission or behaviorist paradigms advocated in many education programs. Experiential learning, self-directed learning, discovery learning, inquiry training, problem-based learning, and reflective practice are examples of constructivist learning models (Gillani 2003; McLeod 2003; Slavin 2000).

Constructivism is explained in terms of its relation to teaching. According to Fosnot (1996), teaching based on constructivism discounts the idea that symbols or concepts can be taken apart as discrete entities and taught out of context. Rather, constructivist teaching affords learners meaningful, concrete experiences in which they can look for patterns, construct their own questions, and structure their own models, concepts, and strategies. The classroom becomes a micro-society in which learners jointly engage in activity, discourse, and reflection. Teachers facilitate

and guide rather than dictate autocratically. Autonomy, mutual reciprocity of social relations, and empowerment characterize a constructively conducted classroom (Fosnot 1996, pp. ix–x). Students can develop in-depth understandings of the instructional materials, understand the nature of knowledge construction, and construct complex cognitive maps to connect bodies of knowledge and understandings (Richardson 2003).

Because meaning, knowledge, and conceptual structures are constructed differently by each individual, teachers should be cognizant that students may view curricula, textbooks, didactic props, and microworlds differently than they do. Accordingly, teachers should not attempt to transfer conceptual knowledge to students through words (Glasersfeld 1995); instead, they should be concerned with how learners understand the process of knowing and how they justify their beliefs (McLeod 2003). Constructivist teachers challenge students to justify and defend their positions so that they can change their conceptual frameworks (e.g., beliefs, assumptions, and conceptions). In the constructivist classroom, learning emphasizes the process, not the product. How one arrives at a particular answer is what matters. The teacher also recognizes the pivotal importance of discourse.

Richardson (2003) identifies several principles as the premises of the constructivist pedagogy. These principles suggest that the teacher first recognize and respect students' backgrounds, beliefs, assumptions, and prior knowledge; provide abundant opportunities for group dialogue aimed at fostering shared understanding of the topic under study; establish a learning environment that encourages students to examine, change, and even challenge their existing beliefs and understandings through meaningful, stimulating, interesting, and relevant instructional tasks; help students develop meta-awareness of their own understandings and learning processes; and introduce the formal domain of knowledge or subject matter into the conversation through a sort of loosely structured instruction and the use of technological tools such as Web sites.

Other educators have also attempted to elaborate on the characteristics of constructivist teaching and learning. Brooks and Brooks (1993) describe both the pillars of constructivist pedagogy and the characteristics of constructivist teaching practices in *In Search of Understanding: The Case for Constructivist Classrooms,* which remains one of the most-cited books on the constructivist approach to teaching. The authors enumerate five pillars on which constructivist classrooms are based: (1) posing problems of emerging relevance to learners; (2) structuring learning around primary concepts; (3) seeking and valuing students' points of view; (4) adapting curricula to address students' suppositions; and (5) assessing student learning in the context of teaching. Translating these principles into instructional practices, these authors argue that teachers in a constructively planned and conducted classroom environment should have students engage in raw data or primary sources, aiming to develop students' cognitive and higher-order thinking skills. Taking into account students' concepts, misconceptions, modes of thinking, and responses, these teachers accordingly shift their teaching methods or content when needed. By asking thoughtful and open-ended questions, constructivist teachers also encourage students to elaborate on their initial responses through such interactive methods as discussion, debate, and Socratic dialogue.

Conclusion

Constructivist theories are of great value to teachers in their efforts to help students grasp the substantive and syntactic components of the subjects they are teaching. This article has explained constructivism in terms of its epistemological, philosophical, and theoretical underpinnings, and its implications for instructional practices. Even though the constructivist view of learning and teaching has dominated the educational literature for more than two decades, constructivist pedagogy in its entirety has not yet penetrated actual classrooms. It should be kept in mind that putting constructivist pedagogical ideas into practice effectively and with integrity first necessitates teachers' willingness to embrace and practice principles of constructivist pedagogy. And doing so in turn requires teachers to examine their deeply held philosophies of teaching—more precisely, their conceptions of teaching—to become conscious of whether they tend to value traditional teacher-centered or constructivist learner-centered conceptions of teaching. Rather than examine technical aspects of teaching, they first can reflect on and formulate their answers to such important conceptual questions as how learning occurs; how the teacher can facilitate the learning process or what roles the teacher should play in student learning; what kinds of learning environments help realize the goals of schooling in general and of school subjects in particular; and how students' learning should be evaluated.

If the goals of teaching school subjects are to be successfully accomplished, teachers of different subject areas should transform students' engagement in subject matters from rote recall and comprehension to more meaningful analysis, synthesis, application, and evaluation via constructivist teaching models and methods.

References

Baxter Magolda, M. B. 1992. "Students' Epistemologies and Academic Experiences: Implications for Pedagogy." *Review of Higher Education* 15 (3): 265–287.

Boethel, M., and K. V. Dimock. 2000. *Constructing Knowledge with Technology.* Austin, Texas: Southwest Educational Development Laboratory.

Brooks, J. G., and M. G. Brooks. 1993. *In Search of Understanding: The Case for Constructivist Classrooms.* Alexandria, Va.: Association for Supervision and Curriculum Development.

Crotty, M. 1998. *The Foundations of Social Research: Meaning and Perspective in the Research Process.* Thousands Oaks, Calif.: Sage Publications.

Fosnot, C. T. 1996. "Constructivism: A Psychological Theory of Learning." In *Constructivism: Theory, Perspectives and Practice,* ed. C. T. Fosnot, 8–33. New York: Teachers College Press.

Fox, R. 2001. "Constructivism Examined." *Oxford Review of Education* 27 (1): 23–35.

Gergen, K. J. 1995. "Social Construction and the Educational Process." In *Constructivism in Education,* ed. L. P. Steffe and J. Gale, 17–39. Hillsdale, N.J.: Lawrence Erlbaum Associates.

Gillani, B. B. 2003. *Learning Theories and the Design of E-learning Environments.* Lanham, Md.: University Press of America.

Glasersfeld, E. von. 1995. "A Constructivist Approach to Teaching." In *Constructivism in Education,* ed. L. P. Steffe and J. Gale, 3–15. Hillsdale, N.J.: Lawrence Erlbaum Associates.

————. 1996. "Introduction: Aspects of Constructivism." In *Constructivism: Theory, Perspectives and Practice,* ed. C. T. Fosnot, 3–7. New York: Teachers College Press.

Hendry, D. G., M. Frommer, and R. A. Walker. 1999. "Constructivism and Problem-based Learning." *Journal of Further and Higher Education* 23 (3): 359–371.

Kamii, C., M. Manning, and G. Manning. 1991. *Early Literacy: A Constructivist Foundation for Whole Language.* Washington, D.C.: National Education Association Professional Library.

Kivinen, O., and P. Ristele. 2003. "From Constructivism to Pragmatist Conception of Learning." *Oxford Review of Education* 29 (3): 363–375.

Lambert, L., D. Walker, D. P. Zimmerman, J. E. Cooper, M. D. Lambert, M. E. Gardner, and P. J. Slack. 1995. *The Constructivist Leader.* New York: Teachers College Press.

Maclellan, E., and R. Soden. 2004. "The Importance of Epistemic Cognition in Student-centered Learning." *Instructional Science* 32: 253–268.

Matthews, M. R. 2000. "Appraising Constructivism in Science and Mathematics." In *Constructivism in Education,* ed. D. Phillips, 161–192. Chicago: University of Chicago Press.

McLeod, G. 2003. "Learning Theory and Instructional Design." *Learning Matters* 2: 35–53. Retrieved February 27, 2005, from <http://courses.durhamtech.edu/tlc/www/html/Resources/Learning_Matters.htm>.

Molebash, P. 2002. "Constructivism Meets Technology Integration: The Cufa Technology Guidelines in an Elementary Social Studies Methods Course."

Theory and Research in Social Education 30 (3): 429–55.

Moshman, D. 1982. "Exogenous, Endogenous, and Dialectical Constructivism." *Developmental Review* 2: 371–384.

Palincsar, A. S. 1998. "Social Constructivist Perspective on Teaching and Learning." *Annual Review of Psychology* 49: 345–375.

Phillips, D. C. 1995. "The Good, the Bad, and the Ugly: The Many Faces of Constructivism." *Educational Researcher* 24 (7): 5–12.

———. 2000. *Constructivism in Education.* Chicago: University of Chicago Press, 6. Quoted in Richardson 2003, 1624–25.

Richardson, V. 1997. "Constructivist Teaching and Teacher Education: Theory and Practice." In *Constructivist Teacher Education: Building a World of New Understandings,* ed. V. Richardson, pp. 3–14. Bristol, Pa.: Falmer Press.

———. 2003. "Constructivist Pedagogy." *Teachers College Record* 105 (9): 1623–1640.

Schunk, D. H. 2004. *Learning Theories: An Educational Perspective.* 4th ed. Upper Saddle River, N.J.: Pearson Prentice Hall.

Slavin, R. E. 2000. *Educational Psychology: Theory and Practice.* Boston: Allyn and Bacon.

Terhart, E. 2003. "Constructivism and Teaching: A New Paradigm in General Didactics?" *Journal of Curriculum Studies* 35 (1): 25–44.

Wasson, B. 1996. "Instructional Planning and Contemporary Theories of Learning: Is This a Self-contradiction?" In *Proceedings of the European Conference on Artificial Intelligence in Education,* ed. P. Brna, A. Paiva, and J. Self, 23–30. Lisbon: Colibri.

KAYA YILMAZ, PHD, is a member of the faculty of the College of Education, Marmara University in Istanbul, Turkey.

Richard E. Clark, Paul A.
Kirschner, and John Sweller

 **NO**

Putting Students on the Path to Learning:
The Case for Fully Guided Instruction

Disputes about the impact of instructional guidance during teaching have been ongoing for more than a half century.[1] On one side of this argument are those who believe that all people—novices and experts alike—learn best when provided with instruction that contains unguided or partly guided segments. This is generally defined as instruction in which learners, rather than being presented with all essential information and asked to practice using it, must discover or construct some or all of the essential information for themselves.[2] On the other side are those who believe that ideal learning environments for experts and novices differ: while experts often thrive without much guidance, nearly everyone else thrives when provided with full, explicit instructional guidance (and should not be asked to discover any essential content or skills).[3]

Our goal in this article is to put an end to this debate. Decades of research clearly demonstrate that *for novices* (comprising virtually all students), direct, explicit instruction is more effective and more efficient than partial guidance.[4] So, when teaching new content and skills to novices, teachers are more effective when they provide explicit guidance accompanied by practice and feedback, not when they require students to discover many aspects of what they must learn. As we will discuss, this does not mean direct, expository instruction all day every day. Small group and independent problems and projects can be effective—not as vehicles for making discoveries, but as a means of *practicing* recently learned content and skills.

Before we describe this research, let's clarify some terms. Teachers providing explicit instructional guidance *fully explain* the concepts and skills that students are required to learn. Guidance can be provided through a variety of media, such as lectures, modeling, videos, computer-based presentations, and realistic demonstrations. It can also include class discussions and activities—if the teacher ensures that through the discussion or activity, the relevant information is explicitly provided and practiced. In a math class, for example, when teaching students how to solve a new type of problem, the teacher may begin by showing students how to solve the problem and fully explaining the how and why of the mathematics

involved. Often, in following problems, step-by-step explanations may gradually be faded or withdrawn until, through practice and feedback, the students can solve the problem themselves. In this way, before trying to solve the problem on their own, students would already have been walked through both the procedure and the concepts behind the procedure.

In contrast, those teachers whose lessons are designed to offer partial or minimal instructional guidance expect students to discover on their own some or all of the concepts and skills they are supposed to learn. The partially guided approach has been given various names, including discovery learning,[5] problem-based learning,[6] inquiry learning,[7] experiential learning,[8] and constructivist learning.[9] Continuing the math example, students receiving partial instructional guidance may be given a new type of problem and asked to brainstorm possible solutions in small groups with or without prompts or hints. Then there may be a class discussion of the various groups' solutions, and it could be quite some time before the teacher indicates which solution is correct. Through the process of trying to solve the problem and discussing different students' solutions, each student is supposed to discover the relevant mathematics. (In some minimal guidance classrooms, teachers use explicit instruction of the solution as a backup method for those students who did not make the necessary discoveries and who were confused during the class discussion.) Additional examples of minimally guided approaches include (1) inquiry-oriented science instruction in which students are expected to discover fundamental principles by mimicking the investigatory activities of professional researchers,[10] and (2) medical students being expected to discover well-established solutions for common patient problems.[11]

Two bodies of research reveal the weakness of partially and minimally guided approaches: research comparing pedagogies, and research on how people learn. The past half century of empirical research has provided overwhelming and unambiguous evidence that, for everyone but experts, partial guidance during instruction is significantly less effective and efficient than full guidance. And, based on our current knowledge of how people learn, there is no reason to expect that partially guided instruction in K–12 classrooms would be as effective as explicit, full guidance.

Research Comparing Fully Guided and Partially Guided Instruction

Controlled experiments almost uniformly indicate that when dealing with novel information (i.e., information that is new to learners), students should be explicitly shown what to do and how to do it, and then have an opportunity to practice doing it while receiving corrective feedback.[12] A number of reviews of empirical studies on teaching novel information have established a solid research-based case against the use of instruction with minimal guidance. Although an extensive discussion of those studies is outside the scope of this article, one recent review is worth noting: Richard Mayer (a cognitive scientist at the University of California, Santa Barbara) examined evidence from studies conducted from 1950 to the late 1980s comparing pure discovery learning (defined as unguided, problem-based instruction) with guided forms of instruction.[13] He suggested that in each decade since the mid-1950s, after empirical studies provided solid evidence that the then-popular unguided approach did not work, a similar approach soon popped up under a different name with the cycle repeating itself. Each new set of advocates for unguided approaches seemed unaware of, or uninterested in, previous evidence that unguided approaches had not been validated. This pattern produced discovery learning, which gave way to experiential learning, which gave way to problem-based and inquiry learning, which has recently given way to constructivist instructional techniques. Mayer concluded that the "debate about discovery has been replayed many times in education, but each time, the research evidence has favored a guided approach to learning."[14] . . .

Evidence from well-designed, properly controlled experimental studies from the 1980s to today also supports direct instructional guidance.[15] Some researchers[16] have noted that when students learn science in classrooms with pure-discovery methods or with minimal feedback, they often become lost and frustrated, and their confusion can lead to misconceptions. Others[17] found that because false starts (in which students pursue misguided hypotheses) are common in such learning situations, unguided discovery is most often inefficient. In a very important study, researchers not only tested whether science learners learned more via discovery, compared with explicit instruction, but also, once learning had occurred, whether the quality of learning differed.[18] Specifically, they tested whether those who had learned through discovery were better able to transfer their learning to new contexts (as advocates for minimally guided approaches often claim). The findings were unambiguous. Direct instruction involving considerable guidance, including examples, resulted in vastly more learning than discovery. Those relatively few students who learned via discovery showed no signs of superior quality of learning.

In real classrooms, several problems occur when different kinds of minimally guided instruction are used. First, often only the brightest and most well-prepared students make the discovery. Second, many students, as noted above, simply become frustrated. Some may disengage, others may copy whatever the brightest students are doing—either way, they are not actually discovering anything. Third, some students believe they have discovered the correct information or solution, but they are mistaken and so they learn a misconception that can interfere with later learning and problem solving.[19] Even after being shown the right answer, a student is likely to recall his or her discovery—not the correction. Fourth, even in the unlikely event that a problem or project is devised that all students succeed in completing, minimally guided instruction is much less efficient than explicit guidance. What can be taught directly in a 25-minute demonstration and discussion, followed by 15 minutes of independent practice with corrective feedback by a teacher, may take several class periods to learn via minimally guided projects and/or problem solving.

As if these four problems were not enough cause for concern, there is one more problem that we must highlight: *minimally guided instruction can increase the achievement gap.* A review[20] of approximately 70 studies, which had a range of more- and less-skilled students as well as a range of more- and less-guided instruction, found the following: more-skilled learners tend to learn more with less-guided instruction, but less-skilled learners tend to learn more with more-guided instruction. Worse, a number of experiments found that less-skilled students who chose or were assigned to less-guided instruction received significantly *lower* scores on posttests than on pretest measures. For these relatively weak students, the failure to provide strong instructional support produced a *measurable loss of learning.* The implication of these results is that teachers should provide explicit instruction when introducing a new topic, but gradually fade it out as knowledge and skill increase.

Even more distressing is evidence[21] that when learners are asked to select between a more-guided or less-guided version of the same course, less-skilled learners who choose the less-guided approach tend to like it even though they learn less from it. It appears that guided instruction helps less-skilled learners by providing task-specific learning strategies. However, these strategies require learners to engage in explicit, attention-driven effort and so tend not to be liked, even though they are helpful to learning.

Similarly, more-skilled learners who choose the more-guided version of a course tend to like it even though they too have selected the environment in which they learn less. The reason more guidance tends to be less effective with these learners is that, in most cases, they have already acquired task-specific learning strategies that are more effective for them than those embedded in the more-guided version of the course. And some evidence suggests that they like more guidance because they believe they will achieve the required learning with minimal effort.

If the evidence against minimally guided approaches is so strong, why is this debate still alive? We cannot say with any certainty, but one major reason seems to be that many educators mistakenly believe partially and minimally guided instructional approaches are based on solid cognitive science. Turning again to Mayer's review of the literature, many educators confuse "constructivism," which is a theory of how one learns and sees the world, with a prescription for how to teach.[22] In the field of cognitive science, constructivism is a widely accepted theory of learning; it claims that learners must construct mental representations of the world by engaging in active cognitive processing. Many educators (especially teacher education professors in colleges of education) have latched on to this notion of students having to "construct" their own knowledge, and have *assumed* that the best way to promote such construction is to have students try to discover new knowledge or solve new problems without explicit guidance from the teacher. Unfortunately, this assumption is both widespread and incorrect. Mayer calls it the "constructivist teaching fallacy." Simply put, cognitive activity can happen with or without behavioral activity, and behavioral activity does not in any way guarantee cognitive activity. In fact, the type of active cognitive processing that students need to engage in to "construct" knowledge can happen through reading a book, listening to a lecture, watching a teacher conduct an experiment while simultaneously describing what he or she is doing, etc. Learning requires the construction of knowledge. Withholding information from students does not facilitate the construction of knowledge.

The Human Brain: Learning 101

In order to really comprehend why full instructional guidance is more effective and efficient than partial or minimal guidance for novices, we need to know how human brains learn. There are two essential components: long-term memory and working memory (often called short-term memory). Long-term memory is that big mental warehouse of things (be they words, people, grand philosophical ideas, or skateboard tricks) we know. Working memory is a limited mental "space" in which we think. The relations between working and long-term memory, in conjunction with the cognitive processes that support learning, are of critical importance to developing effective instruction.

Our understanding of the role of long-term memory in human cognition has altered dramatically over the last few decades. It is no longer seen as a passive repository of discrete, isolated fragments of information that permit us to repeat what we have learned. Nor is it seen as having only peripheral influence on complex cognitive processes such as critical thinking and problem solving. Rather, long-term memory is now viewed as the central, dominant structure of human cognition. Everything we see, hear, and think about is dependent on and influenced by our long-term memory.

A seminal series of studies[23] on chess players, for example, demonstrated that expert players perform well even in "blitz" games (which are played in five minutes) because they are not actually puzzling through each move. They have tens of thousands of board configurations, and the best move for each configuration, stored in long-term memory. Those configurations are learned by studying previous games for 10 years or more. Expert players can play well at a fast pace because all they are doing is recalling the best move—not figuring it out. Similar studies of how experts function have been conducted in a variety of other areas.[24] Altogether, the results suggest that expert problem solvers derive their skill by drawing on the extensive experience stored in their long-term memory in the form of concepts and procedures, known as mental schemas. They retrieve memories of past procedures and solutions, and then quickly select and apply the best ones for solving problems. We are skillful in an area if our long-term memory contains huge amounts of information or knowledge concerning the area. That information permits us to quickly recognize the characteristics of a situation and indicates to us, often immediately and unconsciously, what to do and when to do it. (For instance, think about how much easier managing student behavior was in your fifth year of teaching than in your first year of teaching.) Without our huge store of information in long-term memory, we would be largely incapable of everything from simple acts such as avoiding traffic while crossing a street (information many other animals are unable to store in their long-term memory), to complex activities such as playing chess, solving mathematical problems, or keeping students' attention. In short, our long-term memory incorporates a massive knowledge base that is central to all of our cognitively based activities.

What are the instructional consequences of long-term memory? First and foremost, long-term memory provides us with the ultimate justification for instruction: the aim of all instruction is to add knowledge and skills to long-term memory. If nothing has been added to long-term memory, nothing has been learned.

Working memory is the cognitive structure in which conscious processing occurs. We are only conscious of the information currently being processed in working memory and are more or less oblivious to the far larger amount of information stored in long-term memory. When processing novel information, working memory is very limited in duration and capacity. We have known at least since the 1950s that almost all information stored in working memory is lost within 30 seconds[25] if it is not rehearsed and that the capacity of working memory is limited to only a very small number of elements.[26] That number is usually estimated at about seven, but may be as low as four, plus or minus one.[27] Furthermore, when processing (rather than merely storing) information, it may be reasonable to conjecture that the number of items that can be processed may only be two or three, depending on the nature of the processing required.

For instruction, the interactions between working memory and long-term memory may be even more important than the processing limitations.[28] The limitations of working memory only apply to new, to-be-learned information (that has not yet been stored in long-term memory). When dealing with previously learned, organized information stored in long-term memory, these limitations disappear. Since information can be brought back from long-term memory to working memory as needed, the 30-second limit of working memory becomes irrelevant. Similarly, there are no known limits to the amount of such information that can be brought into working memory from long-term memory.

These two facts—that working memory is very limited when dealing with novel information, but that it is not limited when dealing with organized information stored in long-term memory—explain why partially or minimally guided instruction typically is ineffective for novices, but can be effective for experts. When given a problem to solve, novices' only resource is their very constrained working memory. But experts have both their working memory and all the relevant knowledge and skill stored in long-term memory.

One of the best examples of an instructional approach that takes into account how our working and long-term memories interact is the "worked-example effect." A worked example is just what it sounds like: a problem that has already been solved (or "worked out") for which every step is fully explained and clearly shown; it constitutes the epitome of direct, explicit instruction. The "worked-example effect" is the name given to the widely replicated finding that novice learners who try to learn by being required to solve problems perform worse on subsequent test problems, including transfer problems different from the ones seen previously, than comparable learners who learn by studying equivalent worked examples.

The worked-example effect was first demonstrated in the 1980s.[29] Researchers found that algebra students learned more by studying worked examples than by solving equivalent problems. Since those early demonstrations of the effect, it has been replicated on numerous occasions using a large variety of learners studying an equally large variety of materials—from mathematics and science to English literature and world history.[30] For novices, studying worked examples seems invariably superior to discovering or constructing a solution to a problem.

Why does the worked-example effect occur? The limitations of working memory and the relations between working memory and long-term memory discussed earlier can explain it. Solving a problem requires searching for a solution, which must occur using our limited working memory. If the learner has no relevant concepts or procedures in long-term memory, the only thing to do is blindly search for possible solution steps that bridge the gap between the problem and its solution. This process places a great burden on working-memory capacity because the problem solver has to continually hold and process the current problem state in working memory (e.g., Where am I right now in the problem solving process? How far have I come toward finding a solution?) along with the goal state (e.g., Where do I have to go? What is the solution?), the relations between the goal state and the problem state (e.g., Is this a good step toward solving the problem? Has what I've done helped me get nearer to where I need to go?), the solution steps that could further reduce the differences between the two states (e.g., What should the next step be? Will that step bring me closer to the solution? Is there another solution strategy I can use that might be better?), and any subgoals along the way. Thus, searching for a solution overburdens limited working memory and diverts working-memory resources away from storing information in long-term memory. As a consequence, novices can engage in problem-solving activities for extended periods and learn almost nothing.[31]

In contrast, studying a worked example reduces the burden on working memory (because the solution only has to be comprehended, not discovered) and directs attention (i.e., directs working-memory resources) toward storing the essential relations between problem-solving moves in long-term memory. Students learn to recognize which moves are required for particular problems, which is the basis for developing knowledge and skill as a problem solver.[32]

It is important to note that this discussion of worked examples applies to novices—not experts. In fact, the worked-example effect first disappears and then *reverses* as the learners' expertise increases. That is, for experts, solving a problem is more effective than studying a worked example. When learners are sufficiently experienced, studying a worked example is a redundant activity that places a greater burden on working memory than retrieving a known solution from long-term memory.[33] This reversal in effectiveness is not limited to worked examples; it's true of many explicit, fully guided instructional approaches and is known as the "expertise reversal effect."[34] In general, the expertise reversal effect states that "instructional techniques that are highly effective with inexperienced learners can lose their effectiveness and even have negative consequences when used with more experienced learners."[35] This is why, from the very beginning of this article, we have emphasized that guidance is best for teaching *novel* information and skills. This shows the wisdom of instructional techniques that begin with lots of guidance and then fade that guidance as students gain mastery. It also shows the wisdom of using minimal guidance techniques to reinforce or practice previously learned material.

Recommending partial or minimal guidance for novices was understandable back in the early 1960s, when the acclaimed psychologist Jerome Bruner[37] proposed discovery learning as an instructional tool. At that time, researchers knew little about working memory, long-term memory, and how they interact. We now are in a quite different environment; we know much more about the structures, functions, and characteristics of working memory and long-term memory, the relations between them, and their consequences for learning, problem solving, and critical thinking. We also have a good deal more experimental evidence as to what constitutes effective instruction: controlled experiments almost uniformly indicate that when dealing with novel information, learners should be explicitly shown all relevant information, including what to do and how to do it. We wonder why many teacher educators who are committed to scholarship and research ignore the evidence and continue to encourage minimal guidance when they train new teachers.

After a half century of advocacy associated with instruction using minimal guidance, it appears that there is no body of sound research that supports using the technique with anyone other than the most expert students. Evidence from controlled, experimental (a.k.a., "gold standard") studies almost uniformly supports full and explicit instructional guidance rather than partial or minimal guidance for novice to intermediate learners. These findings and their associated theories suggest teachers should provide their students with clear, explicit instruction rather than merely assisting students in attempting to discover knowledge themselves.

References

1. David P. Ausubel, "Some Psychological and Educational Limitations of Learning by Discovery," *The Arithmetic Teacher* 11 (1964): 290–302; Robert C. Craig, "Directed versus Independent Discovery of Established Relations," *Journal of Educational Psychology* 47, no. 4 (1956): 223–234; Richard E. Mayer, "Should There Be a Three-Strikes Rule against Pure Discovery Learning? The Case for Guided Methods of Instruction," *American Psychologist* 59, no. 1 (2004): 14–19; and Lee S. Shulman and Evan R. Keislar, eds., *Learning by Discovery: A Critical Appraisal* (Chicago: Rand McNally, 1966).
2. See, for example, Jerome S. Bruner, "The Art of Discovery," *Harvard Educational Review* 31 (1961). 21–32; Seymour Papert, *Mindstorms: Children, Computers, and Powerful Ideas* (New York: Basic Books, 1980); and Leslie P. Steffe and Jerry Gale, eds., *Constructivism in Education* (Hillsdale, NJ: Lawrence Erlbaum Associates, 1995).
3. See, for example, Lee J. Cronbach and Richard E. Snow, *Aptitudes and Instructional Methods: A Handbook for Research on Interactions* (New York: Irvington, 1977); David Klahr and Milena Nigam, "The Equivalence of Learning Paths in Early Science Instruction: Effects of Direct Instruction and Discovery Learning," *Psychological Science* 15 (2004): 661–667; Mayer, "Three-Strikes Rule"; Shulman and Keislar, *Learning by Discovery*, and John Sweller, "Evolution of Human Cognitive Architecture," in *The Psychology of Learning and Motivation,* ed. Brian Ross, vol. 43 (San Diego: Academic, 2003), 215–266.
4. John Sweller, Paul Ayres, and Slava Kalyuga, *Cognitive Load Theory* (New York: Springer, 2011).
5. W. S. Anthony, "Learning to Discover Rules by Discovery," *Journal of Educational Psychology* 64, no. 3 (1973): 325–328; and Bruner, "The Art of Discovery."
6. Howard S. Barrows and Robyn M. Tamblyn, *Problem-Based Learning: An Approach to Medical Education* (New York: Springer, 1980); and Henk G. Schmidt, "Problem-Based Learning: Rationale and Description," *Medical Education* 17, no. 1 (1983): 11–16.
7. Papert, *Mindstorms;* and F. James Rutherford, "The Rofe of Inquiry in Science Teaching," *Journal of Research in Science Teaching* 2, no. 2(1964): 80–84.
8. David Boud, Rosemary Keogh, and David Walker, eds., *Reflection: Turning Experience into Learning* (London: Kogan Page, 1985); and David A. Kolb and Ronald E. Fry, "Toward an Applied Theory of Experiential Learning," in *Studies Theories of Group Processes,* ed. Cary L. Cooper (New York: Wiley, 1975), 33–57.
9. David Jonassen, "Objectivism vs. Constructivism," *Educational Technology Research and Development* 39, no. 3 (1991): 5–14; and Leslie P. Steffe and Jerry Gale, eds., *Constructivism in Education* (Hillsdale, NJ: Lawrence Erlbaum Associates, 1995).
10. Wouter R. van Joolingen, Ton de Jong, Ard W. Lazonder, Elwin R. Savelsbergh, and Sarah Manlove, "Co-Lab: Research and Development of an Online Learning Environment for Collaborative Scientific Discovery Learning," *Computers in Human Behavior* 21, no. 4 (2005): 671–688.
11. Henk G. Schmidt, "Problem-Based Learning: Does It Prepare Medical Students to Become Better Doctors?" *Medical Journal of Australia* 168, no. 9 (May 4, 1998): 429–430; and Henk G. Schmidt, "Assumptions Underlying Self-Directed Learning May Be False," *Medical Education* 34, no, 4 (2000): 243–245.
12. Jeroen J. G. van Merriënboer and Paul A. Kirschner, *Ten Steps to Complex Learning* (Mahwah, NJ: Lawrence Erlbaum Associates, 2007).
13. Mayer, "Three-Strikes Rule."
14. Mayer, "Three-Strikes Rule," 18.
15. See, for example, Roxana Moreno, "Decreasing Cognitive Load in Novice Students: Effects of Explanatory versus Corrective Feedback in Discovery-Based Multimedia," *Instructional Science* 32, nos. 1–2 (2004): 99–113; and Juhani E. Tuovinen and John Sweller, "A Comparison of Cognitive Load Associated with Discovery Learning and Worked Examples," *Journal of Educational Psychology* 91, no. 2 (1999): 334–341.

16. Ann L. Brown and Joseph C. Campione, "Guided Discovery in a Community of Learners," in *Classroom Lessons: Integrating Cognitive Theory and Classroom Practice,* ed. Kate McGilly (Cambridge, MA: MIT Press, 1994), 229–270; and Pamela Thibodeau Hardiman, Alexander Pollatsek, and Arnold D. Well, "Learning to Understand the Balance Beam," *Cognition and Instruction* 3, no. 1 (1986): 63–86.

17. See, for example, Richard A. Carlson, David H. Lundy, and Walter Schneider, "Strategy Guidance and Memory Aiding in Learning a Problem-Solving Skill," *Human Factors* 34, no. 2 (1992): 129–145; and Leona Schauble, "Belief Revision in Children: The Role of Prior Knowledge and Strategies for Generating Evidence," *Journal of Experimental Child Psychology* 49, no. 1 (1990): 31–57.

18. Klahr and Nigam, "The Equivalence of Learning Paths."

19. Eve Kikas, "Teachers' Conceptions and Misconceptions Concerning Three Natural Phenomena," *Journal of Research in Science Teaching* 41, no. 5 (2004): 432–448.

20. Richard E. Clark, "When Teaching Kills Learning: Research on Mathemathantics," in *Learning and Instruction: European Research in an International Context,* ed. Heinz Mandl, Neville Bennett, Erik De Corte, and Helmut Friedrich, vol. 2 (London: Pergamon, 1989), 1–22.

21. Richard E. Clark, "Antagonism between Achievement and Enjoyment in ATI Studies," *Educational Psychologist* 17, no. 2 (1982): 92–101.

22. Mayer, "Three-Strikes Rule"; and Richard E. Mayer, "Constructivism as a Theory of Learning versus Constructivism as a Prescription for Instruction," in *Constructivist Instruction: Success or Failure?* ed. Sigmund Tobias and Thomas M. Duffy (New York: Taylor and Francis, 2009), 184–200.

23. See Adriaan D. de Groot, *Thought and Choice in Chess* (The Hague, Netherlands: Mouton Publishers, 1965) (original work published in 1946); followed by William G. Chase and Herbert A. Simon, "Perception in Chess," *Cognitive Psychology* 4, no. 1 (1973): 55–81; and Bruce D. Burns, "The Effects of Speed on Skilled Chess Performance," *Psychological Science* 15, no. 7 (2004): 442–447.

24. See, for example, Dennis E. Egan and Barry J. Schwartz, "Chunking in Recall of Symbolic Drawings," *Memory and Cognition* 7, no. 2 (1979): 149–158; Robin Jeffries, Althea A. Turner, Peter G. Polson, and Michael E. Atwood, "The Processes Involved in Designing Software," in *Cognitive Skills and Their Acquisition,* ed. John R. Anderson (Hillsdale, NJ: Lawrence Erlbaum Associates, 1981), 255–283; and John Sweller and Graham A. Cooper, "The Use of Worked Examples as a Substitute for Problem Solving in Learning Algebra," *Cognition and Instruction* 2, no. 1 (1985): 59–89.

25. Lloyd Peterson and Margaret Jean Peterson, "Short-Term Retention of Individual Verbal Items," *Journal of Experimental Psychology: General* 58, no. 3 (1959): 193–198.

26. George A. Miller, "The Magical Number Seven, Plus or Minus Two: Some Limits on Our Capacity for Processing Information," *Psychological Review* 63, no. 2 (1956): 81–97.

27. See, for example, Nelson Cowan, "The Magical Number 4 in Short-Term Memory; A Reconsideration of Mental Storage Capacity," *Behavioral and Brain Sciences* 24, no. 1 (2001): 87–114.

28. Sweller, "Evolution of Human Cognitive Architecture"; and John Sweller, "Instructional Design Consequences of an Analogy between Evolution by Natural Selection and Human Cognitive Architecture," *Instructional Science* 32, no. 1–2 (2004): 9–31.

29. Sweller and Cooper, "The Use of Worked Examples"; and Graham Cooper and John Sweller, "Effects of Schema Acquisition and Rule Automation on Mathematical Problem-Solving Transfer," *Journal of Educational Psychology* 79, no. 4 (1987): 347–362.

30. William M. Carroll, "Using Worked Examples as an Instructional Support in the Algebra Classroom," *Journal of Educational Psychology* 86, no. 3 (1994): 360–367; Craig S. Miller, Jill Fain Lehman, and Kenneth R. Koedinger, "Goals and learning in Microworlds," *Cognitive Science* 23, no. 3 (1999): 305–336; Fred Paas, "Training Strategies for Attaining Transfer of Problem-Solving Skill in Statistics: A Cognitive-Load Approach," *Journal of Educational Psychology* 84, no. 4 (1992): 429–434; Fred Paas and Jeroen J. G. van Merriënboer, "Variability of Worked Examples and Transfer of Geometrical Problem-Solving Skills: A Cognitive-Load Approach," *Journal of Educational Psychology* 86, no. 1 (1994): 122–133; Hitendra K. Pillay, "Cognitive Load and Mental Rotation: Structuring Orthographic Projection for Learning and Problem Solving," *Instructional Science* 22, no. 2 (1994): 91–113; Jill L. Quilici and Richard E. Mayer, "Role of Examples in How Students Learn to Categorize Statistics Word Problems," *Journal of Educational Psychology* 88, no. 1 (1996): 144–161; Arianne Rourke and John Sweller, "The Worked-Example Effect Using Ill-Defined Problems: Learning to Recognise Designers' Styles," *Learning and Instruction* 19, no. 2 (2009): 185–199; and J. Gregory Trafton and Brian J. Reiser, "The Contributions of Studying Examples and Solving Problems to Skill Acquisition," in *Proceedings of the Fifteenth Annual Conference of the Cognitive Science Society* (Hillsdale, NJ: Lawrence Erlbaum Associates, 1993), 1017–1022.

31. John Sweller, Robert F. Mawer, and Walter Howe, "Consequences of History-Cued and Means-End Strategies in Problem Solving," *American Journal of Psychology* 95, no. 3 (1982): 455–483.

32. Michelene T. H. Chi, Robert Glaser, and Ernest Rees, "Expertise in Problem Solving," in *Advances in the Psychology of Human Intelligence,* ed. Robert J. Sternberg, vol. 1 (Hillsdale, NJ: Lawrence Erlbaum Associates, 1982), 7–75.

33. Slava Kalyuga, Paul Chandler, Juhani Tuovinen, and John Sweller, "When Problem Solving Is Superior to Studying Worked Examples," *Journal of Educational Psychology* 93, no, 3 (2001): 579–588.
34. Kalyuga et al., "When Problem Solving Is Superior."
35. Slava Kalyuga, Paul Ayres, Paul Chandler, and John Sweller, "Expertise Reversal Effect," *Educational Psychologist* 38, no. 1 (2003): 23.
36. Bruner, "The Art of Discovery."

RICHARD E. CLARK is professor of educational psychology and director of the Center for Cogntive Technology in the Rossier School of Education at the University of Southern California.

PAUL A. KIRSCHNER is professor of psychology and lifelong learning, Netherlands laboratory for Lifelong Learning (NeLLL)/Department of Psychology at the Open University of the Netherlands.

JOHN SWELLER is emeritus professor at the University of New South Wales.

EXPLORING THE ISSUE

Is a Constructivist Approach to Teaching Effective?

Critical Thinking and Reflection

1. Imagine that you are the teacher in a constructivist classroom. What are some of the objections to your teaching style that you might expect to get from parents of your students? How would you respond to these objections?
2. What is the evidence that Clark and colleagues amass against constructivist approaches? How would you defend the constructivist approach in the face of this evidence?
3. Are the fully guided and constructivist approaches incompatible? Why or why not?

Is There Common Ground?

Clark, Kirschner, and Sweller point to dozens of studies that they argue demonstrate the superiority of a teacher-centered, fully guided approach to instruction over a learner-centered, constructivist approach. Why, then, do Ilmaz and other constructivists adhere so firmly to their position? How can they ignore the empirical evidence amassed by Clark and colleagues? In part, many constructivists would argue that the so-called constructivist classrooms examined in many studies did little more than insert a few hands-on activities into an otherwise teacher-centered classroom. They would question whether the classrooms that were evaluated really provided a fair test of the impact constructivism has on student learning and achievement.

An even more vexing problem in interpretation, however, is that the two approaches appear to value very different types of outcomes for students. Some suggest that a teacher-centered, fully guided approach values acquisition of a large quantity of decontextualized skills and facts, whereas the constructivist approach values the acquisition of more particular forms of knowing and acting. In other words, the two approaches seem to be designed to teach very different things. This raises the possibility that deciding between them cannot be done solely by relying on empirical data. Instead, we must decide what outcomes are most valuable for students—large collections of facts and skills or the particular modes of thought and action described by the constructivists. Only when that is decided can empirical research be conducted to determine whether the teacher-centered approach, the constructivist approach, or some other approach is best suited to reaching those outcomes in a timely and cost-effective manner.

Complicating matters further is the fact that both the fully guided approach and the constructivist approach are composed of many elements, and it may turn out to be that some elements of each may be most effective. In fact, this possibility has been suggested by a number of cognitive scientists.

Create Central

www.mhhe.com/createcentral

Additional Resources

Jacqueline G. Brooks and Martin G. Brooks, *The Case for Constructivist Classrooms* (Association for Supervision & Curriculum Development, 1993).

James Francis Hesser, "Personal Perspectives on Constructivsim in a High School Art Class," *Art Education* (July 2009).

Katherine J. Janzen, Beth Perry, Margaret Edwards, "Viewing Learning through a New Lens: The Quantum Perspective of Learning," *Creative Education* (vol. 3, 2012).

Michael Grady, Sandra Watkins, and Greg Montalvo, "The Effect of Constructivist Mathematics on Achievement in Rural Schools," *Rural Educator* (Spring/Summer 2012).

Internet References . . .

The Kennedy Center ArtsEdge

http://artsedge.kennedy-center.org/educators.aspx

National School Reform Faculty

www.nsrfharmony.org

Association for Constructivist Teaching

https://sites.google.com/site /assocforconstructteaching/

Selected, Edited, and with Issue Framing Material by:
Leonard Abbeduto, *University of California, Davis*
and
Frank Symons, *University of Minnesota*

ISSUE

Can Howard Gardner's Theory of Multiple Intelligences Transform Educational Practice?

YES: Seana Moran, Mindy Kornhaber, and Howard Gardner, from "Orchestrating Multiple Intelligences," *Educational Leadership* (September 2006)

NO: Lynn Waterhouse, from "Multiple Intelligences, the Mozart Effect, and Emotional Intelligence: A Critical Review," *Educational Psychologist* (vol. 41, no. 4, 2006)

Learning Outcomes

After reading this issue, you will be able to:

- Identify the different forms of intelligence proposed by Gardner.
- Understand the types of empirical evidence claimed to support the theory of multiple intelligences.
- Describe the implications of the theory of multiple intelligences for classroom practice.
- Understand the main criticism leveled against the theory of multiple intelligences.

ISSUE SUMMARY

YES: Seana Moran, Mindy Kornhaber, and Howard Gardner, who originally proposed the theory of multiple intelligences, argue that the theory can transform the ways in which teachers teach and students view themselves. Indeed, the theory should lead to changes in what is assessed, what is valued as educational outcomes, and how teaching should occur.

NO: Lynn Waterhouse argues that there are serious inconsistencies in the theory of multiple intelligences, there is a lack of empirical evidence to support the specific intelligences proposed, and that there is compelling psychometric evidence for a general intelligence.

For the better part of the twentieth century, scholars, policymakers, and laypeople have debated the nature of intelligence. This issue considers one theory of the nature of intelligence that has been embraced by educators around the United States, namely, the theory of multiple intelligences proposed by Howard Gardner. The centerpiece of Gardner's theory is the idea of independent domains (components, or modules) of cognitive ability, which he refers to as "frames of mind." Gardner has proposed, at various times, that there are seven, eight, or even nine intelligences. These are separate areas of ability in the sense that a person can do well in one area but not in another. In fact, although Gardner relies on other forms of evidence as well, the most compelling evidence supporting the existence of independent intelligences comes from cases of people with special talents (e.g., musical prodigies who are otherwise "average") or with a circumscribed loss or limitation of abilities (e.g., savants, who are highly

skilled painters, musicians, etc., despite having autism, intellectual disability, or another pervasive disability). The intelligences proposed by Gardner include the linguistic, spatial, and logical-mathematical. These are the forms of intelligence that are most directly assessed by IQ tests, such as the Stanford-Binet. Also included on Gardner's list, however, are less traditional intelligences: bodily-kinesthetic, musical, interpersonal, intrapersonal, and the most recently proposed intelligences of the naturalist and the existentialist. These latter intelligences as argued by Gardner and colleagues are unlikely to be measured in a meaningful way by current IQ tests.

Gardner's theory has inspired calls for dramatic changes in education. Here are but a few examples of the changes called for in the name of the theory of multiple intelligences:

1. Education has focused too narrowly on tasks that fall within the linguistic and logical-mathematic

intelligences. The scope of education should be expanded to value and nurture the development of the other intelligences as well.

2. Recent calls for a return to "basic skills" will only lead to a further narrowing of the scope of education and will marginalize many children whose talents fall within Gardner's nontraditional intelligences.

3. Evaluations of each intelligence should be made regularly so as to measure the effectiveness of educational efforts. Traditional psychometric methods of assessment are likely to be inadequate and should be replaced by more product-oriented methods, such as student portfolios of their classroom work.

4. Education must extend beyond the classroom and include nontraditional experiences, such as apprenticeships, mentorships, and participation in community-based volunteer programs.

5. Education should be structured to allow students to make discoveries on their own and to construct their own knowledge. A teacher-centered, fact-based, drill-and-practice approach bypasses the discovery process and, thus, is to be avoided.

6. Students may differ in how they approach the same academic content. Those differences should be honored and even encouraged.

Although the response from educators has been largely positive, some have been critical of Gardner's claims and have wondered whether or not the theory really has any significant implications for educational practice. The two selections that follow take very different views about the educational importance of the theory. In the first selection, Seana Moran and her colleagues argue that the theory of multiple intelligences dictates that teachers should create lessons and activities that engage and challenge all the intelligences so that all students will benefit, albeit in different ways depending on each student's profile of relative strengths and weaknesses. In the second selection, Lynn Waterhouse argues that there are serious inconsistencies in the theory of multiple intelligences, that there is a lack of empirical evidence to support the specific intelligences proposed, and that there is compelling psychometric evidence for a general intelligence.

YES ←

Seana Moran, Mindy Kornhaber, and Howard Gardner

Orchestrating Multiple Intelligences

Education policymakers sometimes go astray when they attempt to integrate multiple intelligences theory into schools. They mistakenly believe that teachers must group students for instruction according to eight or nine different intelligence scores. Or they grapple with the unwieldy notion of requiring teachers to prepare eight or nine separate entry points for every lesson.

Multiple intelligences theory was originally developed as an explanation of how the mind works—not as an education policy, let alone an education panacea. Moreover, when we and other colleagues began to consider the implications of the theory for education, the last thing we wanted to do was multiply educators' jobs ninefold. Rather, we sought to demonstrate that because students bring to the classroom diverse intellectual profiles, one "IQ" measure is insufficient to evaluate, label, and plan education programs for all students.

Adopting a multiple intelligences approach can bring about a quiet revolution in the way students see themselves and others. Instead of defining themselves as either "smart" or "dumb," students can perceive themselves as potentially smart in a number of ways.

Profile Students, Don't Score Them

Multiple intelligences theory proposes that it is more fruitful to describe an individual's cognitive ability in terms of several relatively independent but interacting cognitive capacities rather than in terms of a single "general" intelligence. Think of LEGO building blocks. If we have only one kind of block to play with, we can build only a limited range of structures. If we have a number of different block shapes that can interconnect to create a variety of patterns and structures, we can accomplish more nuanced and complex designs. The eight or nine intelligences work the same way.

The greatest potential of a multiple intelligences approach to education grows from the concept of a *profile* of intelligences. Each learner's intelligence profile consists of a combination of relative strengths and weaknesses among the different intelligences: linguistic, logical-mathematical, musical, spatial, bodily-kinesthetic, naturalistic, interpersonal, intrapersonal, and (at least provisionally) existential (Gardner, 2006).

Most people have jagged profiles; they process some types of information better than other types. Students who exhibit vast variation among their intelligences—with one or two intelligences very strong and the others relatively weak—have what we call a *laser* profile. These students often have a strong area of interest and can follow a clear path to success by developing their peak intelligences. Given the ubiquity of high-stakes testing, educators' challenge with laser-profile students is deciding whether to accentuate the students' strengths through advanced opportunities to develop their gifts or to bolster their weak areas through remediation so that they can pass the tests. Policy and funding currently favor the second option unless the student is gifted in the traditional academic areas.

Other students have a *searchlight* profile: They show less pronounced differences among intelligences. The challenge with searchlight-profile students is to help them choose a career and life path. Time and resource limitations often preclude developing all intelligences equally, so we need to consider which intelligences are most likely to pay off for a particular student. Policy and funding currently favor developing primarily linguistic and logical-mathematical intelligences at the expense of the others.

Intelligences are not isolated; they can interact with one another in an individual to yield a variety of outcomes. For example, a successful dancer must combine musical, spatial, and bodily-kinesthetic intelligences; a science fiction novelist must use logical-mathematical, linguistic, interpersonal, and some existential intelligences; an effective trial lawyer must combine linguistic and interpersonal intelligences; a skillful waiter uses linguistic, spatial, interpersonal, and bodily-kinesthetic intelligences; and a marine biologist needs strong naturalistic and logical-mathematical intelligences. In the education setting, the different intelligences can interact in two ways: within the student and across students.

An Internal Orchestra

Just as the sounds of string, woodwind, and percussion instruments combine to create a symphony, the different intelligences intermix within a student to yield meaningful scholastic achievement or other accomplishments. And as in an orchestra, one intelligence (instrument) in an individual can interfere with others, compensate for others, or enhance others.

Interference. Intelligences may not always work in harmony; sometimes they create discord. For example, even a student who has good social skills (strong interpersonal intelligence), may have trouble making friends if she cannot talk with others easily because she has weak linguistic intelligence. Another student who loves to read and receives frequent praise in English class may sit in the back row and bury her head in a novel during math class, where she feels less confident. Thus, her linguistic strength is a bottleneck for the development of her logical-mathematical intelligence. A third student's weakness in intrapersonal intelligence, which makes it difficult for him to regulate his moods or thoughts, may prevent him from completing his math homework consistently and thus mask his strong logical-mathematical intelligence.

Compensation.   Sometimes one intelligence compensates for another. A student may give great class presentations because he can effectively use his body posture and gestures even though his sentence structure is somewhat convoluted. That is, his bodily-kinesthetic intelligence compensates for his linguistic limitations. (We can think of more than one U.S. president who fits this profile.) Or a student may earn a high mark on a paper for writing with a powerful rhetorical voice, even though her argument is not quite solid: Her linguistic intelligence compensates for her logical-mathematical limitations.

Enhancement. Finally, one intelligence may jumpstart another. Strong spatial intelligence may improve a student's ability to conceptualize a mathematical concept or problem. This was certainly the case with Einstein. Strong musical intelligence may stimulate interest and playfulness in writing poetry. Understanding how intelligences can catalyze one another may help students—and teachers—make decisions about how to deploy the intellectual resources they have at their disposal.

The profile approach to multiple intelligences instruction provides teachers with better diagnostic information to help a particular student who is struggling. Before providing assistance, we need to ask *why* the student is having difficulty. For example, consider three beginning readers who have trouble comprehending a story. The first is struggling because of poor reading comprehension skills (a linguistic intelligence challenge). The second has poor social understanding of the dynamics among the story's characters (an interpersonal intelligence challenge). The third has such strong spatial intelligence that he has trouble seeing beyond the physical pattern of the letter symbols (a challenge that Picasso, for example, faced in his early years). More reading practice, which is often the default intervention, may not help all of these students.

A student's potential is not the sum of his or her intelligence "scores," as some multiple intelligence inventory measures on the market imply. If one intelligence is a bottleneck for others, then the student's overall potential may be lower than the straight sum. If intelligences are compensating for or enhancing one another, the student's overall potential may be higher than the straight sum. Intelligences have multiplicative as well as additive effects.

An Effective Ensemble

Intelligences can also work across students. The information explosion has greatly escalated the amount of information that each person must assimilate and understand—frequently beyond what we can handle by ourselves. Work teams, institutional partnerships, and interdisciplinary projects have increasingly become the norm. These ensembles support individuals as they seek to learn, understand, and perform well.

Multiple intelligences theory encourages collaboration across students. Students with compatible profiles (exhibiting the same patterns of strengths and weaknesses) can work together to solidify and build on strengths. For example, two students highly capable in storytelling can support each other by moving beyond the basics of plot to explore and develop twists in the narrative. A group of students who are skilled in numerical computation might extend a statistics lesson beyond mean, median, mode, and range to understand correlation or regression.

Students with complementary profiles (in which one student's weak areas are another student's strengths) can work together to compensate for one another. Such students can approach material in different but equally valid ways. For example, a student who is strong in logical-mathematical intelligence and sufficient in spatial intelligence might be able to translate abstract math problems into dance choreography or sculpture contexts to make them understandable to a student with strong spatial and bodily-kinesthetic intelligences.

Provide Rich Experiences

The eminent psychologist L. S. Vygotsky (1978) emphasized that *experience*—the idiosyncratic way each individual internalizes the environment's information—is important in both cognitive and personality development. If we give all students the same material, each student will have a different experience according to his or her background, strengths, and challenges. Thus, to promote learning across student intelligence profiles, teachers need to offer students rich experiences—activities in which they can engage with the material personally rather than just absorb it in an abstract, decontextualized way.

Rich experiences enable students to learn along several dimensions at once—socially, spatially, kinesthetically, self-reflectively, and so on. Often, these experiences cross subject-area lines. At Searsport Elementary School in Searsport, Maine, a 5th grade teacher who had strong storytelling abilities and an avid interest in history joined forces with her colleague, an expert in hands-on science, to develop an archaeology unit. Students studied history and geography as well as scientific method and archaeology techniques. They investigated local history, conducted a state-approved archaeological dig, identified and classified objects, and displayed the artifacts in a museum exhibit that met real-world curatorial standards (Kornhaber, Fierros, & Veenema, 2004).

Rich experiences also provide diagnostic information. Teachers can observe student performances to find root causes of misunderstandings and to figure out how students can achieve superior understandings. One small group of 2nd and 3rd graders in Chimene Brandt's class at Pittsburgh's McCleary Elementary School produced a mural depicting a rainy street scene. Their spatial portrayal of material was ambiguous: The connection to the unit's topic of rivers and the lesson's topic of the water cycle laws was not obvious. The students' understanding came through linguistically, however, when they presented in class how the water from the street would evaporate, condense into clouds, and again produce rain. By giving the students multiple ways to express the concepts, Brandt was able to confirm that the students understood the material even though their linguistic skills outstripped their spatial skills (Kornhaber, Fierros, & Veenema, 2004).

Two programs exemplify how rich experiences can serve as venues for developing and assessing multiple intelligences. The first, Project Spectrum, is an interactive assessment process for preschool children developed in the 1980s at Harvard Project Zero (Gardner, Feldman, & Krechevsky, 1998). This process evaluates each intelligence directly, rather than funneling the information through a linguistic paper-and-pencil test. Spatial orientation and manipulation tasks evaluate spatial intelligence; group tasks evaluate interpersonal intelligence; self-assessments paired with the other assessments evaluate intrapersonal intelligence. Project Spectrum environments do not segment tasks strictly into one intelligence or another. Instead, they set up situations in which a student can interact with rich materials—and teachers can observe these interactions—to see which intelligences come to the fore and which are relegated to the background.

A naturalist's corner provides biological specimens for students to touch and move (using bodily-kinesthetic intelligence), arrange (naturalistic), create relationships among (logical-mathematical), tell stories about (linguistic), or even compare themselves with (intrapersonal). In a storytelling area, students can tell tales (linguistic), arrange props and character figurines (spatial and possibly bodily-kinesthetic), make characters interact (interpersonal), and design their own storyboards (spatial). Fifteen other activities provide opportunities for evaluating intelligences through reliable scoring rubrics that have been used widely in early childhood education in the United States, Latin America, Europe, and Asia (Gardner, Feldman, & Krechevsky, 1998).

Another environment providing rich experiences using a multiple intelligences approach is the Explorama

at Danfoss Universe, a science park in Nordborg, Denmark. . . . Designed according to multiple intelligences theory, this interactive museum is used by people of all ages—from school groups to corporate teams. The designers have devised separate exhibits, games, and challenges for each intelligence and for numerous combinations of intelligences. One experience asks participants to balance themselves (bodily-kinesthetic); another asks them to balance in a group (bodily-kinesthetic and interpersonal). A computer program encourages participants to add, subtract, or combine different musical qualities and see on screen how the tone frequencies change, tapping into musical, spatial, and logical-mathematical intelligences.

Three activities deserve particular attention for their innovativeness in assessing several intelligences concurrently and in emphasizing intelligences that are often neglected in mainstream academic testing. One game involves manipulating a joystick to control a robot that can lift and move a cube to a target space. When played alone, this exhibit primarily assesses bodily-kinesthetic and spatial intelligence. But when two to four people each control a different joystick—one that controls the left wheel of the robot, another that controls the right wheel, another that raises the cube, and another that lowers the cube—they must coordinate their play to accomplish the task, employing linguistic, logical-mathematical, and interpersonal intelligences.

Another game has two players sitting opposite each other at a table, with a ping-pong ball in the center. Each player tries to move the ball toward the opponent by relaxing. Relaxing reduces the player's stress level, creating alpha waves in the brain that sensors pick up to move the ball forward. This task requires self-control, and thus taps into intrapersonal intelligence. However, the players must also employ interpersonal intelligence, paying attention to each other and trying to produce more alpha waves than the opponent does.

A third notable Explorama activity is a computerized questionnaire in which participants assess their own intelligence profiles. Participants take the self-assessment before entering the Explorama and again after they have engaged in the various activities and tasks. Participants thus get an idea of how well they know their own capabilities. They also can compare their self-assessments before and after the Explorama experience to learn whether their self-perceptions stayed constant or changed. This process develops participants' intrapersonal intelligence.

Get Personal

The orientation toward profiles, interactions, and experience emphasizes a need to develop, in particular, the two personal intelligences.

Intrapersonal intelligence involves knowing yourself— your talents, energy level, interests, and so on. Students who strengthen their intrapersonal intelligence gain a better understanding of areas in which they can expect to excel, which helps them plan and govern their own learning.

Interpersonal intelligence involves understanding others through social interaction, emotional reactions, conversation, and so on. An individual's interpersonal intelligence affects his or her ability to work in groups. Group projects can create environments for students to improve their interpersonal intelligence as they develop other skills and knowledge.

Donna Schneider, a 3rd grade teacher at the John F. Kennedy Elementary School in Brewster, New York, developed a real-world publishing company in her classroom: "Schneider's Ink." Each spring when the school puts on performances and events, Schneider's 3rd graders create programs, banners, advertisements, and other publicity materials for their clients, the sponsoring teachers. Each student assumes a different job—editor, sales manager, typist, accountant, customer service representative, or designer. Before taking on a given position, each student writes a resumé and cover letter, obtains letters of recommendation, and is interviewed by the teacher. Students explore their own strengths and become aware of how those strengths can enable them to succeed in various jobs.

Schneider's Ink also engages students' interpersonal intelligence. For example, the quality-control manager, who is responsible for handling customer complaints, has to work with both clients and the editor to review problems. As company employees, the students juggle simultaneous print orders, coordinating the sequencing of tasks among themselves to produce high-quality work on time. They must understand others through social interaction, emotional reactions, and conversation. Through this process, students acquire a better understanding of the interdependence of individual strengths (Kornhaber, Fierros, & Veenema, 2004).

Building Active Learners

The multiple intelligences approach does not require a teacher to design a lesson in nine different ways so that all students can access the material. Rather, it involves creating rich experiences in which students with different intelligence profiles can interact with the materials and ideas using their particular combinations of strengths and weaknesses.

Often, these experiences are collaborative. As the amount of information that students—and adults—must process continues to increase dramatically, collaboration enables students to learn more by tapping into others' strengths as well as into their own. In ideal multiple intelligences instruction, rich experiences and collaboration provide a context for students to become aware of their own intelligence profiles, to develop self-regulation, and to participate more actively in their own learning.

References

Gardner, H. (2006). *Multiple intelligences: New horizons*. New York: Basic Books.

Gardner, H., Feldman, D. H., & Krechevsky, M. (Eds.). (1998). *Project Zero frameworks for early childhood education: Volume 1. Building on children's strengths: The experience of Project Spectrum*. New York: Teachers College Press.

Kornhaber, M., Fierros, E., & Veenema, S. (2004). *Multiple intelligences: Best ideas from research and practice*. Boston: Pearson.

Vygotsky, L. S. (1978). *Mind in society: The development of higher psychological processes*. Cambridge, MA: Harvard University Press.

SEANA MORAN is a research assistant professor at Clark University.

MINDY KORNHABER is a faculty member in educational theory and policy at Pennsylvania State University.

HOWARD GARDNER is the John H. and Elisabeth A. Hobbs Professor of Cognition and Education at Harvard University and the developer of the theory of multiple intelligences.

Lynn Waterhouse

 **NO**

Multiple Intelligences, the Mozart Effect, and Emotional Intelligence: A Critical Review

. . .

MI Theory

MI theory was first outlined by Gardner in 1983. He proposed the existence of seven distinct intelligences: linguistic, musical, logical-mathematical, spatial, bodily-kinesthetic, intrapersonal sense of self, and interpersonal. In 1999 Gardner revised his model, combining intrapersonal and interpersonal into a single intelligence and adding another intelligence, naturalistic intelligence, the empathy for, and categorization of, natural things. Gardner (1999) also proposed a possible additional intelligence, called existential intelligence, the ability to see oneself "with respect to the further reaches of the cosmos . . . or total immersion in a work of art" (p. 60). More recently Gardner (2004) proposed two additional intelligences, the "mental searchlight intelligence" and the "laser intelligence" (p. 217). Gardner (2004) claimed that people with high IQ test scores have "a *mental searchlight,* which allows them to scan wide spaces in an efficient way thus permitting them to run society smoothly" (p. 217), whereas specialists in the arts, sciences, and trades are more likely to have a *laser intelligence* that permits them to generate "the advances (as well as the catastrophes) of society" (p. 217). Gardner has not yet theorized a connection between laser intelligence, mental searchlight intelligence, and his eight other intelligences. If he does so he will face the problem of reconciling the use of standard IQ scores as the basis for the mental searchlight intelligence while arguing that MI theory reveals the standard IQ measure to be a flawed concept (Gardner, 1983, 1999).

Gardner (1999) posited that "each intelligence comprises constituent units" (p. 103) and stated that "there are several musical, linguistic, and spatial subintelligences" (p. 103). Similarly, Gardner and Connell (2000) proposed that all eight of the intelligences are supermodules that organize 50 to 100 micromodules (p. 292). Gardner (1999) argued that specifying subintelligences "would be more accurate scientifically, but the construct would be unwieldy for educational uses" (p. 103).

Gardner (2004) asserted that his intelligences were "consistent with how most biologists think about the mind and brain" (p. 214). Gardner (1999) claimed that each intelligence operates from a separate area of the brain, arguing that "MI theory demands that linguistic processing, for example, occur via a different set of neural mechanisms than does spatial or interpersonal processing" (p. 99). Gardner (1999) further posited that if "musical and spatial processing were identically represented" in the cortexes of individuals "that fact would suggest the presence of one intelligence, and not two separate intelligences" (p. 99). Similarly, in addressing the 2004 National Dance Association meeting Gardner claimed that "parts of the brain are dedicated to the arts, and it's a shame not to develop these parts" (Hildebrand, 2004, p. 59). Gardner (1999) asserted that not only are the intelligences brain-based but they are also innate and that if tests for the intelligences were developed, "mathematical, spatial, and musical intelligences would have higher heritabilities than linguistic, naturalist, and personal intelligences" (p. 88). Gardner (1999) concluded that "accumulating neurological evidence is amazingly supportive of the general thrust of MI theory. Research supports the particular intelligences I have described" (p. 99). He also reported that neuroscientists "are in the process of homing in on the nature of core operations for each of the intelligences" (Gardner, 2004, p. 217).

The Lack of Empirical Evidence for MI Theory

To date there have been no published studies that offer evidence of the validity of the MI. In 1994 Sternberg reported finding no empirical studies. In 2000 Allix reported finding no empirical validating studies, and at that time Gardner and Connell (2000) conceded that there was "little hard evidence for MI theory" (p. 292). In 2004, Sternberg and Grigorenko stated that there were no validating studies for MI, and in 2004 Gardner asserted that he would be "delighted were such evidence to accrue" (p. 214), and he admitted that "MI theory has few enthusiasts among psychometricians or others of a traditional psychological background" because they require "psychometric or experimental evidence that allows one to prove the existence of the several intelligences" (p. 214).

Defending the Lack of Empirical Evidence for MI Theory

Chen (2004) defended MI theory against the claim that it lacks empirical support arguing that "a theory is not necessarily valuable because it is supported by the results of empirical tests" (p. 22) and that "intelligence is not a tangible object that can be measured" (p. 22). She also claimed that the novelty of the intelligences requires new measures and that MI theory has already been validated in its successful classroom application. Chen further claimed that MI theory better accounts for cognitive skill profiles in both brain-injured and typical individuals than do IQ measures.

Argument 1: Empirical evidence for MI is not necessary. Chen (2004) claimed that as the 20th century debate over scientific method showed that "the absolute objectivity of any methodology is illusory" (p. 17), therefore concern over the lack of evidence for MI theory is mistaken. However, although both Kuhn and Popper recognized that experimental methods may be subject to bias, nothing in the debate between Kuhn and Popper and their followers argued *against* the need for empirical data collection (Fuller, 2004; Nersessian, 1998). In fact, Kuhn's thesis rested on the observation that "the track records" of validating experiments are the normative basis for evaluating theories (Fuller, 2004, p. 29). MI theory has no such track record.

Argument 2: Intelligence is not a tangible object. Chen (2004) asserted that "intelligence is not a tangible object that can be measured; it is a construct that psychologists define" (p. 22). Yes, MI, like general intelligence, memory, or attention, are defined constructs and not tangible objects. However, defined constructs can be measured if they have clearly specified testable components (Allix, 2000; Ceci, 1996; Johnson & Bouchard, 2005). Although Gardner (2004) admitted that "it is important to identify defining features" (p. 214), he stated that he has not proposed testable components for the intelligences because his "basic paradigm clashes with that of psychometrics" (p. 214). Without defined components the intelligences cannot be tested for validity (Allix, 2000; Fuller, 2004).

Argument 3: MI are novel constructs requiring new measures. Chen (2004) argued that because the MI are not abilities but are instead "biological potential with an emergent, responsive, pluralistic nature" (p. 19), they can only be validated with new measures that identify "the different facets" of each intelligence as it functions over time (p. 20). However, because, as noted previously, Gardner's (2004) paradigm stands against defining testable components ("facets") for his intelligences (p. 214), this may prove difficult.

In addition, Allix (2000) argued that even if Gardner were to generate testable components, the validity of individual intelligences still could not be explored because Gardner has not specified the functional links he has theorized to exist between the intelligences. Gardner (1999) proposed that the intelligences are only "semi-independent" (p. 89), that they function together in development, that the

linguistic intelligence operates by receiving input from the other intelligences (Gardner, 1983), and that there is likely to be a "Central Intelligences Agency" that "emerges from other intelligences" (Gardner, 1999, p. 106). Gardner responded to Allix (2000) that "it is difficult to specify how multiple intelligences work synergistically on complex tasks" (Gardner & Connell, 2000, p. 292).

Argument 4: MI theory has been validated by its classroom applications. Chen (2004) claimed that "MI theory can also be validated by evaluating the results of applying the theory in a range of educational settings" (p. 20), and Gardner, too, asserted that the positive outcomes of education methods based on MI can be viewed as empirical support for MI theory (Gardner, 2004, p. 214; Gardner & Connell, 2000, p. 292). However, the successful application of MI theory in education practice (Hoerr, 2003; Shearer, 2004) cannot provide a test of the validity of the intelligences because the act of applying MI theory *assumes* the validity of the intelligences. Moreover, any improvement in student learning under an MI framework is confounded with the positive effects of the novelty of a new method engendered by teacher enthusiasm and student excitement. Furthermore, it is also possible that some MI applications have been successful by serendipity, that is, they have induced improved learning because, coincidentally, some aspect of that method was effective independent of the MI framework of the application.

Argument 5: MI theory profiles cognitive skills better than do IQ subtests. Chen (2004) claimed that MI theory better accounts for cognitive skill profiles of typical students, savants, prodigies, individuals with brain injuries, and individuals in specialized professions than do IQ measures (p. 18). However, no empirical research has been published to support this claim (Allix, 2000; Chen, 2004; Gardner, 2004; Sternberg, 1994; Sternberg & Grigorenko, 2004). Equally important, Watkins and Canivez (2004) argued that IQ subtest profiles are not stable, not reliable, do not adequately discriminate "among diagnostic groups and do not covary with socially important academic and psychosocial outcomes"(p. 137). Therefore, if the discriminating power of MI cognitive skill profiles were to be empirically compared with a standard system, it should not be IQ cognitive profiles. The current standard for assessing variation in an individual's cognitive skills is a battery of valid and reliable fine-grained independent measures of specific aspects of skills such as language, perception, memory, attention, and reasoning (See Lezak, 1995, and C. R. Reynolds & Kamphaus, 2003, for examples of batteries).

Summary: The Lack of Empirical Evidence for MI Theory Remains a Problem

None of Chen's five arguments can serve to exempt MI theory from the need for validating empirical data. Nothing in the Kuhn-Popper debate suggested that theories should not be tested by experimental methods. MI are intangible theorized constructs, but, if their components are specified, they can be tested. MI may require new measures, but new measures depend on clearly defined components for the intelligences, and Gardner (1999, 2004) stated that he will not define such components. MI theory cannot be validated through application research because such research assumes the validity of the intelligences and because positive application effects may be caused by confounding independent factors such as novelty and excitement. No published research has reported that the cognitive skill profiles generated by MI are more discriminating than those generated by IQ subtests. Moreover, for reasons outlined previously, IQ subtest profiles are not an appropriate comparison, should such an empirical comparison be conducted,

Cognitive Psychology and Neuroscience Are Not Exploring MI Theory

Gardner asserted that his intelligences were developed "from an evolutionary perspective" (2004, p. 214) and were supported by research (1999, p. 99) and that neuroscientists were "in the process of homing in on the nature of core operations for each of the intelligences" (2004, p. 217). However, there are no publications from cognitive psychologists, cognitive neuroscientists, or evolutionary psychologists to suggest that they have conducted research directed at defining or validating Gardner's intelligences. Research has explored the nature of human perceptual processes such as vision, hearing, smell, and taste, but these processes have not been determined to be a *seeing intelligence, smelling intelligence, tactile intelligence,* or the like (Born & Bradley, 2005; Eibenstein et al., 2005; Goodwin & Wheat, 2004; J. H. Reynolds & Chelazzi, 2004). Research has also explored language skills, reading skills, music skills, mathematics skills, reasoning skills, spatial skills, and social skills, but these skills have not been found to be functioning as separate intelligences (Cacioppo & Berntson, 2004; Josse & Tzourio-Mazoyer, 2004; R. C. Martin, 2003; Miller, 1999; Parris, 2005; Peretz & Zatorre, 2005; Shafir & LeBoeuf, 2002; Singer-Dudek & Greer, 2005; see also Gazzaniga, 2004).

The majority of recent cognitive psychology, cognitive neuroscience, and evolutionary psychology research programs on human mental abilities have focused on three core explanatory paradigms for human cognition, These are general intelligence, multiple information processing systems, and adapted cognition modules.

Research Findings for General Intelligence "g" Theory

The theory of g claims that a unitary general intelligence exists that is identified by an IQ test factor g (Geake & Hansen, 2005; Johnson & Bouchard, 2005; Johnson, Bouchard, Krueger, McGue, & Gottesman, 2004; McRorie & Cooper, 2004). Gardner (1983) devised MI theory against this paradigm of a unitary general intelligence. Whether g

has two forms, *a fluid* intelligence that reflects mental ability independent of culture and a *crystallized* intelligence that reflects both fluid intelligence and learning, remains a matter of empirical debate (Johnson & Bouchard, 2005). General intelligence has been theorized to reflect overall brain efficiency or the close interconnection of a set of mental skills or working memory.

There are many lines of evidence supporting a general intelligence function. Individual cognitive skills have been shown to be significantly correlated with g (Larson & Saccuzzo, 1989; Watkins & Cavinez, 2004), and g has been shown to predict intellectual performance across different sets of measures (Johnson et al., 2004). Oberauer, Schulze, Wilhelm, and Suss (2005) reported that a substantial portion of g variance is predicted by working memory skill. Colom, Rebolloa, Palaciosa, Juan-Espinosaa, and Kyltonenb (2004) reported that measures of g predicted nearly all the variance in a measure of working memory, and they concluded that g is likely to be working memory, a function of the frontal lobe of the brain that maintains and manipulates information in a limited timeframe.

Toga and Thompson (2005) reported that there is considerable evidence for the heritability of general intelligence, for the heritability of MRI-measured brain volumes, and for the significant positive correlation of IQ measures and brain volumes. McDaniel (2005) reported that a meta-analysis of 37 studies including 1,530 men and women found whole brain volume to be significantly positively correlated with full scale IQ in both men and women, but the correlation between IQ and brain volume was higher in women than in men (p. 343). This sex difference may be linked to the finding that although men, on average, have larger brains than women, women have more brain gray matter than do men (Luders et al., 2005).

Thatcher, North, and Biver (2005) reported that frontal lobe brain activity was positively correlated with IQ. Frontal lobe activity level, as measured by fMRI was also reported to be positively associated with verbal IQ (Geake and Hansen, 2005). McRorie and Cooper (2004) found that motor reaction speed of removing the hand following electric shock correlated significantly with Wechsler full scale IQ and verbal IQ and with a measure of visual search speed. Moreover, it has been argued that the number of cortical neurons combined with conduction velocity of cortical fibers is the best correlate for intelligence in phylogenetic cross-taxon comparisons (Roth & Dicke, 2005).

How do research findings for general intelligence argue against MI theory? Although the empirical evidence for general intelligence does not exclude the possibility of MI, it identifies serious difficulties for MI theory. The significant intercorrelations of IQ subskills (Johnson et al., 2004; Larson & Saccuzzo 1989; Watkins & Cavinez, 2004) argue against the possibility of discrete intelligence-by-intelligence content processing that

Gardner (1999) claimed was a requirement of MI theory (p. 99). The findings for a significant positive correlation between intelligence and the size of the human brain (McDaniel, 2005; Toga & Thompson, 2005) and the level of brain activity (Geake & Hansen, 2005) argue against Gardner's (1999) criticism that g is merely the abstraction of a statistical factor (p. 14).

Equally important, because evidence has suggested that g represents working memory, and working memory is the core frontal lobe executive function (Colom et al., 2004; Oberauer et al., 2005), therefore, g is likely to be the same entity as Gardner's (1999) "Central Intelligences Agency," which he defined as the frontal lobe executive function (pp. 105–106). This stands against Gardner's (1999) assertion that "MI theory is incompatible with 'g'" (p. 87). Furthermore, evidence that g may be working memory also argues that Gardner's (2004) proposed high-IQ "mental searchlight" intelligence (p. 217) would be a high g working-memory ability. As there is nothing inherent in working memory that allows individuals "to scan wide spaces in an efficient way thus permitting them to run society smoothly" (Gardner, 2004, p. 217), the definition of the mental searchlight intelligence becomes problematic. Finally, logically, if g is a measure of working memory, then the "Central Intelligences Agency" may *be* the mental searchlight intelligence. If so, then this would need clarification.

Research Findings for Multiple Information Processing Systems

Although much research investigating possible brain processing systems has concentrated on the functions of specific regions of the brain (Born & Bradley, 2005; Squire, Craig, & Clark, 2005), research has identified two large-scale information processing pathways or processing streams in the brain. One pathway synthesizes the perceptual analyses of what we see and hear to answer the question *"What* is it?" In this processing pathway the "it" is an object, animal, person, place, or other element in our environment. The other processing pathway synthesizes the perceptual analyses of what we see, hear, and feel to answer the question *"Where* is it?" (Arnott, Binns, Grady, & Alain, 2004; Himmelbach & Karnath, 2005; Irwin & Brockmole, 2004).

These two processing pathways might themselves seem to be two "intelligences"—the "What is it?" object intelligence and the "Where is it?" place intelligence. However these processing pathways are not functionally isolated from one another. Gardner (1999) asserted that "MI theory demands that linguistic processing, for example, occur via a different set of neural mechanisms than does spatial or interpersonal processing" (p. 99), but the "What is it?" and the "Where is it?" processing pathways are interconnected. For example, Prather, Votaw, and Sathian (2004) reported that touching things activates not only the "Where is it?" pathways but also the "What is it?"

processing pathway. Similarly, Himmelbach and Karnath (2005) argued that there is systematic interactive switching between the "What is it?" pathway and the "Where is it?" pathway. It has also been suggested that these two processing pathways may actually be different activity patterns of the same overall anatomical processing stream (Deco, Roils, & Horwitz, 2004).

Cognitive neuroscience research also has reported that many other cognitive skills share brain processing pathways. Researchers reported evidence for shared and overlapping processing pathways for language and music (Koelsch et al., 2004). Norton et al. (2005) found associations between the music perceptual skills and both nonverbal reasoning and phonemic awareness in children, and they argued that these correlations suggest a shared neural substrate for language and music processing. A research review suggested that the same aggregations of subcortical neurons in basal ganglia and cerebellum, and the same aggregations of neurons in many separate cortical regions together share control of many different complex behaviors including walking, talking, gesturing, reasoning, speaking, tool-making, and comprehending the meaning of sentences (Lieberman, 2002). Evidence has been reported to suggest that brain circuits for emotions share in a distributed network of processing pathways for reasoning, memory, and action (Adolphs, Tranel, & Damasio, 2003; Morgane, Galler, & Mokler, 2005; Phelps, 2006).

The shared and overlapping brain pathways for cognitive skills may be the result of genes that determine shared pathways. Kovas, Harlaar, Petrill, and Plomin (2005) reported that "most of the genes that contribute to individual differences in mathematics ability also affect reading and g" (p. 485). The researchers argued that because reading, mathematics, and g are complex skills, therefore "a great variety of non-specific abilities, such as long-term memory, working memory and attention" (p. 485) must be involved in these skills. Kovas et al. asserted that *generalist genes* are responsible for the "genetic overlap between mathematics, reading, and g" (p. 485). They predicted that future studies will find more *generalist genes* that determine shared pathways for different forms of cognition.

In addition to the "What is it?" and "Where is it?" pathways model, there is another model that has claimed the existence of a set of distinctive functional brain systems. Kahneman (2003) concluded that there are two separate decision-making systems in the brain: System 1 generates fast, intuitive, automatic decision making; System 2 generates slow, effortful, consciously monitored decision making. Kahneman argued that System 1 and System 2 interact, with System 1 as primary: "impressions produced by System 1 control judgments and preferences, unless modified or overwritten by the deliberate operations of System 2" (p. 20). Kahneman further claimed that System 1 judgments improve with practice, such that experts can make System 1 judgments that are both faster and more accurate than they would using the slow, conscious System 2.

Kahneman's (2003) Systems 1 and 2 might, like the "What is it?" and "Where is it?" pathways, also seem to be potential intelligences: the "intuitive intelligence," and the "deliberative intelligence." However, these two systems each process all the varied types of content information—language, music, numbers, social information—that Gardner argued are channeled into the separate intelligences. Moreover, Kahneman's two theorized systems each have only one task—to compute a decision. Conversely, Gardner's MI each have many tasks. For example, the musical intelligence determines "the performance, composition, and appreciation of musical patterns" (Gardner, 1999, p. 42). Neither System 1 nor System 2 is theorized to create, compose, appreciate, or perform.

How does evidence for these processing systems argue against MI theory? Evidence for the neural processing systems reviewed here argues against the core of MI theory in two important ways. First, the evidence for the functional overlap of the "What is it?" and the "Where is it?" processing pathways, along with the evidence for the shared and overlapping neural pathways for emotion, music, language, logic-mathematics, spatial, body sense, and social skills (Koelsch et al., 2004; Lieberman, 2002; Morgane et al., 2005; Norton et al., 2005) argue against Gardner's (1999) theoretical provision that each intelligence must have its own separate neural processing pathway (p. 99). Second, the basic operating plan of the "What is it?" and "Where is it?" pathways and System 1 and 2 works in a manner that is the direct opposite of the basic operating plan theorized for the MI. Each multiple intelligence is a multipurpose processor that operates on a single content. Conversely, the "What is it?" and "Where is it?" pathways and System 1 and 2 are each unipurpose processors operating on multiple contents.

Research Findings for Adapted Cognition Theory

Evolutionary psychologists have proposed the existence of innate cognitive modules that generate specific adaptive behavior patterns (Cosmides & Tooby, 1992; Cummins, 2002; Gallistel, 1998; Hauser & Spelke, 2004). Gallistel argued that "Because different representations have different mathematical structure and because they are computed from sensory inputs with widely differing properties, learning mechanisms must be domain- or problem-specific" (p. 55). Gallistel speculated that there may be 100 human domain-specific cognition modules wherein each evolved to solve a different environmental computational problem.

Many unique neural computational devices have been found in animals (Burghardt, 2002; Hauser, 2000). Research on possible human adapted cognition modules is not as extensive but is increasing. Evidence has offered support for the existence of a range of adapted cognition modules including one for detecting social cheating (Cummins, 2002; Velicer, 2005), one for knowledge of number (Gelman & Gallistel, 2005; Xu, Spelke, & Goddard, 2005), and one for the mental imitation of others through automatic firing of mirror neurons (Fadiga, Craighero, & Olivier, 2005; Mottonen, Jarvelainen, Sams, & Hari, 2005; Rizzolatti & Craighero, 2004).

Social cheating occurs in many species. Cheating bacteria do not make the beneficial extracellular compounds that their noncheating neighbors do (Velicer, 2005). Insect queens engage in social cheating when they steal workers from other colonies to tend their own larvae. Birds engage in social cheating when they deposit their eggs in other nests thus avoiding the effort of raising their own chicks. Although humans are unusual in their altruistic cooperation (Fehr & Fischbacher, 2003), human social cheating includes theft, sexual infidelity, and shirking group work. Evidence has suggested that humans are better at detecting cheaters than they are at solving parallel detection problems that do not involve cheating (Gigerenzer & Hug, 1992).

Evidence that human number knowledge may be innate has been accumulating (Hauser & Spelke, 2004). Studies have reported that children's acquisition of number knowledge is separate from their initial language development (Xu et al., 2005) and that number knowledge exists in primates (Gelman & Butterworth, 2005).

In addition to cheater detection and number knowledge, still another proposed adapted cognition module is that of the mirror neuron system. The mirror neuron system was first discovered in monkeys, but there is now clear evidence that humans have a mirror neuron system (Rizzolatti & Craighero, 2004). When we observe the behavior of another person, mirror neurons automatically fire, triggering neurons in our brains to copy or "mirror" the observed person's mouth movements (Mottonen et al., 2005), gestures, and actions (Rizzolatti & Carighero, 2004). However, because this firing is below the threshold needed to engage our muscles, we rarely explicitly mimic those we observe (Fadiga et al., 2005). The mirror neuron system of mental imitation enables us to more easily understand the emotional state of those around us and also learn complex behaviors from others.

Adapted cognition theory has engendered a lively debate (Butler, 2005). Hernandez, Li, and MacWhinney (2005) argued that modules are not innate but emerge in development. Lickliter and Honeycult (2003) argued that it was unlikely that adapted cognition modules could sit dormant in the brain waiting to be activated by life experience. Bjorklund (2003) countered that most adapted cognition modules are likely to be *architectural,* resulting from genes that determine the structure of brain regions, or *chronotopic,* resulting from genes that determine critical periods of development.

Bjorkland posited that very few adapted cognition modules, such as the module for number, would be *content-representational,* that is resulting from genes that determine specific innate knowledge. In another entry in this ongoing debate Kanazawa (2004) argued that g itself is an adaptive module that evolved to enable humans to solve new or more general problems in the environment, and other modules such as the detection of social cheating and number knowledge evolved to solve specific recurring problems in the environment.

How do research findings for adapted cognition theory argue against MI theory? The research findings for the adapted cognition modules of detecting social cheating, number knowledge, and the mirror neuron system might seem to suggest that such modules are themselves "intelligences," thus indirectly supporting Gardner's construct of MI. However, adapted cognition modules operate both more narrowly and more broadly than do Gardner's intelligences. For example, mirror neurons do nothing more than activate an observer's brain circuits for those motor patterns that are being enacted by the observed individual. This narrow function argues that mirror neurons are not an "intelligence." At the same time, however, because mirror neurons are activated by a very wide range of behaviors including facial motor movements of others, gesturing, grasping, touching, and tool use (Rizzolatti & Craighero, 2004; Mottonen et al., 2005), the mirror neuron system operates over a much broader range of content than that identified by Gardner for each of his intelligences.

More specifically, evidence for the module of number knowledge might appear to provide support for Gardner's logical-mathematical intelligence. However, the numerosity module is a much narrower cognitive specialization than Gardner's logical-mathematical intelligence. The module includes only counting using the natural numbers (1, 2, 3, 4, . . .) and estimating the numerosity of objects in groups (Gelman & Butterworth, 2005). Neither logic nor mathematics as a system of operations on numbers is included in the number knowledge module. Equally important, because numerosity estimations could occur in all of Gardner's intelligences, the numerosity module operates much more broadly than was theorized by Gardner for his intelligences.

Like the mirror neuron system and number knowledge module, the theorized social cheating detection module also involves processing that would operate across most of Gardner's theorized intelligences and would also, nonetheless, focus on a problem much narrower—who is cheating?—than that assumed by Gardner for each of the MI.

In fact, adapted cognition modules are theorized to have evolved to aid us in solving quite specific recurrent problems in our environment. Mirror neurons can help us learn what our neighbor is doing and feeling by providing automatic mental imitation of our neighbor's behaviors. Innate numerosity skill can assist in quickly counting resources or elements of danger. Social cheating detection can help us discern unjust access to resources.

Although Gardner argued that MI are evolved brain specializations (1999, p. 88; 2004, p. 214), he claimed that "each intelligence probably evolved to deal with *certain kinds of contents* in a predictable world" (1999, p. 95). Thus, the linguistic, musical, logical-mathematical, bodily-kinesthetic, spatial, personal, and naturalistic intelligences were not theorized to each solve a specific environmental problem but to each deal with a different general content. If MI are innate brain specializations, as claimed by Gardner, and if they have not each evolved to solve a particular recurrent problem in our environment, why did they evolve? For example, if the musical intelligence is a cognitive brain specialization that evolved to determine "skill in the performance, composition, and appreciation of musical patterns" (Gardner, 1999, p. 42), what recurrent human environmental problem did music performance, composition, and appreciation evolve to solve? Despite Gardner's (1999) assertion that once an intelligence "emerged, there is nothing that mandates that it must remain tied to the original inspiring content" (p. 95), nothing in MI theory answers the following question: How could the *content* of music *inspire* the evolution of the musical intelligence as a distinct brain specialization?

Summary: Cognition Research Evidence Does Not Support MI Theory

Albeit neuroscience researchers have not claimed that individual human perceptual processes such as taste or vision are intelligences or that innate skills, such as spatial navigation, or learned skills, such as music composition, are intelligences, nonetheless, this provides no evidence against MI theory. However, the empirical evidence reviewed here does argue that the human brain is unlikely to function via Gardner's MI. Taken together the evidence for the intercorrelations of subskills of IQ measures; the evidence for a shared set of genes associated with mathematics, reading, and g; and the evidence for shared and overlapping "What is it?" and "Where is it?" neural processing pathways and shared neural pathways for language, music, motor skills, and emotions suggest that it is unlikely that that each of Gardner's intelligences could operate "via a different set of neural mechanisms" (Gardner, 1999, p. 99). Equally important, the evidence for the "What is it?" and "Where is it?" processing pathways, for Kahneman's two decision-making systems, and for adapted cognition modules suggests that these cognitive brain specializations have evolved to address very specific problems in our environment. Because Gardner claimed that that the intelligences are innate potentialities related to a general content area, MI theory lacks a rationale for the phylogenetic emergence of the intelligences.

MI theory should not be taught without consideration of the absence of empirical validating evidence for MI theory or without consideration of alternate evidence-based models of human cognition. . . .

References

Adolphs, R., Tranel, D., & Damasio, A. R. (2003). Dissociable neural systems for recognizing emotions. *Brain and Cognition, 52,* 61–69.

Allix, N. M. (2000). The theory of multiple intelligences: A case of missing cognitive matter. *Australian Journal of Education, 44,* 272–288.

Arnott, S. R., Binns, M. A., Grady, C. L., & Alain, C. (2004). Assessing the auditory dual-pathway model in humans. *Neuroimage, 22,* 401–408.

Bjorklund, D. (2003). Evolutionary psychology from a developmental systems perspective: Comment on Lickliter and Honeycutt. *Psychological Bulletin, 129,* 836–841.

Born, R. T., & Bradley, D. C. (2005). Structure and function of visual area MT. *Annual Review of Neuroscience, 28,* 157–189.

Burghardt, G. M. (2002). Genetics, plasticity, and the evolution of cognitive processes. In M. Bekoff, C. Allen., & G. M. Burghardt (Eds.), *The cognitive animal: Empirical and theoretical perspectives on animal cognition* (pp. 115–122). Cambridge, MA: MIT Press.

Butler, D. J. (2005). *Adapting minds.* Cambridge, MA: MIT Press.

Cacioppo, J. T., & Berntson, G. G. (2004). Social neuroscience. In M. Gazzaniga (Ed.), *The cognitive neurosciences III* (3rd ed., pp. 977–996). Cambridge, MA: MIT Press.

Ceci, S. J. (1996). *On intelligence* (2nd ed.). Cambridge, MA: Harvard University Press.

Chen, J.-Q. (2004). Theory of multiple intelligences: Is it a scientific theory? *Teachers College Record, 106,* 17–23.

Colom, R., Rebolloa, I., Palaciosa, A., Juan-Espinosaa, M., & Kyllonenb, P. C. (2004). Working memory is (almost) perfectly predicted by g. *Intelligence, 32,* 277–296.

Cummins, D. D. (2002). The evolutionary roots of intelligence and rationality. In R. Elio (Ed.), *Common sense, reasoning and rationality* (pp. 132–147). New York: Oxford University Press.

Deco, G., Rolls, E. T., & Horwitz, B. (2004). "What" and "where" in visual working memory: A computational neurodynamical perspective for integrating FMRI and single-neuron data. *Journal of Cognitive Neuroscience, 16,* 683–701.

Eibenstein, A., Fioretti, A, B., Lena, C., Rosati, N., Amabile, G., et al. (2005). Modern psychophysical tests to assess olfactory function. *Neurological Science, 26,* 147–155.

Fadiga, L., Craighero, L., & Olivier, E. (2005). Human motor cortex excitability during the perception of others' action. *Current Opinion in Neurobiology, 2,* 213–218.

Fehr, E., & Fischbacher, U. (2003). The nature of human altruism. *Nature, 425,* 785–791.

Gardner, H. (1983). *Frames of mind: The theory of multiple intelligences.* New York: Basic Books.

Gardner, H. (1999). *Intelligence reframed.* New York: Basic Books.

Gardner, H. (2004). Audiences for the theory of multiple intelligences. *Teachers College Record, 106,* 212–220.

Gardner, H., & Connell, M. (2000). Response to Nicholas Allix. *Australian Journal of Education, 44,* 288–293.

Gazzaniga, M. S. (Ed.). (2004). *The cognitive neurosciences III* (3rd ed.). Cambridge, MA: MIT Press.

Geake, J. G., & Hansen, P. C. (2005). Neural correlates of intelligence as revealed by fMRI of fluid analogies. *Neuroimage, 26,* 555–564.

Gelman, R., & Butterworth, B. (2005). Number and language: How are they related? *Trends in Cognitive Sciences, 9,* 6–10.

Gelman, R., & Gallistel, C. R. (2005). Language and the origin of numerical concepts. *Science, 306,* 441–443.

Gigerenzer, G., & Hug, K. (1992). Domain-specific reasoning: Social contracts, cheating, and perspective change. *Cognition, 43,* 127–171.

Goodwin, A. W., & Wheat, H. E. (2004). Sensory signals in neural populations underlying tactile perception and manipulation. *Annual Review of Neuroscience, 27.* 53–77.

Hartley, D. R. (2004). Management, leadership and the emotional order of the school. *Journal of Education Policy, 19,* 583–594.

Hauser, M. (2000). *Wild minds.* New York: Holt.

Hauser, M. D., & Spelke, E. S. (2004). Evolutionary and developmental foundations of human knowledge: A case study of mathematics. In M. Gazzaniga (Ed.), *The cognitive neurosciences III* (3rd ed., pp. 853–864). Cambridge, MA: MIT Press.

Hernandez, A., Li, P., & MacWhinney, B. (2005). The emergence of competing modules in bilingualism. *Trends in Cognitive Neuroscience, 5,* 220–225.

Hildebrand, K. (2004). Making a better argument. *Dance Magazine, 78,* 59.

Himmelbach, M., & Karnath, H. O. (2005). Dorsal and ventral stream interaction: Contributions from optic ataxia. *Journal of Cognitive Neuroscience, 4,* 632–640.

Hoerr, T. R. (2003). It's no fad: Fifteen years of implementing multiple intelligences. *Educational Horizons, 81,* 92–94.

Jackson, C. S., & Tlauka, M. (2004). Route-learning and the Mozart effect. *Psychology of Music, 32,* 213–220.

Johnson, W., & Bouchard, T. J., Jr. (2005). The structure of human intelligence: It is verbal, perceptual, and image rotation (VPR), not fluid and crystallized. *Intelligence, 33,* 393–416.

Johnson, W., Bouchard, T. J., Jr., Krueger, R. J., McGue, M., & Gottesman, I, J. (2004). Just one *g*: Consistent results from three test batteries. *Intelligence, 32,* 95–107.

Josse. G., & Tzourio-Mazoyer, N. (2004). Hemispheric specialization for language. *Brain Research Reviews, 44,* 1–12.

Kahneman, D. (2003). A perspective on judgment and choice: Mapping bounded rationality. *American Psychologist, 58,* 697 720.

Kanazawa, S. (2004). General intelligence as a domain-specific adaptation. *Psychological Review, 111,* 512–523.

Koelsch, S., Kasper, E., Sammler, D., Schulze, K., Gunter, T., & Friederici, A. T. (2004). Music, language and meaning: Brain signatures of semantic processing. *Nature Neuroscience, 7,* 302–307.

Larson, G. E., & Saccuzzo, D. P. (1989). Cognitive correlates of general intelligence: Toward a process theory of g. *Intelligence, 13,* 5–31.

Lezak, M. D. (1995). *Neuropsychological assessment.* New York: Oxford University Press.

Lickliter, R., & Honeycutt, H. (2003). Developmental dynamics: Towards a biologically plausible evolutionary psychology. *Psychological Bulletin, 129,* 819–835.

Lieberman, P. (2002). On the nature and evolution of the neural bases of human language. *American Journal of Physical Anthropology, 235,* 36–62.

Martin, R. C. (2003). Language processing: Functional organization and neuroanatomical basis. *Annual Review of Psychology, 54,* 55–89.

McDaniel, M. A. (2005). Big-brained people are smarter: A meta-analysis of the relationship between in vivo brain volume and intelligence. *Intelligence, 33,* 337–346.

McRorie, M., & Cooper, C. (2004). Synaptic transmission correlates of general mental ability. *Intelligence, 32,* 263–275.

Miller, G. A. (1999). On knowing a word. *Annual Review of Psychology, 50,* 1–19.

Morgane, P. J., Galler, J. R., & Mokler, D. J. (2005). A review of systems and networks of the limbic forebrain/limbic midbrain. *Progress in Neurobiology, 75,* 143–60.

Mottonen, R., Jarvelainen, J., Sams, M., & Hari, R. (2005). Viewing speech modulates activity in the left SI mouth cortex. *Neuroimage, 24,* 731–737.

Nersessian, N. J. (1998). Kuhn and the cognitive revolution. *Configurations 6.1,* 87–120. Retrieved December 15, 2004, from http://muse.jhu.edu/journals/configurations/

Oberauer, K., Schulze, R., Wilhelm, O., & Suss, H. M. (2005). Working memory and intelligence—their correlation and their relation: Comment on Ackerman, Beier, and Boyle (2005). *Psychological Bulletin, 131,* 61–65.

Parris, S. G. (2005). Reinterpreting the development of reading skills. *Reading Research Quarterly, 40,* 184–202.

Peretz, I., & Zatorre, R. J. (2005). Brain organization for music processing. *Annual Review of Psychology, 56,* 89–114.

Phelps, E. A. (2006). Emotion and cognition: Insights from studies of the human amygdala. *Annual Review of Psychology, 57,* 27 53.

Reynolds, C. R., & Kamphaus, R. (Eds.). (2003). *Handbook of psychological and educational assessment of children* (2nd ed.). New York: Guilford.

Reynolds, J. H., & Chelazzi, L. (2004). Attentional modulation of visual processing. *Annual Review of Neuroscience, 27,* 611–647.

Rizzolatti G., & Craighero, L. (2004). The mirror-neuron system. *Annual Review of Neuroscience, 27,* 169–182.

Roth, G., & Dicke, U. (2005). Evolution of the brain and intelligence. *Trends in Cognitive Sciences, 9,* 250–257.

Shafir, E, & LeBoeuf, R. A. (2002). Rationality. *Annual Review of Psychology, 53,* 491–517.

Shearer, B., (2004). Multiple intelligence theory after 20 years. *Teachers College Record, 106,* 2–16.

Singer-Dudck, J., & Greer, R. D. (2005). A long term analysis of the relationship between fluency and the training and maintenance of complex math skills. *Psychological Record, 55,* 361–376.

Squire, L. R., Craig, E. L., & Clark, R. E. (2005). The medial temporal lobe. *Annual Review of Neuroscience, 28,* 279–316.

Sternberg, R. J. (1994). Commentary: Reforming school reform: Comments on *Multiple intelligences: The theory in practice. Teachers College Record, 95,* 561–569.

Sternberg, R. J., & Grigorenko, E. L. (2004). Successful intelligence in the classroom. *Theory Into Practice, 43,* 274–280.

Thatcher, R. W., North, D., & Biver, C. (2005). EEG and intelligence: Relations between EEG coherence, EEG phase delay and power. *Clinical Neurophysiology, 116,* 2129–2141.

Toga, A. W., & Thompson, P. M. (2005). Genetics of brain structure and intelligence. *Annual Review of Neuroscience, 28,* 1–23.

Velicer, G. J. (2005). Evolution of cooperation: Does selfishness restraint lie within? *Current Biology, 15,* 173–175.

Watkins, M. W., & Canivez, G. L. (2004). Temporal stability of WISC-III composite strengths and weaknesses. *Psychological Assessment, 16,* 133–138.

Xu, F., Spelke, F. S., & Goddard, S. (2005). Number sense in human infants. *Development Science, 8,* 88–101.

LYNN WATERHOUSE was a faculty member at the College of New Jersey.

EXPLORING THE ISSUE

Can Howard Gardner's Theory of Multiple Intelligences Transform Educational Practice?

Critical Thinking and Reflection

1. How might you measure each of Gardner's intelligences in an elementary school student and in a high school student?
2. Can you summarize the criticisms directed at Gardner's theory? For each criticism, indicate whether or not you agree with it and why.
3. Explain either how you would implement Gardner's theory in your classroom or why you would not implement Gardner's theory in your classroom.

Is There Common Ground?

It may not be possible to answer the question posed by this issue at the current time. In part, this reflects the fact that Gardner's theory of multiple intelligences has been proposed relatively recently and is still evolving. It also reflects the fact that Gardner's theory, like many other psychological theories, was originally formulated as a description of an important dimension of the human mind and was not intended as a theory of pedagogy. This means that there is considerable theoretical and empirical work to be done before the educational implications of the theory are completely understood.

Unfortunately, there is considerable pressure to reform our educational system now. This has led to a number of initiatives that claim to have been inspired by Gardner's theory but that, on careful analysis, have little to do with the theory. Some reformers, for example, have used Gardner's theory to advocate teaching in a way that accommodates a variety of learning styles, including differences between left- and right-brain learners, verbal and visual-spatial learners, and reflective and intuitive learners. See "Multiple Intelligences: Seven Keys to Opening Closed Minds," by Shirley E. Jordan, *NASSP Bulletin*

(November 1996). Other reformers have advocated the creation of formal tests for each of the proposed intelligences. It is also important to recognize that there is not universal support for Gardner's view of intelligence among scholars of the human mind. Many continue to point to the ubiquitous correlations that exist between a wide range of tasks that most of us would agree must tap "intelligence." See "Spearman's g and the Problem of Educational Equality," by Arthur R. Jensen, *Oxford Review of Education* (vol. 17, no. 2, 1991).

Create Central

www.mhhe.com/createcentral

Additional Resources

Branton Shearer, "Multiple Intelligences Theory after 20 Years," *Teachers College Record* (2004).

Howard Gardner, *Multiple Intelligences: New Horizons* (Basic Books, 2006).

John White, "Illusory Intelligences," *Journal of Philosophy of Education* (vol. 42, no. 3–4, 2008).

Internet References . . .

Howard Gardner

http://howardgardner.com/multiple-intelligences/

Multiple Intelligences Research and Consulting Inc.

http://www.miresearch.org/

Multiple Intelligences Oasis

http://multipleintelligencesoasis.org/

Selected, Edited, and with Issue Framing Material by:
Leonard Abbeduto, *University of California, Davis*
and
Frank Symons, *University of Minnesota*

ISSUE

Should Schools Teach Students Self-Control?

YES: **Daniel T. Willingham**, from "Can Teachers Increase Students' Self-Control?" *American Educator* (Summer 2011)

NO: **Alfie Kohn**, from "Why Self-Discipline Is Overrated: The (Troubling) Theory and Practice of Control from Within," *Phi Delta Kappan* (vol. 90, no. 3, 2008)

Learning Outcomes

After reading this issue, you will be able to:

- Define the different facets of self-control.
- Describe the ways in which parents and teachers can promote self-control.
- Summarize the potential advantages and disadvantages of promoting self-control in students.

ISSUE SUMMARY

YES: Daniel T. Willingham argues that individuals with enhanced self-control are more likely to be successful in school and beyond and that healthy self-control arises from genetic factors as well as a warm, structured, and supportive home and school environment.

NO: Alfie Kohn argues that teaching self-control creates conformity and potential mental health challenges for students. Kohn also argues that a focus on self-control detracts attention from more legitimate concerns, such as including students as partners in their own learning and creating a curriculum that is inherently engaging to students.

"**I** need more self-control." Each of us has stated this as a personal goal at some point, most likely immediately after we have failed to achieve some other goal or expectation that we have set for ourselves or others have set for us. "I need more self-control" to stop . . . watching so much television, eating high-calorie foods, losing my temper, drinking alcohol, and so on. Or, "I need more self-control" so that I . . . eat only healthy foods, exercise regularly, read more books, take on more responsibilities at the office, and so on. In everyday language, we seem to want to do the "right thing" (whatever that may be), but often are tempted by short-term pleasures or experiences that get in the way, like eating a favorite sugary snack rather than choosing a healthy food option when we want to lose a pound or two. If only we could control our behavior better and always do the right thing.

Psychologists, educators, and philosophers have also focused on self-control and in some cases made the concept central to their theories of human development and functioning. Sigmund Freud, the founder of psychoanalysis, for example, argued that mental illness could arise from a failure to fully resolve psychological conflicts between our instinctual desires for physical gratification and internalized societal norms and prohibitions against such gratification. Philosophers, too, have argued about the essence of the human, with many seeing the newborn infant as being inherently filled with negative urges that he or she must learn through parents, religion, and the like, to hold in check or to replace with more positive learned desires and behaviors. Central to many religions is the notion of self-sacrifice, which requires effort, diligence, and the forgoing of "earthly" rewards in the service of a more valued reward, such as eternal peace, entry into heaven, and the like.

Our educational system also places considerable emphasis on self-control. We want students to exert self-control over the attention. Students are expected to attend to the academic tasks at hand rather than being distracted by irrelevant stimuli, such as what a peer is doing a few desks away or what they can see happening on the playground out the window. Indeed, children who have excessive problems controlling their attention may be diagnosed with attention deficit disorder (ADD) or attention deficit hyperactivity disorder (ADHD) and provided with treatments ranging from training in behavioral strategies to stimulant medication (e.g., Ritalin). We also want students to exert self-control over their emotions and the behavioral reactions they engender. How many preschool teachers have uttered the phrase "use your words next time" to a student who has just reacted to an injustice or perceived injustice by pushing or hitting the transgressor? We also want students to exert self-control in the form of adhering to the norms, practices, and rules of the classroom. Students are expected to come to class on time, request permission to leave the classroom, wait to take a turn at the sand table, raise their hands when they have a question, return borrowed books from the library, study the topic they are assigned during the appointed class period, and so on. Encouraging this form of behavioral self-control helps to ensure that the teacher can manage the learning of a class filled with as many as 30 or more students and also, perhaps, to prepare the students for participating in the adult world of norms, expectations, and rules. In all these forms of self-control, however, there is the belief that (a) students must learn or develop their self-control skills, (b) these skills are essential for their success in school, the workplace, and beyond, and (c) adult intervention is essential to the acquisition of self-control skills.

In a more general sense, many educators and policymakers tacitly view self-control as the cornerstone of the educational process. In particular, self-control is needed to engage in academic activities that require considerable effort and whose "payoff" is often stated in terms of long-term rather than short-term rewards. One must study and do homework rather than "hang out" with friends so that the academic skills needed to get into college are acquired. College in turn prepares one for a more fulfilling and financially rewarding career, which makes possible owning a nice home, and so on. Along the way, of course, there are short-term rewards like feeling pleased to learn a new idea after struggling hard to grasp it or receiving a good grade or other form of praise from a respected teacher; however, at each step the self is faced with the need to engage in work, which typically means forgoing another pleasurable activity.

Thus, many believe that much of the difference between students who succeed in school and those who fail can be traced to differences in self-control skills. In fact, there are empirical data to support his assertion. Preschoolers who are rated as having better self-control are more successful in elementary school in basic academic domains. Later, during the teenage years, better self-control is associated not only with better academic performance, but also with better peer relations and the avoidance of high-risk behaviors, such as taking illegal drugs. Self-control also has a basis in biology, with maturation of the prefrontal cortex thought to be particularly central in setting the stage to acquire the sorts of self-control needed to be planful and strategic.

But is self-control always positive for the individuals? For society? Should the task of teaching self-control fall on schools? Does working so hard at teaching students to exercise self-control mask inadequacies in pedagogical content or practices that would allow self-control to arise more naturally? These questions and other questions about self-control are considered in the two selections presented. In the first selection, making the case for teaching self-control, Daniel T. Willingham points to the association between self-control skills and indicators of academic success and emotional well-being. He also identifies the characteristics of homes and classrooms that support the development of adaptive self-control, which include characteristics such as warmth and support. In the second selection, Alfie Kohn argues that teaching self-control actually leads to conformity of thought that is detrimental to innovation and to a free democratic society. Kohn also provides evidence of the emotional downside to the individual for whom self-control becomes a central all-consuming vision.

YES

Daniel T. Willingham

Can Teachers Increase Students' Self-Control?

How does the mind work—and especially how does it learn? Teachers' instructional decisions are based on a mix of theories learned in teacher education, trial and error, craft knowledge, and gut instinct. Such knowledge often serves us well, but is there anything sturdier to rely on?

Cognitive science is an interdisciplinary field of researchers from psychology, neuroscience, linguistics, philosophy, computer science, and anthropology who seek to understand the mind. In this regular American Educator *column, we consider findings from this field that are strong and clear enough to merit classroom application.*

Question: Some children seem to have very little difficulty staying on task, but others, try as they might, get distracted easily. And those seem to be the same students whose tempers [flare] at what seem to be small provocations. Why is it that some children have so much trouble controlling themselves? Is mere anything I can do to help them?

Answer: Among cognitive scientists, this quality is usually called "self-regulation" and it has been the subject of intense study in the last five years. The idea is that there is often a rapid, automatic response to a situation, but that automatic response may not be the one that the individual, upon reflection, would want to make. Self-regulation refers to the ability to inhibit the automatic response and to do something else; more generally, it refers to the ability to control one's emotions, to control attention and other cognitive processes, and to plan and control behavior. This capacity turns out to have enormous consequences for academic and social success. And, as teachers observe daily, children differ widely in how much of this capacity they seem to have. Recent research indicates that teachers can help students—especially students having the most trouble—by providing an organized classroom environment, and by removing elements in the environment that can trigger impulsive behavior.

What do the following three scenarios have in common?

- Construction workers pour cement for a sidewalk outside your fifth-grade classroom, clearly visible through the windows, but Vincent manages to ignore this interesting scene and focus on his work.
- Fourteen-year-old Rosalind practices her piano scale exercises faithfully, even though she'd rather hang out with her friends, because she dreams of playing Chopin.

- Malik has been carefully building a block structure for five minutes when another preschooler walks by and accidentally knocks it over. Malik manages to swallow his disappointment and starts to build the structure again.

In each scenario, the child is showing *self-regulation.* Self-regulation refers to being able to control and plan emotions, cognitions, and behaviors.[1] Each child has an automatic inclination to do one thing—watch the construction workers, socialize with friends, mourn the fallen tower—but overcomes that impulse and chooses to do something else that serves longer-term goals.[2]

It seems obvious that self-regulation would be a prized trait. But researchers interested in understanding self-regulation (and trying to boost it) quickly run into complications. The three examples provided above seem to have something in common, but it's easy to see some differences as well. Vincent is regulating his attention in the face of external distractions. Some researchers have emphasized this feature of self-regulation, and measure it with laboratory tasks that require rapid shifts of attention.[3] A related idea is that self-regulation can be measured via the successful inhibition of responses that would come naturally or automatically. For example, in the Head-Toes-Knees-Shoulders task,[4] preschoolers are asked to touch a body part when the experimenter names a different body part (e.g., to touch their toes when the experimenter says "knees," and to touch their knees when the experimenter says "toes").

Other researchers have emphasized emotional regulation like that shown by Malik. It would not be ethical to frustrate small children for the sake of observing their reactions, so emotional regulation is sometimes measured by observing children in natural situations, and more often via a parental questionnaire.[5] Parents (or teachers) are asked to reflect on a child's typical behavior, and to rate a series of statements for how well they apply to the child: for example, "Tends to fall to pieces under stress," and "Is easily irritated."

Still other researchers have thought of self-regulation as more like Rosalind's piano practice. They have emphasized the ability to delay gratification; that is, to persist in a task that is unrewarding in anticipation of a greater reward in the future. A landmark study of delayed gratification among preschoolers was conducted by Walter Mischel.[6] A child was left alone in a room with a treat such as a marshmallow. He could, at any time, ring a bell to summon the experimenter, and then he would be allowed to eat the marshmallow. But if the child could refrain from eating the marshmallow until the experimenter returned on her own, a second marshmallow would be added and the child could eat both. Thus, like Rosalind, the child had the choice of having something pleasurable immediately, or forgoing it in anticipation of gaining an even greater reward later.

Finally, some researchers have trusted that when you describe self-regulation, people know what you mean. People generally feel confident in judging whether an individual is rather impulsive or more measured in his or her responses. These judgments seem to be correct, or at me very least, there is agreement among them: kindergarten teachers' ratings of their students' self-regulation agree pretty well with the ratings of the same children by their first-grade teacher a year later.[7] And, perhaps more surprisingly, people seem to be honest when asked to rate their own self-regulation; self-ratings correspond with ratings provided (anonymously) by friends and coworkers.[8]

Are we really talking about the same thing in these various examples of self-regulation? To some extent, yes. Recent studies have administered a variety of self-regulation tests to the same set of individuals to test the obvious prediction: if the tests all measure the same thing, then individuals scoring well on one should score well on the others, and individuals scoring poorly on one will score poorly on the others. Different measures of self-regulation are associated, but only moderately so.[9] In addition, neuroscientists have pointed out that different self-regulation tasks seem to depend on the same parts of the brain (more specifically, the prefrontal cortex controlling subcortical regions, which are associated with reward and emotion). This anatomic commonality is some indication that these diverse tasks are somewhat related.[10] For the sake of simplicity, I will talk about these perhaps different types of self-regulation as though they are the same thing.

Why Is Self-Regulation Good, and Where Does It Come From?

The usefulness of self-regulation seems intuitive, and indeed, higher levels of self-regulation are associated with a variety of positive outcomes in schooling. Controlling for other factors (such as family income, parents' education, and the like), preschoolers with good self-regulation have higher levels of school readiness—they are more likely to come to school physically healthy, with age-appropriate social and emotional functioning, and with a good attitude toward learning.[11] Good self-regulation in preschool predicts reading and math proficiency in kindergarten,

over and above intelligence,[12] but poor self-regulation is associated with a greater likelihood of expulsion from preschool classrooms.[13]

The association of self-regulation and academic achievement continues into elementary school[14] and middle school.[15] We might wonder whether this association is just a byproduct of the student-teacher relationship; kids who are low in self-regulation are more likely to have behavior problems, whereas kids who are high in self-regulation are probably better liked by their teachers—little wonder that the latter learn more. But studies show that even when one accounts for these factors, self-regulation is still a strong predictor of academic achievement.[16]

Teachers' ratings of kids' self-regulation are also associated with children's social competence, including measures of their empathy,[17] as well as the extent to which they take classroom rules to heart[18] and show socially appropriate behavior.[19] Further, a lack of inhibitory control is associated with social problems. Students who are low in self-regulation are at greater risk for persistent disobedience, aggression, and temper tantrums.[20] In teens, poor self-regulation is associated with delinquency, drug and alcohol abuse, and risky sexual behavior.[21]

Given that it is so desirable, how can we help our students improve their self-regulation? To answer that question, we must first understand its source. One's success in self-regulation is partly due to genetics—you inherit a propensity toward impulsivity or self-regulation from your parents.[22] But that's only part of the story, and it's important to bear in mind that inherited traits can be changed. On occasion, people think of genetics as predestination, but consider that height is highly heritable—tall parents tend to have tall kids, and short parents short kids—but height is also susceptible to environmental factors. We grow to greater or lesser height depending on nutrition. In the case of self-regulation, the "nutrition" concerns the nature of the home and of parenting practices. In particular, two broad factors emerge as important in parenting: emotional support and cognitive support.

Several studies indicate that emotional supports from parents—meaningful praise,* affection, sensitivity to the child's needs, and encouragement—are associated with more successful self-regulation, and their opposites—criticism, coldness, indifference to the child's needs, and physical or verbal control—are associated with poor self-regulation in the child.[23] In studies like these, parent-child interaction is typically measured through direct observation. The researcher might visit the home, or the parent and child might come to the laboratory and be asked to perform a collaborative task, such as assembling a figure from Legos. Whether at home or in the lab, the parent-child interaction is categorized on several dimensions, using a set coding scheme (which is somewhat similar to a detailed rubric that a teacher may use to assess students'

---

*To find out what constitutes meaningful praise, see "How Praise Can Motivate—or Stifle," which I wrote for the Winter 2005–2006 issue of *American Educator*. www.aft.org/newspubs/periodicals/ae/winter0506/willingham.cfm.

presentations). This finding—that parental warmth is associated with the child's self-regulation—complements other work showing that positive interactions with adults help children understand their own emotional experiences, the emotional experiences of others, and how to interact in a responsive, sensitive manner.[24]

In addition to emotional support, studies show that cognitive support from parents is also important. As you might expect, one source of cognitive support is intellectual stimulation from parents (e.g., posing questions to the child, using complex sentence structures) and intellectual resources in the home (e.g., books, engaging toys). Other data show that kids gain self-regulation skills when their parents encourage them to be autonomous, and provide support for that autonomy.[25] Somewhat more subtle is the cognitive support that comes from the principles of behavior and limits that parents set Children appear to develop better self-regulation skills in homes where there are well-structured and consistent rules.[26] We might speculate that when the daily routine inside the home is predictable (and both the rules and their enforcement are predictable), children are more likely to adjust their own behavior to conform to the routine, and that repeated practice in this sort of adjustment yields long-term increases in self-regulation. The bending of one's own wishes to the rules of the house constitutes practice in self-regulation.

This research is still relatively new; a detailed picture of the particular influences that shape self-regulation is not yet apparent. It is difficult to be more specific about which features of an emotionally warm and cognitively supportive home are crucial, because many features of such homes are themselves correlated, making it difficult to pinpoint the influence of any one of them.[27] The influence of different parenting practices is also difficult to specify, because parenting does not just affect kids—kids affect parenting practices. That is, different children elicit different parenting strategies from the same parents.[28] Parents often feel that they had a pretty well-thought-out philosophy of parenting, but then the children came along with different plans! Thus, we can easily imagine a situation in which kids have (perhaps small) differences in self-regulation due to genetic factors, and these small differences lead parents to make different choices in parenting strategies, which in turn influence the child's behavior, which then influences the parents, and so on.

What Can Teachers Do?

Students begin preschool with a set of self-regulation skills that are a product of their genetic inheritance and their family environment. Can their experiences at school change their self-regulation, for better or worse?

There have been some promising attempts to write school curricula that improve self-regulation in children. One example is Tools of the Mind, an early childhood program comprised of 40 activities meant to improve a set of three mental functions, one of which is self-regulation. (The others are working memory—the mental "space" in which thought happens—and cognitive flexibility, that is, the ability to adjust to change.) The 40 activities include, for example, dramatic play, aids to improve memory, activities that encourage collaborative turn-taking, and activities meant to encourage talking to oneself as a self-regulatory strategy. The curriculum takes up 80 percent of the school day, and interventions of one or two years have been shown to have positive effects on children's self-regulation.[29] Another example that helps develop self-regulation while focusing on social and emotional learning is the Promoting Alternative Thinking Strategies curriculum for preschool and elementary school children.[30] These two programs have some evidence of effectiveness, but more research needs to be done.

Suppose a teacher wants to improve the self-regulation of the children in her classroom, and she is not free to adopt a wholesale curriculum (or is not sure she wants to do so). What steps might she take?

Several studies indicate that teachers actually have minimal impact on the development of children's self-regulation.[31] But these overall effects may be minimal because schooling affects self-regulation for just a subset of children (since those who come to school with good self-regulation will show no improvement in the studies). One study[32] that did find that teachers can have an impact focused on kindergartners who, at age 15 months, had been categorized as "socially bold" (which previous studies have found is an indicator that children are more likely to be off task in kindergarten). The researchers categorized the teachers as sensitive, overcontrolling, or detached. Sensitive teachers were consistent, positive, warm, and appropriately responsive to children's cues. Overcontrolling teachers imposed their own learning agenda on children without heeding their cues. Detached teachers were frequently unaware of what children were doing, and responded only halfheartedly when the children needed adult supervision. When paired with an overcontrolling or detached teacher, kids who had been socially bold at 15 months were likely to be off task and to act in impulsive, inappropriate ways. But if paired with a sensitive teacher, these children showed fewer negative behaviors, less time off task, and more self-reliance. In short, teachers can have an impact on the kids who need it most.

Similar results were observed in a more recent study of first-graders.[33] An intervention with their teachers emphasized (1) improving planning and organization, (2) making classroom management more consistent, and (3) facilitating students' independent and small-group work. As in the study just described, it was only students who started the year with poor self-regulation who were helped by being in the classroom of a teacher who had undergone the training.[34] Students who started the year with average or better self-regulation skills showed no special advantage from being in these classrooms. (All students did improve, as self-regulation would be expected to improve with age.) These findings dovetail with earlier findings that students learn more in classrooms that are well organized,[35] and that teachers who devote more time to classroom organization in the fall have more student-managed activities in the spring.[36]

Thus, in the final analysis, the factors that improve self-regulation in the home—warmth, organization, and predictability—also seem to be important in classrooms. Children learn to self-regulate through practice. A well-organized classroom requires that children practice inhibiting their own moment-to-moment desires in favor of acting in accordance with the pace set by the teacher. In addition, a well-organized classroom minimizes chaos and distractions. But with all this talk of organization, let's not imagine a police state—warmth is just as important, both to the benefit of the classroom atmosphere, and to help students learn empathy and emotional regulation. The fact that students with initially poor self-regulation benefit most indicates that these children are learning at school something that other children learned at home.

Creating an organized classroom with a warm atmosphere is something that every teacher strives for; knowing that it may have a positive impact on students' self-regulation may put it even higher on a teacher's (long) list of priorities. But improving classroom organization and atmosphere is also a long-term project. Are there strategies available in the short term that can help students better self-regulate? A different body of research is relevant to this question, and it does offer some suggestions. Researchers have posed the following relevant question: when confronted with a challenge to self-regulation—for example, a dieter offered a sumptuous dessert—what factors in the *immediate environment* predict whether self-regulation will reign, or whether the dieter will succumb to temptation? Researchers have identified three factors that predict yielding: negative emotions, lapses, and cue exposure. Let's briefly explore each, then turn to the possible implications for the classroom.

Negative emotions such as anger, depression, stress, or frustration are likely to make adults act impulsively.[37] When people are upset, they are more likely to overindulge in food[38] or alcohol,[39] or to abuse drugs.[40] They are more likely to act aggressively,[41] to impulsively spend too much money,[42] or to engage in risky sexual behavior.[43] Even just being tired makes adults more likely to lie.[44] Negative emotions seem to make people act in the moment, and to disregard future consequences. The reason is not known with any certainty; it's been suggested that the negative emotion draws much of their attention, and so compromises decision making,[45] or that indulging provides short-term relief from anxiety, and so seems rational in the moment.[46]

A second problem for self-regulation is lapses (that is, "falling off the wagon"). It is familiar to us in the form of the dieter eating a brownie or the reforming alcoholic having a drink; once the abstainer has lapsed, it seems not only easy to lapse again, but pointless to abstain any

longer. This phenomenon has been repeated several times in the laboratory. If subjects can eat as much or as little as they care to during the experiment, dieters will eat less than nondieters, as one might expect. But if, as part of the experiment, everyone is *required* to eat a high calorie food, dieters *don't* eat less in order to compensate for the calories just consumed. On the contrary, dieters in that situation eat *more* than nondieters.[47]

A third feature of the environment that can make self-regulation challenging is cues (that is, subtle or overt reminders of the appeal of the thing to be avoided). Simply put, if I'm dieting, it's harder for me to turn down a sundae if I actually *see* it.[48] The visual appeal might make me think about how marvelous it would taste. Similarly, actually seeing drugs or drug paraphernalia makes it more likely that substance abusers will relapse.[49]

These three factors that confound self-regulation—negative emotions, lapses, and cues—suggest some classroom changes that might help students. First, teachers can try to be mindful of the effect of negative emotions on students' ability to self-regulate. When a student does act impulsively, a calm, warm correction and redirection of the student is more likely to prevent further impulsive acts than a rebuke that makes the student feel bad. In addition, teachers should expect that a student who is depressed or is having a hard time at home will have more difficulty working on his own, controlling his temper, and other tasks that require self-regulation. The student might need more support from the environment—a quiet environment in which to work, for example, or more monitoring and guidance than other students on independent work. Needless to say, such support must be provided in a sensitive manner so that the student does not feel singled out among her peers.

The data on negative emotions also provide some insight into what can be the cyclical nature of misbehavior. Many misbehaviors—fighting, teasing, breaking rules—are associated with negative emotions, and negative emotions reduce the ability to self-regulate. For example, the child who gets in a fight will be angry and probably frustrated. When the fight is broken up, those negative emotions will make it harder for the child to do anything requiring self-regulation—including staying out of another fight.

The finding that lapses can lead to people more or less giving up their attempts to self-regulate points again to the importance of the student-teacher relationship. With a warm, trusting relationship in place, the teacher will have the credibility to encourage the student to put the lapse behind him, and to resolve again to behave as he knows he should: attend to his work, refrain from fighting, or avoid whatever the trouble spot may be.

The importance of cues in self-regulation failures yields a straightforward classroom application: get rid of the cues. In his celebrated marshmallow study, Mischel noted that the children who did not eat the marshmallow often used a strategy of eliminating the cue: they turned around in their seats, for example, so that the marshmallow was no longer visible, and thus, less tempting. I once visited a first-grade classroom that had just acquired a rabbit as a class pet. In the hour I was there, children sitting near the bunny found it almost impossible to concentrate on anything else. When I visited the next week, the teacher had hung an attractive wall hanging from the ceiling, hiding the rabbit's cage. Problem solved. When students are distracted, it's always worth considering removing the distraction altogether, rather than counting on the students to ignore it. More generally, when there is a trigger in the environment that prompts poor self-regulation in one or more students, it's worth weighing the pros and cons of removing the trigger.

Helping students better self-regulate is a daunting task because it seems such a personal, permanent quality of an individual. But researchers have shown that it is open to change, and they also have shown that good self-regulation is associated with a broad spectrum of positive academic and social outcomes, and that poor self-regulation is associated with greater risk for correspondingly bad outcomes. These facts highlight the urgency for teachers to do all they can to help students grow in this area.

References

1. Janet Metcalfe and Walter Mischel, "A Hot/Cool-System Analysis of Delay of Gratification: Dynamics of Willpower," *Psychological Review* 106, no. 1 (1999): 3–19; and Dale H. Schunk and Barry J. Zimmerman, "Social Origins of Self-regulatory Competence" *Educational Psychologist* 32, no. 4 (1997): 195–208.

2. Wilhelm Hofmann, Malte Friese, and Fritz Strack, "Impulse and Self-Control from a Dual-Systems Perspective," *Perspectives on Psychological Science* 4, no. 2 (2009): 162–176; and William James, *The Principles of Psychology* (New York: Henry Holt, 1890).

3. See, for example, Bridget M. Gaertner, Tracy L. Spinrad, and Nancy Eisenberg, "Focused Attention in Toddlers: Measurement, Stability, and Relations to Negative Emotion and Parenting," *Infant and Child Development* 17, no. 4 (2008): 339–363.

4. Claire Cameron Panitz, Megan M. McClelland, J. S. Matthews, and Frederick J. Morrison, "A Structured Observation of Behavioral Self-Regulation and Its Contribution to Kindergarten Outcomes," *Developmental Psychology* 45, no. 3 (2009): 605–619.

5. See, for example, Ann Shields and Dante Cicchetti," Emotion Regulation among School-Age Children: The Development and Validation of a New Criterion Q-Sort Scale," *Developmental Psychology* 33, no. 6 (1997): 906–916.

6. Walter Mischel, Ebbe B. Ebbesen, and Antonette Raskoff Zeiss, "Cognitive and Attentional Mechanisms in Delay of Gratification," *Journal of Personally and Social Psychology* 21, no. 2 (1972): 204–218.

7. Christopher J. Trentacosta and Carroll E. Izard, "Kindergarten Children's Emotion Competence as a Predictor of Their Academic Competence in First Grade," *Emotion* 7, no. 1 (2007): 77–88.

8. Angela Lee Duckworth and Margaret L. Kern, "A Meta-Analysis of the Convergent Validity of Self-Control Measures," *Journal of Research in Personality* 45, no. 3 (2011): 259–268.

9. Duckworth and Kern, "Convergent Validity of Self-Control Measures"; and Traci Sitzmann and Katherine Ely, "A Meta-Analysis of Self-Regulated Learning in Work-Related Training and Educational Attainment: What We Know and Where We Need to Go," *Psychological Bulletin* 137. no. 3 (2011): 421–442.

10. Jessica R. Cohen and Matthew D. Lieberman, "The Common Neural Basis of Exerting Self-Control in Multiple Domains," in *Self Control in Society, Mind, and Brain*, ed. Ran Hassin, Kevin Ochsner, and Yaacov Trope (Oxford: Oxford University Press, 2010), 141–162; Todd F. Heatherton and Dylan D. Wagner, "Cognitive Neuroscience of Self-Regulation Failure." *Trends in Cognitive Science* 15, no. 3 (2011): 132–139; and Nora D. Volkow, Gene-Jack Wang, Joanna S. Fowler, and Frank Telang, "Overlapping Neuronal Circuits in Addiction and Obesity: Evidence of Systems Pathology," *Philosophical Transactions of the Royal Society B: Biological Sciences* 363, no. 1507 (2008): 3191–3200.

11. Nancy Eisenberg, Carlos Valiente, and Natalie D. Eggum, "Self-Regulation and School Readiness," *Early Education and Development* 21, no. 5 (2010): 681–698.

12. Clancy Blair and Rachel Peters Razza, "Relating Effortful Control, Executive Function, and False Belief Understanding to Emerging Math and Literacy Ability in Kindergarten," *Child Development* 78, no. 2 (2007): 647–663; and Megan M. McClelland, Claire E. Cameron, Carol McDonald Connor, Carrie L. Farris, Abigail M. Jewkes, and Frederick J. Morrison, "Links between Behavioral Regulation and Preschoolers' Literacy, Vocabulary, and Math Skills," *Developmental Psychology* 43, no. 4 (2007): 947–959.

13. Walter S. Gilliam and Golan Shahar, "Preschool and Child Care Expulsion and Suspension: Rates and Predictors in One State," *Infants and Young Children* 19, no. 3 (2006): 228–245.

14. Karl L. Alexander, Doris R. Entwisle, and Susan L. Dauber, "First-Grade Classroom Behavior. Its Short- and Long-Term Consequences for School Performance," *Child Development* 64, no. 3 (1993): 801–814; and Carlos Valiente, Kathryn Lemery-Chalfant, Jodi Swanson, and Mark Reiser, "Prediction of Children's Academic Competence from Their Effortful Control, Relationships, and Classroom Participation," *Journal of Educational Psychology* 100, no. 1 (2008): 67–77.

15. Angela Lee Duckworth and Martin E. P. Seligman, "Self-Discipline Outdoes IQ in Predicting Academic Performance of Adolescents." *Psychological Science* 16, no. 12 (2005): 939–944.

16. Paulo A. Graziano, Rachael D. Reavis, Susan P. Keane, and Susan D. Calkins. "The Role of Emotion Regulation in Children's Early Academic Success," *Journal of School Psychology* 45, no. 1 (2007): 3–19.

17. Mary K. Rothbart, Stephan A. Ahadi, and Karen L. Hershey, "Temperament and Social Behavior in Childhood," *Merrill-Palmer Quarterly* 40, no. 1 (1994): 21–39.

18. Grazyna Kochanska, "Multiple Pathways to Conscience for Children with Different Temperaments: From Toddlerhood to Age 5," *Developmental Psychology* 33, no. 2 (1997): 228–240.

19. Nancy Eisenberg, Richard A. Fabes, Mariss Karbon, Bridget C. Murphy, Marek Wosinski, Lorena Polazzi, Gustavo Carlo, and Candy Juhnke, "The Relations of Children's Dispositional Prosocial Behavior to Emotionality, Regulation, and Social Functioning," *Child Development* 67, no. 3 (1996): 974–992.

20. Sheryl L. Olson, Arnold J. Sameroff, David C. R. Kerr, Nestor L. Lopez, and Henry M. Wellman, "Developmental Foundations of Externalizing Problems in Young Children: The Role of Effortful Control," *Development and Psychopathology* 17, no. 1 (2005): 25–45; and Ann-Margret Rydell, Lisa Berlin, and Gunilla Bohlin, "Emotionality, Emotion Regulation, and Adaptation among 5- to 8-Year-Old Children," *Emotion* 3, no. 1 (2003): 30–47.

21. Kris N. Kirby, Nancy M. Petry, and Warren K. Bickel, "Heroin Addicts Have Higher Discount Rates for Delayed Rewards Than Non-Drug-Using Controls," *Journal of Experimental Psychology: General* 128, no. 1 (1999): 78–87; Robert F. Krueger. Avshalom Caspi. Terrie E. Moffitt, Jennifer White, and Magda Stouthamer-Loeber, "Delay of Gratification, Psychopathology, and Personality: Is Low Self-Control Specific to Externalizing Problems?" *Journal of Personalty* 64. no. 1 (1996): 107–129; and Patrick D. Quinn and Kim Fromme, "Self-Regulation as a Protective Factor against Risky Drinking and Sexual Behavior," *Psychology of Addictive Behaviors* 24, no. 3 (2010): 376–385.

22. H. Hill Goldsmith, Kristin A. Buss, and Kathryn S. Lemery, "Toddler and Childhood Temperament Expanded Content, Stronger Genetic Evidence, New Evidence for the Importance of Environment," *Developmental Psychology* 33, no. 6 (1997): 891–905; Michael I. Poster. Mary K. Rothbart, and Brad E. Sheese, "Attention Genes," *Developmental Science* 10, no. 1 (2007): 25–29; and Mary K. Rothbart, and John E. Bates, "Temperament," in *Handbook of Child Psychology, Vol. 3: Social, Emotional, and Personality Development.* ed. Nancy Eisenberg, William Damon, and Richard M. Lerner, 6th ed. (Hoboken, NJ: John Wiley and Sons, 2006), 99–166.

23. See, for example, Susan D. Calkins, Cynthia L. Smith, Kathryn L. Gill, and Mary C. Johnson, "Maternal Interactive Style across Contexts: Relations to Emotional, Behavioral and Physiological Regulation during Toddlerhood," *Social Development* 7, no. 3 (1998): 350–369; Nancy Eisenberg, Qing Zhou, Tracy L. Spinrad, Carlos Valiente, Richard A. Fabes, and Jeffrey Liew, "Relations among Positive Parenting, Children's Effortful Control, and Externalizing Problems: A Three-Wave Longitudinal Study," *Child Development* 76, no. 5 (2005): 1055–1071; National Institute of Child Health and Human Development (NICHD) Early Child Care Research Network, "Do Children's Attention Processes Mediate the Link between Family Predictors and School Readiness?" *Developmental Psychology* 39, no. 3 (2003): 581–593; and NICHD Early Child Care Research Network, "Predicting Individual Differences in Attention, Memory, and Planning in First Graders from Experiences at Home, Child Care, and School," *Developmental Psychology* 41, no. 1 (2005): 99–114.

24. See, for example, Carollee Howes, Catherine C. Matheson, and Claire E. Hamilton, "Maternal, Teacher, and Child Care History Correlates of Children's Relationships with Peers," *Child Development* 65, no. 1 (1994): 264–273.

25. Annie Bernier, Stephanie M. Carlson, and Natasha Whipple, "From External Regulation to Self-Regulation: Early Parenting Precursors of Young Children's Executive Functioning," *Child Development* 81, no. 1 (2010): 326–339.

26. Liliana J. Lengua, Elizabeth Honorado, and Nicole R. Bush, "Contextual Risk and Parenting as Predictors of Effortful Control and Social Competence in Preschool Children," *Journal of Applied Developmental Psychology* 28, no. 1 (2007): 40–55; and Valarie Schroeder and Michelle L. Kelley, "Family Environment and Parent-Child Relationships as Related to Executive Functioning in Children," *Early Child Development and Care* 180, no. 10 (2010): 1285–1298.

27. Rachel A. Razza, Anne Martin, and Jeanne Brooks-Gunn, "Associations among Family Environment, Sustained Attention, and School Readiness for Low-Income Children," *Developmental Psychology* 46, no. 6 (2010): 1528–1542.

28. Nancy Eisenberg, Masa Vidmar, Tracy L Spinrad, Natalie D. Eggum, Alison Edwards, Bridget Gaertner, and Anne Kupfer, "Mothers' Teaching Strategies and Children's Effortful Control: A Longitudinal Study," *Developmental Psychology* 46, no. 5 (2010): 1294–1308; and Samuel P. Putnam, Becky L. Spritz, and Cynthia A. Stifter, "Mother-Child Coregulation during Delay of Gratification at 30 Months," *Infancy* 3, no. 2 (2002): 209–225.

29. W. Steven Barnett, Kwanghee Jung, Donald J. Yarosz, Jessica Thomas, Amy Hornbeck, Robert Stechuk, and Susan Burns, "Educational Effects of the Tools of the Mind Curriculum: A Randomized Trial," *Early Childhood Research Quarterly* 23, no. 3 (2008): 299–313; and Adele Diamond, W. Steven Barnett, Jessica Thomas, and Sarah Munro,

"Preschool Program Improves Cognitive Control," Science 318, no. 5855 (2007): 1387–1388.

30. See, for example, Mark T. Greenberg, Carol A. Kusche, Elizabeth T. Cook, arid Julie P. Quamma, "Promoting Emotional Competence in School-Aged Children: The Effects of the PATHS Curriculum," *Development and Psychopathology* 7, no. 1 (1995): 117–136; and Celene E. Domitrovich, Rebecca C. Cortes, and Mark T. Greenberg, "Improving Young Children's Social and Emotional Competence: A Randomized Trial of the Preschool 'PATHS' Curriculum," *Journal of Primary Prevention* 28, no. 2 (2007): 67–91.

31. Marie S. Burrage, Claire Cameron Ponitz, Elizabeth A. McCready, Priti Shah, Brian C. Sims, Abigail M. Jewkes, and Frederick J. Morrison, "Age- and Schooling-Related Effects on Executive Functions in Young Children: A Natural Experiment," *Child Neuropsychology* 14, no. 6 (2008): 510–524; NICHD, "Predicting Individual Differences"; and Lori E. Skibbe, Carol McDonald Connor, Frederick J. Morrison, and Abigail M. Jewkes, "Schooling Effects on Preschoolers' Self-Regulation. Early Literacy, and Language Growth," *Early Childhood Research Quarterly* 26, no. 1 (2011): 42–49.

32. Sara E. Rimm-Kaufman, Diane M. Early, Martha J. Cox, Gitanjali Saluja, Robert C. Pianta, Robert H. Bradley, and Chris Payne, "Early Behavioral Attributes and Teachers' Sensitivity as Predictors of Competent Behavior in the Kindergarten Classroom," *Journal of Applied Developmental Psychology* 23, no. 4 (2002): 451–470.

33. Carol McDonald Connor, Claire Cameron Ponitz, Beth M. Phillips, Q. Monét Travis, Stephanie Glasney, and Frederick J. Morrison, "First Graders' Literacy and Self-Regulation Gains: The Effect of Individualizing Student Instruction," *Journal of School Psychology* 48, no. 5 (2010): 433–455; for a different intervention with some of the same spirit, see also C. Cybele Raver, Stephanie M. Jones, Christine Li-Grining, Fuhua Zhai, Kristen Bub, and Emily Pressler, "CSRP's Impact on Low-Income Preschoolers' Preacademic Skills: Self-Regulation as a Mediating Mechanism," *Child Development* 82, no. 1 (2011): 362–378.

34. Rimm-Kaufman et al., "Early Behavioral Attributes."

35. See, for example, Catherine M. Bohn, Alysia D. Roehrig, and Michael Pressley, "The First Days of School in the Classrooms of Two More Effective and Four Less Effective Primary-Grades Teachers," *Elementary School Journal* 104, no. 4 (2004): 269–287.

36. Claire E. Cameron, Carol McDonald Connor, and Frederick J. Morrison, "Effects of Variation in Teacher Organization on Classroom Functioning," *Journal of School Psychology* 43, no. 1 (2005): 61–85.

37. For a review, see Heatherton and Wagner, "Cognitive Neuroscience of Self-Regulation Failure."

38. Eric Stice, Katherine Presnell, and Diane Spangler, "Risk Factors for Binge Eating Onset in Adolescent Girls: A 2-Year Prospective Investigation," *Health Psychology* 21, no. 2 (2002): 131–138.

39. Ned L. Cooney, Mark D. Litt, Priscilla A. Morse, Lance O. Bauer, and Larry Gaupp, "Alcohol Cue Reactivity, Negative-Mood Reactivity, and Relapse in Treated Alcoholic Men," *Journal of Abnormal Psychology* 106, no. 2 (1997): 243–250.

40. Yavin Shaham, Uri Shalev, Lin Lu, Harriet de Wit, and Jane Stewart, "The Reinstatement Model of Drug Relapse: History, Methodology, and Major Findings," *Psychopharmacology* 168, nos. 1–2 (2003): 3–20.

41. Menno R. Kruk, Jozsef Halasz, Wout Meelis, and Jozsef Haller, "Fast Positive Feedback between the Adrenocortical Stress Response and a Brain Mechanism Involved in Aggressive Behavior," *Behavioral Neuroscience* 118, no. 5 (2004): 1062–1070.

42. Sabrina D. Bruyneel, Siegfried Dewitte, Philip Hans Franses, and Marnik G. Dekimpe, "I Felt Low and My Purse Feels Light: Depleting Mood Regulation Attempts Affect Risk Decision Making," *Journal of Behavioral Decision Making* 22, no. 2 (2009): 153–170.

43. Kathleen A. Ethier, Trace S. Kershaw, Jessica B. Lewis, Stephanie Milan, Linda M. Niccolai, and Jeannette Ickovics, "Self-Esteem, Emotional Distress, and Sexual Behavior among Adolescent Females: Inter-Relationships and Temporal Effects," *Journal of Adolescent Health* 38, no. 3 (2006): 268–274.

44. Nicole L. Mead, Roy F. Baumeister, Francesca Gino, Maurice E. Schweitzer, and Dan Ariely, "Too Tired to Tell the Truth: Self-Control Resource Depletion and Dishonesty," *Journal of Experimental Social Psychology* 45, no. 3 (2009): 594–597.

45. Andrew Ward and Traci Mann, "Don't Mind If I Do: Disinhibited Eating Under Cognitive Load," *Journal of Personality and Social Psychology* 78, no. 4 (2000): 753–763.

46. Rajita Sinha, "Chronic Stress, Drug Use, and Vulnerability to Addiction," *Annals of the New York Academy of Sciences* 1141 (2008): 105–130.

47. C. Peter Herman and Janet Polivy, "The Self-Regulation of Eating: Theoretical and Practical Problems," in *Handbook of Self-Regulation: Research, Theory, and Applications,* ed. Roy F. Baumeister and Kathleen D. Vohs (New York: Guilford, 2004), 492–508.

48. See, for example, Carlos M. Grilo, Saul Shiffman, and Rena R. Wing, "Relapse Crisis and Coping among Dieters," *Journal of Consulting and Clinical Psychology* 57, no. 4(1989): 488–495.

49. Shaham et al., "The Reinstatement Model of Drug Relapse."

DANIEL T. WILLINGHAM, PHD, is a professor in the Department of Psychology at the University of Virginia. He is a cognitive psychologist with interests in the intersection of cognitive neuroscience and K–12 education.

Alfie Kohn    **NO**

Why Self-Discipline Is Overrated: The (Troubling) Theory and Practice of Control from Within

If there is one character trait whose benefits are endorsed by traditional and progressive educators alike, it may well be self-discipline. Just about everyone wants students to override their unconstructive impulses, resist temptation, and do what needs to be done. True, this disposition is commended to us with particular fervor by the sort of folks who sneer at any mention of self-esteem and deplore what they insist are today's lax standards. But even people who don't describe themselves as conservative agree that imposing discipline on children (either to improve their behavior or so they'll apply themselves to their studies) isn't nearly as desirable as having children discipline themselves. For teachers—indeed, for anyone in a position of relative power—it's appealing the people over whom they have authority will do what they're supposed to do on their own. The only question is how best to accomplish this.

Self-discipline might be defined as marshalling one's willpower to accomplish things that are generally regarded as desirable, and *self-control* as using that same sort of willpower to prevent oneself from doing what is seen to be *un*desirable or to delay gratification. In practice, these often function as two aspects of the same machinery of self-regulation, so I'll use the two terms more or less interchangeably. Do a search for them in indices of published books, scholarly articles, or Internet sites, and you'll quickly discover how rare it is to find a discouraging word, or even a penetrating question, about their value.

While I readily admit that persevering at worthwhile tasks is good—and that some students seem to lack this capacity—I want to suggest that the concept is actually problematic in three fundamental ways. To inquire into what underlies the idea of self-discipline is to uncover serious misconceptions about motivation and personality, controversial assumptions about human nature, and disturbing implications regarding how classroom and society are arranged. Let's call these challenges *psychological, philosophical,* and *political,* respectively. All of them apply to self-discipline in general, but they're particularly relevant to what happens in our schools.

Psychological Issues: Critical Distinctions

If our main goal for students is just to get them to complete whatever tasks, and obey whatever rules, they're given, then self-discipline is undeniably a useful trait. But if we're interested in the whole child—if, for example, we'd like our students to be psychologically healthy—then self-discipline might not deserve a privileged status compared to other attributes. In some contexts, it may not be desirable at all.

Several decades ago, the eminent research psychologist Jack Block described people in terms of their level of "ego control"—that is, the extent to which impulses and feelings are expressed or suppressed. Those who are undercontrolled are impulsive and distractible; those who are overcontrolled are compulsive and joyless. The fact that educators are more irritated by the former, and thus more likely to define it as a problem, doesn't mean the latter is any less troubling. Nor should we favor "the replacement of unbridled impulsivity with categorical, pervasive, rigid impulse control," Block warned. It's not just that self-control isn't always good; it's that a *lack* of self-control isn't always bad because it may "provide the basis for spontaneity, flexibility, expressions of interpersonal warmth, openness to experience, and creative recognitions." So what does it say about our society that "the idea of self-control is generally praised" even though it may sometimes be "maladaptive and spoil the experience and savorings of life"?[1]

The idea that either extreme can be unwise shouldn't be particularly controversial, yet the possibility of unhealthy overcontrol is explicitly rejected by some researchers who double as cheerleaders for self-discipline.[2] Moreover, a reluctance to acknowledge this important caution is apparent in the array of published materials on the subject. Such discussions typically contain unqualified assertions such as "The promotion of self-discipline is an important goal for all schools" or "Teaching self-discipline to students should be something all teachers strive for."[3]

It's hard to square those statements with research that finds "disciplined and directed behavior, which can be advantageous in some situations . . . is likely to be detrimental" in others.[4] Not only has it been shown that "the consequences of impulsivity are not always negative,"[5] but a high degree of self-control tends to go hand-in-hand with less spontaneity and a blander emotional life[6]—and, in some cases, with more serious psychological problems.[7]

"Overcontrollers tend to be complete abstainers from drug use, but they are less well-adjusted than individuals who have lower ego control and may have experimented briefly with drugs, [while] a tendency toward overcontrol puts young women (but not young men) at risk for the development of depression."[8] A preoccupation with self-control is also a key feature of anorexia.[9]

Consider a student who always starts her homework the moment it's assigned. What might look like an admirable display of self-discipline, given that there are other things she'd rather be doing, may actually be due to an acute discomfort with having anything unfinished. She wants—or, more accurately, *needs*—to get the assignment out of the way in order to stave off anxiety. (The fact that something resembling self-discipline is required to complete a task doesn't bode well for the likelihood of deriving any intellectual benefit from it. Learning, after all, depends not on what students do so much as on how they regard and construe what they do.[10] To assume otherwise is to revert to a crude behaviorism long since repudiated by serious scholars.)

More generally, it can be less a sign of health than of vulnerability. Self-discipline might reflect a fear of being overwhelmed by external forces, or by one's own desires, that must be suppressed through continual effort. In effect, such individuals suffer from a fear of being *out* of control. In his classic work, *Neurotic Styles*, David Shapiro described how someone might function as "his own overseer, issuing commands, directives, reminders, warnings, and admonitions concerning not only what is to be done and what is not to be done, but also what is to be wanted, felt, and even thought."[11] Secure, healthy people can be playful, flexible, open to new experiences and self-discovery, deriving satisfaction from the process rather than always focused on the product. An extremely self-disciplined student, by contrast, may see reading or problem solving purely as a means to the end of a good test score or a high grade. In Shapiro's more general formulation, such people "do not feel comfortable with any activity that lacks an aim or a purpose beyond its own pleasure, and usually they do not recognize the possibility of finding life satisfying without a continuous sense of purpose and effort."[12]

A couple of interesting paradoxes follow from this analysis. One is that while self-discipline implies an exercise of the will, and therefore a free choice, many such people are actually not free at all, psychologically speaking. It's not that they've disciplined themselves so much as that they can't allow themselves to be undisciplined. Likewise for the deferral of gratification, as one researcher observed: Those who put off the payoff "were not just 'better' at self-control, but in a sense they seemed to be unable to avoid it."[13]

A second paradox is that impressive self-discipline may contain the seeds of its own undoing: an explosive failure of control, which psychologists call "disinhibition." From one unhealthy extreme (even if it's not always recognized as such), people may suddenly find themselves at the other: The compliant student abruptly acts out in appalling fashion; the pious teetotaler goes on a dangerous drinking binge or shifts from absolute abstinence to reckless, unprotected sex.[14] Moreover, making an effort to inhibit potentially undesirable behaviors can have other negative effects. A detailed review of research concerning all sorts of attempts to suppress feelings and behaviors concludes that the results often include "negative affect (discomfort or distress) [and] cognitive disruption (including distractibility and intrusive, obsessive thoughts about the proscribed behavior)."[15]

In short, we shouldn't always be reassured to learn that a student is remarkably self-disciplined, or apt to delay gratification (since delayers "tend to be somewhat overcontrolled and unnecessarily inhibited"[16]), or always inclined to persist at a task even when he or she is unsuccessful. The last of these tendencies, commonly romanticized as tenacity or "grit," may actually reflect a "refusal to disengage" that stems from an unhealthy and often counterproductive need to continue with something even when it clearly doesn't make sense to do so.[17]

Of course, not every child who exhibits self-discipline, or something similar, is doing so in a worrisome way. So what distinguishes the healthy and adaptive kind? Moderation, perhaps, but also flexibility, which Block calls "adaptively responsive variability."[18] What counts is the capacity to choose whether and when to persevere, to control oneself, to follow the rules—rather than the simple tendency to do these things in every situation. This, rather than self-discipline or self-control per se, is what children would benefit from developing. But such a formulation is very different from the uncritical celebration of self-discipline that we find in the field of education and throughout our culture.

Good Self-Discipline

What can be problematic about self-discipline, it seems, isn't just a matter of how much but what kind. One of the most fruitful ways of thinking about this issue emerges from the work of motivational psychologists Edward Deci and Richard Ryan. To begin with, they invite us to reconsider the casual way that we talk about the concept of motivation, as if it were a single thing that one possessed in a certain quantity. We want students to have more, so we try to "motivate" them—perhaps with the strategic use of rewards or punishments.

In fact, though, there are different types of motivation, and the type matters more than the amount. *Intrinsic* motivation consists of wanting to do something for its own sake—to read, for example, just because it's exciting to lose oneself in a story. *Extrinsic* motivation exists

ON MARSHMALLOWS AND GENDER DIFFERENCES:
REREADING SELF-DISCIPLINE RESEARCH

Four decades ago, in the Stanford University laboratory of Walter Mischel, preschool-age children were left alone in a room after having been told they could get a small treat (say, a marshmallow) by ringing a bell at any time to summon the experimenter—or, if they held out until he returned on his own, they could have a bigger treat (two marshmallows). As the results of this experiment are usually summarized, the children who were able to wait scored better on measures of cognitive and social skills about a decade later and also had higher SAT scores. The lesson is simple, as conservative commentators tell the story: We ought to focus less on "structural reforms" to improve education or reduce poverty, and look instead at traits possessed by individuals—specifically, the ability to exert good old-fashioned self-control.[1]

But the real story of these studies is a good deal more complicated. For starters, the causal relationship wasn't at all clear, as Mischel acknowledged. The ability to delay gratification might not have been responsible for the impressive qualities found 10 years later; instead, both may have resulted from the same kind of home environment.[2]

Second, what mostly interested Mischel wasn't *whether* children could wait for a bigger treat—which, by the way, most of them could—and whether waiters fared better in life than non-waiters, but *how* children go about trying to wait and which strategies help.[3] Mischal discovered that kids waited longer when they were distracted by a toy. What worked best wasn't "self-denial and grim determination" but doing something enjoyable while waiting so that self-control wasn't needed at all![4]

Third, the specifics of the situation—that is, the design of each experiment—were more important than the personality of a given child in predicting the outcome.[5] This is precisely the opposite of the usual lesson drawn from these studies, which is that self-control is a matter of individual character, which we ought to promote.

Fourth, even to the extent Mischel did look at stable individual characteristics, he was primarily concerned with "cognitive competencies"—strategies for how to think about (or stop thinking about) the goody—and how they're related to other skills that are measured down the road. In fact, those subsequent outcomes weren't associated with the ability to defer gratification, per se, but only with the ability to distract oneself when those distractions weren't provided by the experimenters.[6] And that ability was significantly correlated with plain old intelligence.[7]

Finally, most people who cite these experiments simply assume that it's better to take a bigger payoff later than a smaller payoff now. But is that always true? Mischel, for one, didn't think so. "The decision to delay or not to delay hinges, in part, on the individual's values and expectations with regard to the specific contingencies," he and his colleagues wrote. "In a given situation, therefore, postponing gratification may or may not be a wise or adaptive choice."[8]

No Benefit but Higher Grades

If the conservative spin on Mischel's work is mostly attributable to how others have (mis)interpreted it, the same can't be said of a more recent study, where the researchers themselves are keen to blame underachievement on the "failure to exercise self-discipline." Angela Duckworth and Martin Seligman attracted considerable attention (in *Education Week*, the *New York Times*, and elsewhere) for their experiment, published in 2005 and 2006, purporting to show that self-discipline was a strong predictor of academic success, and that this trait explained why girls in their sample were more successful in school than boys.[9]

Once again, the conclusion is a lot more dubious once you look more closely. For one thing, all of the children in this study were 8th graders at an elite magnet school with competitive admissions, so it's not at all clear that the findings can be generalized to other populations or ages. For another thing, self-discipline was mostly assessed by how the students described themselves, or how their teachers and parents described them, rather than being based on something they actually did. The sole behavioral measure—making them choose either $1 today or $2 in a week—correlated weakly with the other measures and showed the smallest gender difference.

Most tellingly, though, the only beneficial effect of self-discipline was higher grades. Teachers gave more A's to the students who said, for example, that they put off doing what they enjoyed until they finished their homework. Suppose it had been discovered that students who nodded and smiled at everything their teacher said received higher grades. Would that argue for teaching kids to nod and smile more, or might it call into question the significance of grades as a variable? Or suppose it was discovered that self-discipline on the part of adults was associated with more positive evaluations from workplace supervisors. We'd have to conclude that employees who did what their bosses wanted, regardless of whether it was satisfying or sensible, elicited a favorable verdict from those same bosses. But so what?

We already know not only that grades suffer from low levels of validity and reliability, but that students who are led to focus on grades tend to be less interested in what they're learning, more likely to think in a superficial fashion (and to retain information for a shorter time), and apt to choose the easiest possible task.[10] Moreover, there's some evidence that students with high grades are, on average, overly conformist and not particularly creative.[11] That students who are more self-disciplined get better grades, then, constitutes an endorsement of self-discipline only for people who don't understand that grades are a terrible marker for the educational qualities we care about. And if girls in our culture are socialized to control their impulses and do what they're told, is it really a good thing that they've absorbed that lesson well enough to be rewarded with high marks?   —A.K.

Notes

1. For example, see David Brooks, "Marshmallows and Public Policy," *New York Times*, 7 May 2006, p. 13.
2. Walter Mischel, "From Good Intentions to Willpower," in Peter M. Gollwitzer and John A. Bargh, eds., *The Psychology of Action: Linking Cognition and Motivation to Behavior* (New York: Guillford, 1996), p. 212.
3. A "remarkably consistent finding" in delay-of-gratification studies, at least those designed so that waiting yields a bigger reward, is that "most children and adolescents do manage to delay." In one such experiment, "83 out of the 104 subjects delayed the maximum number of times" (David C. Funder and Jack Block, "The Role of Ego-Control, Ego-Resiliency, and IQ in Delay of Gratification in Adolescence," *Journal of Personality and Social Psychology,* vol. 57, 1989, p. 1048). This suggests either that complaints about the hedonism and self-indulgence of contemporary youth may be exaggerated or that these studies of self-control are so contrived that *all* of their findings are of dubious relevance to the real world.
4. Mischel, p. 209.
5. Ibid., p. 212. See also Walter Mischel, Yuichi Shoda, and Philip K. Peake, "The Nature of Adolescent Competencies Predicted by Preschool Delay of Gratification," *Journal of Personality and Social Psychology*, vol. 54, 1988, p. 694.
6. Mischel, p. 211.
7. Ibid., p. 214. This finding is interesting in light of the fact that other writers have treated self-discipline and intelligence as very different characteristics. See, for example, the title of the first article in note 9, below.
8. Yuichi Shoda, Walter Mischel, and Philip K. Peake, "Predicting Adolescent Cognitive and Self-Regulatory Competencies from Preschool Delay of Gratification," *Developmental Psychology*, vol. 26, 1990, p. 985. They add that the *ability* to put up with delay so one can make that choice is valuable, but of course this is different from arguing that the exercise of self-control in itself is beneficial.
9. Angela L. Duckworth and Martin E. P. Seligman, "Self-Discipline Outdoes IQ in Predicting Academic Performance of Adolescents," *Psychological Science*, vol. 16, 2005, pp. 939–44; and Angela Lee Duckworth and Martin E. P. Seligman, "Self-Discipline Gives Girls the Edge," *Journal of Educational Psychology*, vol. 98, 2006, pp. 198–208.
10. I've reviewed the evidence on grades in *Punished by Rewards* (Boston: Houghton Mifflin, 1993) and *The Schools Our Children Deserve* (Boston: Houghton Mifflin, 1999).
11. Consider one of the studies that Duckworth and Seligman cite to prove that self-discipline predicts academic performance—that is, high grades. It found that such performance "seemed as much a function of attention to details and the rules of the academic game as it was of intellectual talent." High-achieving students "were not particularly interested in ideas or in cultural or aesthetic pursuits. Moreover, they were not particularly tolerant or empathic; however, they did seem stable, pragmatic, and task-oriented, and lived in harmony with the rules and conventions of society. Finally, relative to students in general, these superior achievers seemed somewhat stodgy and unoriginal" (Robert Hogan and Daniel S. Weiss, "Personality Correlates of Superior Academic Achievement," *Journal of Counseling Psychology*, vol. 21, 1974, p. 148).

when the task isn't really the point; one might read in order to get a prize or someone's approval. Not only are these two kinds of motivation different—they tend to be inversely related. Scores of studies have shown that the more you reward people for doing something, the more they're apt to lose interest in whatever they had to do to get the reward. Researchers keep finding that offering children "positive reinforcement" for being helpful and generous ends up undermining those very qualities, and encouraging students to improve their grades results in their becoming less interested in learning.[19]

Yet children do some things that aren't intrinsically appealing even in the absence of extrinsic inducements. They have, we might say, *internalized* a commitment to doing them. And here we return to the idea of self-discipline (with the emphasis on "self"). Indeed, this is exactly where many educators have placed their bets: We want kids to get busy without needing an adult to stand next to them, carrots and sticks at the ready; we want them to act responsibly even when no one is watching.

But Deci and Ryan are not finished complicating our lives. Having shown that there are different kinds of motivation (which are not equally desirable), they go on to suggest that there are also different kinds of internalization (ditto). This is a possibility that few of us have considered; even an educator who can distinguish intrinsic from extrinsic will insist that children should be helped to internalize good values or behaviors, period. But what exactly is the nature of that internalization? On the one hand, a rule or standard can be swallowed whole, or "introjected," so that it controls children from the inside: "Behaviors are performed because one 'should' do them, or because not doing so might engender anxiety, guilt, or loss of esteem." On the other hand, internalization can take place more authentically, so the behavior is experienced as "volitional or self-determined." It's been fully integrated into one's value structure and feels chosen.

Thus, a student may study either because she knows she's supposed to (and will feel lousy about herself if she doesn't) or because she understands the benefits of doing so and wants to follow through even if it's not always pleasurable.[20] This basic distinction has proved relevant to academics, sports, romantic love, generosity, political involvement, and religion—with research in each case demonstrating that the latter kind of internalization leads to better outcomes than the former. With education in particular, it's possible for teachers to promote the more positive version by minimizing "externally imposed evaluations, goals, rewards, and pressures" as well as proactively supporting students' sense of autonomy."[21]

The moral of this story is that just because motivation is internal doesn't mean it's ideal. If kids feel controlled, even from within, they're likely to be conflicted, unhappy, and perhaps less likely to succeed (at least by meaningful criteria) at whatever they're doing. Dutiful students may be suffering from what the psychoanalyst Karen Horney famously called the "tyranny of the should"—to the point that they no longer know what they really want or who they really are. So it for teenagers who have mortgaged their present lives to the future: noses to the grindstone, perseverant to a fault, stressed to the max. High school is just preparation for college, and college consists of collecting credentials for whatever comes next. Nothing has any value or provides any gratification in itself. These students may be skilled test-takers and grade grubbers and gratification delayers, but they remind us just how mixed the blessing of self-discipline can be.

Philosophical Issues: Underlying Beliefs

In light of all these reasons for caution, why do we find ourselves so infatuated with self-discipline and self-control? The answer may involve basic values that pervade our culture. Let's ask a different question: What must be true about children—or people in general—if self-discipline is required to make oneself do valuable things?

Consider this recent reflection by David Brooks, a conservative newspaper columnist:

> In Lincoln's day, to achieve maturity was to succeed in the conquest of the self. Human beings were born with sin, inflected with dark passions and satanic temptations. The transition to adulthood consisted of achieving mastery over them. You can read commencement addresses from the 19th and early 20th centuries in which the speak-

ers would talk about the beast within and the need for iron character to subdue it. Schoolhouse readers emphasized self-discipline. The whole character-building model was sin-centric.[22]

Brooks has it right with one important caveat: The emphasis on self-discipline isn't just an historical relic. These days we're spared the florid and exhortatory rhetoric, but a few minutes on-line reminds us that the concept itself is alive and well in contemporary America—to the tune of 3 million hits on Google. It's also a key element in the character education movement.[23] Brooks offers a useful if disconcerting reminder about the sin-centric assumptions on which the gospel of self-discipline still rests. It's because our preferences are regarded as unworthy, our desires as shameful, that we must strive to overcome them. Taken to its logical conclusion, human life is a constant struggle to stifle and transcend ourselves. Morality consists of the triumph of mind over body, reason over desire, will over want.[24]

What's interesting about all of this is how many secular institutions and liberal individuals, who would strenuously object to the notion that children are self-centered little beasts that need to be tamed, nevertheless embrace a concept that springs from just such a premise. Some even make a point of rejecting old-fashioned coercion and punishment in favor of gentler methods.[25] But if they're nevertheless engaged in ensuring that children internalize our values—in effect, by installing a policeman inside each child—then they ought to admit that this isn't the same as helping them develop their own values, and it's diametrically opposed to the goal of helping them become independent thinkers. Control from within isn't inherently more humane than control from without, particularly if the psychological effects aren't all that different, as it appears they aren't.

Control from Within Isn't Inherently More Humane Than Control from Without

Even beyond the vision of human nature, a commitment to self-discipline may reflect a tacit allegiance to philosophical conservatism with its predictable complaint that our society—or its youth—has forgotten the value of hard work, the importance of duty, the need to accept personal responsibility, and so on. (Never mind that older people have been denouncing youthful slackers and "modern times" for centuries.) And this condemnation is typically accompanied by a prescriptive vision that endorses self-denial and sarcastically dismisses talk about self-exploration or self-esteem.

In his fascinating book *Moral Politics*, the linguist and social critic George Lakoff argued that self-discipline plays a critical role in a conservative worldview.[26] Obedience to authority is what produces self-discipline, and self-discipline, in turn, is required for achievement.[27] Its absence is seen as a sign of self-indulgence and therefore of moral weakness. Thus, any time a child receives something desirable, including our approval, without having *earned* it, any time competition is removed (so that success is possible without having to defeat others), any time he or she receives too much assistance or nurturance, then we are being "permissive," "overindulgent," failing to prepare the child for the Real World. Interestingly, this kind of conservatism isn't limited to talk radio or speeches at the Republican convention. It's threaded through the work of key researchers who not only study self-discipline but vigorously insist on its importance.[28]

Of course, fundamental questions about morality and human nature can't be resolved in an article; it's clear that the point of departure for some of us is radically different than it is for others. But for educators who casually invoke the need to teach children self-discipline, it may make sense to explore the philosophical foundation of that concept and to reconsider it if that foundation gives us pause.

Political Issues: Practical Implications

When we want to understand what's going on in a given environment—say, a classroom—it often makes sense to look at its policies, norms, and other structural features. Unfortunately, many of us tend to ignore the way the system works and attribute too much significance to the personalities of the individuals involved—a phenomenon that social psychologists have dubbed the Fundamental Attribution Error.[29] Thus, we assume that self-control is just a feature that a person might possess, even though it's probably more accurate to think of it as "a situational concept, not an individual trait" given that "an individual will display different degrees of self-control in different situations." Exactly the same is true of delaying gratification.[30]

It's not just that attending to individuals rather than environments hampers our ability to understand. Doing so also has practical significance. Specifically, the more we fault people for lacking self-discipline and spend our efforts helping them develop the ability to control their impulses, the less likely we are to question the structures (political, economic, or educational) that shape their actions. There is no reason to work for social change if we assume that people just need to buckle down and try harder. Thus, the attention paid to self-discipline is not only philosophically conservative in its premises, but also politically conservative in its consequences.

Our society is teeming with examples. If consumers are over their heads in debt, the effect of framing the problem as a lack of self-control is to deflect attention from the concerted efforts of the credit industry to get us hooked on borrowing money from the time we're children.[31] Or consider the Keep America Beautiful campaign launched in the 1950s that urged us to stop being litterbugs—a campaign financed, it turns out, by the American Can Company and other corporations that had the effect of blaming individuals and discouraging questions about who profits from the production of disposable merchandise and its packaging.[32]

But let's return to the students sitting in our classrooms. If the question is: "How can we get them to raise their hands and wait to be called on rather than blurting out the answer?" then the question *isn't*: "Why does the teacher ask most of the questions in here—and unilaterally decide who gets to speak, and when?" If the question is: "What's the best way to teach kids self-discipline so they'll do their work?" then the question *isn't*: "Are these assignments really worth doing?" In other words, to identify a lack of self-discipline as the problem is to focus our efforts on making children conform to a status quo that is left unexamined and is unlikely to change. Each child, moreover, has been equipped with "a built-in supervisor," which may not be in his or her best interest but is enormously convenient for creating "a self-controlled—not just controlled—citizenry and work force."[33]

Not every objection or piece of evidence reviewed here will apply to every example of self-discipline. But it makes sense for us to take a closer look at the concept and the ways in which it's applied in our schools. Aside from its philosophical underpinnings and political impact, there are reasons to be skeptical about anything that might produce overcontrol. Some children who look like every adult's dream of a dedicated student may in reality be anxious, driven, and motivated by a perpetual need to feel better about themselves, rather than by anything resembling curiosity. In a word, they are workaholics in training.

Notes

1. Jack Block, *Personality as an Affect-Processing System: Toward an Integrative Theory* (Mahway, N.J.: Erlbaum, 2002), pp. 195, 8–9. Or, as a different psychologist puts it, "One person's lack of self-control is another person's impetus for a positive life change" (Laura A. King, "Who Is Regulating What and Why?" *Psychological Inquiry*, vol. 7, 1996, p. 58).

2. "Our belief [is] that there is no true disadvantage of having too much self-control," Christopher Peterson and Martin Seligman wrote in their book *Character Strengths and Virtues* (Oxford University Press, 2004), p. 515. June Tangney, Roy Baumeister, and Angie Luzio Boone similarly declared that "self-control is beneficial and adaptive in a linear fashion. We found no evidence that any psychological problems are linked to high self-control" ("High Self-Control Predicts Good Adjustment, Less Pathology, Better Grades, and Interpersonal Success," *Journal of Personality*, vol. 72, 2004, pp. 271–324). This conclusion—based on questionnaire responses by a group of undergraduates—turns out to be a trifle misleading, if not disingenuous. First, it's supported by the fact that Tangney and her colleagues found

an inverse relationship between self-control and negative emotions. Other research, however, has found that there's also an inverse relationship between self-control and *positive* emotions. (See, for example, Darya L. Zabelina et al., "The Psychological Tradeoffs of Self-Control," *Personality and Individual Differences,* vol. 43, 2007, pp. 463–73.) Even if highly self-controlled people aren't always unhappy, they're also not particularly happy; their emotional life in general tends to be muted. Second, the self-control questionnaire used by Tangney and her colleagues "includes items reflective of an appropriate level of control and [of] undercontrol, but not overcontrol. It is therefore not surprising that the correlates of the scale do not indicate maladaptive consequences associated with very high levels of control" (Tera D. Letzring et al., "Ego-Control and Ego-Resiliency," *Journal of Research in Personality,* vol. 39, 2005, p. 3). In other words, the clean bill of health they award to self-control was virtually predetermined by the design of their study. At the very end of their article, Tangney et al. concede that some people may be rigidly overcontrolled but then immediately try to define the problem out of existence: "Such overcontrolled individuals may be said to lack the ability to control their self-control" (p. 314).

3. The first sentence is from Joseph F. Rogus, "Promoting Self-Discipline: A Comprehensive Approach," *Theory Into Practice,* vol. 24, 1985, p. 271. The second is from http://wik.ed.uiuc.edu/index.php/Self-Discipline, a web page of the Curriculum, Technology, and Education Reform program at the University of Illinois at Urbana-Champaign. Rogus's article appeared in a special issue of the journal *Theory Into Practice* devoted entirely to the topic of self-discipline. Although it featured contributions by a wide range of educational theorists, including some with a distinctly humanistic orientation, none questioned the importance of self-discipline.

4. Letzring et al., p. 3.

5. Scott J. Dickman, "Functional and Dysfunctional Impulsivity," *Journal of Personality and Social Psychology,* vol. 58, 1990, p. 95.

6. Zabelina et al.

7. Daniel A. Weinberger and Gary E. Schwartz, "Distress and Restraint as Superordinate Dimensions of Self-Reported Adjustment," *Journal of Personality,* vol. 58, 1990, pp. 381–417.

8. David C. Funder, "On the Pros and Cons of Delay of Gratification," *Psychological Inquiry,* vol. 9, 1998, p. 211. The studies to which he alludes are, respectively, Jonathan Shedler and Jack Block, "Adolescent Drug Use and Psychological Health," *American Psychologist,* vol. 45, 1990, pp. 612–30; and Jack H. Block, Per E. Gjerde, and Jeanne H. Block, "Personality Antecedents of Depressive Tendencies in 18-Year-Olds," *Journal of Personality and Social Psychology,* vol. 60, 1991, pp. 726–38.

9. For example, see Christine Halse, Anne Honey, and Desiree Boughtwood, "The Paradox of Virtue: (Re)thinking Deviance, Anorexia, and Schooling," *Gender and Education,* vol. 19, 2007, pp. 219–35.

10. This may explain why the data generally fail to show any academic benefit to assigning homework—which most students detest—particularly in elementary or middle school. (See Alfie Kohn, *The Homework Myth* [Cambridge, Mass.: Da Capo Press, 2006] and an article based on that book in the September 2006 issue of *Kappan.*) Remarkably, most people assume that students will somehow benefit from performing tasks they can't wait to be done with, as though their attitudes and goals were irrelevant to the outcome.

11. David Shapiro, *Neurotic Styles* (New York: Basic, 1965), p. 34.

12. Ibid., p. 44.

13. Funder, op. cit., p. 211.

14. Regarding the way that "disinhibition [is] occasionally manifested by some overcontrolled personalities," see Block, p. 187.

15. Janet Polivy, "The Effects of Behavioral Inhibition," *Psychological Inquiry,* vol. 9, 1998, p. 183. She adds: "This is not to say that one should never inhibit one's natural response, as, for example, when anger makes one want to hurt another, or addiction makes one crave a cigarette" (ibid.). Rather, it means one should weigh the benefits and costs of inhibition in each circumstance—a moderate position that contrasts sharply with our society's tendency to endorse self-discipline across the board.

16. Funder, op. cit., p. 211. Walter Mischel, who conducted the so-called "marshmallow" experiments (see sidebar), put it this way: The inability to delay gratification may be a problem, but "the other extreme—excessive delay of gratification—also has its personal costs and can be disadvantageous. . . . Whether one should or should not delay gratification or 'exercise the will' in any particular choice is often anything but self-evident" ("From Good Intentions to Willpower," in Peter M. Gollwitzer and John A. Bargh, eds., *The Psychology of Action: Linking Cognition and Motivation to Behavior* [New York: Guilford, 1996], p. 198).

17. See, for example, King, op. cit.; and Alina Tugend, "Winners Never Quit? Well, Yes, They Do," *New York Times,* 16 August 2008, p. B5, for data that challenge an unqualified endorsement of perseverance such as is offered by psychologist Angela Duckworth and her colleagues: "As educators and parents we should encourage children to work not only with intensity but also with stamina." That advice follows their report that perseverance contributed to higher grades and better performance at a spelling bee (Angela L. Duckworth et al., "Grit: Perseverance and Passion for Long-Term Goals," *Journal of Personality and Social Psychology,* vol. 92, 2007; quotation on

p. 1100). But such statistical associations mostly point up the limitations of these outcome measures as well as of grit itself, a concept that ignores motivational factors (that is, *why* people persevere), thus conflating genuine passion for a task with a desperate need to prove one's competence, an inability to change course when appropriate, and so on.

18. Block, op cit., p. 130.
19. See, for example, my book *Punished by Rewards*, rev. ed. (Boston: Houghton Mifflin, 1999); and Edward L. Deci et al., "A Meta-Analytic Review of Experiments Examining the Effects of Extrinsic Rewards on Intrinsic Motivation," *Psychological Bulletin*, vol. 125, 1999, pp. 627–68.
20. Richard M. Ryan, Scott Rigby, and Kristi King, "Two Types of Religious Internalization and Their Relations to Religious Orientations and Mental Health," *Journal of Personality and Social Psychology*, vol. 65, 1993, p. 587. This basic distinction has been explicated and refined in many other writings by Ryan, Deci, Robert J. Vallerand, James P. Connell, Richard Koestner, Luc Pelletier, and others. Most recently, it has been invoked in response to Roy Baumeister's claim that the capacity for self-control is "like a muscle," requiring energy and subject to being depleted—such that if you resist one sort of temptation, you'll have, at least temporarily, less capacity to resist another. The problem with this theory is its failure to distinguish "between self-regulation (i.e., autonomous regulation) and self-control (i.e., controlled regulation)." Ego depletion may indeed take place with the latter, but the former actually "maintains or enhances energy or vitality" (Richard M. Ryan and Edward L. Deci, "From Ego Depletion to Vitality," *Social and Personality Psychology Compass*, vol. 2, 2008, pp. 709, 711).
21. See, for example, Richard M. Ryan, James P. Connell, and Edward L. Deci, "A Motivational Analysis of Self-determination and Self-regulation in Education," in *Research on Motivation in Education*, vol. 2, (Orlando, Fla.: Academic Press, 1985); and Richard M. Ryan and Jerome Stiller, "The Social Contexts of Internalization: Parent and Teacher Influences on Autonomy, Motivation, and Learning," *Advances in Motivation and Achievement*, vol. 7, 1991, pp. 115–49. The quotation is from Ryan and Stiller, p. 143.
22. David Brooks, "The Art of Growing Up," *New York Times,* 6 June 2008, p. A23.
23. See Alfie Kohn, "How Not to Teach Values: A Critical Look at Character Education," *Phi Delta Kappan*, February 1997, pp. 429–39.
24. One educator based his defense of the need for self-discipline on "our natural egoism [that threatens to] lead us into 'a condition of warre one against another'"—as though Thomas Hobbes's dismal view of our species was universally accepted. This was followed by the astonishing assertion that "social class differences appear to be largely a function of the ability to defer gratification"

and the recommendation that we "connect the lower social classes to the middle classes who may provide role models for self-discipline" (Louis Goldman, "Mind, Character, and the Deferral of Gratification," *Educational Forum*, vol. 60, 1996, pp. 136, 137, 139). Notice that this article was published in 1996, not 1896.
25. To whatever extent internalization or self-discipline *is* desired, this gentler approach—specifically, supporting children's autonomy and minimizing adult control—has consistently been shown to be more effective. (I reviewed some of the evidence in *Unconditional Parenting* [New York: Atria, 2005], especially chap. 3.) Ironically, many of the same traditionalists who defend the value of self-control also promote a more authoritarian approach to parenting or teaching. In any case, my central point here is that we need to reconsider the goal, not merely the method.
26. George Lakoff, *Moral Politics: How Liberals and Conservatives Think*, 2nd ed. (Chicago: University of Chicago Press, 2002).
27. For a discussion of the relationship between obedience and self-control, see Block, esp. pp. 195–96.
28. I'm thinking specifically of Roy Baumeister and his collaborator June Tangney, as well as Martin Seligman and Angela Duckworth, and, in a different academic neighborhood, criminologists Michael R. Gottfredson and Travis Hirschi, who argued that crime is due simply to a lack of self-control on the part of criminals. For a critique of that theory, see the essay by Gilbert Geis and other chapters in Erich Goode, ed., *Out of Control: Assessing the General Theory of Crime* (Stanford, Calif.: Stanford University Press, 2008).
29. I discussed the Fundamental Attribution Error in an article about academic cheating, which is typically construed as a reflection of moral failure (one often attributed to a lack of self-control), even though researchers have found that it is a predictable response to certain educational environments. See "Who's Cheating Whom?" *Phi Delta Kappan*, October 2007, pp. 89–97.
30. Per-Olof H. Wikström and Kyle Treiber, "The Role of Self-Control in Crime Causation," *European Journal of Criminology*, vol. 4, 2007, pp. 243, 251. Regarding delay of gratification, see Walter Mischel et al., "Cognitive and Attentional Mechanisms in Delay of Gratification," *Journal of Personality and Social Psychology*, vol. 21, 1972, pp. 204–18.
31. For example, see CBS News, "Meet 'Generation Plastic,'" 17 May 2007, available at www.cbsnews.com/stories/2007/05/17/eveningnews/main2821916.shtml.
32. See Heather Rogers, *Gone Tomorrow: The Hidden Life of Garbage* (New York: New Press, 2005).
33. Samuel Bowles and Herbert Gintis, *Schooling in Capitalist America* (New York: Basic, 1976), p. 39. Perhaps it shouldn't be surprising that the conservative *National Review* published an

essay strongly supporting homework because it teaches "personal responsibility and self-discipline. Homework is practice for life" (John D. Gartner, "Training for Life," 22 January 2001). But what aspect of life? The point evidently is not to train children to make meaningful decisions, or become part of a democratic society, or learn to think critically. Rather, what's being prescribed are lessons in doing whatever one is told.

ALFIE KOHN is a writer, lecturer, and commentator who focuses on education, child development, and human behavior.

EXPLORING THE ISSUE

Should Schools Teach Students Self-Control?

Critical Thinking and Reflection

1. Both Willingham and Kohn identify various types of skills or activities that fall within the construct of self-control. Is it possible that some types of self-control are positive and should be taught and that other types are negative and should not be taught? Why?
2. What is the evidence that Willingham marshals to support the need to teach self-control?
3. What is the evidence that Kohn marshals against teaching self-control?
4. Reflect on your own experiences in school. Can you give examples in which self-control was emphasized in a negative way and in a positive way?

Is There Common Ground?

Both Willingham and Kohn present compelling empirical data in support of the potential benefits and dangers of self-control. Can the positions and data be reconciled? On the one hand, it seems that Willingham is not arguing for self-control "at all costs." In fact, he points out that adaptive self-control is inspired by parents and teachers who provide a rationale for learning self-control, embed their teaching in a warm and supportive environment, and appear driven by an interest in the emotional health and lifelong adaptation of the child. On the other hand, Kohn provides an important caution about an approach that focuses on self-control as an end onto itself and that is devoid of the warmth, rationale, and support encouraged by Willingham. Thus, Willingham and Kohn might not differ too dramatically on the types of characteristics they wish to instill in schools and homes. Warmth, discussion with respect, and support are optimal environments for learning and healthy development.

At the same time, there does seem to be a real difference in the papers of Willingham and Kohn regarding the outcomes that are valued by each of them; that is, the types of people they hope children will grow up to be. The focus of Willingham, or at the least studies he chooses to cite, is on traditional measures of academic success and of emotional health, largely as defined by parents and teachers. In contrast, the focus of Kohn is on independence and critical thinking, which may overlap with, but is not identical to traditional measures of academic success and emotional health. Here again, we see an instance in which a controversy may not be resolved solely by data as it also depends on differences in values and perspectives on the ideal educated citizen.

Create Central

www.mhhe.com/createcentral

Additional Resources

Walter Mischel, "From Good Intentions to Willpower," in Peter M. Gollwitzer and John A. Bargh, eds., *The Psychology of Action: Linking Cognition and Motivation to Behavior* (Guilford, 1996).

Nancy Eisenberg, Carlos Valiente, and Natalie D. Eggum, "Self-Regulation and School Readiness," *Early Education and Development* (vol. 21, no. 5, 2010).

Grazyna Kochanska, "Multiple Pathways to Conscience for Children with Different Temperaments: From Toddlerhood to Age 5," *Developmental Psychology* (vol. 33, no. 2, 1997).

Internet References . . .

Alfie Kohn

http://alfiekohn.org

KidsHealth from Nemours

http://kidshealth.org

Parenting Science

http://www.parentingscience.com

Selected, Edited, and with Issue Framing Material by:
Leonard Abbeduto, *University of California, Davis*
and
Frank Symons, *University of Minnesota*

ISSUE

Do Recent Discoveries About the Brain Have Implications for Classroom Practice?

YES: Judy Willis, from "Building a Bridge from Neuroscience to the Classroom," *Phi Delta Kappan* (February 2008)

NO: Dan Willingham, from "When and How Neuroscience Applies to Education," *Phi Delta Kappan* (February 2008)

Learning Outcomes

After reading this issue, you will be able to:

- Understand the nature of the questions being asked about the human brain by neuroscientists and the technologies they use to answer those questions.
- Become familiar with examples of the translation of brain science findings into educational practices.
- Understand the potential of brain science to inform educational practice.
- Understand the challenges of translating brain science findings into concrete educational practices.

ISSUE SUMMARY

YES: Judy Willis argues that current research on brain function does inform educational practice and she provides some examples from recent brain science findings. Willis cautions, however, that we are truly in the infancy of brain science and the "hard facts" are still scarce and that many people misinterpret and misuse the brain science findings.

NO: Dan Willingham argues that not every finding about how the brain works can or should lead to an accommodation of educational practice. Moreover, Willingham argues that some of the ways in which brain science is conducted, while sensible for learning about the brain and the scientific questions of interest, actually obscure or mislead about the importance of the findings for the classroom.

Research in the brain sciences has proceeded at a rapid pace since the 1970s, due in large measure to the advent of some amazing new technologies, including positron emission tomography (PET), single photon emission computed tomography (SPECT), magnetic resonance imaging (MRI), functional magnetic imaging (fMRI), diffusion tensor imaging (DTI), and high-density event-related potentials (HD-ERP). These technologies provide high-resolution images of the human brain, yielding information about not only structural characteristics but also about how the brain functions "online" as an individual processes perceptual information, solves complex problems, or makes responses as simple as a button press or as complex as planning and producing a sentence. Some of these techniques require sedation, exposure to radiation, and injections and are thus of limited utility with young children. Other techniques, however, are noninvasive, typically requiring only that the individual whose brain is being "imaged" sit motionless in a special apparatus while performing the cognitive task being studied. Moreover, many

of these technologies can be contextualized as games or as involving pretend play, which means that many of these techniques can provide a window into the brains of even very young children.

A few of the findings that have captured the attention of educators (not to mention the news media) in recent years follow:

1. In contrast to what was believed only a few years ago, the structure and function of the human brain is not fixed at birth. It now appears that the brain undergoes dramatic changes in connectedness during infancy. The many neurons (nerve cells) in the baby's brain establish increasing information-exchanging links with each other. The number of connections, or synapses, increases more than 20 times during the first few months of life.
2. The timing of synaptic development varies across different parts of the human brain, which may account in part for the different behavioral capabilities of children at different ages. For example,

at 18 to 24 months, a dramatic increase in synaptic density and changes in the metabolic activity of the brain may help to produce the burst in vocabulary learning normally seen at this time.

3. At the same time that synaptic growth is providing the foundation for new skills and capabilities, it is closing off other avenues of learning. For example, there is evidence that early in infancy neurons in the auditory cortex are responsive to a range of speech sounds. As the infant gains exposure to his or her native language, however, neurons become more specialized, responding only to specific, frequently heard sounds, which leaves them "unresponsive" to unfamiliar speech sounds, such as those included in other languages. This seems to occur by 12 months of age.

4. There is evidence that brain regions that are normally responsible for one function can assume other functions depending on the experiences available to the individual. For example, portions of the temporal lobe that are responsive to sound in individuals with normal hearing are sensitive to visual stimuli in congenitally deaf individuals.

5. Chronic traumatic experiences during periods of rapid brain growth can lead to greatly elevated levels of stress hormones, which then flood the brain, altering its structure and function, with serious long-lasting consequences for subsequent learning and behavior.

6. Individuals with neurodevelopmental disorders, such as autism, appear to process information differently, activating different parts of their brains compared to typically developing individuals performing the same cognitive tasks.

Educators have enthusiastically embraced findings emerging from work in the brain sciences. After all, our understanding of the brain informs us about learning. Presumably, it should follow that our understanding of the brain will inform us about teaching as well. In the first of the following selections, Judy Willis argues that current research on brain function does inform educational practice and she provides some examples from recent brain science findings. Willis cautions, however, that we are truly in the infancy of brain science and the "hard facts" are still scarce. In the second selection, Dan Willingham argues that not every finding about how the brain works can or should lead to an accommodation of educational practice. Morever, Willingham argues that some of the ways in which brain science is conducted, while sensible for learning about the brain and the scientific questions of interest, actually obscure or mislead about the importance of the findings for the classroom.

YES

Judy Willis

Building a Bridge from Neuroscience to the Classroom

Knowledge of the underlying science, Dr. Willis argues, will enable educators to make good use of all that neuroscientists are learning about our brains, young and old. It is also the best defense against misleading assertions put forth by opportunists.

Neuroscience and cognitive science relating to education are hot topics. They receive extensive but simplified coverage in the mass media, and there is a booming business in "brain-booster" books and products, which claim to be based on the research.

Eric Jensen advocates more collaboration among scientists from the full variety of disciplines engaged in brain research. This collaboration, with corresponding evaluations using cognitive and classroom research, can offer educators more coherent knowledge that they can use in teaching. And educators want this knowledge, as shown by a communication I received from Lisa Nimz, a fifth-grade teacher in the Chicago suburb of Skokie, in response to my May 2007 *Kappan* article.

> We know how important it is for relevant research from the scientific community to be shared with and used in the education community. We are anxious for neurological research to become more a part of educators' thinking and wonder how to make it so. There seem to be only a few people in the unique position of being able to understand the research, figure out its implications for the classroom, and use those implications to direct their teaching. We are actively pondering how a sturdy and wide enough bridge can be built between the scientific community and the education community.
>
> There are many obstacles to building such a construct. Reading the primary sources of neurological research can be challenging even for the brightest of us. And even if someone can comprehend these primary sources, there are many highly educated people who don't seem to approach scientific evidence with the caution and skepticism necessary to make fair judgments about the implications of that evidence. There are also many members of the scientific community and academia who haven't studied pedagogy. We are thankful for books, articles, and presentations that mitigate some of that disconnect.

Ms. Nimz' quandary reflects educators' increasing concern about how to keep up with the exponential growth of the body of information coming from the varied scientific specialties about the structure and function of the brain with regard to learning and memory. Of equal concern is how to interpret the multitude of claims, usually by nonscientists, that the effectiveness of various "brain-based strategies" has been "proven by brain research."

The interdisciplinary collaboration of neuroscientists, molecular geneticists, cellular biologists, cognitive scientists, and education professionals can be the "wide, sturdy bridge" Ms. Nimz seeks to connect scientific knowledge of the human brain to applications of that research in the classroom. But before that bridge is completed, we need to allow some flexibility. In order to help educators make sense of the massive amounts of information, I propose a two-tiered structure in which factual, collaborative brain research is designated as such and educational strategies strongly *suggested* by neuroscientific data are identified as *interpretations* of that research. The resulting structure will change with time because the interpretive tier will become more concrete as initial interpretations are supported or contradicted by subsequent neuroscience.

The first step is to debunk the neuromyths. Even some of the purest, most accurately reported neuroscience research has been misinterpreted. People trying to capitalize on research with their elixirs, books, cure-all learning theories, and curriculum packages have perpetrated much of the damage. Other folks have unintentionally made errors of interpretation when they have been unfairly asked for scientific evidence to support the strategies they have been using successfully for years.

But it is important to understand that some research findings can be applied to education now. For example, a review of neuroplasticity research shows how collaboration across fields, with certain checks and balances, can lead to classroom strategies that can add to teaching success.

Brain research has not yet provided a direct connection between classroom interventions and brain function or structure, but that does not mean it is irrelevant. Its use is akin to the "off-label" uses of medications by doctors. While Food and Drug Administration regulations require that the label information and advertising of a medication indicate the drug's use only for specific, approved conditions, physicians, based on their *knowledge and available current information,* may prescribe a medication for a use not indicated in the approved labeling. In the same way, educators should use their understanding of brain-learning research to evaluate, develop, and use strategies that are neuro-*logical,* based on *knowledge and available current information.*

Neuromyths

We study history, in part, so that we can learn from the mistakes of the past. Analyzing the errors in interpretation that led to brain-learning myths helps us evaluate the interpretive strengths and limitations of neuroimaging and other current neuroscientific research and avoid misinterpretation.

I go through the research in my fields of neuroscience and education with the goal of finding scientific studies that relate to learning and that adhere to the medical model of limiting the variables and confining interpretation to objective data. Then I seek cognitive testing of the conclusions neuroscientists make from their data. Do the study's data about how the brain responds to a specific input or stimulus correlate with the cognitive test? When I find a valid fit between the neuroscience and the cognitive testing, I go in search of the holy grail: objective evaluation of the effect of the intervention on statistically appropriate numbers of students in their classrooms. To my knowledge, there has not yet been a strategy or intervention that has made it through all three of these filters.

Misinterpreted neuroscientific data have led to beliefs that some people cling to despite objective evidence to the contrary. For example, it has taken more than a decade to debunk the left brain/right brain oversimplification of learning styles, even though neuroimaging studies have, for more than a decade, demonstrated that human cognition is far too complex to be controlled by a single hemisphere. We now know that although parts of the brain are particularly active during certain memory or learning activities, these regions do not work in isolation. There are networks throughout both hemispheres of the brain that constantly communicate, and even these neural networks change in response to genetics and environment throughout our lives.

In the December 1999 *Kappan,* John Bruer reviewed several decades of biological and neuroimaging research and revealed important unconnected dots between laboratory findings and the theories that hitchhiked on the research. For example, Bruer took on the popular assumptions "correlating" synaptic-density growth, high brain metabolism, critical brain-growth periods, and their proposed long-range effects on intelligence and found several weak foundations. He pointed out the flaws in the assumption that critical brain-growth periods of rapid synapse formation are windows of opportunity for instruction geared to those parts of the brain. He reported contradictory research, such as findings that brains build knowledge and store memories with no drop in efficiency long after

peak rates of synaptic, axonal, and dendritic growth have leveled off in adolescence.

Bruer also questioned whether increased cortical-glucose metabolism, as measured by PET scans, is direct evidence of rapid growth in synaptic density during the so-called critical periods. This, in turn, called into question the correlations between high metabolic activity measured by neuroimaging and periods of increased potential for learning that were the basis for claims that brain research *proved* that increased environmental stimulation of students during critical brain-growth phases resulted in more learning.

Neuroplasticity and Pruning

It is important for educators to remember that the absence of a positive correlation between neuroimaging data and environmental stimulation does not mean that stimulating classrooms are not valuable for learning. It is likely that environmental stimulation does influence learning. However, that theory has not yet been proved by brain research. I remain hopeful, as does Bruer, that the indirect evidence from neuroimaging and other neuroscience research has the potential to suggest teaching strategies and environmental stimuli that are valuable for learning. One promising area of ongoing study is neuroplasticity and pruning.

One longtime misconception held that brain growth stops with birth and is followed by a lifetime of brain-cell death. Now we know that, though most of the neurons where information is stored are present at birth, there is lifelong growth of the support and connecting cells that enrich the communication between neurons (axons, dendrites, synapses, glia) and even some brain regions that continue to form new neurons (neurogenesis) throughout life, such as in the dentate nucleus of the hippocampus and the olfactory cortex.[1] Even after the last big spurt of brain growth in early adolescence, neurotrophins (growth-stimulating proteins) appear elevated in the brain regions and networks associated with new learning and memory formation.[2]

Neuroplasticity is the genetically driven overproduction of synapses and the environmentally driven maintenance and pruning of synaptic connections.[3] Once neural networks are formed, it is the brain's plasticity that allows it to reshape and reorganize these networks, at least partly, in response to increased or decreased use of these pathways.[4] After repeated practice, the connections grow stronger, that is, repeated stimulation makes each neuron more likely to trigger the next connected neuron.[5] The most frequently stimulated connections also become thicker with more myelin coating, making them more efficient.[6]

While active cells require blood to bring nourishment and clear away waste, cells that are inactive do not send messages to the circulatory system to send blood. This reduced blood flow means that calcium ions accumulate around the cell and are not washed away. This calcium ion build-up triggers the secretion of the enzyme calpain, which causes cells to self-destruct, in what is called the pruning process.[7] When unused memory circuits break down, the brain becomes more efficient as it no longer metabolically sustains the pruned cells.

As neurological research provides information about various stages of brain maturation through neuroplasticity and pruning, we come full circle to Jean Piaget's theories regarding the developmental stages of the thought processes of children. If neuroplasticity and pruning represent stages of brain maturation, this may be indirect evidence in support of Piaget's theory that, until there is maturation of brain neural networks, children do not have the circuitry to learn specific things or perform certain tasks.[8]

These neuroplasticity findings allow us to consider which strategies and classroom environments promote increased stimulation of memory or strengthening of cognitive neural networks. For example, appealing to a variety of learning styles when we review important instructional information could provide repeated stimulation to multiple neural networks containing this information. Each type of sensory memory is stored in the lobe that receives the input from that sensory system. Visual memory is stored in the occipital lobes, auditory memory is stored in the temporal lobes, and memories of tactile experiences are stored in the parietal lobes. There could be greater potential for activation, restimulation, and strengthening of these networks with practice or review of the information through multi-sensory learning, resulting in increased network efficiency for memory storage and retrieval.

Off-Label Prescribing

Jensen cautions, "Brain-based education suggests that we not wait 20 years until each of these correlations is proven beyond any possible doubt." The toll of one-size-fits-all education with its teaching to the standardized tests is so high that it calls for a compromise of the pure medical research model. We do need to take some temporary leaps of faith across the parts of the bridge that are not yet sturdy and try interventions before the research is complete.

When a patient has exhausted all the regular treatments for epilepsy or a brain tumor, neurologists try investigative therapies or "off-label" uses of medications. While off-label medications have not completed FDA testing for the condition in question, the physician believes, through experience and knowledge of pharmacology, that the risk is worth taking in order to treat the patient's disease. For students at risk in our schools, we should use a similar strategy, that is, trying new methods even though they are not yet proven.

However, educators need to use these methods prudently. We need to discuss our successes and acknowledge what doesn't work. Our successful strategic interventions may not yet be proven by brain research, but that doesn't mean they are not valuable. Nevertheless, educators need

to beware of opportunists who claim that their strategies are proven by brain research.

Until There Is Hard Evidence

The brain-research evidence for certain instructional strategies continues to increase, but there still is no sturdy bridge between neuroscience and what educators do in the classroom. But educators' knowledge and experience will enable them to use the knowledge gained from brain research in their classrooms. For example, choice, interest-driven investigation, collaboration, intrinsic motivation, and creative problem solving are associated with increased levels of such neurotransmitters as dopamine, as well as the pleasurable state dopamine promotes.[9] Novelty, surprise, and teaching that connects with students' past experiences and personal interests and that is low in threat and high in challenge are instructional strategies that appear to be correlated with increased information passage through the brain's information filters, such as the amygdala and reticular activating system. Lessons in which students are engaged and invested in goals they helped to create have the potential to stimulate and restimulate networks of new memories as students actively process information in the construction of knowledge.[10] These instructional strategies date back to theories developed decades before neuroimaging. But they are consistent with the increasing pool of neuroimaging, behavioral, and developmental psychology.

We can look forward to a time when human brain mapping, correlated with the other areas of neuroscience, will reveal additional brain mechanisms involved in memory and learning to help us define the most successful teaching strategies for the variety of learners we teach. We are likely to have neuroimaging tools to identify presymptomatic students at risk and genetic testing that will isolate the precise genes that predispose children to such conditions as ADHD or the various dyslexias. With these powerful diagnostic tools, cognitive and education professionals will be able to design strategies to provide at-risk children with the interventions needed to strengthen areas of weakness before they enter school and to develop differentiated instruction allowing all learners to achieve to their highest potentials.

University psychology and education departments are already obtaining neuroimaging scanners. This will increase educators' influence on what is studied. Teachers will communicate with researchers about the strategies they find successful, so researchers can investigate what is happening in students' brains when those strategies are used. Researchers will need to make their data accessible to teachers who can develop new strategies that bring the fruits of the research to the students in their classrooms.

With time, collaboration, and greater integration of the neuroscience of learning into schools of education and into professional development, educators who stay on top of the science will play leading roles in designing and implementing curriculum and classroom strategies that are effective and consistent with the discoveries of how the brain learns best.

For now, the most powerful asset we educators have to influence the direction of education policy is our up-to-date knowledge and understanding of the most accurate, collaborative, neuroscientific research. With that knowledge, we can remain vigilant in our scrutiny of any premature or misleading assertions about interventions claimed to be proven by brain research. And we will be ready to create, evaluate, and implement the best, truly brain-based instruction in our classrooms. These will be important challenges to meet, but the next decade will reward us with extraordinary opportunities. It may not seem like it now, but we are on the brink of the most exciting time in history to be an educator.

References

1. Peter Eriksson et al., "Neurogenesis in the Adult Human Hippocampus," *Nature Medicine,* vol. 4, 1998, pp. 1313–17.
2. Soo Kyung Kang et al., "Neurogenesis of Rhesus Adipose Stromal Cells," *Journal of Cell Science,* vol. 117, 2004, pp. 4289–90.
3. Dante Cicchetti and W. John Curtis, "The Developing Brain and Neural Plasticity: Implications for Normality, Psychopathology, and Resilience," in Dante Cicchetti and D. J. Cohen, eds., *Developmental Psychopathology: Developmental Neuroscience,* 2nd ed. (New York: Wiley, 2006), p. 11.
4. Jay N. Giedd et al., "Brain Development During Childhood and Adolescence: A Longitudinal MRI Study," *Nature Neuroscience,* vol. 2, 1999, pp. 861–63.
5. Harry Chugani, "Biological Basis of Emotions: Brain Systems and Brain Development," *Pediatrics,* vol. 102, 1998, pp. 1225–29.
6. Nitin Gogtay, "Dynamic Mapping of Human Cortical Development During Childhood Through Early Adulthood," *Proceedings of the National Academy of Sciences,* vol. 101, 2004, pp. 8174–79.
7. Philip Seeman, "Images in Neuroscience: Brain Development, X: Pruning During Development," *American Journal of Psychiatry,* vol. 156, 1999, p. 168.
8. Jean Piaget, "Intellectual Evolution from Adolescence to Adulthood," *Vita Humana,* vol. 15, 1972, pp. 1–12.
9. Panayotics Thanos et al., "The Selective Dopamine Antagonist," *Pharmacology, Biochemistry and Behavior,* vol. 81, 2005, pp. 190–97.
10. Alfie Kohn, "The Cult of Rigor and the Loss of Joy," *Education Week,* 15 September 2004, available at www.alfiekohn.org/articles_subject.htm.

JUDY WILLIS, MD, MED, was a practicing neurologist and more recently an elementary and middle school teacher.

Dan Willingham

 **NO**

When and How Neuroscience Applies to Education

I agree with Eric Jensen on several important points, among them: that neuroscientific data are relevant to educational research, that these data have already proved useful, and that neuroscience alone should not be expected to generate classroom-ready prescriptions. I sharply disagree with him, however, on the prospects for neuroscience to make frequent and important contributions to education.

I set two criteria for a "contribution" to education: the data must tell us something that we did not already know, and that something must hold the promise of helping teachers or students. For example, I expect that most teachers know that students do not learn well if they are hungry or uncomfortably warm. What then does an understanding of the neurobiology of hunger and its effect on cognition add to a teacher's practice?

One might argue that teachers should understand *why* they do what they do, for example, why they ensure that the room is comfortable. I disagree. All of us make use of technologies that we do not understand, and we do so without concern because understanding or ignorance wouldn't change practice. I don't understand what my computer hardware is doing as I type this reply, but if I did, that knowledge would not change how I typed or what I wrote. Thus, while it might be rewarding for a teacher to understand some neurobiology, I argue that education has not moved forward unless that knowledge improves his or her teaching.

So under what conditions do neuroscientific findings improve education? How do we integrate neuroscientific data with educational theory and practice? It's not enough to say that "the brain is intimately involved in and connected with everything educators and students do at school," which is Jensen's premise. That statement is true, but trivially so, because the brain is intimately involved in *anything* related to human affairs. The question is how we leverage what we know about the brain to help us better understand the processes of education. Jensen relies too heavily on his intuition that, because education relies on the brain, knowledge of the brain is *bound* to help.

But knowledge of the brain is not bound to help. This is where the problem of levels of analysis proves vital. Let's set neuroscience aside for a moment and consider how the levels problem plays out in cognitive psychology, using a simple example.

We know that memory is more enduring if you "overlearn" material—that is, continue studying it after

you've mastered it.[1] So why not apply that knowledge to the classroom? Why not have students rehearse important facts (for example, multiplication tables) and not quit even when they have mastered them? Any classroom teacher knows that it's not that simple, because continuous practice will be purchased at considerable cost to motivation. So here's the rub: for the sake of simplicity, cognitive psychologists intentionally isolate one component of the mind (e.g., memory or attention) when they study it. But in the classroom, all of the components operate simultaneously. So a principle from the cognitive lab might backfire when it's put into the more complex classroom environment. That's the problem of levels of analysis. Cognitive psychologists study one level—individual components of the mind—but educators operate on a different level—the entire mind of the child. (Or, better put, the mind of the child in the context of a classroom, which complicates things still further.)

Now, how can we add neuroscientific data to this picture? Parts of the brain don't map onto the cognitive system, one for one. There is not a single part of the brain for "learning" and one for "attention." Each of those cognitive functions is served by a network of brain structures. "Memory" relies on the hippocampus, entorhinal cortex, thalamus, and frontal cortex, at the least. Suppose I take an observation about the hippocampus—which I know contributes to memory—and try to draw a classroom application from that. In so doing, I'm assuming that whatever happens in the hippocampus is a reliable guide to what is happening in the memory system as a whole, even though the hippocampus is just one part of that system. And on top of that, I'm still making the other assumption—that if I do something known to benefit memory when the memory system is isolated (as in the laboratory), it will still benefit memory when applied to the mind taken as a whole in the classroom.

But, of course, Jensen never advocated going straight from hippocampus to classroom! He explicitly emphasized that brain-based learning must be multidisciplinary. He's simply arguing that neuroscience should have a place at the table, so to speak. What I argue, in turn, is that the levels-of-analysis problem greatly reduces the likelihood that neuroscience will offer educators much of a payoff. Educators should use these data, by all means, but they should also expect that they won't find occasion to do so very often. As one gets more distant from the desired level of analysis (the child in the classroom), the probability of learning anything useful diminishes. That's true because the interactions between components at one level of analysis make it difficult to predict what's going to happen at the next level of analysis. That is, if you care about whether a child is learning, knowing conditions that make the memory system in isolation operate more efficiently (which is what a cognitive psychologist might contribute) is no guarantee that you will know whether the child in the classroom will learn more quickly. And knowing whether conditions are right for neurogenesis (which is what a neuroscientist might contribute) is no guarantee that you know that the child's memory system will operate more efficiently.

Let's further consider Jensen's example—that exercise is correlated with neurogenesis. It is perfectly plausible that a daily exercise period would benefit learning. But it's just as plausible that exercise would, at the same time, have a negative effect on attention or on motivation. We wouldn't know until we examined the effect of exercise in a real-life school setting. Jensen agrees. And presumably if we couldn't detect a positive effect of exercise on educational outcomes, we would conclude that, neurogenesis notwithstanding, the cognitive system as a whole does not benefit from exercise. Likewise, if careful behavioral research indicated that exercise *did* help in a school setting and neuroscientists protested that it ought not to, we would consider the data from the classroom to be decisive.

So what has neuroscience done for us? In this case, not much, because it's the classroom data that really matter. In principle, neuroscientists might suggest something that we could try in the classroom, and then we would decide—by behavioral (not neuroscientific) measures— whether it works or doesn't work. That would be a valuable contribution, but I don't believe that there will be many such situations—that is, one in which neuroscientists say, "Hey, maybe you should try this at school," and educational researchers say, "Never thought of that!" The notion that exercise helps cognition, for example, is hardly new.

Still, there are other, more indirect, ways that neuroscience can illuminate educational theory. Although space limitations preclude a thorough treatment, I will mention three techniques.[2]

First, there are times when two well-developed behavioral theories make very similar predictions, making them difficult to separate with behavioral data. But at the neural level, it might be possible to make different predictions. For example, the nature of dyslexia was, for some time, controversial. Although some behavioral research indicated that it had a phonological basis,[3] other researchers argued that phonology was not the fundamental problem in the disorder. Behavioral data were not conclusive.[4] Brain-imaging data showed dyslexics to have decreased activation in brain regions known to support phonological coding,[5] thus providing support to the phonological theory.

Second, neuroscientific data can show us that there is diversity where there appeared to be unity, or unity where one might suspect diversity. That is, we might discover that what seemed like a single type of behavior (e.g., "learning") is actually supported by two anatomically distinct brain systems. That indicates (but doesn't prove) that what we thought was a single function is in fact two different functions, operating in different ways. The study of learning and memory was revolutionized in the 1980s by such observations.[6] Neuroscientific data might also support the opposite conclusion. That is, we might suspect that two cognitive functions are separate but find that they rely on the same anatomical circuit. For example, although dyslexics show some diversity of behavioral symptoms across cultures and languages, the anatomical locus is quite consistent (at least in alphabetic languages), which indicates that the disorder is the same.[7]

Third, neuroscientific data might prove useful for the diagnosis of some learning disabilities. Researchers know that dyslexic readers show patterns of brain activity on electroencephalograms that differ from those of average readers.[8] Several laboratories are attempting to discern whether abnormal brain activity is measurable *before* reading instruction begins, and there have been some promising results.[9] Early diagnosis would allow early intervention, which could be an enormous advance.

In summary, I agree with Jensen that neuroscientific data can be of use to education. Indeed, they already have been. However, careful specification of how neuroscientific data and theory would actually apply to educational affairs leads to a more sober estimate of their value. The path to the improvement of education has proved steep and thorny. Neuroscience offers an occasional assist, not a significant shortcut.

References

1. Thomas F. Gilbert, "Overlearning and the Retention of Meaningful Prose," *Journal of General Psychology,* vol. 56, 1957, pp. 281–89.
2. For more details, see Daniel T. Willingham and Elizabeth Dunn, "What Neuroimaging and Brain Localization Can Do, Cannot Do, and Should Not Do for Social Psychology," *Journal of Personality and Social Psychology,* vol. 85, 2003, pp. 662–71; and Daniel T. Willingham and John W. Lloyd, "How Can Brain Imaging Research Help Education?," paper presented at the annual meeting of the American Educational Research Association, Chicago, 2007.
3. Richard K. Wagner and Joseph K. Torgesen, "The Nature of Phonological Processing and Its Causal Role in the Acquisition of Reading Skills," *Psychological Bulletin,* vol. 101, 1987, pp. 192–212.
4. For a review of theories, see Peggy McCardle, Hollis S. Scarborough, and Hugh W. Catts, "Predicting, Explaining, and Preventing Children's Reading Difficulties," *Learning Disabilities Research & Practice,* vol. 16, 2001, pp. 230–39.

5. Judith M. Rumsey et al., "Failure to Activate the Left Temporoparietal Cortex in Dyslexia: An Oxygen 15 Positron Emission Tomographic Study," *Archives of Neurology,* vol. 49, 1992, pp. 527–34.

6. For a review, see Daniel B. Willingham, "Memory Systems in the Human Brain," *Neuron,* January 1997, pp. 5–8.

7. Eraldo Paulesu et al., "Dyslexia: Cultural Diversity and Biological Unity," *Science,* vol. 291, 2001, pp. 2165–67.

8. Gal Ben-Yehudah, Karen Banai, and Merav Ahissar, "Patterns of Deficit in Auditory Temporal Processing Among Dyslexic Adults," *Neuroreport,* vol. 15, 2004, pp. 627–31.

9. Kimberly A. Espy, Dennis L. Molfese, and Victoria J. Molfese, "Development of Auditory Event-Related Potentials in Young Children and Relations to Word-Level Reading Abilities at Age 8 Years," *Annals of Dyslexia,* June 2004, pp. 9–38.

DAN WILLINGHAM, PHD, is a professor of psychology at the University of Virginia, Charlottesville.

EXPLORING THE ISSUE

Do Recent Discoveries About the Brain Have Implications for Classroom Practice?

Critical Thinking and Reflection

1. We have discussed whether and how research on brain function informs educational practice. Could the study of classroom practices also inform brain research? Why or why not? Provide examples to support your conclusion.
2. Assume that children with dyslexia (a reading disorder) are born with brains "wired" differently than those of other children. What would this mean for the teaching of reading?
3. Do you think that Willis and Willingham really differ in their views about how to translate brain science findings into educational practices? Or do they differ in the views of specific findings and their implications? Why or why not?

Is There Common Ground?

Any plausible theory of learning must include the assumption that learning involves the brain. Why, then, is there any controversy about the implications of brain research for educational practice? Doesn't any finding about the brain tell us something useful about how to teach? Unfortunately, it is not always possible to move directly from knowledge about the brain to recommendations for educational practice. This is because learning always involves more than the activity of the brain. Learning results from the interaction of the child (and, of course, his or her brain) with the environment.

Consider, for example, the finding that the "spurt" in children's vocabulary seen at 18 to 24 months of age is associated with a rather dramatic increase in the synaptic density and activity of the brain. This finding is important because it suggests that something may "click" in children's brains at this time that increases their preparedness to learn words. But this finding does not by itself tell us very much about what parents and educators should do during this time to assist children. On the one hand, it may be that children are so prepared at this time that they can pick up words effortlessly from just about any sort of interaction and in any environment. In this case, there might little we can or should do to help with vocabulary learning. On the other hand, what adults do when children are ready to "spurt" may matter a great deal. In that case, there might need to be a tightly orchestrated match between biology and what parents, teachers, and other people do when they talk to and interact with the child. Deciding between these alternatives is not always clear based on studies of the brain; we need studies of the environment as well.

Create Central

www.mhhe.com/createcentral

Additional Resources

Nancy Frey and Douglas Fisher, "Reading and the Brain: What Early Childhood Educators Need to Know," *Early Childhood Education Journal* (vol. 38, 2010).

Kenneth W. Gasser, "Five Ideas for 21st Century Math Classrooms," *American Secondary Education* (vol. 39 Summer 2011).

Mark H. Johnson, *Developmental Cognitive Neuroscience*, 2nd ed. (Blackwell, 2005).

Robert J. Sternberg, "The Answer Depends on the Question: A Reply to Eric Jensen," *Phi Delta Kappan* (February 2008).

Internet References . . .

National Institutes of Health

> http://NIH.gov

Centre for Neuroscience in Education, Cambridge University

> http://www.cne.psychol.cam.ac.uk/

Neuroscience Education Institute

> http://www.neiglobal.com/

Selected, Edited, and with Issue Framing Material by:
Leonard Abbeduto, *University of California, Davis*
and
Frank Symons, *University of Minnesota*

ISSUE

Do Video Games Promote Violent Behavior in Students?

YES: Brad J. Bushman, Hannah R. Rothstein, and Craig A. Anderson, from "Much Ado about Something: Violent Video Game Effects and a School of Red Herring: Reply to Ferguson and Kilburn (2010)" *Psychological Bulleting* (vol. 136, no. 2, 2010)

NO: Christopher J. Ferguson and John Kilburn, from "Much Ado about Nothing: The Misestimation and Overinterpretation of Violent Video Game Effects in Eastern and Western Nations: Comment on Anderson et al. (2010)" *Psychological Bulletin* (vol. 136, no. 2, 2010)

Learning Outcomes

After reading this issue, you will be able to:

- Describe the general idea behind and a number of issues related to synthesizing research.
- Compare different perspectives on the seriousness of the problem in relation of other "high-risk" behaviors in childhood and youth.
- Describe the range of possible effects of video game violence on children and youth development.

ISSUE SUMMARY

YES: Brad Bushman, Hannah Rothstein, and Craig Anderson argue that the research-based evidence synthesized statistically across multiple studies—a meta-analysis—is clear and that violent video game exposure is causally related to later aggression.

NO: Christopher Ferguson and John Kilburn argue that the meta-analysis of research studies examining the effects of violent video game exposure is flawed and that there is not a compelling collection of evidence supporting a causal link between exposure and later aggression.

T wo sides of the same coin are highlighted by the selections addressing the issue of whether exposure to violent video games (violent video games, VVG) is causally related to later aggression. One side is the substantive issue manifest, in part, as the latest iteration of the role of technology (modern media) and its relation to child and youth development and outcomes (e.g., exposure to television violence, exposure to movie violence, and now exposure to video game violence and later aggression and violence). More on the substantive side of the coin later; the other side of the coin is methodological.

One need not be a statistical expert to appreciate the points raised by the authors of the papers and their different perspectives. What is striking is how clearly different their conclusions are about the proposition that viewing VVG is causally related to later violent behavior. The stakes are high, with public policy decisions determined and parent practices affected, in part, by what the studies "say,"

or maybe more accurately what the experts conclude about what the studies "say." When there are numerous studies in a given area, one way to give them a collective "voice" is to statistically synthesize them by creating common metrics such that study results can be pooled and compared. The process is referred to as meta-analysis. Specifically, a meta-analysis is an "analysis of analyses" and proceeds by identifying a common effect size across studies in relation to their primary outcomes. An effect size is a way to quantify the strength or magnitude of a relation between two variables (e.g., the treatment and effect, the input and output, the exposure and the outcome, etc.). In the present context, the Anderson et al. meta-analysis, which the two selections are discussing, was based on calculating effect sizes from studies investigating the relation between exposure to VVG and later violent behavior and related outcomes. Each study-level effect size (i.e., indicators of magnitude of effect or strength of the relationship) can then be statistically "handled" (weighted depending on certain characteristics of a study), and combined to generate an estimate of the overall effect size.

Herein lies part of the problem; the effect size is an estimate of the strength of the relation. Estimates can be biased by a variety of factors. There are differences of opinion regarding the degree to which different factors bias estimates and perhaps more importantly what to do about them. One example highlighted by the two selections is the problem of publication bias. Publication bias refers to statistically significant results being more likely to be published. In other words, if a study is well designed and executed but does not find a statistically significant result, there is a bias against its publication. Think about this issue with respect to meta-analysis as a procedure and also a process to help ascertain the state of our knowledge in a given area. Procedurally, part of the task is to identify and gather up all of the research conducted in a given area. So, in this instance, all of the studies that have been conducted to test the relation between VVG exposure and later violent behavior. Not all of that work is published; some of it will be in the form of conference proceedings, abstracts, doctoral dissertations, etc. (the so-called "gray literature"). And there will be instances of "file drawer" problems—studies that were conducted but the results were not statistically significant and the study was not published. Depending on the approach to meta-analysis used, a "file drawer" study may or may not make it into the meta-analysis. As a process to get to the best judgment of what we know, it is problematic to think that there are results that may be missed, particularly if the studies that are included versus those missed (because of publication bias) differ in systematic ways. As the two selections and their authors illustrate, there are differences of opinion about how publication bias is considered and the methods used to reduce or at least expose the bias. The issue highlights the complexity underlying a seemingly straightforward empirical issue—whether exposure to VVG is causally related to later violent or aggressive behavior.

There are definitional issues, as well, that matter and lead into measurement differences across studies that can undermine our confidence in "hearing" what the evidence "has to say." Ferguson and Kilburn make the point that the way in which aggression is measured in many of the studies is unstandardized (i.e., the construct "aggression" is operationalized and measured in different ways). From the meta-analytic perspective, one potential problem is that unstandardized measures may influence effect size estimates, yet another way of introducing bias into the process. Bushman, Rothstein, and Anderson acknowledge the issue, but disagree that it is necessarily operating in the research on aggression and VVG and cite evidence supporting their perspective.

Substantively, then, what are we—as educators, clinicians, researchers, policymakers, consumers, parents, students—to make of this? That there is disagreement about the evidence base regarding the issue of whether VVG exposure is a causal risk factor for later violent and aggressive behavior. In developed countries there is considerable exposure to violence in the media through television programming, movies, and video games. The issue has, in different ways, been acknowledged, addressed, and investigated for many decades. Many professional organizations and associations (e.g., American Psychological Association) and government agencies (e.g., U.S. Office of the Surgeon General) have reached similar conclusions that media violence exposure leads to increases in violent and aggressive behavior (see D. A. Gentile and colleague's paper in the journal *Social Issues and Policy Review*, vol. 1, pp. 15–61). At the same time, as Ferguson and Kilburn point out, youth violence overall is trending down while VVG use is increasing, which does not immediately suggest a clear link at a societal level. Clearly, the issue is complex but important. Considerable resources have been invested in resolving it. And yet, as exemplified by the exchange, reaching a uniform consensus with absolute certainty or complete agreement will be difficult (if not impossible). The best we can hope for, though, is that the process of science will continue to shed light on the problem so that evidence can be evaluated and weighted fairly and decisions made based on our best judgment of the available empirical evidence.

Brad J. Bushman, Hannah R. Rothstein, and Craig A. Anderson

Much Ado about Something: Violent Video Game Effects and a School of Red Herring: Reply to Ferguson and Kilburn (2010)

We appreciate the opportunity to reply to the Ferguson and Kilburn (2010) critique of our meta-analysis on violent video game effects (Anderson et al., 2010). Healthy debate about such issues is how scientific knowledge progresses. In this reply we address the criticisms Ferguson and Kilburn have raised about our meta-analysis.

Author Expertise in Violent Media Research and Meta-Analysis

The three authors who wrote this reply have considerable expertise in conducting violent media research, in meta-analysis, or in both (as do the other authors on our meta-analysis). Two of us (Anderson and Bushman) have been conducting research on violent media (including violent video games) for at least 20 years (e.g., Anderson & Ford, 1986; Bushman & Geen, 1990). Two of us (Bushman and Rothstein) teach graduate-level courses on meta-analysis, have written meta-analysis books (Borenstein, Hedges, Higgins, & Rothstein, 2009; Wang & Bushman, 1999), have contributed chapters to reference books on meta-analysis (Bushman & Wang, 2009; Rothstein, 2003; Rothstein & Hopewell, 2009; Rothstein, McDaniel, & Borenstein, 2001), and have written peer-reviewed articles that advance meta-analytic theory and methods (Bushman & Wang, 1995, 1996; Hedges, Cooper, & Bushman, 1992; Ioannidis, Patsopoulos, & Rothstein, 2008; Rothstein, 2008b; Rothstein & McDaniel, 1989; Schmidt et al., 1993; Valentine, Pigott, & Rothstein, in press; Wade, Turner, Rothstein, & Lavenberg, 2006; Wang & Bushman, 1998). One of us (Rothstein) is an expert on publication bias in meta-analysis (McDaniel, Rothstein, & Whetzel, 2006; Rothstein, 2004, 2008a, 2008b; Rothstein & Hopewell, 2009; Rothstein, Sutton, & Borenstein, 2005).

Excluding Unpublished Studies from Meta-Analytic Reviews

The term *unpublished study* means that the study was not published in a peer-reviewed journal, although it could have been published in another outlet (e.g., book). In their comment on our meta-analysis, Ferguson and Kilburn (2010) stated that "Anderson et al. failed to note that many scholars have been critical of the inclusion of unpublished studies in meta-analyses" (p. 175). This is simply false, at least when considering the writings of meta-analytic scholars. Consider the following statements from individuals who have written books on how to conduct meta-analytic reviews. Lipsey and Wilson (2001) stated that including only published material because it is refereed and represents "higher quality research" is "generally not very convincing" (p. 19). Petticrew and Roberts (2005) recommended searching for journal articles, books and book chapters, conference proceedings, dissertations, and other "gray" literature. Cooper (2009) specifically pointed out the limitations of relying only on peer-reviewed journal articles, stating that

> *bias against null findings and confirmatory bias means that quality-controlled journal articles (and conference presentations) should not be used as the sole source of information for a research synthesis* unless you can convincingly argue that these biases do not exist in the specific topic area. (p. 63, italics in the original)

Borenstein et al. (2009) stated that "publication status cannot be used as a proxy for quality; and in our opinion should not be used as a basis for inclusion or exclusion of studies" (p. 279). Littell, Corcoran, and Pillial (2008) urged individuals who conduct a meta-analysis to invest the extra effort needed to obtain gray or unpublished studies.

The view advanced by Egger and Smith, who are cited by Ferguson and Kilburn (2010) as arguing that inclusion of unpublished studies increases bias, was taken out of context. In fact, what Egger and Smith said is that inclusion of data from unpublished studies can, under some conditions, introduce bias, but they did not recommend limiting meta-analyses to peer-reviewed journal articles (see also Egger, Dickersin, & Smith, 2001). The Cook et al. article (1993) cited by Ferguson and Kilburn is the report of an opinion survey conducted almost 20 years ago among journal editors. This survey is out of date, and more recent surveys indicate that opinions have changed (e.g., Tetzlaff, Moher, Pham, & Altman 2006).

In summary, the current consensus among meta-analysis experts is that publication status is not a good proxy for methodological rigor and that any study that (otherwise) meets the inclusion criteria for a meta-analysis should not be excluded because it was not published in a peer-reviewed journal. There is absolutely no support for Ferguson and Kilburn's position that unpublished studies should not be included in a meta-analysis.

Publication Bias

There is ample evidence from multiple sources that publication bias is pervasive. That is why meta-analysts are urged to try to track down unpublished studies. Even when a researcher sets out to locate all potentially eligible studies, and unpublished articles such as dissertations and conference proceedings are included in a review, it is possible that some studies meeting the inclusion criteria were not found, and that these studies differed in some systematic way from those that were found. The purpose of conducting publication bias analyses is to assess the likelihood that, if such studies exist, they would threaten the validity of the results obtained by meta-analyzing only the retrieved studies.

In their meta-analytic reviews (Ferguson, 2007a, 2007b; Ferguson & Kilburn, 2009), Ferguson and his colleagues claimed that the trim and fill technique produces a "corrected" coefficient; it does not. In fact, the trim and fill technique produces an estimate of the effect adjusted for imputed missing studies. Both the originators of trim and fill technique (cf. Duval, 2005) and other meta-analysis experts who advocate its use have stated unequivocally that one should not view the adjusted estimate as a corrected or more accurate estimate of the effect, because it is based on imputed data points. Trim and fill is most appropriately considered a useful sensitivity analysis that assesses the potential impact of missing studies on the meta-analysis. It does this by examining the degree of divergence between the original effect-size estimate and the trim and fill adjusted effect-size estimate. This point is made numerous times in the key reference source for publication bias in meta-analysis (Rothstein et al., 2005), including in chapters cited by Ferguson and his colleagues.

Additionally, the key assumption of trim and fill is that the observed asymmetry in effects is due to publication bias rather than to real differences between effects found in small- versus large-sample studies. Sterne and Egger (2001) noted that it is possible that studies with smaller samples actually do have larger effects, perhaps because the smaller studies used different populations or designs than did the larger ones. Sterne and Egger coined the term *small study effect* to denote this alternative explanation for the results of the trim and fill and other publication bias procedures (e.g., Begg and Mazumder and Egger tests). Ferguson and his colleagues do not mention this critical caveat, even though these are the procedures they are relying upon.

Finally, it has been established that under conditions of heterogeneity, trim and fill may "impute" missing studies that do not actually exist in file drawers or anywhere else (Peters, Sutton, Jones, Abrams, & Rushton, 2007;

Terrin, Schmid, Lau, & Olkin, 2003). The results of both our and Ferguson's work show that the effect sizes are quite heterogeneous. This is yet another reason to interpret the trim and fill results as a test of the robustness of the observed effects to the threat of publication bias, rather than as the correct effects.

We endorse Ferguson and Kilburn's (2010) observation that the politicization of this research area increases the risk for bias. Unlike the typical scenario in which publication bias is created by censoring on the basis of statistical significance, in politicized areas of research, there is at least the possibility that data are censored on the basis of political or other personal interests of researchers, reviewers, or editors. Thus, unlike typical publication bias, where one is concerned that the small effect size, nonsignificant results are missing (i.e., the ones that show that violent video games have no or minimal effects), in cases such as the current one, there is equal cause for concern that some large effect size results could be missing due to deliberate suppression. Because we considered both possibilities, we used the trim and fill method to look for putatively missing studies higher than the mean effect, as well as to look for putatively missing studies lower than the mean effect. We conducted these analyses on relatively homogeneous subgroups, in an attempt to avoid the problems that can occur when trim and fill is used when there is a lot of between study heterogeneity. The results, noted as sensitivity analyses and reported in Table 10 of Anderson et al. (2010), show that for some outcomes it appeared that low-effect studies were missing (the trim and fill adjusted correlation was lower than the observed correlation), whereas for other outcomes it appeared that high-effect studies were missing (the trim and fill adjusted correlation was higher than the observed correlation). We therefore do not understand Ferguson and Kilburn's (2010) objection to our conclusion that, overall "there is no evidence that publication or selection bias had an important influence on the results" (p. 167).

Inclusion Criteria and Classification of Studies as "Best Practice"

As stated in our article, unpublished studies were retrieved from PsycINFO and MEDLINE databases in the United States and from proceedings and annual reports in Japan. In addition, there were a number of "unpublished" Japanese studies from proceedings compilations. The publication bias analyses we conducted confirm that if we missed any unpublished studies, they would not have significantly influenced our findings.

Ferguson and Kilburn disagreed with our classification of some studies as "best practice." Agreement among coders was 93% for best practice studies. More important, the pattern of results was the same for best practice studies and for all studies. Ferguson and Kilburn (2010) stated that we were "disinclined toward Williams and Skoric (2005), despite the fact that this study does indeed (contrary to

Anderson et al.'s assertions) include a measure of verbal aggression at least as ecologically valid, if not more so, than many of those nominated as best practices." This study did not meet our inclusion criteria because it measured verbal rather than physical aggression.

There are a host of other problems with Ferguson and Kilburn's (2010) claims about what was (or was not) included in our meta-analysis. Indeed, detailing all of them would take more space than is allocated for such replies. None of the studies that they claimed we missed were in fact missed. Several studies that are now available were not available at the time of the cutoff for the meta-analysis (i.e., Ferguson & Rueda, in press; Ferguson, San Miguel, & Hartley, in press; Olson et al, 2009; Przybylski, Weinstein, Ryan, & Rigby, 2009). We could redo all the meta-analyses again, including these and other recent studies, but by the time we finished there would be still more studies. Besides, adding all of the newly available studies would not change the results of our meta-analysis in even a minor way, for two reasons: (a) the effect sizes are similar in size to the ones in our meta-analysis and (b) their sample sizes are not large enough to change the average effect size much, even if the new studies had effect sizes around zero (which they do not).

Posters, such as Barnett, Coulson, and Foreman (2008), are not included in PsycINFO or MEDLINE, so there could be no bias in our selection of posters. Furthermore, although Ferguson and Kilburn claimed that these authors had a published report in 2008, they failed to provide a reference for it and there is no record of it in PsycINFO or MEDLINE. Also, we did not ask any research groups for unpublished studies or posters.

It is unclear why Ferguson and Kilburn think that work by Ryan and his colleagues (Przybylski et al., 2009; Ryan, Rigby, & Przybylski, 2006) contradicts our meta-analysis findings. They studied why people are attracted to video games, not the effects of violent video games on aggression. The relevant data from all of the remaining research groups that "arguably, have presented research not in line with Anderson et al.'s hypotheses" (Ferguson & Kilburn, 2010, p. 175) were in fact included in our meta-analysis. Furthermore, even though each of these remaining studies failed to meet one or more best practice inclusion criteria, their effects were similar in size to those obtained in other studies ($r+ = .184$, $K = 7$, $N = 2,080$, $Z = 8.45$, $p < .001$). In summary, Ferguson and Kilburn failed to identify any biased search processes, any biased search outcomes, or any studies that should have been but were not included in our meta-analysis.

Magnitude of Effect of Violent Video Games on Aggressive Behavior

Ferguson and Kilburn (2010) stated, "Our analyses agree that the uncorrected estimate for violent video game effects is quite small ($r = .15$ in both analyses)." We are not sure where Ferguson and Kilburn came up with the $r = .15$

value. Perhaps they used the "best partials" estimate for all study designs, an estimate that actually does "correct" for gender differences in all studies and initial aggression levels in longitudinal studies (see Anderson et al., 2010, Table 4). The overall estimate of the effect of violent video games on aggression was $r = .19$ for all studies and $r = .24$ for studies of higher methodological quality.

Ferguson and Kilburn claimed that the .15 estimate is too liberal because it does not control for other risk factors, such as depression, peer group influence, and family environment. There are at least four problems with this claim. First, it is irrelevant to experimental studies in which participants are randomly assigned to groups. Second, the point estimates for cross-sectional studies were all larger than $r = .15$ ($rs = .26$, .17, and .19 for best raw, best partials, and full sample, respectively). Third, one cannot combine correlations from studies unless all studies controlled for exactly the same variables. Fourth, Ferguson and Kilburn do not mention that some well-known cross-sectional studies controlled for several individual-difference risk factors and still found significant violent video game effects (e.g., Anderson et al., 2004).

Ferguson and Kilburn (2010) considered the effects we obtained to be so small that they are not worth worrying about. Other meta-analyses cited by Ferguson and Kilburn as supposedly refuting the effect of violent video games on aggressive and violent behavior have found correlations in the same range (e.g., Sherry, 2001). What differs is not the magnitude of the obtained effects but rather how the effects are interpreted.

By conventional standards (Cohen, 1988), our correlations are between "small" ($r = .1$) and "medium" ($r = .3$) in size. However, this is the range of effects most commonly observed in social psychology. For example, one meta-analysis examined the magnitude of effects obtained in social psychology studies during the past century. The average effect obtained from 322 meta-analyses of more than 25,000 social psychology studies involving over 8 million participants was about $r = .2$ (Richard, Bond, & Stokes-Zoota, 2003). This not surprising, because human behavior is extremely complex and has multiple causes. For this reason Hemphill (2003) recommended a reconceptualization of effect size, in which $r = .1$ is small, $r = .2$ is medium, and $r = .3$ is large. Similarly, Lipsey (1990) recommended a reconceptualization of effect-size conventions, based on reviews of effects of social science interventions, in which $r = .07$ is small, $r = .22$ is medium, and $r = .41$ is large.

The effects we obtained for violent video games are similar in size to the effects of risk factors for physical health, such as exposure to lead, asbestos, or secondhand smoke (Bushman & Anderson, 2001). They are also similar in size to other risk factors for violent and aggressive behavior, such as poverty, substance abuse, and low IQ (U.S. Department of Health and Human Services, 2001). We do not consider the magnitude of these effects to be trivial. Neither do professional physical and mental health organizations, which issued the *Joint Statement on the Impact of Entertainment Violence on Children*. According to the statement, "Entertainment violence can lead to increases in aggressive attitudes, values, and behavior, particularly in children" (Congressional Public Health Summit, 2000, p. 1). The six organizations that signed the statement were the American Academy of Child and Adolescent Psychiatry, American Academy of Family Physicians, American Academy of Pediatrics, American Medical Association, American Psychiatric Association, and American Psychological Association. More recently, the American Psychological Association (2005) issued a similar statement on violent video game effects.

Finally, there are circumstances in which small effect sizes warrant serious concern: "When effects accumulate across time, or when large portions of the population are exposed to the risk factor, or when consequences are severe, statistically small effects become much more important (Abelson, 1985; Rosenthal, 1986, 1990). All three of these conditions apply to violent video game effects" (Anderson et al., 2010, p. 170).[1]

Effects of Violent Video Games on Serious Acts of Aggression or Violence

Ferguson and Kilburn (2010) probably are correct in noting that violent video games have a weaker effect on serious acts of aggression and violence than on less serious acts.[2] This is no surprise. Because serious acts of aggression and violence are relatively rare, they are difficult to predict using violent video game exposure or any other single risk factor. Violent crimes typically result from a combination of multiple risk factors. No single risk factor accounts for a large proportion of variance, but that does not mean that the risk factors are trivial and should be ignored.[3]

Unstandardized Aggression Measures

Ferguson and Kilburn (2010) raised a potentially valid point about the use of unstandardized aggression measures. Variations of the competitive reaction time task developed by Taylor (1967) have been used by aggression researchers for over 40 years. Different researchers have used different measures of aggression from this task, and this practice could increase the probability of a Type I error if researchers were systematically choosing a measure on the basis of the size of the media violence effect. If the overall meta-analytic experimental effect size is inflated by such a reporting bias in competitive reaction time studies, these studies should yield systematically larger effect sizes than experimental studies using other aggressive behavior measures, but they did not. This is not surprising. A previous meta-analysis found that different laboratory measures of aggressive behavior produce similar results and are highly correlated (Carlson, Marcus-Newhall, & Miller, 1989). For example, the correlation between physical punishment intensity and duration was .76 across 92 experimental studies.

Is Psychology Inventing a Phantom Youth Violence Crisis?

There are at least five problems with Ferguson and Kilburn's (2010) claims in this section of their comment. First, we have never claimed that national violent crime data are a good test of media violence effects. Because violent crime is influenced by so many risk factors, simple studies of national crime rate changes are difficult to interpret (Anderson & Bushman, 2002). Second, there is evidence that certain types of youth violence rates are increasing (Escobar-Chaves & Anderson, 2008). The data are not definitive yet and are not relevant to testing media violence effects. They do, however, suggest that there may be some selectivity in Ferguson and Kilburn's choice of violence indicators. Third, the only studies we have seen in which controls for a variety of "third" variables wiped out the video game violence effect have done so by "controlling" for variables that themselves could be conceptualized as additional outcomes of high exposure to violent video games, such as trait aggressiveness. Fourth, the experimental studies yielded significant effects, and they used random assignment to control for the types of third variables that Ferguson and Kilburn claimed explain video game violence effects. Fifth, media violence researchers do not claim that violent media are the most important risk factor for aggressive and violent behavior. However, of all the risk factors linked to aggressive and violent behavior, exposure to violent media may be the easiest factor for parents to control. In summary, claims that the mainstream media violence research community is trying to invent a phantom youth violence crisis have no basis in fact.

Overlapping Meta-Analyses

This is not the place to go through a long list of concerns we have about the violent video game meta-analyses conducted by Ferguson and his colleagues, but we would like to mention briefly one concern. Ferguson and his colleagues provide very little information about the studies included in their three meta-analyses (Ferguson, 2007a, 2007b; Ferguson & Kilburn, 2009). This too goes against current practice. Most important, no list of included studies is provided for any of the meta-analyses. We asked Ferguson for a list of the studies included in each of his meta-analyses, and he graciously provided us these lists. The percentages of overlapping studies in the meta-analyses ranged from 54% to 100%. Thus, their meta-analytic results are not independent.

Summary

In summary, we conducted a state-of-the art meta-analysis on violent video game effects, one that includes data from more that 10 times as many participants as in meta-analyses conducted by Ferguson and his colleagues. We included unpublished studies, as recommended by virtually all meta-analysis experts. We created and tested stringent inclusion criteria. We conducted appropriate analyses to assess the impact of publication bias and found minimal bias. One could still argue that the magnitude of effects we observed was so small that it is trivial, but most meta-analysis experts, physicians, psychologists, and psychiatrists would disagree with Ferguson and Kilburn on this point as well. Our results suggest that violent video games increase aggressive thoughts, angry feelings, and aggressive behaviors and decrease empathic feelings and prosocial behaviors. Moreover, we obtained similar effects in Western and Eastern countries. Violent video game exposure is a causal risk factor for later aggression.

Notes

1. For example, Rosenthal (1990) noted the case involving the effects of taking a daily aspirin (vs. a placebo) on the occurrence of a heart attack. The original, double-blind placebo-randomized experiment was stopped early because the preliminary results were so strong that it was deemed unethical to continue giving placebos. The effect size was $r = .034$.
2. But seriousness of aggression was not a significant moderator in our meta-analysis.
3. For example, in a longitudinal study (Anderson, Gentile, & Buckley, 2007, Chapter 7), a fairly extreme behavior (getting into a physical fight at school) was affected by a risk factor of small size. After controlling for Time 1 fighting behavior, sex, and hostile attribution bias, those who played a lot of violent video games early in the school year were about 20% more likely to be involved in a subsequent physical fight.

References

American Psychological Association. (2005, August 17). *Resolution on violence in video games and interactive media.* Retrieved from http://www.apa.org/pubs/jounials/releases/resolutiononvideoviolence.pdf

Anderson, C. A., & Bushman, B. J. (2002). Media violence and the American public revisited. *American Psychologist, 57,* 448–450.

Anderson, C. A., Carnagey, N. L., Flanagan, M., Benjamin, A. J., Eubanks, J., & Valentine, J. C. (2004). Violent video games: Specific effects of violent content on aggressive thoughts and behavior. *Advances in Experimental Social Psychology, 36,* 199–249.

Anderson, C. A., & Ford, C. M. (1986). Affect of the game player: Short-term effects of highly and mildly aggressive video games. *Personality and Social Psychology Bulletin, 12,* 390–402.

Anderson, C. A., Gentile, D. A., & Buckley, K. E. (2007). *Violent video game effects on children and adolescents: Theory, research, and public policy.* New York, NY: Oxford University Press.

Anderson, C. A., Shibuya, A., Ihori, N., Swing, E. L., Bushman, B. J., Sakamoto, A., . . . Saleem, M. (2010). Violent video game effects on aggression, empathy, and prosocial behavior in Eastern and Western countries. *Psychological Bulletin, 136,* 151–173.

Barnett, J., Coulson, M., & Foreman, N. (2008, April). *The WoW! factor: Reduced levels of anger after violent on-line play.* Poster session presented at the annual meeting of the British Psychological Society, Dublin, Ireland.

Borenstein, M., Hedges, L. V., Higgins, J. P. T., & Rothstein, H. R. (2009). *Introduction to meta-analysis.* New York, NY: Wiley.

Bushman, B. J., & Anderson, C. A. (2001). Media violence and the American public: Scientific facts versus media misinformation. *American Psychologist, 56,* 477–489.

Bushman, B. J., & Geen, R. G. (1990). The role of cognitive–emotional mediators and individual differences in the effects of media violence on aggression. *Journal of Personality and Social Psychology, 58,* 156–163.

Bushman, B. J., & Wang, M. C. (1995). A procedure for combining sample correlations and vote counts to obtain an estimate and a confidence interval for the population correlation coefficient. *Psychological Bulletin, 117,* 530–546.

Bushman, B. J., & Wang, M. C. (1996). A procedure for combining sample standardized mean differences and vote counts to estimate the population standardized mean difference in fixed effects models. *Psychological Methods, 1,* 66–80.

Bushman, B. J., & Wang, M. C. (2009). Vote counting methods in meta-analysis. In H. M. Cooper, L. V. Hedges, & J. C. Valentine (Eds.), *Handbook of research synthesis* (2nd ed., pp. 207–220). New York, NY: Russell Sage Foundation.

Carlson, M., Marcus-Newhall, A., & Miller, N. (1989). Evidence for a general construct of aggression. *Personality and Social Psychology Bulletin, 15,* 377–389.

Cohen, J. (1988). *Statistical power analysis for the behavioral sciences* (2nd ed.). New York, NY: Academic Press.

Congressional Public Health Summit. (2000, July 26). *Joint statement on the impact of entertainment violence on children.* Retrieved from www.aap.org/advocacy/releases/jstmtevc.htm

Cooper, H. (2009). *Research synthesis and meta-analysis: A step-by-step approach* (4th ed.). Thousand Oaks, CA: Sage.

Duval, S. (2005). The trim and fill method. In H. R. Rothstein, A. J. Sutton, & M. Borenstein (Eds.),

Publication bias in meta-analysis: Prevention, assessment and adjustments (pp. 127–144). Chichester, England: Wiley.

Egger, M., Dickersin, K., & Smith, G. (2001). Problems and limitations in conducting systematic reviews. In M. Egger, G. Davey-Smith, & D. Altaian (Eds.), *Systematic reviews in health care: Meta-analysis in context* (pp. 43–68). London, England: BMJ Books.

Escobar-Chaves, S. L., & Anderson, C. A. (2008). Media and risky behaviors. *The Future of Children, 18,* 147–180.

Ferguson, C. J. (2007a). Evidence for publication bias in video game violence effects literature: A meta-analytic review. *Aggression and Violent Behavior, 12,* 470–482.

Ferguson, C. J. (2007b). The good, the bad and the ugly: A meta-analytic review of positive and negative effects of violent video games. *Psychiatric Quarterly, 78,* 309–316.

Ferguson, C. J., & Kilburn, J. (2009). The public health risks of media violence: A meta-analytic review. *Journal of Pediatrics, 154,* 759–763.

Ferguson, C. J., & Kilburn, J. (2010). Much ado about nothing: The misestimation and overinterpretation of violent video game effects in Eastern and Western nations: Comment on Anderson et al. (2010). *Psychological Bulletin, 136,* 174–178.

Ferguson, C. J., & Rueda, S. M. (in press). The Hitman study: Violent video game exposure effects on aggressive behavior, hostile feelings and depression. *European Psychologist.*

Ferguson, C. J., San Miguel, C., & Hartley, R. D. (in press). A multivariate analysis of youth violence and aggression: The influence of family, peers, depression, and media violence. *Journal of Pediatrics.*

Hedges, L. V., Cooper, H. M., & Bushman, B. J. (1992). Testing the null hypothesis in meta-analysis. A comparison of combined probability and confidence interval procedures. *Psychological Bulletin, 111,* 188–194.

Hemphill, J. F. (2003). Interpreting the magnitudes of correlation coefficients. *American Psychologist, 58,* 78–79.

Ioannidis, J. P. A., Patsopoulos, N. A., & Rothstein, H. R. (2008). Reasons or excuses for avoiding meta-analysis in forest plots. *British Medical Journal, 336,* 1413–1415.

Lipsey, M. W. (1990). *Design sensitivity: Statistical power for experimental research.* Newbury Park, CA: Sage.

Lipsey, M. W., & Wilson, D. B. (2001). *Practical meta-analysis.* Thousand Oaks, CA: Sage.

Littell, J. H., Corcoran, J., & Pillai, V. (2008). *Systematic reviews and meta-analysis.* Oxford, England: Oxford University Press.

McDaniel, M. A., Rothstein, H. R., & Whetzel, D. (2006). Publication bias: A case study of four test vendor manuals. *Personnel Psychology, 59,* 927–953.

Olson, C., Kutner, L., Baer, L., Beresin, E., Warner, D., & Nicholi, A. (2009). M-rated video games and aggressive or problem behavior among young adolescents. *Applied Developmental Science, 13* (4), 1–11.

Peters, J. L., Sutton, A. J., Jones, D. R., Abrams, K. R., & Rushton, L. (2007). Performance of the trim and fill method in the presence of publication bias and between-study heterogeneity. *Statistics in Medicine, 26,* 4544–4562.

Petticrew, M., & Roberts, H. (2005). *Systematic reviews in the social sciences: A practical guide.* Chichester, England: Wiley-Blackwell.

Przybylski, A., Weinstein, N., Ryan, R., & Rigby, C. (2009). Having to versus wanting to play: Background and consequences of harmonious versus obsessive engagement in video games. *Cyber-Psychology & Behavior, 12,* 485–492.

Richard, F. D., Bond, C. F., Jr., & Stokes-Zoota, J. J. (2003). One hundred years of social psychology quantitatively described. *Review of General Psychology, 7,* 331–363.

Rosenthal, R. (1990). How are we doing in soft psychology? *American Psychologist, 45,* 775–777.

Rothstein, H. R. (1990). Interrater reliability of job performance ratings: Growth to asymptote level with increasing opportunity to observe. *Journal of Applied Psychology, 75,* 322–327.

Rothstein, H. R. (2003). Progress is our most important product: Contributions of validity generalization and meta-analysis to the development and communication of knowledge in I/O psychology. In K. R. Murphy (Ed.), *Validity generalization: A critical review* (pp. 115–154). Mahwah, NJ: Erlbaum.

Rothstein, H. R. (2004). File drawer analysis. In M. Lewis-Beck (Ed.), *The encyclopedia of research methods for the social sciences.* Thousand Oaks, CA: Sage.

Rothstein, H. R. (2008a). Publication bias. In *Wiley encyclopedia of clinical trials.* Chichester, England: Wiley.

Rothstein, H. R. (2008b). Publication bias as a threat to the validity of meta-analytic results. *Journal of Experimental Criminology, 4,* 61–81.

Rothstein, H. R., & Hopewell, S. (2009). Grey literature. In H. M. Cooper, L. V. Hedges, & J. C. Valentine (Eds.), *Handbook of research synthesis* (2nd ed., pp. 103–125). New York, NY: Russell Sage Foundation.

Rothstein, H. R., & McDaniel, M. A. (1989). Guidelines for conducting and reporting meta-analyses. *Psychological Reports, 65,* 759–770.

Rothstein, H. R., McDaniel, M. A., & Borenstein, M. (2001). Meta-analysis: A review of quantitative cumulation methods. In N. Schmitt & F. Drasgow (Eds.), *Advances in measurement and data analysis* (pp. 534–570). San Francisco, CA: Jossey-Bass.

Rothstein, H. R., Sutton, A. J., & Borenstein, M. (2005). *Publication bias in meta-analysis: Prevention, assessment and adjustments.* Hoboken, NJ: Wiley.

Ryan, R., Rigby, C. S., Przybylski, A. (2006). The motivational pull of video games: A self-determination theory approach. *Motivation and Emotion, 30,* 344–360.

Schmidt, F. L., Law, K., Hunter, J. E., Rothstein, H. R., Pearlman, K., & McDaniel, M. (1993). Refinements in validity generalization methods: Implications for the situational specificity hypothesis. *Journal of Applied Psychology, 78,* 3–12.

Sherry, J. L. (2001). The effects of violent video games on aggression: A meta-analysis. *Human Communication Research, 27,* 409–431.

Sterne, J. A. C., & Egger, M. (2001). Funnel plots for detecting bias in meta-analysis: Guidelines on choice of axis. *Journal of Clinical Epidemiology, 54,* 1046–1055.

Taylor, S. P. (1967). Aggressive behavior and physiological arousal as a function of provocation and the tendency to inhibit aggression. *Journal of Personality, 35,* 297–310.

Terrin, N., Schmid, C. H., Lau, J., & Olkin, I. (2003). Adjusting for publication bias in the presence of heterogeneity. *Statistics in Medicine, 22,* 2113–2126.

Tetzlaff, J., Moher, D., Pham, B., & Altman, D (2006, October). *Survey of views on including grey literature in systematic reviews.* Paper presented at the 16th Cochrane Colloquium, Dublin, Ireland.

U.S. Department of Health and Human Services. (2001). *Youth violence: A report of the Surgeon General.* Rockville, MD: U.S. Government Printing Office.

Valentine, J. C., Pigott, T. D., & Rothstein, H. R. (in press). How many studies do you need? A primer on statistical power for meta-analysis. *Journal of Educational and Behavioral Statistics.*

Wade, C. A., Turner, H. M., Rothstein, H. R., & Lavenberg, J. (2006). Information retrieval and the role of the information specialist in producing high-quality systematic reviews in the social, behavioral, and education sciences. *Evidence & Policy: A Journal of Research, Debate and Practice, 2,* 89–108.

Wang, M. C., & Bushman, B. J. (1998). Using normal quantile plots to explore meta-analytic data sets. *Psychological Methods, 3,* 46–54.

Wang, M. C., & Bushman, B. J. (1999). *Integrating results through meta-analytic review using SAS software.* Gary, NC: SAS Institute.

BRAD J. BUSHMAN, Institute for Social Research, University of Michigan, and VU University, Amsterdam, the Netherlands.

HANNAH R. ROTHSTEIN, Department of Management, Baruch College, City University of New York.

CRAIG A. ANDERSON, Center for the Study of Violence, Department of Psychology, Iowa State University.

Christopher J. Ferguson
and John Kilburn

 **NO**

Much Ado about Nothing: The Misestimation and Overinterpretation of Violent Video Game Effects in Eastern and Western Nations: Comment on Anderson et al. (2010)

Over the last two decades, society has expressed concern that violent video games (VVGs) may play some role in youth violence. To answer some of these questions, we engaged in a series of precise meta-analyses of VVG studies that most closely related to violent outcomes (e.g., Ferguson, 2007; Ferguson & Kilburn, 2009). Indeed, we were well aware that less precise measures tend to overestimate effects (Paik & Comstock, 1994). We also had questions regarding whether journals had been selectively publishing significant studies and potentially ignoring nonsignificant studies. Our results were clear: The influence of VVGs on serious acts of aggression or violence is minimal, and publication bias is a problem in this research field. We also noted (as did Paik & Comstock, 1994) that the best measures of aggression and violence produced the weakest effects and that problematic unstandardized use of some aggression measures, particularly in experimental studies, tended to inflate effects.

Points of Agreement and Disagreement with Anderson et al.

Anderson et al. (2010) critiqued our analyses and offered an alternative of their own. Our analyses agree that the uncorrected estimate for VVG effects is quite small ($r = .15$ in both analyses). We also agree that meta-analytic researchers must take careful steps to minimize the influence of publication bias. But our research groups disagree on many points: whether to include unpublished studies, how best to analyze and correct for publication bias, whether bivariate correlations are a proper estimate of VVG effects, how precise standardized and valid aggression measures need to be to adequately answer research questions, and how effect size estimates should be interpreted. We have concerns that Anderson et al. have made several misstatements about our meta-analyses and meta-analyses more generally and have also made significant errors in their own analyses that render their results difficult to interpret.

Building the Perfect Meta-Analytic Beast

We are honored that Anderson et al. (2010) selected our analyses to contrast with their own. However, readers should be aware that other recent meta-analyses on VVGs and media violence more broadly have been no more supportive of Anderson et al.'s position than our own (Savage & Yancey, 2008; Sherry, 2001, 2007). Anderson et al. surprisingly cite Sherry (2001) as if supportive of their position, but in fact he is quite clear that he does not find the results of his analyses persuasive for the causal position. Indeed, he is specifically critical of the Anderson et al. research group, stating, "Further, why do some researchers (e.g., Gentile & Anderson, 2003) continue to argue that video games are dangerous despite evidence to the contrary?" (Sherry, 2007, p. 244).

Anderson et al. (2010) suggested that we should have included unpublished studies in our analyses and that the best way to negate publication bias issues is to "conduct a search for relevant studies that is thorough, systematic, unbiased, transparent, and clearly documented" (p. 152). We note that, given that one of our questions specifically regarded the amount of bias in the published literature, including unpublished studies would be counterintuitive. Although including unpublished studies in meta-analyses is certainly common, is it really as "widely accepted" as they claim? Further, does their meta-analysis live up to their own rhetoric?

First, Anderson et al. (2010) failed to note that many scholars have been critical of the inclusion of unpublished studies in meta-analyses. Baumeister, DeWall, and Vohs (2009) noted that one weakness of meta-analysis is that the inclusion of dubious unpublished works can "muddy the waters" (p. 490). Smith and Egger (1998), echoing our own concerns, noted that including unpublished studies increases bias, particularly when located studies are not representative of the broader array of studies. Others have noted that inclusion of unpublished studies remains controversial, although certainly common, and it is not uncommon for meta-analyses to avoid unpublished studies (Cook et al., 1993). Thus, Anderson et al.'s implication that we essentially invented the notion of avoiding unpublished studies is fanciful, much as we would like to take credit.

Despite the comments of Anderson et al. (2010) supporting a search for unpublished studies that is "thorough, systematic, unbiased, transparent, and clearly documented," they actually provide little information about how they located unpublished studies. However, one common procedure, although certainly not sufficient in and of itself, is to request unpublished studies from known researchers in the field (Egger & Smith, 1998). It is surprising then that, although the Anderson et al. researchers were in contact with us (i.e., C. J. Ferguson), they neither mentioned their meta-analysis nor requested in-press or unpublished studies. As such, they missed several in-press studies (e.g., Ferguson & Rueda, in press; Ferguson, San Miguel, & Hartley, 2009) as well as a larger number of "on review" papers and papers for which data had been collected but not yet written up. We express the concern that other research groups that, arguably, have presented research not in line with Anderson et al.'s hypotheses have also not have been contacted (e.g., Barnett, Coulson, & Foreman, 2008; Colwell & Kato, 2003; Kutner & Olson, 2008; Ryan, Rigby, & Przybylski, 2006; Unsworth, Devilly, & Ward, 2007; Williams & Skoric, 2005). For example, we note that several published reports (e.g., Barnett et al., 2008; Olson et al., 2009; Przybylski, Weinstein, Ryan, & Rigby, 2009) from this group of authors have been missed. Thus, from only a small group of researchers, albeit those who differ from Anderson et al. in perspective, a considerable number of published, in-press, and unpublished studies were missed. One can only speculate at the number of other missed studies from unknown authors. On the other hand, when examining the appendix of included studies, one finds that unpublished studies from Anderson et al.'s research group and colleagues are well represented. For example, of two unpublished studies, both are from Anderson et al.'s broader research group. Of three in-press manuscripts included, two (67%) are from the Anderson et al. group. Of conference presentations included, 9 of 12 (75%) are from the Anderson et al. group and colleagues. Whatever techniques used by Anderson et al. to garner unpublished studies, these techniques worked very well for their own unpublished studies but poorly for those from other groups. We do not conclude that this was purposeful on the part of Anderson et al.; rather, this matter highlights our concerns about including unpublished studies.

Publication Bias Exists in VVG Studies

Our original meta-analyses indicated that published studies of VVGs are products of publication bias. Anderson et al. (2010) does not appear to have disputed this but suggested

we should have included unpublished studies instead of our publication bias analyses. Anderson et al. focused on our use of the "trim and fill" procedure. As Anderson et al. indicated, the trim and fill is not without imperfections. However, they failed to mention that we actually used a wide range of publication bias analyses and looked for concordance between these analyses. Indeed, we found a general agreement between publication bias tests for studies of aggressive behavior and VVGs. The trim and fill procedure can function as an estimate for the degree of publication bias, particularly when there are sound theoretical reasons to expect publication bias. As Egger and Smith (1998) indicated, publication bias is quite common. Ioannidis (2005) observed that bias is particularly prevalent in new or "hot" research fields, as that on VVGs certainly is. Other scholars have expressed concern that VVG studies have become politicized, which increases the risk for bias (e.g., Grimes, Anderson, & Bergen, 2008; Kutner & Olson, 2008; Sherry, 2007). We find suggestions that VVG studies are immune to publication bias effects to be naive. However, the reader need not take our word for it. Publication bias appears evident in a previous meta-analysis by this research team (Anderson, 2004). Of the published studies ($n = 32$) in this analysis, 19 were supportive of the causal view, nine were inconclusive, and four were nonsupportive. Of the unpublished studies ($n = 11$), one was supportive, one was inconclusive, and nine were nonsupportive. The difference between published and unpublished studies is obvious.

Best Practices or Best of the Worst?

Some of the suggestions offered by Anderson et al. (2010) concerning "best practices" appear reasonable, but we express concern that they did not raise the issue of unstandardized aggression measures used in many VVG studies. A measure of aggression (or any other construct) is unstandardized when the method for calculating outcomes scores is not clearly set; this allows different scholars to calculate outcomes in very different ways (or the same author may calculate outcomes differently between studies). By contrast, a measure may be considered standardized when measurements taken from it (as well as its administration) are "set in stone" and do not vary across studies or across researchers (the aggression score developed from the Child Behavior Checklist is an example of a standardized aggression measure). The benefit of standardized measures is that researchers must accept the outcomes from these measures whether or not the outcomes are favorable to their hypothesis. Unstandardized assessments potentially allow researchers to select from among multiple outcomes those which best fit their a priori hypotheses. For instance, the Anderson et al. research group has assessed the "noise blast" aggression measure differently across multiple studies, with little explanation as to why (for a discussion, see Ferguson, 2007). Our previous analyses have suggested that unstandardized measures tend to inflate effect size estimates, as noted, potentially because researchers may ignore the "worst" outcomes and select the "best" outcomes to interpret (we argue that this is human nature and do not mean to imply any purposeful unethical behavior). Standardization is a basic tenet of psychometrics; thus, it is unfortunate that it has been so ignored in this research field. Unfortunately, the best practices-nominated studies are populated with manuscripts in which unstandardized assessments were used. This fact, rather than the quality of those reports, probably explains why the effect sizes seen for this group or paper were higher than those for other papers.

We also find that Anderson et al. (2010) did not rigidly apply their own standards. For instance, they nominated at least one paper (Konijn, Nije Bijvank, & Bushman, 2007) as best practices, although it included several games with violent content descriptors (The Sims 2, Tony Hawk's Underground 2, Final Fantasy) in its nonviolent game condition, thus making its results uninterpretable. Panee and Ballard (2002) were nominated as best practices even though all participants played the same game. Similarly, Anderson et al. seem particularly disinclined toward Williams and Skoric (2005), despite the fact that this study does indeed (contrary to Anderson et al.'s assertions) include a measure of verbal aggression at least as ecologically valid, if not more so, than that of many of those studies nominated as best practices.

Anderson et al. (2010) included several studies from which it is unclear how effect size estimates meaningful to the basic hypotheses were calculated. For example (and this is a partial list), Hagell and Newburn (1994) provided only descriptive percentiles and no analyses from which a meaningful effect size estimate could be calculated. Hind (1995) reported only the degree to which offender and nonoffender youths liked different kinds of games, not their reaction to playing these games or any correlation between play and behavior. Kestenbaum and Weinstein (1985) reported p values, but no other statistics, and these for some outcomes but not all. In the Panee and Ballard (2002) study, all participants played the same violent game without any variation in game violence content. Silvern and Williamson (1987) reported only a pretest/posttest design in which all children played the same video game (Space Invaders). We do not believe that these studies (or many others included in Anderson et al.) provide meaningful information related to VVGs and youth violence.

Is Psychology Inventing a Phantom Youth Violence Crisis?

Anderson et al. (2010) neglected to report on one very basic piece of information. Namely, as VVGs have become more popular in the United States and elsewhere, violent crime rates among youths and adults in the United States, Canada, United Kingdom, Japan, and most other industrialized nations have plummeted to lows not seen since the 1960s. Even the Anderson et al. group appears

to have acknowledged that this kind of data is important to consider: "Nonetheless, dramatic reductions in media violence exposure of children should, over a several year period, lead to detectible reductions in real world aggression by those children. This would further provide evidence for a strong media violence link to aggression" (Barlett & Anderson, 2009, p. 10). In fact, we are seeing the opposite relationship, in which dramatic increases in VVGs are correlated with dramatic decreases in youth violence. The correlation coefficient for this data is $r = -.95$, a near-perfect correlation in the wrong direction. We agree with Barlett and Anderson (2009) that this kind of evidence is strong. Barlett and Anderson, of course, cannot have it both ways, with crime data important only so long as they are consistent with Barlett and Anderson's beliefs.

Last, Anderson et al. (2010) suggested that the $r = .15$ relationship is too conservative and, nonetheless, as strong as that seen in other areas of criminology. The $r = .15$ estimate includes only basic controls; therefore, this estimate is probably too liberal. Our own research suggests that when other risk factors (e.g., depression, peers, family) are controlled, video game effects drop to near zero (Ferguson et al., 2009). Indeed, focusing on bivariate correlations is problematic, as they overestimate relationships due to third variables. Males both play more VVGs and are more aggressive than females. Thus, aggression will tend to correlate with VVGs and with any other male-dominated activity, such as growing beards, dating women, and wearing pants rather than dresses. Anderson et al. noticed this themselves. It is obvious that controlling other important risk factors related to personality, family, and even genes (if one could) would further reduce the unique predictive value of VVGs. Anderson et al. ignored this third variable effect, although it has been well known for some time. It is also not true that the $r = .15$ estimate— even if we were to believe that it is accurate—is on par with other criminological effect size estimates. Furthermore, Anderson et al. claimed that small effects may accumulate over time yet found the weakest effects from longitudinal studies, in contradiction to this claim. It should be noted that this 2.25% coefficient of determination reflects a change of nonpathological aggression to the tune of 2.25% within individuals; it does not mean that 2.25% of normal children became antisocial or any other such alarmist interpretation of this effect. We observe that Anderson et al. themselves acknowledged that this effect is for nonserious aggression (Footnote 12) due to the limitations of many of the measures included in this analysis.

In conclusion, we believe that Anderson et al. (2010) are sincere in their concerns for children and beliefs about VVGS. However, their current meta-analysis contains numerous flaws, all of which converge on overestimating and overinterpreting the influence of VVGs on aggression. Nonetheless, they find only weak effects. Given that discussions of VVGs tend to inform public policy, both scientists and policymakers need to consider whether these results will get the "bang for their buck" out of any forthcoming policy recommendations. There are real risks that the exaggerated focus on VVGs, fueled by some scientists, distracts society from much more important causes of aggression, including poverty, peer influences, depression, family violence, and Gene × Environment interactions. Although it is certainly true that few researchers suggest that VVGs are the sole cause of violence, this does not mean they cannot be wrong about VVGs having any meaningful effect at all. Psychology, too often, has lost its ability to put the weak (if any) effects found for VVGs on aggression into a proper perspective. In doing so, it does more to misinform than inform public debates on this issue.

References

Anderson, C. (2004). An update on the effects of playing violent video games. *Journal of Adolescence, 27,* 113–122.

Anderson, C. A., Shibuya, A., Ihori, N., Swing, E. L., Bushman, B. J., Sakamoto, A., . . . Saleem, M. (2010). Violent video game effects on aggression, empathy, and prosocial behavior in Eastern and Western countries. *Psychological Bulletin, 136,* 151–173.

Barlett, C. P., & Anderson, C. A. (2009). *Violent video games and public policy.* Retrieved from http://www.psychology.iastate.edu/faculty/caa/abstracts/2005–2009/09BA2english.pdf

Barnett, J., Coulson, M., & Foreman, N. (2008, April). *The WoW! factor: Reduced levels of anger after violent on-line play.* Poster session presented at the annual meeting of the British Psychological Society, Dublin, Ireland.

Baumeister, R., DeWall, C., & Vohs, K. (2009). Social rejection, control, numbness and emotion: How not to be fooled by Gerber and Wheeler (2009). *Perspectives on Psychological Science, 4,* 489–493.

Colwell, J., & Kato, M. (2003). Investigation of the relationship between social isolation, self-esteem, aggression and computer game play in Japanese adolescents. *Asian Journal of Social Psychology, 6,* 149–158.

Cook, D., Guyatt, G., Ryan, G., Clifton, J., Buckingham, L., Willan, A., . . . Oxman, A. (1993, June 2). Should unpublished data be included in meta-analyses? Current convictions and controversies. *JAMA, 269,* 2749–2753.

Egger, M., & Smith, G. (1998, January 3). Meta-analysis: Bias in location and selection of studies. *British Medical Journal, 315,* 61–66. Retrieved from http://www.BritishMedicalJournal.com/archive/7124/7124ed2.htm

Ferguson, C. J. (2007). Evidence for publication bias in video game violence effects literature: A meta-analytic review. *Aggression and Violent Behavior, 12,* 470–482.

Ferguson, C. J. (2008). The school shooting/violent video game link: Causal link or moral panic? *Journal of Investigative Psychology and Offender Profiling, 5,* 25–37.

Ferguson, C. J. (Ed.). (2009). *Violent crime: Clinical and social implications.* Thousand Oaks, CA: Sage.

Ferguson, C. J., & Kilburn, J. (2009). The public health risks of media violence: A meta-analytic review. *Journal of Pediatrics, 154,* 759–763.

Ferguson, C. J., & Rueda, S. M. (in press). The Hitman study: Violent video game exposure effects on aggressive behavior, hostile feelings and depression. *European Psychologist.*

Ferguson, C. J., San Miguel, C., & Hartley, R. D. (2009). A multivariate analysis of youth violence and aggression: The influence of family, peers, depression and media violence. *Journal of Pediatrics, 155,* 904–908.

Grimes, T., Anderson, J., & Bergen, L. (2008). *Media violence and aggression: Science and ideology.* Thousand Oaks, CA: Sage.

Hagell, A., & Newburn, T. (1994). *Young offenders and the media: Viewing habits and preferences.* London, England: Policy Studies Institute.

Hind, P. A. (1995). A study of reported satisfaction with differentially aggressive computer games amongst incarcerated young offenders. *Issues in Criminological and Legal Psychology, 22,* 28–36.

Ioannidis, J. P. (2005). Why most published research findings are false. *PLoS Medicine, 2,* e124. Retrieved from http://www.plosmedicine.org/article/info:doi/10.1371/journal.pmed.0020124

Kestenbaum, G. I., & Weinstein, L. (1985). Personality, psychopathology and developmental issues in male adolescent video game use. *Journal of the American Academy of Child Psychiatry, 24,* 329–333.

Konijn, E. A., Nije Bijvank, M., & Bushman, B. J. (2007). I wish I were a warrior: The role of wishful identification in effects of violent video games on aggression in adolescent boys. *Developmental Psychology, 43,* 1038–1044.

Kutner, L., & Olson, C. (2008). *Grand theft childhood: The surprising truth about violent video games and what parents can do.* New York, NY: Simon & Schuster.

Olson, C., Kutner, L., Baer, L., Beresin, E., Warner, D., & Nicholi, A. (2009). M-rated video games and aggressive or problem behavior among young adolescents. *Applied Developmental Science, 13,* 188–198.

Paik, H., & Comstock, G. (1994). The effects of television violence on antisocial behavior: A meta-analysis. *Communication Research, 21,* 516–539.

Panee, C. D., & Ballard, M. E. (2002). High versus low aggressive priming during video game training:

Effects on violent action during game play, hostility, heart rate, and blood pressure. *Journal of Applied Social Psychology, 32,* 2458–2474.

Przybylski, A., Weinstein, N., Ryan, R., & Rigby, C. S. (2009). Having to versus wanting to play: Background and consequences of harmonious versus obsessive engagement in video games. *CyberPsychology & Behavior, 12,* 485–492.

Ryan, R., Rigby, C. S., & Przybylski, A. (2006). The motivational pull of video games: A self-determination theory approach. *Motivation and Emotion, 30,* 344–360.

Savage, J., & Yancey, C. (2008). The effects of media violence exposure on criminal aggression: A meta-analysis. *Criminal Justice and Behavior, 35,* 1123–1136.

Sherry, J. (2001). The effects of violent video games on aggression: A meta-analysis. *Human Communication Research, 27,* 409–431.

Sherry, J. (2007). Violent video games and aggression: Why can't we find links? In R. Preiss, B. Gayle, N. Burrell, M. Allen, & J. Bryant (Eds.), *Mass media*

effects research: Advances through meta-analysis (pp. 231–248). Mahwah, NJ: Erlbaum.

Silvern, S. B., & Williamson, P. A. (1987). The effects of video game play on young children's aggression, fantasy and prosocial behavior. *Journal of Applied Developmental Psychology, 8,* 453–462.

Smith, G., & Egger, M. (1998, January 17). Meta-analysis: Unresolved issues and future developments. *British Medical Journal, 316,* 221–225. Retrieved from http://www.BritishMedicalJournal.com/archive/7126/7126ed8.htm

Unsworth, G., Devilly, G., & Ward, T. (2007). The effect of playing violent videogames on adolescents: Should parents be quaking in their boots? *Psychology, Crime & Law, 13,* 383–394.

Williams, D., & Skoric, M. (2005). Internet fantasy violence: A test of aggression in an online game. *Communication Monographs, 72,* 217–233.

CHRISTOPHER J. FERGUSON AND JOHN KILBURN, Department of Behavioral, Applied Sciences, and Criminal Justice, Texas A&M International University .

EXPLORING THE ISSUE

Do Video Games Promote Violent Behavior in Students?

Critical Thinking and Reflection

1. For a sound policy to be created, what level of disagreement among the research experts can reasonably be tolerated?
2. What steps could or should federal funding agencies take with regard to expecting or requiring some degree of uniformity in the approaches different research groups take in studying VVG and aggression?
3. How much of an issue do you think is created by the different definitions of aggression being used?
4. What makes it difficult to determine whether there is a causal link between viewing violent video games and later aggressive or violent behavior?

Is There Common Ground?

The selections highlight a scientific exchange between groups with differing perspectives on matters of opinion as much as fact in regard to a particular data analytic approach—meta-analysis. How to properly conduct and interpret a meta-analysis is as much at issue as the substantive issue. In one sense, the two issues are not separable as such—how the problem is approached to be solved—that is, the methods one chooses will lead to certain substantive conclusions. If groups cannot agree on the methods or the interpretation of their results, it is difficult to see how conclusions are going to be agreed upon. In most areas of research and study, if different methods produce the same or comparable findings, then that is considered an indicator of robustness. In other words, the relations between variables and their outcomes will be "discovered" or "established" in spite of using different methods. Here, though, the two selections are a "point-counterpoint" disagreement in regard to a meta-analytic study published previously by one of the groups (the original meta-analytic study was published in the *Psychological Bulletin*, vol. 136, pp. 151–173 by Craig Anderson and his colleagues, the group arguing "Yes" in the exchange).

There are definitional issues that matter and lead to measurement differences across studies that can undermine our confidence in "hearing" what the evidence "has to say." Ferguson and Kilburn make the point that the way in which aggression is measured in many of the studies is unstandardized (i.e., the construct "aggression" is operationalized and measured in different ways). From the meta-analytic perspective, one potential problem is

that unstandardized measures may influence effect size estimates yet another way of introducing bias into the process. Bushman, Rothstein, and Anderson acknowledge the issue, but disagree that it is necessarily operating in the research on aggression and VVG and cite evidence supporting their perspective.

Create Central

www.mhhe.com/createcentral

Additional Resources

C. A. Anderson, A. Shibuya, N. Ihori, E. L. Swing, E. L., B. J. Bushman, A. Sakamoto, . . . M. Saleem (2010). "Violent Video Game Effects on Aggression, Empathy, and Prosocial Behavior in Eastern and Western Countries," *Psychological Bulletin* (vol. 136, pp. 151–173).

D. Cook, G. Guyatt, G. Ryan, J. Clifton, L. Buckingham, A. Willan, . . . A. Oxman, "Should Unpublished Data Be Included in Meta-Analyses? Current Convictions and Controversies," JAMA (vol. 269, pp. 2749–2753, June 1993).

C. J. Ferguson (2008). "The School Shooting/Violent Video Game Link: Causal link or Moral Panic?" *Journal of Investigative Psychology and Offender Profiling* (vol. 5, pp.25–37).

L. Berkowitz, *Aggression: Its Causes, Consequences, and Control* (McGraw-Hill 1993).

Internet References . . .

The Final Report and Findings of the Safe School Initiative: Implications for the Prevention of School Attacks in the United States

http://videogames.procon.org/sourcefiles/the-final
-report-and-findings-of-the-safe-school-initiative.pdf

Resolution on Violence in Video Games and Interactive Media

http://videogames.procon.org/sourcefiles/resolution
-on-violence-in-video-games-and-interactive-media.pdf

Teens, Video Games, and Civics

http://videogames.procon.org/sourcefiles/teens
-video-games-and-civics-pew-research.pdf

Unit 3

UNIT

Effective Teaching and the Evaluation of Learning

*P*edagogical practice is shaped by many factors. As illustrated in the other units of this book, the nature of the students being taught and the particular theory of learning adopted by a teacher both help to determine what and how students are taught; however, instructional practices are shaped by many other factors. A number of logistical and organizational factors also are likely to affect teacher practices, school experience, and student outcome. Would there be a benefit to increased uniformity in curricular goals across schools? Does assigning grades to student work facilitate or hinder learning? As resources have become increasingly scarce, our classes have become larger, with more students per teacher. Would a move to smaller classes have a benefit? Does homework have a benefit in terms of the impact on learning? Should we follow the lead of Japan and other nations and increase the amount of time that students spend in school? In this section, we consider the controversies that have arisen as our schools and society have tried to define effective teaching and effective evaluation of learning.

Selected, Edited, and with Issue Framing Material by:
Leonard Abbeduto, *University of California, Davis*
and
Frank Symons, *University of Minnesota*

ISSUE

Should Schools Adopt a Common Core Curriculum?

YES: E. D. Hirsch, Jr., from "Beyond Comprehension," *American Educator* (Winter 2010–2011)

NO: Tom Loveless, from "The Common Core Initiative: What Are the Chances of Success?" *Educational Leadership* (December 2012/January 2013)

Learning Outcomes

After reading this issue, you will be able to:

- Describe the basic principles of the common core curriculum movement.
- Summarize the history of and motivation for the proposed common core curriculum.
- Summarize the main tenets of the arguments of proponents and oponents of the common core curriculum.

ISSUE SUMMARY

YES: E. D. Hirsch, Jr., argues in favor of a common core curriculum, one in which language arts is infused with a requirement to gain a broad base of domain-specific knowledge about the world that is assumed by writers of newspapers, magazine articles, and other everyday texts. Hirsch contrasts this approach to language arts with one that teaches general literacy skills devoid of content knowledge about the world. He also argues that adoption of a common curriculum better meets the needs of an increasingly mobile student body than does a curriculum that is variable and idiosyncratic across schools.

NO: Tom Loveless argues that a common core curriculum is unlikely to lead to the promised improvements in educational outcomes. In part, this argument is based on the failure of past large-scale efforts to adopt a common set of educational targets at each grade, but with little impact on outcomes. He also points out that the common core entails adoption of common set of target skills but not a single approach to teaching those skills and thus individual variation is likely to continue to characterize education in the United States.

The past few decades have seen numerous calls for overhauling K–12 education in the United States. These calls for change have been motivated by a number of concerning trends regarding student achievement, including the fact that the proficiency of students in mathematics and science continues to lag behind that of students in other industrialized nations, that the number of students scoring at proficient levels on standardized tests of achievement in reading continues to be quite low, and that drop out rates continue to climb, particularly in urban areas and among ethnic and racial minority youth. Business leaders also add to the crescendo of criticisms suggesting that schools are not preparing students for twenty-first-century jobs.

Critics point to many practices within the educational system as contributing to poor student outcomes. Two practices, however, have gained considerable traction among critics: the perceived failure to focus sufficiently on basic academic skills and the failure to hold all teachers, classrooms, and schools to the same high standards. In short, teachers and schools have been left to their own devices when it comes to choosing what to teach and they have made poor choices, focusing on domains that are not truly related to academics (e.g., emotional intelligence) and they are not held accountable for whether their students progress as they should.

The Common Core State Standards Initiative is an attempt to address these concerns. The initiative was sponsored by the National Governors Association and the Council of Chief State School Officers. The initiative led to a set of prescriptions for what knowledge and skills students should acquire at each grade in the areas of language arts and mathematics so that they will be adequately prepared for college or a skilled workforce after high school. Standards for other academic domains are also being developed. The standards emerged out of the efforts of a commission led by leading scholars and content experts in the academic domains of interest (e.g., mathematics). Various incentives to use the copyrighted standards have been implemented, including the awarding of "Race to the Top" federal grants for state-based educational reform and a liberal use license provided that the standards are adopted as a whole rather than in a piecemeal fashion.

What types of skills and knowledge do these standards embody? In mathematics, for example, the standards specify that at the first grade, students should understand the concepts of addition and subtraction and develop strategies for adding and subtracting within 20. First graders should also develop an understanding of linear measurement and the iterative units underlying that measurement. These general prescriptions are accompanied by considerable detail in terms of the specific types of problems the students should be able to solve if they have acquired the targeted concepts and strategies. (See http://www.corestandards.org/Math/Content/1/introduction for more details regarding the examples provided here.)

Thus far, 45 states and the District of Columbia have adopted the full set of Common Core State Standards. It is important to note, however, that the Standards initiative specifies what students must learn at each grade level for life after high school, either in college or in a skilled job. The standards do not, however, prescribe the pedagogical activities for teaching the targeted skills. Nor does the initiative specify how to assess student progress. Decisions about curriculum and assessment are left to the states to decide, although the hope is that uniformity of standards may encourage more uniformity in teaching and assessment practices. Indeed, several consortia of states have emerged around the development of assessments and large textbook publishers have been quick to develop curriculum packages that are designed to align with the standards.

The Common Core State Standards are in many respects the natural outgrowth of initiatives launched by several states interested in raising student achievement and increasing teacher and school accountability for that achievement. Nevertheless, the unparalleled scope of the current initiative have led to considerable controversy and discussion, in part because the investment and thus, the stakes are quite high for states, the federal government, textbook publishers, and, of course, students. Several important opposing views are well represented in the two selections presented here. In the first article, E. D. Hirsch, Jr., argues in favor of a common core. Note that Hirsch also argues for a particular approach to implementing language arts standards, one in which language arts is infused with a broad base of domain-specific knowledge about the world that is assumed by writers of newspapers, magazine articles, and other everyday texts. Hirsch contrasts this approach to language arts with one that teaches general literacy skills devoid of content knowledge about the world. In the second article, Tom Loveless argues that a common core curriculum is unlikely to lead to the promised improvements in educational outcomes. In part, Loveless's argument is based on the failure of past large-scale efforts to adopt a common set of educational targets at each grade, but with little impact on outcomes. Loveless also argues that because the common core entails adoption of common set of target skills but not a single approach to teaching those skills, individual variation is likely to continue to characterize education in the United States even after full implementation of the Standards initiative.

YES ↵

E. D. Hirsch, Jr.

Beyond Comprehension

The prevailing view of the American educational community is that no specific background knowledge is needed for reading. Any general background knowledge will do. This innocent-sounding idea, so liberating to the teacher and the student, frees schools from any requirement to teach a specific body of knowledge. This purported liberation from "mere" information and rote learning is one of the most precious principles of American educational thought, and lies at its very core. Its proponents disparage those who favor a definite, cumulative course of study for children as "traditional," "hidebound," and "reactionary," to mention only the more polite terms.

Yet the supposedly liberating and humane idea that any general background knowledge will serve to educate children and make them proficient readers is not only incorrect, it is also very old and tired; it has had its day for at least half a century, during which time American reading proficiency and verbal SAT scores have declined drastically.[1] . . . Scapegoats for the decline, such as television and social forces, have been invoked to explain it, but they cannot fully explain why other nations, equally addicted to television but not to American educational theories that disparage "mere" information, have not suffered a similarly drastic decline in reading proficiency.[2]

It is true that given a good start in decoding, a child will develop fluency and accuracy in decoding with practice. And it is also true that decoding is a skill that can be transferred from one text to another. But the progress of a child's reading comprehension is different. That progress does not follow a reliable course of development. Because comprehension is knowledge dependent, someone who reads well about the Civil War may not necessarily read well about molecular interactions.

One particularly elegant experiment was conducted to find out how important domain-specific knowledge is in actual reading tasks.[3] In two of the groups of students studied, one had good decoding skills but little knowledge of the subject, baseball, while another had poor decoding skills but knew a lot about baseball. As predicted, *the reading comprehension of the low-skills, baseball-knowing group proved superior to the reading comprehension of the high-skills, baseball-ignorant group.* These results have been replicated in other situations and knowledge domains; they show

the powerful effect of prior knowledge on actual reading ability.[4]

Faulty Ideas

Most current reading programs talk about "activating" the reader's background knowledge so she can comprehend a text. But in practice, they are only paying lip service to the finding that background knowledge is essential to reading comprehension. Little attempt is made to *enlarge* children's background knowledge—and, as a direct result, little is accomplished in terms of expanding children's ability to comprehend more complex and varied texts. The disjointed topics and stories that one finds in current reading programs, such as "Going to School" and "Jenny at the Supermarket," seem designed mainly to appeal to the knowledge that young readers probably already have.

For decades, most professional educators have believed that reading is an all-purpose skill that, once learned, can be applied to all subjects and problems. A specific, fact-filled, knowledge-building curriculum, they hold, is not needed for gaining all-purpose cognitive skills and strategies. Instead of burdening our minds with a lot of supposedly dead facts, they call for us to become expert in solving problems, in thinking critically—in reading fluently—and then we will be able to learn anything we need.

This idea sounds plausible. (If it did not, it could not have so thoroughly captured the American mind.) Its surface plausibility derives from the fact that a good education can indeed create very able readers and critical thinkers. The mistake is to think that these achievements are the result of acquiring all-purpose skills rather than broad factual knowledge. As the study of students' abilities to comprehend a text about baseball demonstrated, reading and critical thinking are always based on concrete, relevant knowledge and cannot be exercised apart from what psychologists call "domain-specific" knowledge.[5]

The idea that reading with comprehension is largely a set of general-purpose skills and strategies that can be applied to any and all texts is one of the main barriers to our students' achievement in reading. It leads to activities (like endless drilling in finding the main idea) that are deadening for agile and eager minds, and it carries big opportunity costs. These activities actually slow down the

Reprinted with permission from the Winter 2010–2011 issue of *American Educator,* the quarterly journal of the American Federation of Teachers, AFL-CIO.

acquisition of true reading ability: they take up time that could be devoted to gaining general knowledge, which is the central requisite for high reading ability.

Most current reading programs do not prepare students for high school, higher education, the workplace, or citizenship because they do not make a systematic effort to convey coherently, grade by grade, the knowledge that books (including high school textbooks), newspapers, magazines, and serious radio and TV programs *assume* American readers and listeners possess. (Every newspaper, book, and magazine editor, and every producer for radio and TV is conscious of the need to distinguish what can be taken for granted from what must be explained. The general reader or listener that every journalist or TV newscaster must imagine is somebody whose relevant knowledge is assumed to lie between the total ignorance of a complete novice and the detailed knowledge of an expert.)

How Much Knowledge Do We Need?

Here is the first paragraph of an article by Janet Maslin, taken at random from the books section of the *New York Times* on February 6, 2003. It is an example of writing addressed to a general reader that a literate American high school graduate would be expected to understand.

> When Luca Turin was a boy growing up in Paris, according to Chandler Burr's ebullient new book about him, "he was famous for boring everyone to death with useless, disconnected facts, like the distance between the earth and the moon in Egyptian cubits." Mr. Burr sets out to explain how such obsessive curiosity turned Mr. Turin into a pioneering scientist who, in the author's estimation, deserves a Nobel Prize.

This example shows that the background knowledge required to understand the general sections of the *New York Times,* such as the book review section, is not deep. It is not that of an expert—of course not, for we cannot all be experts on the diverse subjects that are treated by books. If authors want their books to be sold and read, they must not assume that their readers are experts. They may take for granted only the relevant background knowledge that a literate audience can be expected to possess.

What *do* readers need to know in order to comprehend this passage? We need to know first that this is a book review, which aims to tell us what the book is about and whether it is worth reading. We need to understand that the reviewer is favorably disposed to the book, calling it "ebullient," and that it is a nonfiction work about a scientist named Luca Turin. We need to have at least a vague semantic grasp of key words like ebullient, boring, obsessive, pioneering, estimation. We need to know some of the things mentioned with exactness, but not others. It's not necessary to know how long a cubit is. Indeed, the text implies that this is an odd bit of information, and we can infer that it is some form of measurement. We need to

know in general what Paris is, what the moon is and that it circles the earth, that it is not too far away in celestial terms, and we need to have some idea what a Nobel Prize is and that it is very prestigious. Consider the knowledge domains included in this list. Paris belongs to history and geography; so does Egypt. The moon belongs to astronomy and natural history. The Nobel Prize belongs to general history and science.

We may infer from this example that only a person with broad knowledge is capable of reading with understanding the *New York Times* and other newspapers. This fact has momentous implications for education, and for democracy as well. A universal ability of citizens to read newspapers or their equivalent with understanding is the essence of democracy. Thomas Jefferson put the issue unforgettably: "The basis of our government being the opinion of the people, the very first object should be to keep that right; and were it left to me to decide whether we should have a government without newspapers or newspapers without a government, I should not hesitate a moment to prefer the latter. But I should mean that every man should receive those papers and be capable of reading them."[6] The last phrase, "be capable of reading them," is often omitted from the quotation, but it is the crucial one. Reading achievement will not advance significantly until schools recognize and act on the fact that it depends on the possession of a broad but definable range of diverse knowledge. Effectively teaching reading requires schools to systematically teach the diverse, enabling knowledge that reading with comprehension requires.

What Knowledge Do We Need?

But what exactly does that enabling knowledge comprise? That is the nuts-and-bolts question. The practical problem of helping all students achieve adequate reading comprehension depends on our schools being able to narrow down what seems at first glance to be vast amounts of heterogeneous information into a teachable repertory that will enable students to understand the diverse texts addressed to the average citizen. Our sketch of the background knowledge needed to understand Maslin's short passage offers clues to the kind of instruction needed to advance general reading comprehension ability. It will be broad instruction in the worlds of nature and culture as a necessary platform for gaining deeper knowledge through listening and reading. But what, exactly, should that broad general knowledge be?

My colleagues Joseph Kett and James Trefil and I set out to answer that question back in the 1980s. We asked ourselves, "In the American context, what knowledge is taken for granted in the classroom, in public orations, in serious radio and TV, in books and magazines and newspapers addressed to a general audience?" We considered various scholarly approaches to this problem. One was to look at word frequencies. If a word appeared in print quite often, then its meaning was probably not going to be explained by the writer. We looked at a frequency analysis of the Brown Corpus, a collection of passages from very diverse kinds of publications that was lodged at Brown University, but we found that this purely mechanical approach, while partially valid, did not yield altogether accurate or intelligent results. For example, because the Brown Corpus was compiled in the 1950s, "Nikita Khrushchev" was a more frequent vocabulary item than "George Washington."[7]

A much better way of finding out what knowledge speakers and writers take for granted is to ask them whether they assume specific items of knowledge in what they read and write. This direct approach proved to be a sounder way of determining the tacit knowledge, because what we must teach students is the knowledge that proficient readers and writers actually use. From people in every region of the country we found a reassuring amount of agreement on the substance of this taken-for-granted knowledge.

We had predicted this agreement. The very nature of communicative competence, a skill that successful teachers, reporters, doctors, lawyers, book club members, and writers have already shown themselves to have, requires that it be widely shared within the speech community. Shared, taken-for-granted background knowledge is what makes successful communication possible. Several years after our compilation of such knowledge was published, independent researchers investigated whether reading comprehension ability did in fact depend on knowledge of the topics we had set forth. The studies showed an unambiguous correlation between knowledge of these topics and reading comprehension scores, school grades, and other measures of reading ability. One researcher investigated whether the topics we set forth as taken-for-granted knowledge are in fact taken for granted in newspaper texts addressed to a general reader. He examined the *New York Times* by computer over a period of 101 months and found that "any given day's issue of the *Times* contained approximately 2,700 occurrences" of these unexplained terms, which "play a part in the daily commerce of the published language."[8]

An inventory of the tacit knowledge shared by good readers and writers cannot, of course, be fixed at a single point in time. The knowledge that writers and radio and TV personalities take for granted is constantly changing at the edges, especially on issues of the moment. But inside the edges, at the core, the body of assumed knowledge in American public discourse has remained stable for many decades.[9] This core of knowledge changes very slowly, as sociolinguists have pointed out. If we want to bring all students to reading proficiency, this stable core is the enabling knowledge that we must teach.

That's more easily said than done. One essential, preliminary question that we faced was this: how can this necessary knowledge be sequenced in a practical way for use in schools? We asked teachers how to present these topics grade by grade and created working groups of experienced teachers in every region of the country to produce

a sequence independently of the others. There proved to be less agreement on how to present the material grade by grade than there had been in identifying what the critical topics are. That difficulty too was predicted, since the sequencing of many topics is inherently arbitrary. While it's plausible that in math, addition needs to come before multiplication, and that in history, Greece probably ought to come before Rome, maybe it's not plausible that Greece should come before George Washington.

We collected the accumulated wisdom of these independent groups of teachers, made a provisional draft sequence, and in 1990 held a conference where 145 people from every region, scholarly discipline, and racial and ethnic group got together to work extremely hard for two and a half days to agree on an intelligent way to teach this knowledge sequentially. Over time, this Core Knowledge Sequence has been refined and adjusted, based on actual classroom experience. It is now used in several hundred schools (with positive effects on reading scores), and it is distinguished among content standards not only for its interest, richness, and specificity, but also because of the carefully thought-out scientific foundations that underlie the selection of topics. (The Core Knowledge Sequence is available online at www.coreknowledge.org.)

Today, in response to requests from educators, the Core Knowledge Foundation offers a range of instructional supports, including detailed teacher guides, a day-by-day planner, and an anthology of African American literature, music, and art. And . . . we are now offering a complete language arts program for kindergarten through second grade. This program, which was pilot tested in 17 urban, suburban, and rural schools, addresses both the skills and the knowledge that young children need to become strong readers and writers. This new program is our attempt to reconceive language arts as a school subject. In trying to make all students proficient readers and writers, there is no avoiding the responsibility of imparting the specific knowledge they will need to understand newspapers, magazines, and serious books. There is no successful shortcut to teaching and learning this specific knowledge—and there is nothing more interesting than acquiring broad knowledge of the world. The happy consequence is a reading program that is much more absorbing, enjoyable, and interesting than the disjointed, pedestrian programs offered to students today.

Most current programs assume that language arts is predominantly about "literature," which is conceived as poems and fictional stories, often trivial ones meant to be inoffensive vehicles for teaching reading skills. Stories are indeed the best vehicles for teaching young children— an idea that was ancient when Plato reasserted it in *The Republic*. But stories are not necessarily the same things as ephemeral fictions. Many an excellent story is told about real people and events, and even stories that are fictional take much of their worth from the nonfictional truths about the world that they convey.

The new Core Knowledge language arts program contains not only fiction and poetry, but also narratives about the real worlds of nature and history. Since word learning occurs much faster in a familiar context, the program stays on each selected subject matter domain long enough to make it familiar. Such integration of subject-matter content in reading classes enriches background knowledge and enlarges vocabulary in an optimal way.

Constantly Changing Schools—A Critical Issue

Thus far, I've mostly been explaining the need for a fact-filled, knowledge-building curriculum. But the critical issue of student mobility demands more than just each school adopting or adapting such a curriculum. If we are really to serve all of our children to the best of our ability, then nothing short of a common curriculum—one shared by all schools—will do.

Mobility is a term to denote students' moving from one school to another in the middle of the year. The percentage of economically disadvantaged students who migrate during the school year is appallingly high, and the effects are dishearteningly severe. One study has analyzed those effects on 9,915 children. With this large group, the researchers were able to factor out the influences of poverty, race, single-parent status, and lack of parental education in order to isolate just the effects of changing schools. Even with other adverse influences factored out, children who changed schools often were much more likely than those who did not to exhibit behavioral problems and to fail a grade.[10] The researchers found that the adverse effects of such social and academic incoherence are greatly intensified when parents have low educational levels and when compensatory education is not available in the home. But this big fact of student mobility is generally ignored in discussions of school reform. It is as if that elephant in the middle of the parlor is less relevant or important than other concerns, such as the supposed dangers of encouraging uniformity or of allowing an "outsider" to decide what subjects are to be taught at which grade level.

In a typical American school district, the average rate at which students transfer in and out of schools during the academic year is about one-third.[11] In a typical inner-city school, only about half the students who start in the fall are still there in the spring—a mobility rate of 50 percent.[12] Given the curricular incoherence in a typical American school (in which two fourth grade classrooms may cover completely different content), the education provided to frequently moving students is tragically fragmented. The high mobility of low-income parents guarantees that disadvantaged children will be most severely affected by the educational handicaps of changing schools, and that they will be the ones who are most adversely affected by lack of commonality across schools.

The finding that our mobile students (who are preponderantly from low-income families) perform worse than stable ones does not mean that their lower performance is a consequence of poverty. That is to commit the fallacy of social determinism. *Where there is greater commonality of the curriculum, the effects of mobility are less severe.* In a summary of research on student mobility, Herbert Walberg states that "common learning goals, curriculum, and assessment within states (or within an entire nation) . . . alleviate the grave learning disabilities faced by children, especially poorly achieving children, who move from one district to another with different curricula, assessment, and goals."[13] The adverse effects of student mobility are much less severe in countries that use a nationwide core curriculum.

While ignoring important issues like mobility that really do impede learning, some people blame ineffective teachers for students' lackluster performance. But so-called low teacher quality is not an innate characteristic of American teachers; ineffective teaching is the consequence of the ineffective training they have received and of the vague, incoherent curricula they are given to teach, both of which result from most education schools' deemphasis on specific, cumulative content. No teacher, however capable, can efficiently cope with the huge differences in academic preparation among the students in a typical American classroom—differences that grow with each successive grade.[14] In other nations, the differences between groups diminish over time, so that they are closer together by grade 7 than they were in grade 4.[15] Even the most brilliant and knowledgeable American teacher faced with huge variations in student preparation cannot achieve as much as an ordinary teacher can within a more coherent curricular system like those found in the nations that outperform us.

The chief cause of our schools' inefficiency is precisely this curricular incoherence.[16] At the beginning of the school year, a teacher cannot be sure what the entering students know about a subject, because they have been taught very different topics in prior grades, depending on the different preferences of their teachers. Typically, therefore, the teacher must spend a great deal of time at the beginning of each year reviewing the preparatory material students need to know in order to learn the next topic—time that would not need to be so extensive (and so very boring to students who already have the knowledge) if the incoming students had all been taught using a common core curriculum and thus had all gained this knowledge already.

If states would adopt a common core curriculum that builds knowledge grade by grade, reading achievement would rise for all groups of children. So would achievement in math, science, and social studies because, as common sense predicts, reading is strongly correlated with the ability to learn in all subjects. Equally important, the achievement gap between social groups would be greatly narrowed and social justice would be served.

Notes

1. There is a large literature on the decline of verbal SAT scores in the 1960s and 1970s, and on NAEP (National Assessment of Educational Progress) scores when these began to be collected in the 1970s. A summary of these issues with full bibliographical references can be found in E. D. Hirsch, Jr., *Cultural Literacy* (Boston: Houghton Mifflin, 1987), 1–10; and E. D. Hirsch, Jr., *The Schools We Need* (New York: Doubleday, 1996), 39–42, 176–179.

2. See Christopher Jencks, "What's Behind the Drop in Test Scores?" (working paper, Department of Sociology, Harvard University, Cambridge, MA, July–August 1978).

3. Donna R. Recht and Lauren Leslie, "Effect of Prior Knowledge on Good and Poor Readers' Memory of Text," *Journal of Educational Psychology* 80, no. 1 (March 1988): 16–20.

4. Wolfgang Schneider and Joachim Korkel, "The Knowledge Base and Text Recall: Evidence from a Short-Term Longitudinal Study," *Contemporary Educational Psychology* 14, no. 4 (1989): 382–393, "Performance was more a function of soccer knowledge than of aptitude level."

5. For reviews of the scientific literature on these subjects, see Hirsch, *Cultural Literacy;* Hirsch, *The Schools We Need;* Wolfgang Schneider, Joachim Korkel, and Franz Emanuel Weinert, "Expert Knowledge, General Abilities, and Text Processing," in *Interactions among Aptitudes, Strategies, and Knowledge in Cognitive Performance,* ed. Wolfgang Schneider and Franz Emanuel Weinert (New York: Springer-Verlag, 1990).

6. Letter to Colonel Edward Carrington, January 16, 1787, taken from *The Life and Selected Writings of Thomas Jefferson,* ed. Adrienne Koch and William Peden (New York: Random House, 1944), 411–412.

7. Nelson W. Francis and Henry Kucera, *Frequency Analysis of English Usage: Lexicon and Grammar* (Boston: Houghton Mifflin, 1982).

8. John Willinsky, "The Vocabulary of Cultural Literacy in a Newspaper of Substance" (paper presented at the annual meeting of the National Reading Conference, Tucson, AZ, November 29–December 3, 1988).

9. Hirsch, *Cultural Literacy.*

10. Deborah L. Cohen, "Frequent Moves Said to Boost Risk of School Problems," *Education Week,* September 22, 1993, 15. See also David Wood, Neal Halfon, Debra Scarlata, Paul Newacheck, and Sharon Nessim, "Impact of Family Relocation on Children's Growth, Development, School Function, and Behavior," *Journal of the American Medical Association* 270, no. 11 (September 15, 1993): 1334–1338.

11. Deborah Cohen, "Moving Images," *Education Week,* August 3, 1994, 32–39; David Kerbow, "Patterns of Urban Student Mobility and Local School Reform," *Journal of Education for Students Placed at Risk* 1, no. 2 (1996); Shana Pribesh and Douglas B. Downey, "Why Are Residential and School Moves Associated with Poor School Performance?" *Demography* 36, no. 4 (1999): 521–534; Thomas Fowler-Finn, "Student Stability vs. Mobility," *School Administrator* 58, no. 7 (August 2001): 36–40; Russell W. Rumberger, Katherine A. Larson, Robert K. Ream, and Gregory J. Palardy, *The Educational Consequences of Mobility for California Students and Schools,* PACE Policy Brief (Berkeley, CA: Policy Analysis for California Education, 1999); and Del Stover, "The Mobility Mess of Students Who Move," *Education Digest* 66, no. 3 (2000): 61–64.

12. U.S. General Accounting Office, *Elementary School Children: Many Change Schools Frequently, Harming Their Education* (Washington, DC: GAO, 1994).

13. Bruce C. Straits, "Residence, Migration, and School Progress," *Sociology of Education* 60 (1987): 34–43, cited in H. J. Walberg, "Improving Local Control and Learning," preprint 1994.

14. Harold W. Stevenson and James W. Stigler, *The Learning Gap: Why Our Schools Are Failing and What We Can Learn from Japanese and Chinese Education* (New York: Summit, 1992).

15. Hirsch, *The Schools We Need,* 38–41; Centre for Educational Research and Innovation, *Immigrants' Children at School* (Paris: Organisation for Economic Co-operation and Development, 1987).

16. Hirsch, *The Schools We Need,* 22–26.

E. D. HIRSCH, JR., is a professor emeritus of the University of Virginia and the founder of the Core Knowledge Foundation.

Tom Loveless    **NO**

The Common Core Initiative: What Are the Chances of Success?

The Chances Are Slim at Best—and Here's Why.

Advocates of the Common Core State Standards are hopeful. They believe the standards offer a historic opportunity to boost the overall quality of U.S. education.

Hope is important in policy debates, but there's also a role for skepticism. The Common Core State Standards are not the first national education initiative to be launched with the anticipation of success. Nor is it the first time policymakers have called on education standards to guide us toward better schools.

Looking into the Claims

In a recent study (Loveless, 2012), I tried to estimate the probability that the Common Core standards will produce more learning. The study started with the assumption that a good way to predict the future effects of any policy is to examine how well similar policies have worked in the past—in this case, by examining the past effects of state education standards. The study conducted three statistical investigations using state data from the reading and math portions of the National Assessment of Educational Progress (NAEP) at both 4th and 8th grades.

The first investigation looked at whether the quality of state standards is related to past gains in student achievement. It turns out it isn't. States with poor standards have made NAEP gains comparable to states with excellent standards.

A second investigation looked at whether the levels at which states set past proficiency standards made a difference in achievement. They don't. States with low bars for student proficiency posted similar NAEP scores as those with high bars.[1]

Finally, the third analysis looked at variation in achievement. A key objective of the new standards is to reduce glaring inequalities. This doesn't mean to perfectly equalize all learning, of course. However, striving to ensure that all students possess the knowledge and skills necessary for college or careers means, statistically speaking, that a reduction in achievement variation should occur.

So how much reduction can we expect? The Common Core standards will surely not affect variation inside each individual state. Schools and districts in every state have been operating under common standards for years. The real opportunity that the initiative presents is harmonizing differences in standards among states.

How much variation on NAEP achievement is there among states? Not much. In fact, within-state variation on NAEP is four to five times greater than variation among states. Put another way, the NAEP score gap between Massachusetts and Mississippi, one of the widest between any two states, exists among different schools and districts in *every* state. Unless the Common Core standards possess some unknown power that previous standards didn't possess, that variation will go untouched.

On the basis of these findings, the most reasonable prediction is that the Common Core initiative will have little to no effect on student achievement.

How might it defy this prediction and prove successful? Advocates of the initiative are counting on two mechanisms—high-quality professional development and improvements in curriculum—to overcome the many obstacles that lie ahead.

The Problem with Professional Development

So what does high-quality professional development look like? The research on the topic is limited, producing suggestive characteristics rather than definitive prescriptions.

Limited Potential for Strong Effects

A white paper on teacher quality from the National Academy of Education (Wilson, 2009) notes that several studies have identified promising features of effective professional development. These features include a focus on subject-matter knowledge; ample time (more than 40 hours per program) with a year or more of follow-up; clear linkages to teachers' existing knowledge and skills; training that actively engages teachers; and training teams of teachers from the same school. A meta-analysis by the Council of Chief State School

Officers (Blank & de las Alas, 2009) endorses a similar set of characteristics, although the best programs in this study were longer, delivering 100 hours or more of training.

Both reports note the limitations of professional development research. None of the studies that meet commonly recognized criteria for good evaluations involve middle or high school teachers, only elementary teachers. Also, the list of promising features comes from studies of disparate programs. Their effectiveness when combined into a large-scale, comprehensive program is unknown.

The only randomized field trial—the gold standard of program evaluation—of a professional development program embodying many of the recommended features produced disappointing results (Garet et al., 2008). Participants received training on early reading instruction in content-focused summer institutes, with extensive follow-up during the school year. Teachers' knowledge increased and their pedagogy changed, but there was no improvement in student achievement. The National Academy of Education report (Wilson, 2009) observes that professional development programs with strong effects have been associated with small projects, concluding that "the average teacher has a minimal chance of experiencing high-quality professional development targeted to the subjects, grades, and students he or she teaches" (p. 6).

A Word about External Assessments

To evaluate whether professional development programs had an effect on student achievement, the Council of Chief State School Officers' meta-analysis includes some studies that look at assessments specifically designed by the programs themselves as well as studies that use national, state, and local assessments to judge program effectiveness. The latter group is more relevant to the Common Core standards because the success or failure of the programs depended on how much students learned on external assessments, the type of assessments the Common Core initiative will use.

These evaluations detected educationally insignificant, even trivial, effect sizes: .17 for national norm-referenced tests, .01 for statewide assessments, and .05 for studies that used local achievement tests (Blank & de las Alas, 2009). If professional development typically yields such small effects, then expectations that it will have a significant impact in the context of the new standards are probably unwarranted.

There's an important lesson here for educators who, in coming years, will be bombarded with tales of wonderful professional development tied to the Common Core standards. Be on guard. In an extensive Institute for Education Sciences review of 1,300 studies of professional development (Yoon, Duncan, Lee, Scarloss, & Shapley, 2007), the reviewers cautioned:

> The limited number of studies and the variability in their professional development approaches

preclude any conclusions about the effectiveness of specific professional development programs or about the effectiveness of professional development by form, content, and intensity (p. 14).

A "Better" Curriculum—But Which One?

The Common Core website makes a point of differentiating between standards and curriculum. The page "Myths vs. Facts" declares, The Standards are not a curriculum. They are a clear set of shared goals and expectations for what knowledge and skills will help our students succeed. Local teachers, principals, superintendents, and others will decide *how* the standards are to be met. Teachers will continue to devise lesson plans and tailor instruction to the individual needs of the students in their classrooms. (National Governors Association Center for Best Practices & Council of Chief State School Officers, 2012)

The curriculum that fleshes out the new standards will, in the end, determine how teachers, parents, and students actually experience the standards. What will that curriculum contain? Given that curricular content is subject to local discretion, how broad are the boundaries for those choices?

Core Knowledge vs. Partnership for 21st Century Skills

Consider two dramatically different views of curriculum, one supported by the Core Knowledge Foundation and the other by the Partnership for 21st Century Skills. Their philosophies are diametrically opposed, yet both organizations are convinced that the Common Core State Standards embrace their point of view.

Core Knowledge, the brainchild of E. D. Hirsch, holds that content knowledge is king. The author of the Core Knowledge blog, Robert Pondiscio (2012), lauds the Common Core initiative for reminding us "to engage children not just with rote literacy skills work and process writing, but also, and especially, with real content—rich, deep, broad knowledge about the world in which they live." For example, on the Core Knowledge website, model lessons for 8th grade language arts include the study of Greek and Latin root words; William Shakespeare's *Twelfth Night*; Pearl S. Buck's *The Good Earth* (supplemented by a research paper on Chinese culture); and Maya Angelou's *I Know Why the Caged Bird Sings*. The key to becoming a good reader is content knowledge, Pondiscio argues, and he asks, "Yet how many times have we heard it said that we need to deemphasize teaching 'mere facts' and focus on skills like critical thinking, creativity, and problem solving?"

The Partnership for 21st Century Skills promotes exactly what Pondiscio deplores. The partnership has developed a framework of skills it believes are essential to good schooling, including life and career skills; information, media, and technology skills; and what it calls the 4Cs (critical thinking, communication, collaboration, and creativity). The partnership has also published a P21 Common Core Toolkit (Magner, Soulé, & Wesolowski, 2011), which shows how the Common Core initiative and the partnership's framework are aligned. The toolkit also offers vignettes ("lesson starters") to illustrate how the Common Core standards integrate with the partnership's framework.

For example, in contrast with Core Knowledge's 8th grade lesson, an 8th grade English language arts lesson aligned to the partnership's framework proceeds as follows:

After completing a literature circle unit of teen problem novels, students brainstorm a list of significant social, emotional, or health issues that teens face today. Working in groups, students research one issue and create a public service announcement on a closed YouTube channel (viewable only by students in the class) to persuade their peers about one action they should take regarding the issue. Students will select and use references from literary readings (e.g., citing how a particular novel presents the issue) as well as research from nonfiction sources to illustrate major points (Partnership for 21st Century Skills, 2008, p. 8).

This lesson would never occur in a Core Knowledge classroom. The point here is not to settle the argument between Core Knowledge and the Partnership for 21st Century Skills. Rather, it's to illustrate the elasticity of the educational philosophy underpinning the Common Core State Standards. Philosophical ambiguity may be smart politically because it allows for a wide range of supporters—a "big tent" strategy. But if two organizations with such starkly contrasting points of view both see the standards as compatible with their definition of an ideal curriculum, then any guidance about what to teach in local schools is broad indeed.

The Curriculum Conundrum

How will educators make curricular decisions? Hopefully, the effectiveness of curricular materials and programs will factor prominently.

Unfortunately, the research on effective curriculum is as thin as the research on effective professional development. As my Brookings colleagues document in a recent report, educators are "choosing blindly" when making curriculum decisions. Instructional programs can differ dramatically in their effectiveness (Chingos & Whitehurst, 2012).

Mathematica Policy Research conducted a randomized field trial of four primary-grade math textbooks and found huge differences between the most and least effective (Agodini, Harris, Thomas, Murphy, & Gallagher, 2010). Such high-quality studies are rare, and more important, even the most robust studies cannot do the impossible—provide advice on how to choose effective materials from a sea of candidates that have never been rigorously evaluated in the first place.

So what kind of information will inform the selection of local curriculum? Note that the publishers of the four math textbooks just mentioned—both effective and ineffective alike—all advertise that their texts are now aligned with the Common Core standards. As Chingos and Whitehurst (2012) observe:

Publishers of instructional materials are lining up to declare the alignment of their materials with the Common Core standards using the most superficial of definitions. The Common Core standards will only have a chance of raising student achievement if they are implemented with high-quality materials, but there is currently no basis to measure the quality of materials. (p. 1)

Back to Where We Started?

The Common Core State Standards have been adopted by 46 states and the District of Columbia. They enjoy a huge following of well-wishers and supporters who are optimistic that the standards will boost achievement in U.S. schools. Setting aside the cheerleading and fond hopes, what are the real chances of success?

The most reasonable prediction is that the Common Core initiative will have little to no effect on student achievement. Moreover, on the basis of current research, high-quality professional development and "excellent" curricular materials are also unlikely to boost the Common Core standards' slim chances of success.

References

Agodini, R., Harris, B., Thomas, M., Murphy, R., & Gallagher, L. (2010). *Achievement effects of four early elementary school math curricula: Findings for first and second graders*. Princeton, NJ: Mathematica Policy Research.

Blank, R. K., & de las Alas, N. (2009). *Effects of teacher professional development on gains in student achievement*. Washington, DC: Council of Chief State School Officers.

Chingos, M. M., & Whitehurst, G. J. (2012). *Choosing blindly: Instructional materials, teacher effectiveness, and the Common Core*. Washington, DC: Brookings Institution. Retrieved from www.brookings.edu/research/reports/2012/04/10-curriculum-chingos-whitehurst

Garet, M. S., Cronen, S., Eaton, M., Kurki, A., Ledwig, M., Jones, W., et al. (2008). *The impact of two professional development interventions on early reading instruction and achievement*. Washington, DC: Institute of Education Sciences.

Loveless, T. (2012). *The 2012 Brown Center report on American education: How well are American students learning?* Washington, DC: Brookings Institution. Retrieved from www.brookings.edu/~/media/research/files/reports/2012/2/brown%20center/0216_brown_education_loveless.pdf

Magner, T., Soulé, H., & Wesolowski, K. (2011). *P21 Common Core toolkit: A guide to aligning the Common Core State Standards with the Framework for 21st Century Skills.* Washington, DC: Partnership for 21st Century Skills. Retrieved from www.p21 .org/storage/documents/P21CommonCoreToolkit.pdf.

National Governors Association Center for Best Practices & Council of Chief State School Officers. (2012). *Myths vs. Facts.* Washington, DC: Authors. Retrieved from www.corestandards.org/about-the-standards /myths-vs-facts

Partnership for 21st Century Skills. (2008). *21st century skills map.* Tucson, AZ: Author. Retrieved from www .p21.org/storage/documents/21st_century_skills_english _map.pdf

Pondiscio, R. (2012, June 14). Nobody loves standards (and that's OK) [blog post]. Retrieved from *Common Core Watch* at www.edexcellence.net/commentary /education-gadfly-daily/common-core-watch/2012/nobody -loves-standards-and-thats-ok.html

Wilson, S. (Ed., 2009). *Teacher quality* (Education policy white paper). Washington, DC: National Academy of Education. Retrieved from http://naeducation.org /Teacher_Quality_White_Paper.pdf

Yoon, K., Duncan, T., Lee, S., Scarloss, B., & Shapley, K. (2007). *Reviewing the evidence on how teacher professional development affects student achievement* (Issues & Answers Report, REL 2007–No. 033). Washington, DC: Regional Educational Laboratory Southwest. Retrieved from http://ies.ed.gov/ncee /edlabs/regions/southwest/pdf/REL_2007033.pdf

Note

1. States that raised the bar from 2005 to 2009 did show an increase in 4th grade NAEP scores, but the correlation is weak, it does not appear in 8th grade, and the direction of causality is unclear. Rather than loftier expectations driving achievement gains, states may have raised the bar for proficiency because of rising achievement.

Tom Loveless is a senior fellow at the Brown Center on Education Policy at The Brookings Institution. He is a former elementary school teacher.

EXPLORING THE ISSUE

Should Schools Adopt a Common Core Curriculum?

Critical Thinking and Reflection

1. Loveless relies largely on previous attempts to implement standards on a wide scale (e.g., at a state level) to make predictions about the chances of the Common Core Curriculum having an impact on student achievement. Do you think this is a reasonable critique? Why or why not?
2. Hirsch focuses largely on ensuring that all students acquire a reasonable common set of knowledge and skills that are the foundation for everyday literacy activities. Do you think that this approach will help all students equally? Alternatively, will the approach be of greater benefit to struggling students? For students who are already high achievers? Why?
3. Do you think that adoption of the Common Core Curriculum will reduce variability in the educational experiences of students in different classrooms and different schools? Why or why not?

Is There Common Ground?

Are there empirical data to indicate whether the Common Core is working? The State of Kentucky was an early adopter of the standards and thus has been among the first to evaluate its effects. Positive effects have been seen, but the improvements on many indicators are modest at best. Such data are not surprising to critics, such as Tom Loveless, who have seen other attempts at standards specification fail to achieve positive effects when implemented on a smaller scale. Why, he asks, should a larger-scale implementation of the same approach fare any better? But is it fair to make conclusions so early on? In fact, one could argue that a massive change such as the adoption of a new educational approach by virtually the entire nation is bound to meet with unanticipated barriers and missteps and thus, it may take several years for all of the "bugs" to be worked out. Moreover, the adoption of common and effective methods of teaching the standards and of evaluating student progress will require time to "catch up" and align correctly with the standards. Thus, a fair test of the initiative may not be possible until several years of implementation.

At the same time, however, is it wise to adopt the standards and a well-developed curriculum for teaching those standards? Two concerns arise here. First, it may be that the failure of the current system is as much, or more, about teaching practices than content. In this case, changing standards may thus have little effect without curricular development. Second, the development of a curriculum that not only accurately embodies the standards at any one grade level but that also is consistent and synergistic with the curricula at earlier and later grades is a daunting undertaking, which may well take decades to achieve. In this case, one wonders about the wisdom of investing almost exclusively in changing only a part of the educational reform puzzle.

Finally, we are faced with an unsettling truth that the core skills that are needed by a skilled and informed citizenry today may not be the same skills that are needed in a decade or two. Indeed, we have only take a cursory look back at digital technology for evidence of the rapid pace of changes needed to be successful in school and the workforce. How can we create an educational system that can respond quickly to such changes? Is a system controlled at the local or the national level likely to be most flexible and responsive?

Create Central

www.mhhe.com/createcentral

Additional Resources

M. M. Chingos and G. J. Whitehurst, *Choosing Blindly: Instructional Materials, Teacher Effectiveness, and the Common Core* (The Brookings Institution, 2012).

E. D. Hirsch, Jr., *The Schools We Need* (Doubleday, 1996).

Tom Loveless, *The Great Curriculum Debate: How Should We Teach Reading and Math?* (Brookings Institution Press, 2001).

Internet References . . .

Core Knowledge® Foundation

http://www.coreknowledge.org/

Partnership for 21st Century Skills

http://www.p21.org/

Brookings Institution

http://www.brookings.edu/

Common Core State Standards Initiative

http://www.corestandards.org/

Selected, Edited, and with Issue Framing Material by:
Leonard Abbeduto, *University of California, Davis*
and
Frank Symons, *University of Minnesota*

ISSUE

Should Character Education Define the Values We Teach Students?

YES: Merle J. Schwartz, Alexandra Beatty, and Eileen Dachnowicz, from "Character Education: Frill or Foundation?" *Principal Leadership* (December 2006)

NO: Pamela Bolotin Joseph and Sara Efron, from "Seven Worlds of Moral Education," *Phi Delta Kappan* (March 2005)

Learning Outcomes

After reading this issue, you will be able to:

- Compare and contrast the different views of character education proposed by Schwartz and colleagues, on the one hand, and Jospeh and Efron, on the other.
- Summarize the outcomes achieved by students experiencing several popular character education programs.
- Understand the debate about the essential elements or goals of character education.

ISSUE SUMMARY

YES: Merle J. Schwartz, Alexandra Beatty, and Eileen Dachnowicz argue that identifying and teaching core values such as civic engagement and virtue can improve academic performance, school climate, and individual character.

NO: Pamela Bolotin Joseph and Sara Efron argue for a broader moral curriculum, one that goes beyond character education to include cultural competence and a commitment to peace, justice, and social action.

U.S. society is in a state of moral decay, or so say many government officials, politicians, and religious leaders. And, indeed, there are many alarming trends reflecting a tendency of citizens to harm or devalue themselves and others. Crime, violence, and high-risk behaviors (e.g., drug and alcohol abuse) are more common today than they were a few decades ago. In the past, concerns about the moral state of society typically led to a renewed interest in—and dedication to—society's children, who were seen as the hope for the future. What is unique about today's disintegration of the social order is that many of the crimes, acts of violence, and problem behaviors of greatest concern are those perpetrated by children and youth. Perhaps even more startling are the acts of violence committed by children against other children *at school*. In addition to the acts of violence, many social commentators point with concern and outrage to increases in teenage pregnancy, drug and alcohol abuse, gambling, and other problem activities. It often seems that every new report disseminated by the media suggests that children are engaging in risky or criminal behaviors at younger and younger ages.

Many social critics have argued that the solution to this problem is to teach morality, or values, in school. These critics suggest that schools rather than families must be the source of moral education because the American family is itself in disarray. As evidence that many families are poorly prepared to conduct the requisite moral education, critics point to the increasing divorce rate, the fact that the majority of American children live for at least some part of their lives in a single-parent home, and the decline in the amount of time that parents spend with their children. In fact, many believe that this so-called disintegration of the American family is largely responsible for what they see as the dismal moral state of today's youth.

Calls for the inclusion of a moral agenda in the school curriculum harken back to the early history of education in the United States. Prior to the twentieth century, moral education, which often took the form of inculcating a system of values and beliefs reflective of a particular religious ideology, was commonplace. In fact, the Bible was often the primary textbook not only for the curriculum of values but also for the more strictly academic curriculum. It was not until recently that the debate about the separation of church and state led to a more secular and, some would say, less moral curriculum. This movement away from explicit instruction in religiously derived morality was greatly hastened in the 1960s and 1970s by a rejection of "traditional" values and authority and an increased emphasis on personal freedom and autonomy. In more recent years, the increasing cultural diversity of U.S. schools has facilitated the adoption of moral relativism, a belief that there are differences across cultures (and perhaps even between individuals within a culture) with regard to the systems of values held and that all those systems should be seen as equally valid and moral.

Should schools once again incorporate morality into their agendas? What should this moral curriculum look like? Whose values should it reflect? Have American schools really stopped teaching moral values, or have they simply been teaching values that are at odds with the values held by those who call for a return to morality?

These are some of the questions that shape the debate reflected in the following selections. In the first selection, Merle Schwartz, Alexandra Beatty, and Eileen Dachnowicz describe several successful character education programs that not only inculcated specific moral traits and values in students but also improved academic performance. These programs stress the use of role models of, and reinforcement for, engaging in specific behaviors thought to be critical for the functioning of a democratic society such as ours. In the second selection, Pamela Bolotin Joseph and Sara Efron argue that the traits and behaviors at the center of character education represent only one possible instantiation of moral education. Joseph and Efron suggest that equally important as the values of moral education are behaviors and modes of thought derived from non-mainstream or non-U.S. cultures, an ethic of caring and nurturing, an orientation toward peace, an inclination toward social action, and a commitment to justice and ethical inquiry.

YES

Merle J. Schwartz, Alexandra Beatty, and Eileen Dachnowicz

Character Education: Frill or Foundation?

Accountability. The word resounds in states, districts, and schools as educational programs come under close scrutiny. Proof of academic performance often serves as the litmus test for maintaining instructional practices and programs. Just as the national focus on academic improvement has gained momentum, so too has another movement calling for character education. Educators find themselves caught in the middle, questioning whether character education is just another passing fad or a valid educational initiative that will positively affect student performance as well as attitude.

Although character education has gained momentum at the elementary school level and has made considerable strides in middle level schools, high school faculties are still less than enthusiastic about adopting it. It is easy to see how some teachers, long exhausted from serving as the custodians of the prevailing education fashion, look skeptically at this movement. Faced with the formidable challenge of high-stakes testing, they wonder how they can prepare their students for state standardized tests as well as the SAT and AP exams and still find time to accent ethical qualities. Some teachers may listen wistfully to success stories in which character education has transformed school culture. Many can easily point out that a lack of ethical values seems to be the root of many of the problems in schools.

What Does Science Say?

The Character Education Partnership (CEP), a national advocacy group for character education in Washington, DC, aims to help educators and policymakers make informed decisions about character education by identifying and describing strategies that work. Each year for the past nine years, CEP has recognized approximately 10 elementary and secondary schools as National Schools of Character because of their exemplary implementation of character education. Through reading thousands of applications and visiting more than 180 award-winning schools, CEP has collected a wealth of effective strategies and also observed a correlation between the effective implementation of character education and improved school culture and academic advancement.

Interviews and record reviews of middle level and high school award winners showed that character education had positive effects on discipline, student and faculty

member morale, and student performance. For example, Kennedy Middle School in Eugene, OR, showed a 15% improvement in meeting or exceeding the state's academic benchmarks and a 65% decrease in discipline referrals. Halifax (PA) Middle School reported not only the elimination of vandalism but also a total change in student attitude toward academic success. In addition to improved disciplinary statistics, high school winners—such as South Carroll High School in Sykesville, MD, and Cranford (NJ) High School—have reported a steady increase in their SAT averages. Site visitors observed that school size and geographical location did not appear to be the contributing factor to the school's success. Eleanor Roosevelt High School in Greenbelt, MD, which has nearly 3,000 students, and private New Hampton (NH) School, which has 325, have benefited from character education.

The outcomes of character education, however, are difficult to measure. Most studies either have referred to the results of specific commercial programs or have relied heavily on anecdotal accounts. But two recent studies of character education programs, funded largely by the John Templeton Foundation, provide evidence of their effectiveness—and describe strategies that will help middle level and high school educators who want to initiate or improve character education in their schools.

These data-driven studies approach character education scientifically from two different perspectives. The first explores the character education initiatives in 24 high schools that have received recognition for excellence; the second study examines 69 research studies on 33 specific character education programs to provide empirical evidence of what works in character education. The two studies fit together like pieces of a puzzle to confirm what many have long argued: effective character education not only improves school climate and student behavior but also can lead to academic improvement.

What Is Character Education?

The phrase *character education* does not refer to a single approach or even a single list of the values that are taught in character education programs. *Character education* is often the umbrella term that describes concerted efforts to teach a number of qualities, such as civic virtues, respect and responsibility, social and emotional learning, empathy and caring, tolerance for diversity, and service to the community. Citizens need training in each of these areas to develop the moral and ethical stamina that enables them to contribute positively to a democratic society. Because a democratic society depends on a citizenry that shares such values as justice, fairness, responsibility, and caring, many believe that it is the obligation of schools, both public and private, to teach such values.

Lickona and Davidson (2005) point out that strength of character is necessary for the development of civic character: "Becoming a person of civic character, for example, requires the development of ethical thinking, moral agency, and a battery of social and emotional skills" (p. 178). Individual research on character and civic education adds additional characteristics to the definition of *character*. In emphasizing the role of living in an increasingly globalized economy. Nordgren (2002) exhorts schools to foster highly effective teamwork and shared decision making because people's lives are intertwined in a shrinking world.

Although some schools and districts choose commercial programs so staff members and families will be on the same page as far as language and goals are concerned, many schools have developed homegrown programs that address their students' specific needs. Some are comprehensive, and others are a compilation of books, Web sites, and other resources that educators can mine for ideas.

All character education programs share the following goals:

- Increasing students' awareness of moral and ethical questions
- Affecting students' attitudes regarding such questions
- Affecting students' actions.

Some programs target specific behaviors—they aim to reduce rates of disciplinary action, cheating, teen pregnancy, drug use, and the like. Others may aim to promote positive behaviors, such as community involvement and civic participation. Still others focus on developing skills or fostering complex thinking about ethical issues—and many incorporate multiple goals.

The boundaries of character education are imprecise. These goals overlap with those for other efforts, such as civic education programs and service-learning programs. By 2002, however, roughly three-fourths of the states were actively encouraging their versions of character education; 14 states mandated some form of it, another 14 encouraged it through legislation, and another 10 supported it in other ways.

Does It Work? Can We Tell?

Lickona and Davidson (2005) document a three-part effort to identify practices that seem to hold promise for character education at the secondary level. Beginning with a broad review of the literature on adolescent development, high school reform, and character education, the authors developed a framework for thinking about the

characteristics of high schools that integrate ethics and excellence. First, they identified 24 high schools that had received external recognition for excellence. The schools, ranging in size from 300 to 4,300 students, were drawn from every section of the country and included public and private schools in rural, suburban, and urban settings. The researchers examined each school closely to ascertain successful strategies and develop generalizations about effective practice that is based on those strategies. Using focus groups, classroom observations, interviews, and analyses of program materials and archival data, the team developed portraits of the schools and their practices.

The findings are organized around the "promising practices" that the team identified as most effective for developing both individuals with key character traits and an ethical learning community. The authors present their findings in the form of six principles for developing such a community:

1. Develop shared purpose and identity. Explicit expectations for personal behavior as well as academic achievement—such as an honor code, a school motto, and school traditions—provide important direction for students.
2. Align practices with desired outcomes and relevant research. Offering staff members and parents specific guidance about research-based strategies for meeting designated goals reinforces a school's efforts.
3. Have a voice; take a stand. Allowing students to have a voice in the classroom and in school affairs—as well as listening to faculty and staff members, parents, and community members—contributes to excellence and ethics in a school.
4. Take personal responsibility for continuous self-development. Adult members of the school community can set an example for students by promoting the need to strive for excellence and to engage in self-reflection. Thus, a culture of excellence and fostering personal responsibility is created in classrooms and schoolwide.
5. Practice collective responsibility for excellence and ethics. In a community that values ethics and excellence, adults and students intervene right away when others need support to succeed or do the right thing.
6. Grapple with tough issues. Collective responsibility for an ethical learning community entails confronting institutional practices or issues that are at odds with the school's commitment to excellence and ethics.

Promising practices also buttress the "eight strengths of character" identified as integral to "smart and good high schools":

- Lifelong learner and critical thinker
- Diligent and capable performer
- Socially and emotionally skilled person
- Ethical thinker

- Respectful and responsible moral agent
- Self-disciplined person who pursues a healthy lifestyle
- Contributing community member and democratic citizen
- Spiritual person engaged in crafting a life of noble purpose.

After assessing their own school's needs, educators can select from a host of proven instructional strategies, high school reform designs, professional development opportunities, curricular structures, media literacy resources, study skills programs, team challenges, and academic initiatives that they can replicate in their own schools. The report concludes with a question-and-answer section that offers practical advice for initiating or implementing character education programs in schools that have a wide range of concerns.

For teachers who perceive character education as another frill that interferes with the real business of education, namely academic growth, this study shows that teaching ethical values goes hand-in-hand with academic performance. A headmaster of a small, private school interviewed for the study summed up his vision: "'To have an engaging school, you need three things: teachers ready to teach, students ready to learn, and something important to teach.'" Lickona and Davidson's study provides practitioners with verified strategies for character education that have worked in shaping high schools of excellence, strategies that middle level and high school educators can adapt to the needs of their schools.

Berkowitz and Bier (2005), the authors of the second study, look at existing research on character education programs "to help practitioners to be more effective in fostering the development of students' character" (p. 23). They began with a fairly broad definition of *character education:* "any school-based K–12 initiatives either intended to promote the development of some aspect of student character or for which some aspect of student character was measured as a relevant outcome variable" (p. 3). They sought to address four questions:

- For which programs is there research demonstrating effectiveness?
- What are the characteristics of effective programs?
- What do schools generally do that is effective?
- What are the effects of specific character education practices?

To answer the first question, Berkowitz and Bier identified 109 research studies that were potentially relevant and found that 69 of them provided scientifically sound evidence that 33 of the programs studied were effective. This list of programs provided the basis for answering the second question. The team developed lists of pedagogical strategies and other characteristics of the 33 programs for which there was some evidence of successful outcomes and collected data about how prevalent these strategies

were. The question about the effectiveness of these strategies was more difficult to address, and the authors suggest that support for additional research on that question is needed.

On the question of the outcomes of character education, the team found an overall success rate of 51%—approximately half the time, positive change was found to result from the program studied. Among the areas in which the researchers noted the greatest degree of positive change were sociomoral cognition (thinking about ethical and moral issues), prosocial behaviors and attitudes, sexual behavior, problem-solving skills, and drug use. Moreover, the researchers found that cooperative learning and class discussions of moral issues were the most effective practices for producing academic and social outcomes.

From this review, Berkowitz and Bier (2005) concluded that, when effectively implemented, character education programs of many kinds can have a significant impact on young people and that the effects can be quite long lasting. They identified features that were characteristic of effective programs:

- Professional development. All 33 of the effective programs identified incorporated ongoing professional development.
- Peer interaction. All 33 also incorporated strategies for fostering peer interaction, such as discussion, role playing, and cooperative learning.
- Direct teaching and skill training. Many of the programs included direct instruction about character as well as teaching specific intrapersonal (e.g., self-management) and interpersonal (e.g., conflict resolution) skills and capacities.
- Explicit agenda. More than half the programs studied use specific language about character, morality, values, or ethics.
- Family and community involvement. Including parents and other community members—as recipients of character education and as participants in the design and delivery of the programs—was a common strategy.
- Models and mentors. Both peer and adult role models foster character development.
- Integration into academic curricula. Nearly half of the effective programs are integrated with academic curricula in some way, most often through social studies and language arts curricula.
- Multiple strategies. Virtually all of the effective programs use a multistrategy approach, rather than relying on a single model or tool.

How Does It Add Up?

These two studies offer a wealth of detail and descriptions that enrich the picture of how and why particular strategies stand out as effective. The data presented in the two studies indicate that character education initiatives affect student attitudes and behavior, thus setting the stage for improved academic performance.

They also take different but equally important approaches to the challenge of drawing conclusions about what works in character education. What is interesting in comparing the studies is that despite the difference in focus, there was similarity in identifying earmarks of fruitful character education programs at the secondary level, including:

- Goals should be both explicit and ambitious
- Professional development is necessary
- The whole school community should be involved, and everyone should have a voice
- Adults need to be role models.

Transforming the culture of a middle level or high school is not easy. As these studies point out, however, through careful planning, professional development, and involvement of all members of the school community, character education becomes far more than a passing fad; it is the road map to building a caring school culture, a safer and more-nurturing environment, and a more responsible and responsive student body, all of which lay the foundation for improved academic performance.

MERLE J. SCHWARTZ, ALEXANDRA BEATTY, AND EILEEN DACHNOWICZ were all affiliated with Character Education Partnership in Washington, DC, at the time they wrote this article.

Pamela Bolotin Joseph
and Sara Efron

Seven Worlds of Moral Education

In his striking critique of character education, Alfie Kohn suggests that educators might want to "define our efforts to promote children's social and moral development as an *alternative*" to character education.[1] In this article, we address Kohn's question "What does the alternative look like?" by describing the aims, practices, advantages, and difficulties of seven worlds of moral education—of which character education is only one. Lastly, we consider why character education should be the dominant approach to moral education in the United States when there are inspiring alternatives.

Viewing moral education as comprising various "moral worlds" helps us to imagine classrooms and schools that consistently support the beliefs, values, and visions that will shape students into adults and determine the world they will make. In such environments, moral education is a coherent endeavor created with purpose and deliberation. Educators in moral worlds believe that they must create a process through which young people can learn to recognize values that represent prosocial behaviors, engage in actions that bring about a better life for others, and appreciate ethical and compassionate conduct.

We describe below the moral worlds of character education, cultural heritage, caring community, peace education, social action, just community, and ethical inquiry. These worlds do not exist in isolation, nor are their purposes diametrically opposed; they may, in fact, share several characteristics. Classrooms and schools can also create coherent hybrid approaches that combine aspects of several moral worlds. Nonetheless, to clarify and foster conversations about moral education, we explore these approaches to social and ethical development as distinct moral worlds.

Character Education

The moral world of character education rests on the conviction that schooling can shape the behavior of young people by inculcating in them the proper virtues. Proponents of this world argue that children need clear directions and good role models and, implicitly, that schools should shape character when families are deficient in this task. Advocates also recommend giving students numerous opportunities to do good deeds, such as taking part in service learning, which they believe will eventually lead

to moral habits. Moreover, character educators believe in establishing strong incentives for good behavior.[2]

To no small extent, *The Book of Virtues,* by William Bennett, influences many character education programs. The virtues Bennett describes are "self-discipline, compassion, responsibility, friendship, work, courage, perseverance, honesty, loyalty, and faith." Another strong influence is Character Counts, a coalition that posits "six pillars of character": 1) be honest; 2) treat others with respect; 3) do what you are supposed to do; 4) play by the rules; 5) be kind; and 6) do your share to make your school and community better. Communities have also developed their own sets of traits or rules that guide character education programs.[3]

How do schools create a moral world using character traits as starting points? First, modeling virtuous behavior is a key component of character education programs—teachers, administrators, and students are instructed to be role models. Many schools call attention to character traits in public forums and displays such as assemblies, daily announcements, bulletin boards, and banners, as well as in the study of history and literature. School 18 in Albany, New York, uses "positive reinforcement of good character traits" through a Kids for Character program. "Students who are 'caught' doing something that shows good character have their names posted where the entire school community can see. Then, each Friday, those students are called to the office to receive a reward."[4]

Schools may emphasize a different character trait each month in curricular content and assemblies. In the Kent City Schools in Ohio, November is "compassion" month. In social studies classes, students "study those who immigrated to this country at great personal sacrifice, develop a school or community service project, and research the Underground Railroad and consider how people extended help to those escaping slavery." Self-control is the trait for December. In physical education classes, students "devise an exercise chart to help monitor personal fitness." In language arts, they "keep a personal journal of times self-control was used." And in math classes, they "graph the number of times students hand in assignments on time." Teachers may also infuse their classroom management strategies and lessons with respect for aspects of character.[5]

A strength of the character education moral world is educators' belief that it is their responsibility to form character rather than remain indifferent to their students' moral development. Another positive aspect of this approach is the goal of proponents to infuse character education throughout the curriculum and school environment in order for students to experience the consistency of a moral world both academically and socially.

However, character education raises a number of critical questions that its advocates have not satisfactorily addressed. Are behavioral traits in fact the same as moral character? Do displays of virtues or desired traits truly encourage moral behavior? Does the posting of character traits on banners and bulletin boards result in a "marquee mentality" and therefore not reach the hearts and minds of young people? Is character education merely indoctrination of dominant cultural standards that may not represent the values of diverse communities? And finally, do the values chosen by character educators reflect the status quo and encourage compliance with it?[6]

Cultural Heritage

Like character education, the moral world of cultural heritage emphasizes values. These values, however, are not those of the mainstream but, instead, are drawn from the traditions of nondominant cultures. Unlike character education, there are no underlying assumptions that schools may have better values than those of communities and families or that schools need to instill character traits in children that may run counter to students' own cultural values. In the cultural heritage moral world, the spheres of school, home, and community are interconnected. Parents, elders, and cultural leaders educate children within and outside the walls of the school. Moreover, students learn cultural traditions and values not through direct instruction but by deep understanding of and participation in the culture's arts and ceremonies.

One embodiment of the cultural heritage world is the values instruction offered in Afrocentric schools. For example, the mission statement of the African American Academy for Accelerated Learning in Minneapolis affirms the importance of "reconnecting African American families to their cultural heritage, spirituality and history." The mission of the African American Academy, a public school in Seattle, is to instruct students in a way that "embraces the history, culture and heritage of African and African American people by studying and putting into practice the seven principles of Nguzo Saba: Umoja (Unity), Kujichagulia (Self-Determination), Ujima (Collective Work and Responsibility), Ujamaa (Cooperative Economics), Nia (Purpose), Kuumba (Creativity), and Imani (Faith)." Afrocentric schools emphasize parent involvement. In a report to the Kansas City Missouri Board of Education, the African Centered Education Task Force affirmed the African proverb "It takes an entire village to raise just one child" by giving parents an essential role in African-centered schools as "partners of the village."[7]

Native American schools that teach language, customs, and history also create the moral world of cultural heritage. In Native American education, cherished values include "respect [for] people and their feelings, especially respecting elders, and living in harmony with nature." Schools are imbued with a "sense of empathy and kinship with other forms of life" and a belief that "there should be no division between school climate and culture and family and community climate and culture." Parents and elders are present throughout the school, and students and teachers are expected to be in the community and the natural environment as well as in the classroom. The Tulalip Heritage School in Washington State (jointly sponsored by the public school district, the Boys and Girls Club, and the Tulalip Tribe) transmits its ethos to the students by having them learn the stories of ancestors, cultivating respect for Native American culture and "respect for one another," and recognizing the importance of community. The NAWAYEE Center School, an alternative high school in Minneapolis, offers cultural classes that "include art, spirituality, family, community, and oral traditions" but also strives to ensure that "American Indian cultural values and beliefs are modeled and integrated throughout the entire curriculum."[8]

The cultural heritage moral world has a number of advantages. Cultural heritage schools demonstrate respect for the cultures of their students by not just paying lip service to cultural diversity but being seriously committed to the sustenance of cultures. Partnerships with communities and meaningful parent involvement create active stakeholders in these schools and foster greater commitment to education. Continuity between the culture of the home and that of the school allows for moral instruction to use familiar patterns of communication, both verbal and nonverbal. As they learn through culturally congruent education, students do not experience a disjunction between their families' and schools' moral instruction. Furthermore, students have opportunities to learn more about their communities' moral values through the study of their history and culture, so moral learning is embedded within academic scholarship.[9]

A difficulty in implementing this model of moral education is its dependence on educators who come from the students' cultures or who themselves have deep knowledge of the culture. Districts clearly must do all that is possible to attract such educators and to sponsor community members in teacher preparation programs. Also, although all schools benefit from parents' and elders' participation, a fully realized moral world of cultural heritage would be most desired in certain schools or districts in which a significant percentage of the students are from one ethnic culture. it is crucial, however, to be sensitive to the concerns of the community. This model of moral education cannot be imposed upon a community, but it should be provided if the community so desires. Moreover, a focus on the cultural heritage of a community in no way precludes the need to learn the skills required for success in the dominant culture. Indeed, all the schools mentioned here also have a strong academic focus.

Caring Community

The caring community emphasizes the ethic of care—nurturing, closeness, emotional attachment, and respectful, mutually supportive relationships. This moral world also focuses on the social and emotional health of all its community members. As the individuals in the classroom and the school begin to feel like a family, the school's institutional image is replaced by that of a home. Educators' moral influence stems from their caring relationships with students, parents, and one another. In the caring community, students are not rewarded for individual empathic actions; instead, these behaviors are considered the norm of the classroom culture.[10]

Accounts of schools as caring communities describe how teachers, administrators, parents, and students feel that they are members of a community. In these schools, class size is small, teachers are mentored, and all staff members feel and demonstrate genuine concern for students. In the classroom, nurturing peer relationships develop as students care for one another through informal and planned activities and structures such as buddy systems.[11]

In academics, the theme of caring is introduced through service learning projects and the study of literature that accentuates interpersonal and intercultural understanding. The classroom environment features discussions and cooperative learning activities and is defined not by rules but by how students feel about being in the class and being with one another. For example, at the Russ School in California, children developed a list of "Ways We Want to Be in Room Eight" as their classroom rules rather than a list of prohibitions.[12]

Inclusiveness is another theme in the caring community, as schools welcome and nurture diverse populations, including special education students. For instance, when the Lincoln Center Middle School in Milwaukee chose to become a caring community, it expressed caring by selecting students by means of a lottery for all who were interested in its arts-based curriculum rather than by holding auditions or having specific admissions requirements. This moral world also features schoolwide activities that involve parents and community members. Moreover, families and school personnel communicate with one another about students' academic progress, social development, and emotional health.[13]

The caring community has numerous benefits for students. Researchers from the Developmental Studies Center Child Development Project report that children educated in such schools perceive their classrooms as fair, safe, caring places that are conducive to learning. Once more, students "with a strong sense of community [are] more likely to act ethically and altruistically, develop social and emotional competencies, avoid drug use and violent behavior, and [be] academically motivated." Emotional well-being is the catalyst for moral development in the caring community. As students feel respected and cared for in loving classroom and school environments, they are less likely to act out "from feelings of inferiority, cynicism, or egocentrism that blind them to others' feelings." Furthermore, students who are nurtured are more likely to expand their sphere of caring from friends, teachers, and families to others in their communities.[14]

Difficulties for educators who wish to create a caring community occur when school culture—large class size, disruptive pullout programs, and a history of not welcoming families—thwarts the building of caring relationships. Although educators may strive to create a caring classroom, students and teachers may feel "uncared for" when the school environment is hostile. Unfortunately, the students most in need of caring often have schools whose resources cannot support this moral world.[15]

Peace Education

The moral world of peace education stems from an ethic of care that extends beyond the classroom. Moral commitments underpinning peace education include valuing and befriending the Earth, living in harmony with the natural world, recognizing the interrelatedness of all human and natural life, preventing violence toward the Earth and all its peoples, and learning how to create and live in a culture of peace. Peace education promotes "awareness of the interdependence of all things and a profound sense of responsibility for the fate of the planet and for the well-being of humanity."[16]

The components of peace education include:

- conflict resolution—developing skills and appreciation for nonviolent problem solving;
- peace studies—examining the causes of war and its prevention and participating in activities that focus on the meaning of peace and raise peace awareness;
- environmental education—developing an appreciation of and the desire to inquire into the interrelationships of humans, their cultures, their surroundings, and all forms of life;
- global education—recognizing the interdependent nature of the world and studying problems and issues that cut across national boundaries; and
- human rights education—learning about the universal rights of human beings and strengthening respect for fundamental freedoms.[17]

Although many U.S. schools teach violence-reduction skills, few create a holistic moral world that makes a connection between peaceful personal behaviors and promoting peace throughout the world. Maria Montessori's belief that education can contribute to world peace has been a profound influence on some schools that emphasize her vision. One World Montessori School in California is an example of a school devoted to peace as an ultimate moral goal. In its K–8 peace curriculum, "teachers assist the children in developing a common language of peace and work on their own communication, peace making, and peace keeping skills."[18]

Another school that teaches for peace and interconnectedness is the Global Village School in California, which develops materials for home-schoolers. Its "Peacemakers" course "presents role models who work to enact nonviolent social change and concrete examples of such successfully enacted change." And the peace awareness curriculum of the New School at South Shore, a public primary school in Seattle, is inspired by the school's mission to "view each child as a bright spirit on a magnificent journey in our quest to contribute powerfully to the healing of humanity and Mother Earth." The goal of the Environmental and Adventure School, a public school in Washington State, is to develop responsible citizens who are stewards of the Earth. This school's mission is based on the belief that "when students are out in their environment and learn to respect and care for their surroundings, they also learn to respect and care for their classmates and teachers." The theme of "interdependent relationships—people and environments" is woven into the junior high school curriculum both in the classroom and in the many natural settings nearby.[19]

Peace educators teach that all lives and actions matter and that students are connected to all of life through a vision of peace, harmony, and Earth stewardship. Peace educators aim to create "moral sensitivity to others in the immediate classroom [and] concern for local communities and for all life on the planet." Thus the greatest advantage of this moral world is that it nourishes students' desire for personal meaning in increasingly violent times. An academic benefit is that peace education can be integrated into a stimulating curriculum that covers all disciplines, including science, language, and history.[20]

Creating an integrated peace education curriculum is difficult within traditional education systems in which content is taught in discrete disciplines. The greatest hurdle to creating this moral world, however, is the potential for conflict with community values. Undoubtedly, teaching about justice, sustainability, and peace challenges the prevailing world view in the U.S. by promoting values that confront uncontrolled economic development, consumerism, and militarism.

Social Action

In the moral world of social action, the values of justice and compassion guide a curriculum focused on the political nature of society. Educators believe that students are both empathic human beings and social agents who are capable of effecting change by critically examining unjust situations and participating in political processes. Teachers encourage students to ask, "What should I be paying attention to in my world?" The social action approach taps students' idealism for bringing about a better world—to "heal, repair and transform the world."[21]

Students are encouraged to generate ideas, negotiate subject matter, and find learning resources outside of the school setting. They venture into the community to gather documents, conduct interviews, and make observations. Teachers believe that their role is to confront students' ignorance or prejudices by helping the students to understand both privilege and oppression and by cultivating a "critical consciousness" of the perspectives of others.[22]

An example of this moral world occurred at Nova Alternative High School, a public school in Seattle. A junior who works with a human rights group told her classmates and teachers about the difficult situation in East Timor. In response, students began meeting once a week to study East Timor's history, politics, and culture and to raise money for Kay Rala, a small high school in Manatuto that "was burned to the ground by Indonesian soldiers in the late 1990s." Rather than donating money to a charity, the Seattle students established direct contact with Kay Rala and developed a fund-raising system with the students in East Timor. The Seattle students raised thousands of dollars for the school. The student whose concerns sparked the project reported that her "world [had] opened up"—helping her "not only to see people who are less fortunate but instead of accepting dreary situations, to change them."[23]

Another account of the social action moral world is from a fifth-grade class in Aurora, Colorado. When her students were studying the Civil War, teacher Barbara Vogel explained to her pupils that slavery was not merely a defunct system from a bygone era in American history but that people in Sudan and elsewhere were enslaved in the present day. Although the children were horrified and distraught, Vogel did not try to comfort them or to rationalize such horrors. Instead, she sought to channel their feelings of concern and outrage into social action by helping her students start a letter-writing campaign to bring this dire situation to the public's attention. When their letters did not change the fate of Sudanese slaves, the children raised money to buy freedom for a few slaves. As newspapers publicized the children's efforts, donations came in from around the world, and the class eventually purchased the freedom of more than 1,000 people. The class even developed a website to encourage others to stop slavery in Sudan.[24]

A highlight of the social action world is its Integrated curriculum—rich in academic, social, and political knowledge—which reflects the moral concerns of children and adolescents. Educators report that students learn to view themselves as social and political beings with the right to access the systems of influence in communities and the larger world. Through involvement in social action, students come to believe in themselves as moral agents.[25]

Creating this moral world is not without challenges. Teachers are responsible for creating an atmosphere in which students feel comfortable voicing their moral concerns and ensuring that students' ideas are not dismissed. Also, it requires a contemporary, integrated curriculum not constrained by rigid disciplinary boundaries. Moreover, despite the opportunities to make a difference, the social action moral world requires students to encounter misery and critically analyze the reasons for unjust acts and conditions. Accordingly, can students resist pessimism when they cannot easily change the world?

Just Community

In the just community moral world, classrooms and schools become democratic settings that provide students with opportunities to deliberate about moral dilemmas and to participate in cooperative decision making. Students, teachers, and administrators openly discuss and address matters of mutual concern, construct the school community's policies and rules through procedures that are viewed as fair and just, and resolve moral conflicts. In the process of building community, students gain perspectives on the principles of justice and fairness by experiencing moral deliberations and by applying the principles to real and specific problems in the school community.[26]

The just community model, based on the ideas of Lawrence Kohlberg, holds that the goal of moral education is the enhancement of students' development from lower to higher stages of moral reasoning. Advocates for the just community assert that students influence their own moral development by deliberating about and seeking to resolve moral conflicts. Social interactions—i.e., lived moral dilemmas—advance learners' moral judgment as students clarify and refine their thoughts while listening and responding to other points of view. In such environments, "teachers and students engage in philosophical deliberation about the good of the community." Teachers can prepare even young students to participate in a just community by encouraging them to think about rules not as "immutable laws" but as constructed moral guidelines necessary for living in a community.[27]

Two examples of just community schools are in New York State: the Pablo Neruda Academy for Architecture and World Studies in the Bronx and the Scarsdale Alternative School. Both public high schools emphasize students' deliberation about moral dilemmas within real-world situations—freedom combined with responsibility, cooperation over competition, and "how to balance the needs of individuals with those of the community." Features of these schools include community meetings, in which decisions are made about essential school policy; fairness committees, in which conflicts among students or students and teachers are resolved; and advisories, in which students discuss their own problems and plan the agendas for community meetings.[28]

An advantage of the just community is its unequivocal naming of justice as a safeguard of individuals' rights and the community's well-being. The ideal of democracy is both a moral standard and a guiding light, raising awareness of good citizenship within a moral context. Finally, students learn that their views and actions make a difference because their moral inquiries do not seek to resolve hypothetical situations or to prepare them for life outside of school but are focused on the school itself.[29]

One problem with the just community approach is that it takes a great deal of time for students to develop real trust among themselves and to deliberate about and resolve issues. Another difficulty is that most teachers have not been trained to facilitate "an apprenticeship in democracy." Finally, truly democratic school cultures with shared authority have been exceedingly rare, and this moral world cannot exist without students' uninhibited conversations and real decision-making authority.[30]

Ethical Inquiry

In the world of ethical inquiry, moral education is a process by which students engage in "moral conversation" centered on dilemmas. Also influenced by Lawrence Kohlberg's theories, this ethical inquiry approach to moral education is grounded on the premise that deliberation promotes students' moral development. Within respectful, egalitarian, and carefully facilitated discussions, teachers invite students to investigate values or actions and to imagine alternatives. In this world, students consider "how human beings should act," "life's meaning and the human place in the world," "the sources of evil and suffering," and "universal existential concerns and ways of knowing such as the meaning of friendship, love, and beauty."[31]

Teachers guide discussions on the moral dilemmas embedded within subjects across the curriculum. Springboards for ethical inquiry include literature, history, drama, economics, science, and philosophy. In particular, students learn about the consequences of making moral decisions and how fictional characters and real people make choices when aware that a moral question is at stake. Through this process of inquiry, students ponder the effects that moral, immoral, and amoral actions have on themselves and others, empathize with and appreciate the perspectives of others (their classmates as well as fictional characters or historical figures), and construct their understanding of what it means to be a moral human being.[32]

There are numerous accounts of how teachers integrate moral inquiry into their literature, social studies, and science classroom—illustrating that most topics have ethical dimensions. Teachers also use published curricula, such as Philosophy for Children, that provide stories and other media for ethical deliberation. Facing History and Ourselves, a curriculum about 20th-century genocide, focuses on teaching middle and high school students "the meaning of human dignity, morality, law, citizenship, and behavior." This curriculum aims to help students learn to reason morally as they think about their individual decisions and behavior toward others.[33]

A value of the ethical inquiry world is that it is not an "add-on" program but rather a way to integrate genuine moral deliberation into all academic areas—becoming a norm of the classroom culture. Ethical inquiry provides opportunities for students to appreciate others' viewpoints and to bring different perspectives into their own deliberations—important skills for democratic citizenship. This moral world also capitalizes on the process of identity development, making the search for moral identity an explicit goal.[34]

Because it is a process of inquiry and negotiation, a criticism of ethical inquiry is that it does not explicitly teach values. Teachers act as important intellectual role models who care about their students' ideas and their construction of personal ethics, but they do not overtly advocate particular moral standards. Another concern is ethical inquiry's cognitive approach to moral education. Educators do not guide students to help others or to bring about a better society but instead trust that students who think ethically will actively participate in the world beyond the classroom.

Choosing a Moral World

Our description of seven worlds of moral education reveals that there is "no perfect world." All moral worlds have their limitations, and educators face challenges no matter which approach they take to moral education. How then do we select a moral world for classrooms and schools?

Educators face hard choices, but choose they must, as these seven worlds hold dissimilar assumptions about what constitutes best practice for moral education. These worlds also reveal different conceptions of learners. They posit that moral educators can think about students as material to be shaped, as feelers with emotional needs, as thinkers whose judgments can be stimulated, or as villagers who learn from elders. Indeed, these moral worlds hold different understandings of *morality* itself. Does morality mean having good character, nurturing peers, caring for those who suffer (those both near and far), or being stewards of the Earth?

Serious ethical deliberation about the aims and practices of moral education cannot be avoided. It would be a mistake to try to create an approach to moral education that represents the "best of all worlds," because forming an amalgam of many approaches is more likely to result in a haphazard environment in which students receive conflicting messages. Moral educators need to decide on one approach or to create a thoughtfully considered hybrid that has clear aims and coherent practices. Too often, consideration of moral education (as well as any aspect of education) focuses only on the inadequate question of what works rather than on what we define as our utmost hopes for our students and the society in which they will live. When we ask the moral question, not merely the operational one, we allow ourselves to imagine our students having lives of meaning, taking part in genuine and peaceful relationships, and living without violence, cynicism, and despair.

The most popular world of moral education at present is character education. Numerous politicians, organizations, and boards of education advocate its implementation. Yet, as we explore these seven moral worlds, we see that character education has the most limited vision of morality and moral education—despite its advocates' good intentions.

How do we compare naming "the trait of the month" to teaching children to have a deep appreciation for peace and for sustaining the Earth? Why should we select stories in the hope that students will assimilate certain values or emulate heroes when we can teach literature as a springboard for pondering moral dilemmas and developing moral identities? Why should we settle for posting the names of "good" children on a bulletin board when we can aim to create loving, familial classrooms or a village of moral educators? How do we equate mandated service learning with a thoughtfully conceived student-led effort of social action, not only to alleviate suffering but also to stop cycles of poverty and injustice?

We question why the dominant approach to moral education consists of the practice of giving rewards to students just for following rules and for occasional acts of kindness. Instead, should we not help students to engage in profound ethical deliberation, revere peace, be cared for and be caring, and develop as moral agents who can repair the world? Why are these not among the endorsed goals of moral education?

In conclusion, the other six moral worlds hold more humane, imaginative, and profound visions of morality and moral education than those of character education. These compelling alternatives deserve serious consideration on the part of educators.

References

1. Alfie Kohn, "How Not to Teach Values: A Critical Look at Character Education," *Phi Delta Kappan*, February 1997, p. 436.

2. Thomas Lickona, *Educating for Character: How Our Schools Can Teach Respect and Responsibility* (New York: Bantam, 1991); Kevin Ryan and Karen E. Bohlin, *Building Character in Schools: Practical Ways to Bring Moral Instruction to Life* (San Francisco: Jossey-Bass, 1999), p. 11; and Edward A. Wynne and Kevin Ryan, *Reclaiming Our Schools: A Handbook on Teaching Character, Academics, and Discipline* (New York: Macmillan, 1993).

3. William J. Bennett, *The Book of Virtues: A Treasury of Great Moral Stories* (New York: Simon & Schuster, 1993). The six ethical values of the Character Counts Youth Ethics Initiative can be found at. . . . The Kent City Schools in Ohio developed a list of character virtues: cooperation, self-control, trustworthiness, tolerance, compassion, commitment and dedication, work ethic and responsibility, respect for self and others, fairness and justice, and respect for our community and environment, which is available at. . . .

4. For information on the School 18 program, see. . . .

5. For information on these and other character activities, see. . . .

6. See J. Wesley Null and Andrew J. Milson, "Beyond Marquee Morality: Virtue in the Social Studies," *Social Studies,* May/June 2003, pp. 119–22; Don Jacobs, "The Case for the Inclusion of an Indigenous Perspective in Character Education," paper presented at the annual meeting of the American Educational Research Association, New Orleans, April 2002; and David Purpel, "The Politics of Character Education," in idem, ed., *Moral Outrage in Education* (New York: Peter Lang, 1999), pp. 83–97.

7. For more information on these examples, visit . . . ; . . . ; . . . ; and. . . .

8. In this article, we focus on examples from Indian schools that are not strictly tribal schools. For example, see Sandra M. Stokes, "Curriculum for Native American Students: Using Native American Values," *Reading Teacher,* vol. 50, 1997, pp. 576–84; Angayuqaq Oscar Kawagley and Ray Barnhardt, "Education Indigenous to Place: Western Science Meets Native Reality," in Gregory A. Smith and Dilafruz R. Williams, eds., *Ecological Education in Action: On Weaving Education, Culture, and the Environment* (Albany: State University of New York Press, 1998), pp. 117–40; G. Mike Charleston, "Toward True Native Education: A Treaty of 1992: Final Report of the Indian Nations at Risk Task Force," *Journal of American Indian Education,* Winter 1994, pp. 1–23; and Washington Education Association, "Tulalip Heritage School: Linking Cultures and Generations," 9 November 2000, available at. . . . For information on the Center School, see. . . .

9. For discussions on culturally relevant moral education, see Cynthia Ballenger, "Because You Like Us: The Language of Control," *Harvard Educational Review,* vol. 62, 1992, pp. 199–208; Peter Murrell, "Afrocentric Immersion: Academic and Personal Development of African American Males in Public Schools," in Theresa Perry and James W. Frazer, eds., *Freedom's Plow: Teaching in the Multicultural Classroom* (New York: Routledge, 1993), pp. 231–59.

10. Nel Noddings, *The Challenge to Care in Schools* (New York: Teachers College Press, 1992); and Jane Roland Martin, *The Schoolhome: Rethinking Schools for Changing Families* (Cambridge: Harvard University Press, 1992).

11. Victor Battistich et al., "Students and Teachers in Caring Classroom and School Communities," paper presented at the annual meeting of the American Educational Research Association, New Orleans, April 1994; and Rick Weissbourd, "Moral Teachers, Moral Students," *Educational Leadership,* March 2003, pp. 6–11.

12. Lynn H. Doyle and Patrick M. Doyle, "Building Schools as Caring Communities: Why, What, and How?," *The Clearing House,* May/June 2003, pp. 259–61; and Jean Tepperman, "Schooling as a Caring Community," *Children's Advocate,* September/October 1997, available at. . . .

13. Doyle and Doyle, op. cit.

14. Eric Schaps, "Creating a School Community," *Educational Leadership,* March 2003, pp. 31–33.

15. Ibid.; and Weissbourd, op. cit.

16. Ian M. Harris, Mary Lee Morrison, and Timothy Reagan, *Peace Education,* 2nd ed. (Jefferson, N.C.: McFarland & Company, 2002); "What Is Peace Education?," in *A Teachers' Guide to Peace Education* (New Delhi, India: United Nations Educational, Scientific, and Cultural Organization, 2001), available at . . . ; Frans C. Verhagen, "The Earth Community School: A Back-to-Basics Model of Secondary Education," *Green Teacher,* Fall 1999, pp. 28–31; William Scott and Chris Oulton, "Environmental Values Education: An Exploration of Its Role in the School Curriculum," *Journal of Moral Education,* vol. 27, 1998, pp. 209–24; and American Montessori Society, "AMS Position Paper: Holistic Peace Education," available at. . . .

17. Mary Lee Morrison, "Peace Education in Theory and Practice," *Delta Kappa Gamma Bulletin,* Fall 2002, pp. 10–14.

18. For information on the One World Montessori School, see. . . .

19. For more information on these examples, see . . . and. . . .

20. Morrison, op. cit.

21. Peter McLaren, *Life in Schools: An Introduction to Critical Pedagogy in the Foundations of Education* (New York: Longman, 1989); and Henry Giroux, *Border Crossings: Cultural Works and the Politics of Education* (New York: Routledge, 1993), p. 104.

22. Pamela Bolotin Joseph and Mark Windschitl, "Fostering a Critical and Caring Classroom Culture," *Social Education, Middle Level Learning Supplement,* May/June 1999, pp. 14–15.

23. Regine Labossiere, "Nova Sister-School Class Aids East Timor Students," *Seattle Times,* 13 October 2003, p. B-3.

24. See David Field, "Freedom Writers," *Teacher Magazine on the Web,* February 1999; Nat Hentoff, "Fifth-Grade Freedom Fighters," *Washington Post,* 1 August 1998, p. A-15; Mindy Sink, "Schoolchildren Set Out to Buy Freedom for Slaves," *New York Times,* 2 December 1998, p. B-14; and Richard Woodbury, "The Children's Crusade," *Time,* 21 December 1998, p. 44.

25. Joseph and Windschitl, op. cit.

26. Lawrence Kohlberg, *The Psychology of Moral Development: Moral Stages and the Life Cycle,* vol. 2 (San Francisco: Harper & Row, 1984).

27. Clark Power, "Building Democratic Community: A Radical Approach to Moral Education," in William Damon, ed., *Bringing in a New Era in Character Education* (Palo Alto, Calif.: Hoover Institution, 2002), pp. 1–32; and Elsa K. Weber, "Rules, Right and

Wrong, and Children," *Early Childhood Education Journal,* Winter 2000, pp. 107–11.

28. For more information on these examples, see . . . ; and . . .

29. Sara Efron, "Beyond Character Education: Democracy as a Moral Goal," *Critical Issues in Teacher Education,* vol. 8, 2000, pp. 20–28.

30. Barbara J. Thayer-Bacon, "Democratic Classroom Communities," *Studies in Philosophy and Education,* vol. 15, 1996, pp. 333–51; F. Clark Power, "Building Democratic Community: A Radical Approach to Moral Education," in Damon, pp. 129–48; and Edward R. Mikel, "Deliberating Democracy," in Pamela Bolotin Joseph et al., eds., *Cultures of Curriculum* (Mahwah, N.J.: Lawrence Erlbaum, 2000), pp. 115–35.

31. Robert J. Nash, *Answering the "Virtuecrats": A Moral Conversation on Character Education* (New York: Teachers College Press, 1997); and Katherine G. Simon, *Moral Questions in the Classroom: How to Get Kids to Think Deeply about Real Life and Their Schoolwork* (New Haven, Conn.: Yale University Press, 2001), pp. 37–38.

32. Joe Winston, "Theorising Drama as Moral Education," *Journal of Moral Education,* December 1999, pp. 459–71; Vaille Dawson, "Addressing Controversial Issues in Secondary School Science," *Australian Science Teachers Journal,* November 2001, pp. 38–44; and Larry R. Johannessen, "Strategies for Initiating Authentic Discussion," *English Journal,* September 2003, pp. 73–79.

33. Linda Leonard Lamme, "Digging Deeply: Morals and Ethics in Children's Literature," *Journal for a Just and Caring Education,* October 1996, pp. 411–20; Steven Wolk, "Teaching for Critical Literacy in Social Studies," *Social Studies,* May/June 2003, pp. 101–6; Lena Green, "Philosophy for Children: One Way of Developing Children's Thinking," *Thinking,* vol. 13, no. 2, 1997, pp. 20–22; . . . ; Margot Stern Strom, Martin Sleeper, and Mary Johnson, "Facing History and Ourselves: A Synthesis of History and Ethics in Effective History Education," in Andrew Garrod, ed., *Learning for Life: Moral Education Theory and Practice* (Westport, Conn.: Praeger, 1992), pp. 131–53; and Melinda Fine, "Facing History and Ourselves: Portrait of a Classroom," *Educational Leadership,* December 1991, pp. 44–49.

34. Constance M. Perry, "How Do We Teach What Is Right?: Research and Issues in Ethical and Moral Development," *Journal for a Just and Caring Education,* October 1996, pp. 400–10; and Ruth W. Grant, "The Ethics of Talk: Classroom Conversation and Democratic Politics," *Teachers College Record,* Spring 1996, pp. 470–82.

PAMELA BOLOTIN JOSEPH is a senior lecturer at University of Washington Bothell.

SARA EFRON is a professor in the Department of Educational Foundations and Inquiry at National-Louis University.

EXPLORING THE ISSUE

Should Character Education Define the Values We Teach Students?

Critical Thinking and Reflection

1. Briefly summarize the points that Schwartz and colleagues make in arguing in favor of schools taking responsibility for teaching morality. Do you agree or disagree with each point? Why?
2. Briefly summarize the points that Joseph and Efron make in arguing for a broader view of moral education. Do you agree or disagree with each point? Why?
3. Recall your experiences in elementary, middle, and high school. What were some of the moral values that your schools tried to teach you? How did they go about teaching these values? Do you agree with what and how they taught? Why or why not?

Is There Common Ground?

Can we answer the question posed for this issue by gathering and evaluating data through empirical research? In one respect, the answer is yes. It certainly would be possible to compare the relative effectiveness of two curricula, one including a character education component and the other with a strictly academic focus or with a broader moral focus, such as that proposed by Pamela Bolotin Joseph and Sara Efron. In any such study, of course, care would need to be taken to ensure that the students, classes, or schools compared were identical in all respects save the moral, or character, dimensions of the curricula.

In another respect, however, the question may not be answerable by empirical data. It simply may not be possible to reach consensus on what the objectives of a moral education should be. Ultimately, decisions about the content of any moral education curriculum may be decided, not by recourse to empirical investigation or by considerations of universal acceptance, but rather by the beliefs and values of those who have the power to make decisions about the schools; namely, government leaders and policymakers, the educational establishment that trains teachers, and the people who develop and administer the curriculum. Because access to these positions of power has been limited until recently to those of the majority culture, it is likely (2005) that the moral values contained in most educational programs will reflect to a very large degree the values of the majority culture. Whether that is a good or a bad state of affairs, fair or unfair, etc. cannot be solved by conducting an empirical study.

Create Central

www.mhhe.com/createcentral

Additional Resources

James Traub, "The Moral imperative," *Education Digest* (Winter 2005).

Carol Gilligan, *In a Different Voice: Psychological Theory and Women's Development by Carol Gilligan* (Harvard University Press, 1982).

Hunter Brimi, "Academic Instructors or Moral Guides? Moral Education in America and the Teacher's Dilemma," *The Clearing House* (January/February 2009).

Internet References . . .

Character Education Partnership

http://www.character.org/

Character Counts!

http://charactercounts.org/

Markkula Center for Applied Ethics

http://www.scu.edu/ethics/practicing/focusareas/education/

Selected, Edited, and with Issue Framing Material by:
Leonard Abbeduto, *University of California, Davis*
and
Frank Symons, *University of Minnesota*

ISSUE

Does Homework Lead to Improved Student Achievement?

YES: Douglas Fisher and Nancy Frey, from "Homework and the Gradual Release of Responsibility: Making 'Responsibility' Possible," *The English Journal* (vol. 98, no. 2, November 2008)

NO: Dorothy Suskind, from "What Students Would Do if They Did Not Do Their Homework," *Phi Delta Kappan* (September 2012)

Learning Outcomes

After reading this issue, you will be able to:

- Describe what is at issue from a practice perspective.
- Compare different perspectives on what are relevant indicators of homework effects.
- Describe the range of possible effects of homework on achievement and what the differences may be with respect to different definitions of homework.

ISSUE SUMMARY

YES: Douglas Fisher and Nancy Frey argue that there are positive outcomes between homework and achievement, but that it is important to recognize the nuanced nature of the relationship with instruction and be clear about what the goal and specific objectives are.

NO: Dorothy Suskind argues that the "homework default" (automatically assigning homework) is poorly informed practice and that the time spent completing homework is counterproductive with the potential to interfere with family relationships, and, in the long run, reduce student creativity.

In the educational research literature there are two widely cited studies documenting the positive influence of homework on achievement—both papers are quantitative reviews by Cooper and colleagues (H. Cooper [1989, November], "Synthesis on Research of Homework," *Educational Leadership*, 47(3), pp. 85–91, and H. Cooper, J. C. Robinson, and E. A. Patall [2006], "Does Homework Improve Academic Achievement? A Synthesis of Research 1987–2003," *Review of Educational Research*, 76(1), pp. 1–62). Both are important syntheses of the existing research literature of the time and both were designed to find out what the evidence was—one way or the other—about the effects of homework on academic achievement. Overall, the reviews have led to the general conclusion and conventional wisdom that on balance there is an overall net positive association between homework and academic achievement. But there have been popular press critiques of the reviews (see critiques by Alfie Kohn in which he argues [poorly] from an almost ad-hominen position that Cooper and colleagues approached the problem from an "establishment" perspective and were deliberately trying

to find evidence supporting homework). There has also been a sense among the practice community (teachers, school administrators) that while the burden of homework has increased, it is less clear that there is corresponding academic gain, and there is concern that there may well be detrimental effects for some student groups as well as families (see, for example, E. Kralovec and John Buell [2000], *The End of Homework: How Homework Disrupts Families, Overburdens Children, and Limits Learning*, Boston: Beacon).

The most common metric is "time spent on homework." But what if the metric was changed and the question concerned homework frequency (how often assigned), or homework type (of problems), or homework study tactics, or homework effort. Similarly, there are other individual (student) factors that increasingly are recognized as affecting the relationship between homework and achievement including positive/negative homework emotions, motivation, and the subject area and student's interest in it. The net effect of considering definitional differences, measurement differences, and different variables considered in different analytic models is that the answer about whether homework leads to improved student achievement seems to be a nuanced qualified "yes." Yes, but it depends. It has long been recognized that there are age/student level differences such that the associations between homework and achievement are stronger in the secondary grades than primary or middle school. But, even here, there are qualified conclusions—with much of the variability in outcome possibly related to positive or negative homework emotions and amount of effort required as much as the conventional "time spent on homework" metric.

Aside from the general critiques of the previous syntheses, it is a fair question to ask how good is the research evidence from individual studies? There are two really "thorny" issues (see Trautwein and colleagues for an excellent overview and recommended reading). One is referred to as the "multilevel analysis problem" and the other might best be called the "common cause confounder." The multilevel analysis problem refers to the fact that there are at least three levels of analysis that are possible—at the class level (comparing between classes), at the inter-individual level (comparing between students), and at the intra-individual level (comparing within a student; e.g., gains before and after homework). Each of the levels requires a specific and separate analysis model and each can lead to different inferences about the effects of homework on achievement. The common cause confounder refers to overlooking potential confounding variables that may better explain the relationship between homework and academic achievement. For example, imagine a study that included in the sample elite math classes/elite schools with students from privileged backgrounds in which teachers required more homework and a strong positive association between homework and achievement is found. The effect is more likely explained by the "common cause" of a high quality school or related variables rather than the homework, per se. Similarly, there is a "chicken/egg" problem lurking in that the majority of studies are correlational relying on a single time point for measurement often without prior educational achievement controlled for making the "directionality" of the relationship difficult to disentangle—does homework time cause improved achievement or does high prior achievement affect homework time?

Fisher and Frey acknowledged a disruptive or at least "status quo" effect of homework in their classrooms (i.e., homework as default—as per Suskind's observation). To make homework meaningful, they describe a reflective process in which homework is incorporated thoughtfully into the learning cycle, but they are careful to ensure that prerequisite skills are in place prior to assigning homework. In fact, they developed a clear rubric to match the purpose of the homework with the needed student characteristics and response requirement. Overall, they argue that if homework is used, then it should be part and parcel of good instructional design and just one of many components used to support student learning. It should be noted that they were writing from a secondary perspective. Whether the same general framework would "work" in a primary grade context is unknown. But the larger point—homework as part of effective instruction—and acknowledging and recognizing the importance of clearly stated goals, determining where students are in the learning cycle (acquisition, fluency, retention, application, etc.) are critical practice considerations.

Perhaps the best "takeaway" regarding the issue—whether homework leads to improved academic achievement—is to remember the old adage about analytic models—all models are wrong but some are more useful than others. Rather than a simple model (more homework = improved achievement), it seems that a more nuanced view reflecting the complexity of the relation—although less convenient to capture in a "sound bite"—may better reflect reality. For example, homework effort does seem positively associated with achievement outcomes; but it is less clear that there is a uniform positive relation between homework time and achievement outcomes. In fact, homework time combined with negative homework emotions negatively predicts achievement. Conversely, high achievement is positively associated with less homework time but also with homework effort and lower levels of negative homework emotions. Perhaps the next generation of homework research will consistently consider both sides of the equation; "homework" definition/measurement and student performance factors (emotions, academic interests, levels of support) to more accurately reflect the nature of the relation between homework and achievement providing a better road map for school policy and classroom practice.

YES

Douglas Fisher and Nancy Frey

Homework and the Gradual Release of Responsibility: Making "Responsibility" Possible

For several decades, teachers and researchers have argued the value of homework. There have been research reviews suggesting that homework is beneficial, such as the meta-analyses done by Harris Cooper, Jorgianne C. Robinson, and Erika A. Patall. Their analysis concluded, "With only rare exceptions, the relationship between the amount of homework students do and their achievement outcomes was found to be positive and statistically significant" (48). Harris Cooper also notes that homework is more powerful as students get older. In his 1989 meta-analysis, Cooper reported the following effect sizes according to different age groups (71):

- Grades 4–6: ES = .15 (Percentile gain = 6)
- Grades 7–9: ES = .31 (Percentile gain = 12)
- Grades 10–12: ES = .64 (Percentile gain = 24)

This pattern suggests that homework is increasingly beneficial as students get older. However, critics of homework argue that it is not effective and interrupts family interactions and fosters a competitive environment that values work over social interactions (e.g., Kralovec and Buell). Alfie Kohn even suggests that researchers inflate the value of homework. For example, Kohn suggested that Cooper was determined "to massage the numbers until they yield something—anything—on which to construct a defense of homework for younger children" (84).

Homework appears to be deeply embedded in the beliefs about schooling. A survey sponsored by MetLife revealed that homework is viewed as "important" or "very important" by teachers (83%), parents (81%), and students (77%). However, the purposes for homework were more complex. The majority of teachers reported that they used homework to "improve skills in the classroom and for improving life skills beyond high school" (30), especially in establishing effective work habits about assuming responsibility. Notwithstanding, 26% of secondary teachers confessed that they "very often or often" assigned homework because they ran out of time in class (32). We find this worrisome because it suggests that middle school and high school students regularly face homework assignments for which they have received inadequate preparation.

The debate rages on about homework (e.g., Marzano and Pickering) as schools and teachers attempt to meet adequate yearly progress targets with their students. But what if we are asking the wrong question about homework? Or what if we changed the question from a dichotomous one—either a yes or no to homework—and focused on the role that homework plays in building competence? In particular, we'd like to talk about instructional routines and procedures that support learning through homework. Our work with high school students has allowed us to clarify our understanding of how classroom instruction and homework can complement one another to result in deeper understanding and improved skills. We will describe our process for planning instruction and developing homework assignments that allow students to assume responsibility because they are thoroughly prepared for the task.

Before Homework, Consider Instruction

Before thinking about what we want students to do at home, we plan a series of experiences in class. We do so using the gradual release of responsibility model. The gradual release of responsibility model stipulates that the teacher moves from assuming "all the responsibility for performing a task . . . to a situation in which the students assume all of the responsibility" (Duke and Pearson 211). Our operationalization of this model consists of four major components: focus, guided, collaborative, and independent (e.g., Fisher and Frey).

Focus Lesson

Before students can be expected to produce independently, they need to understand the purpose and experience an example. The focus lesson does exactly that. During the focus lesson, the teacher establishes the purpose and models his or her own thinking. Purpose is established in using both content and language objectives (Echevarria, Vogt, and Short). For example, during a recent class meeting our purpose included a content goal (Synthesize and retell information gained from reading multiple sources) and a language goal (Use signal words to guide the reader in understanding).

Once students understand the purpose of the lesson, they need an example of the thinking required to complete the task. As such, teachers model their understanding using think-alouds and demonstrations. The emphasis during the modeling phase of instruction is on explaining one's thinking for learners. Behaviors frequently modeled include comprehension strategies, word solving, using text structure, or gaining information from text features. For example, thinking aloud about the information presented in a graph of the world's population demonstrates for students how text features work. Similarly, demonstrating the use of predicting, visualizing, or summarizing while reading provides students with examples that they can use in their reading. And finally, solving unknown words using context clues, word parts, or resources such as other people and dictionaries helps readers understand that there are ways of figuring out "tricky words."

During the first class session in which students were reading multiple sources of informational text, we modeled our comprehension of a newspaper article written about the Chicago stockyards around the time that Upton Sinclair was working on *The Jungle*. We also thought aloud about a photograph from the time that portrayed the harsh work conditions of meatpackers, explaining what we saw. We drew their attention to the blood and animal body parts on the floor and the men using push brooms to unsuccessfully clear away the mess. We were careful to include academic vocabulary identified for the unit in our modeling, including *meatpacking plant, sanitary, slaughter, muckraker,* and *contamination*.

Guided Instruction

With a purpose and examples, students are ready to assume more of the responsibility for the task at hand. In this phase of instruction, the teacher strategically uses prompts, cues, and questions to get the students to do more of the work. Guided instruction can be done with the whole class, but our experience suggests that teachers can be much more precise when they guide the learning of small groups of students. For example, Nancy met with four students who were struggling to understand a political cartoon related to the publication of Upton Sinclair's book. The cartoon featured President Teddy Roosevelt holding his nose with one hand while using a large rake labeled "investigations" in a stinking pool of detritus labeled "meat scandal."[1] Rather than tell them what it meant, Nancy used a series of questions to get students to do the thinking. She first asked, "What is the biggest image on the page and why might it have been made so large?" The students in the group talked about this for a few minutes, agreeing that both the rake and the pool were dominant. She then reminded them of the term *muckraker* and prompted, "How might this relate to the photograph we examined earlier?" They were able to connect the visual commonalities—the push brooms and rake—as well as the animal body parts. An

outcome of their discussion was a deeper understanding of the impact of photographs and political cartoons in creating the public outcry that resulted from the publication of the book. The goal of guided instruction—for students to assume increased responsibility for their learning while also receiving scaffolds and supports when they experience difficulty—was realized in this exchange.

Collaborative Learning

While the teacher meets with groups of students for guided instruction, other students in the class work collaboratively. The key to this phase of instruction lies in the task. Students need to be held individually accountable for their performance while working together. Collaborative tasks have to be structured such that students work together and each contribute to the product. For example, as part of the class session on reading multiple sources of informational text, students not working with Nancy created collaborative posters. The task that was posted on the board read as follows:

> Create a poster that includes:
>
> - An image that portrays the main idea of the reading
> - A quote that captures the feeling of this reading
> - A statement that summarizes the meaning of this reading
>
> Remember, each group member uses a different color pen and each color pen must appear on the poster.

Working together, students read an assigned newspaper editorial or article and composed a visual and textual summary on poster paper with each student contributing to the poster.

Independent Tasks

The final phase provides students an opportunity to apply what they have learned to a new situation or experience. Ideally, the independent task should align with the other phases of instruction and not be something only tangentially related to the lesson's focus. Unfortunately, this is often not the case and students do not understand the purpose of the homework assignment and thus do not do well on it. This is not to say that students can't propose independent learning tasks or be provided a number of choices in what to complete.

In addition, some homework assignments are given prematurely in the instructional cycle. As a result, students complete tasks independently for which they are not yet ready and often learn things incorrectly as a result. And we all know how long it takes to "unteach" misconceptions and misunderstandings. Learning something incorrectly may be one of the most significant reasons for the lack of consensus in the research on homework's impact on student achievement.

Given that students in our classes were just being introduced to intertextual analysis, we didn't assign homework related to the lesson on this day. Instead, we asked students to continue reading the books they had chosen and to work on their weekly literacy letters, which we had taught them to write at the beginning of the year. Over time, they would be ready to take home a collection of reading materials on a topic and complete an analysis on their own.

The Role That Homework Can and Should Play

In our experience, there are a number of ways that homework can be useful. We use the four systems described below, but we don't use all of them all of the time. Instead, we vary the ways in which students apply what they are learning and invite students to propose ways that they can demonstrate their application of the content. Figure 1 contains a list of questions to consider for each of these four areas of homework.

Fluency Building

One of the things that homework does for students, in the gradual release of responsibility model, is build fluency. Current neurosciences research suggests that readers must develop fluency, or automaticity, with decoding, sight words, word recognition, comprehension strategies, and the like so that they can free up working memory for making meaning (e.g., Wolf).

We know what reading does for the mind in terms of vocabulary and background knowledge (Cunningham and Stanovich). As such, we need to provide students with opportunities to read widely on a daily basis. Therefore, one standing homework assignment we advocate is reading. Understanding the importance of choice and motivation, our reading homework is completed from books students have chosen to read. This provides students a great deal of control in how they complete this homework task.

Similarly, we understand the importance of writing fluency. Of course, we know that simply asking students to write at home, in the absence of instruction, will not make them better writers. We assign reading responses several times a week using the genres that have been taught in class. For example, the summary writing in the above lesson came after many lessons involving the characteristics of effective summaries. Students used strategies such as Anne E. Cunningham's GIST (Generating Interaction between Schemata and Text) to make decisions about key information contained in longer texts. This strategy has been particularly helpful for English language learners (Frey, Fisher, and Hernandez). Therefore, when students write a summary of a book or article they are reading independently, they are using approaches that have been thoroughly taught in the classroom.

Application

Once students have experienced quality instruction and have been apprenticed into the thinking and vocabulary required of a task, they can and should be asked to apply this knowledge on their own. Again, the key is to ensure that this application is not requested prematurely in the instructional cycle. Learners deserve to understand the purpose of the task, have access to models of the thinking

Figure 1

Checklist for Developing Effective Homework Assignments

Purpose of homework	Characteristics	Reflective questions to ask
Fluency Building	• Multiple opportunities for practice • Focuses on one or two skills • Serves as an access point for other skills or knowledge	1. Do students fully understand how the skill is performed? 2. Is the difficulty level low enough so that they can focus on speed/rate/fluency, instead of how it is performed?
Application	• Allows a skill to be used to solve a problem, or apply a rule or principle • Uses previously learned skill for a new situation	1. What rule or principle will the students use to solve the problem? 2. Do the students possess the background knowledge and prior experiences necessary to understand the new or novel situation?
Spiral Review	• Student utilizes previously learned skills or knowledge • Allows students to confirm their understanding and assess their learning • Related conceptually to current learning	1. What previously taught skills or knowledge is important for future learning and assessment? 2. In what ways will this strengthen students' metacognitive awareness of how well they use skills and knowledge? 3. What previously taught skills or knowledge serve as a basis for current classroom instruction?
Extension	• Potential for development of new understandings • Results in a new product or innovation • Requires the use of a variety of skills or knowledge	1. Does the assignment lead to a new knowledge base or set of concepts? 2. Will the students create a new product or innovation that they have not done before? 3. What skills or knowledge will students require to complete the assignment?

required, practice with peers, and receive scaffolded support before being asked to perform independently. Our weekly literacy letters are an example of this type of application.

In our classes, students choose books that they want to read and they read from these books nightly. We have regular, brief conferences with readers, usually a few times each week. These conferences allow us to monitor student reading and engagement as well as get to know students as individuals and guide their understanding of, and reactions to, the things they've chosen to read. In addition, students write a weekly literacy letter for homework. We teach this format in the beginning of the year and expect a weekly letter from every student in our classes. The format is a friendly letter in which the first paragraph updates us on the events in the book and the student's reaction to the book. The second paragraph provides students an opportunity to apply something we've focused on in class to their writing. For example, after analyzing characters for several weeks, the second paragraph prompt provides students an opportunity to use what they had learned and apply it to the book they were reading. Similarly, after some time spent on setting and how authors use setting, the second paragraph prompt provides students an opportunity to apply this independently. Figure 2 contains a sample literacy letter based on the prompt related to setting.

Spiral Review

A third feature of effective homework is to provide a spiral review of past learning. We find this to be an especially important function for students who will be taking major end-of-course and standardized tests in the spring. Students can be challenged to draw on topics that were taught months ago, and homework assignments that require students to apply knowledge from past units of instruction can keep it fresh. Learners can sometimes have difficulty with understanding how the lessons they were taught in the fall of the year can relate to their current lessons. The National Research Council examined the research on effective teaching of secondary history, science, and mathematics and reported that the move from novice to expert is dependent on one's ability to organize factual knowledge into larger core concepts. In English, an example of students' ability to organize factual knowledge into larger core concepts would be students utilizing their knowledge of metaphors and similes from an earlier poetry unit in their persuasive essays later in the year. Assignment of homework that is strategically chosen to refer back to previous learning strengthens students' ability to access background knowledge and build larger "enduring understandings" (Wiggins and McTighe 17).

Extension

A final type of homework invites students to extend their learning across topics and disciplines. We have found that this is particularly useful for students who are struggling with perceiving the relevance of a topic beyond the unit of instruction. For example, after several national reports

Figure 2

Sample Literacy Letter Based on Setting

Dear Reader,

The book that I have been reading for the last week is called *Tyrell* by Coe Booth. In the book the main character, Tyrell, is living in a shelter with his mother and little brother. While living in the shelter, Tyrell meets a girl name Jasmine who he thought was very attractive. Tyrell does something that he regrets because he has a girlfriend already. Tyrell is also having problems with his mom because she is pressuring him to go sell drugs to get them out of the shelter. But Tyrell has another plan. He decides to throw a party that he can charge people money to come to.

One day Tyrell spends the night at his girlfriend's house because of the snowstorm. But the other girl, Jasmine, calls him and tells him that his brother is home alone crying. When Tyrell goes back to the shelter he finds out that his mom left his brother to go shopping with a man name Dante. Dante is Tyrell father's friend (they were in prison together) and Tyrell doesn't trust him at all. That's as far as I got in the book this week.

In *Tyrell*, the setting of the book is in Bronx. The author of the book, Coe Booth, has been working with families and teenagers in the Bronx who are poor and has lived in a shelter before, so she really understands the setting. She was a writing consultant for the New York City Housing Department and received a MFA in creative writing from The New School and that's where she finished *Tyrell*. Because of all of this, the setting really works and helps move the story along. I can picture the places she writes about and I wouldn't change the setting. I don't think that this story, at least what I've read so far, would work in the suburbs or in a smaller city. So far, the setting hasn't provided any symbolic details and is just a backdrop for the story. But I'm on the lookout for details that might be symbolic. I do think that the social class of the characters is important for the setting. There are some people who couldn't survive the life the Tyrell has. I think the time period is modern because of the crises that the family experiences. And finally, for mood, I think that the setting helps me understand the overall mood of the first few chapters, which is worrisome, or ominous as you might say.

Sincerely,

Destini

PS: I rate this book 10/10.

were issued about the dangers of working in meatpacking plants, and several recalls of meat were issued, we linked students' learning about food inspection, the Progressive Era, persuasive essays, and letter writing as a homework assignment to write their representatives in Congress about their concerns regarding working conditions and food safety. Students were able to marshal their knowledge of Upton Sinclair and the Pure Food and Drug Act of 1906 within an accepted business-letter format. They wrote persuasively about human rights and the role of the federal government in protecting its citizens. They utilized argumentation in their writing, balancing the *ethos, pathos,* and *logos* arguments to make their points.

Homework Design and Homework Completion

As we have continued to refine our practice of a gradual release of responsibility model of instruction, we have come to understand that homework can be a meaningful part of the independent phase of learning. However, past experience has taught us that we are often too quick to assign homework before students have had an opportunity to learn the skills and strategies needed to successfully complete it. Instead, we have begun to use homework for four purposes: to build fluency, foster application, provide a spiral review, and offer opportunities for extension. We have noted in our practice that homework completion has risen over the course of the school year. While we would not attribute this increase solely to homework design, we do believe it plays an important role.

Many teachers talk about the importance of students assuming responsibility for their learning and assert that homework builds that habit. We believe that "responsibility" is a two-way street, and more attention to the role of homework as part of our overall instructional design makes it possible for more learners to assume that responsibility.

Note

1. This cartoon is available at http://www.vw.vccs.edu/vwhansd/his122/Teddy/Images/TRtoonMuck.jpg.

References

Cooper, Harris. *Homework*. White Plains: Longman, 1989. Cooper, Harris, Jorgianne C. Robinson, and Erica A. Patall. "Does Homework Improve Academic Achievement? A Synthesis of Research, 1987–2003." *Review of Educational Research* 76. 1 (2006): 1–62.

Cunningham, Anne E., and Keith E. Stanovich. "What Reading Does for the Mind." *American Educator* 22 (1998): 1–8.

Duke, Nell K., and P. David Pearson. "Effective Practices for Developing Reading Comprehension." *What Research Has to Say about Reading Instruction*. Ed. A. E. Farstup and S. J. Samuels. Newark: International Reading Assoc. 205–42.

Echevarria, Jana, Mary Ellen Vogt, and Deborah Short. *Making Content Accessible for English Learners: The SIOP Model*. 3rd ed. Boston: Allyn, 2007.

Fisher, Douglas, and Nancy Frey. *Better Learning through Structured Teaching: A Framework for the Gradual Release of Responsibility*. Alexandria: ASCD, 2008.

Frey, Nancy, Douglas Fisher, and Ted Hernandez. "What's the Gist? Summary Writing for Struggling Adolescent Writers." *Voices from the Middle* 11.*2* (2003): 43–49.

Kohn, Alfie. *The Homework Myth: Why Our Kids Get Too Much of a Bad Thing*. Cambridge: Da Capo, 2006.

Kralovec, Etta, and John Buell. *The End of Homework: How Homework Disrupts Families, Overburdens Children, and Limits Learning*. Boston: Beacon, 2000.

Marzano, Robert J., and Debra J. Pickering. "The Case for and against Homework." *Educational Leadership* 64.6 (2007): 74–79.

MetLife. *The MetLife Survey of the American Teacher: The Homework Experience*. 2008. 7 Mar. 2008 http://www.ced.org/docs/report/report_metlife2008.pdf.

National Research Council. *How Students Learn: History, Mathematics, and Science in the Classroom*. Ed. M. S. Donovan and J. D. Bransford. Division of Behavioral and Social Sciences and Education. Washington, DC: National Academies, 2008.

Sinclair, Upton. *The Jungle*. 1906. New York: Penguin, 2006.

Wiggins, Grant, and Jay McTighe. *Understanding by Design*. 2nd ed. Alexandria: ASCD, 2005.

Wolf, Maryanne. *Proust and the Squid: The Story and Science of the Reading Brain*. New York: Harper, 2007.

DOUGLAS FISHER AND NANCY FREY teach at Health Sciences High and Middle College. They are the authors of numerous books, including the NCTE publication *Language Learners in the English Classroom*.

Dorothy Suskind    **NO**

What Students Would Do if They Did Not Do Their Homework

Questioning the validity of homework calls us to be brave. It charges us as practitioners to review the research and look past the elephants bickering in the corners of our classrooms and kitchens, holding foreboding signs that shout, "We have always done it this way?" "What on earth will the parents say?" "How will children learn self-discipline and study skills?" and "How will my child prepare himself for the rigors of tomorrow's workforce?" To question the homework default prods us to be advocates and stewards of the children we teach and reflect upon our own motives and methodologies for assigning nightly work. We must put on research-laden armor and prepare to speak up and out at faculty meetings, meet-the-teacher nights, and parent-teacher conferences.

As Alfie Kohn suggests, "ultimately, it's not enough just to have less homework or even better homework. We should change the fundamental expectation in our schools so that students are asked to take schoolwork home only when there's a reasonable likelihood that a particular assignment will be beneficial to most of them. The bottom line: No homework except for those occasions when it's truly necessary" (2007, p. 21).

To follow this charge, we need rich and provocative discussions about standardized homework policies, consistent homework schedules, the effect of homework on struggling learners, how homework is killing a nation of readers, and what types of homework meet Kohn's definition of "truly necessary" (Gallagher, 2009; Kohn, 2006). We need discussions that make us sweat just a little bit because our responsibility is to our children, not to politics and precedents.

Just as a doctor can't proclaim that parent pressures, precedents dating back to the 1950s, an increasingly competitive work climate, or threats of global competition made him write that prescription to the over-scheduled and understimulated eight-year-old sitting in the corner of his office, we shouldn't yield to similar pressures unless they're packaged atop a mounting heap of research. Yet, as teachers and administrators, that's exactly what we've done. What if we paused and rethought the homework default based, not on pressures and precedents, but on what the research suggests about homework and achievement, global competiveness, self-discipline and study skills, and family household dynamics—and then took

that as fodder to refocus our discussion on what might benefit students more than homework?

The Homework Default

Since 1981, the time that children have been devoting to organized sports and outside activities has declined substantially while independent reading time remains limited, and time spent on homework has climbed sharply (Juster, Ono, & Stafford, 2004). Cooper's extensive reviews of studies on homework and achievement suggest that "for elementary age students, the effects of homework on achievement is trivial if it exists at all" (2001, p. 36), and only a moderate positive correlation exists in the middle grades, with those correlations pushing into the negative realm when homework exceeds one to two hours per day (Cooper, 1989; Cooper, 2006; Cooper, Robinson, & Patall, 2006).

Correlations, however, represent a relationship, not a causation. If you visit my 1st-grade classroom in March, you'll find a correlation between the outside temperature and the number of children wearing shorts. But, if you overheard me telling students, "Please wear shorts tomorrow because I really want it to be warm for my son's afternoon soccer practice," you'd probably think I'd spent too much time with the glue sticks.

But, as educators, we have seemingly decided that the small correlation between homework and achievement in the middle grades is in fact a causation. But it's just as plausible that students who like school and excel at school are more likely to spend more time doing homework than students who don't like school and don't excel at school, and that motivation and level of achievement result from in-class learning, not time on task outside school. These interpretations, however, don't soothe our trepidations about achievement gaps.

Historically, the United States' educational system has reacted to the perceived threat of global competition by withering autonomy, tightening the bolts of control, and calling for increased homework. This was evident in our response to Sputnik in 1957, the publication of *A Nation at Risk* in the 1980s, and the bipartisan rollout of the No Child Left Behind Act in 2001. But a scan of the global front reveals that teachers in top-performing nations, such as Japan, Denmark, and the Czech Republic,

Suskind, Dorothy. From *Phi Delta Kappan,* September 2012, pp. 52–55. Reprinted with permission of Phi Delta Kappa International. All rights reserved. www.pdkintl.org

assign less homework compared to their low-performing counterparts in Greece, Thailand, and Iran. U.S. teachers lead the charge in making homework a high-stakes event, with nearly 70% selecting to grade homework, compared to 6% in Germany, 14% in Japan, and 28% in Canada, despite research suggesting that grading students on outside work encourages them to limit their focus, cheat, strive for the minimally set standards of success, and produces undue stress on family dynamics (Baker & LeTendre, 2005; Dudley-Marling, 2003; Bennett & Kalish, 2006).

If caught in an unguarded moment, many teachers and parents will attest to the aforementioned perils of homework, yet moments later will redress in political correctness and profess that homework teaches self-discipline and study skills, not realizing there is a void of research supporting such claims. In fact, when Hofferth and Sandberg (2001) examined how time studying, reading, and watching television was linked with behavior and achievement, only reading showed a positive correlation. Their research also identified a correlation between emotional well-being and eating family meals, acquiring adequate sleep, and playing organized sports—practices and conditions often called into jeopardy due to rigorous homework regimens.

Game Changer: A New Default

Most adults work eight- to 10-hour days and expect unstructured time in the evening to complete household chores and connect with families, hobbies, and interests. But homework deprives children of the same use of their nonwork hours. Gerver (2010) invites us to think of school (or homework) as that person who corners you, perhaps at a cocktail party, who "derided all of your interests and told you that they were unimportant, then went on to spend hours telling you about . . . (their) interests and just how important and significant they were and that, really, . . . (their) 'stuff' was far more important to you than the 'stuff' you cared about."

Consider the story of Cal Tech's Jet Propulsion Laboratory (JPL), a premier aerospace research facility. JPL attracts engineers who graduate at the top of their classes at high-prestige universities like MIT and Stanford. But the managers found that engineers who excelled were the childhood tinkerers, the ones who had built with Legos, taken apart clocks, and worked on their dad's car. "The JPL managers discovered through research that there is a kind of magic in play. What might seem like a frivolous or even childish pursuit is ultimately beneficial. It's paradoxical that even a little bit of 'nonproductive' activity can make one enormously more productive and invigorated in other aspects of life" (Brown & Vaughan, 2009, p. 10).

Futurists suggest that successful individuals going forward will be those who have the creativity to make a multiplicity of connections that aren't evident within the boundaries of their own disciplines and instead adapt, view, and combine perspectives previously thought of as unrelated. That's what Einstein did with energy, mass, and speed within his theory of relativity. Such acts of courage have marked the innovators who have pushed our country forward. Those moments are unlikely to come within the current folds of school because, as Csikszentmihalyi (2007) asserts, "It is easier to enhance creativity by changing the environment than by trying to make people creative."

Unfortunately, many students never find that "changed environment" or those spaces at school. Where they do find them is while playing on the ball field, constructing Legos on the living room floor, rummaging through the trash, and rifling through the bushes. They make discoveries when their intrinsic motivation inspires them to press forward. This is a very different lived life than the one teachers currently offer where we send children home with structured assignments, calling for narrow interpretations, arid promising punitive measures if left undone or completed outside the boxes that teachers have outlined for them.

This homework experience is in opposition to what happens when people are engaged in authentic tasks with intrinsic motivations. "It takes a lot of courage to be a research scientist. It really does. I mean you invest an enormous amount of yourself, your life, your time and nothing may come of it . . . so that's the story . . . it's great fun, to come upon something new," said Vera Rubin, a researcher and astronomer (Csikszentmihalyi, pp. 3–4). This search for flow and discovery is what inspired Google executives to ask employees to dedicate 20% of their time pursuing innovation; within this 20% bubble of autonomy, employees created Google News and Gmail (Pink, 2009).

You may want to close your conversation with that pestering cocktail guest by reminding him that the global market has called us to restructure our knowledge economy into a creative economy. Yet homework policies that monopolize students' free time are preparing them "for 20th-century work, assembly-line work, in which workers don't have to be creative or smart. They just have to be able to put their assigned bolt in the assigned hole," with an emphasis on obedience rather than thinking (Brown & Vaughan, 2009; Kohn, 2007). As you get your coat and leave the party guest behind, it would be nice to share with him tomorrow's plan to build a Lego police station, eat dinner with your family, and read a self-selected book for enjoyment.

Think: If the research has consistently failed to link homework with achievement, as narrowly defined by school culture, what would the future hold if children were allowed to move freely after school as they discovered tomorrow's world? Heck, I wrote this article during my holiday vacation, not because I was asked to, needed to, or was paid to, but because I felt called on by my own creative desires, philosophical beliefs, and intrinsic motivation to improve our nation's schools. Imagine what children might do.

References

Baker, D. & LeTendre, G. (2005). *National differences, global similarities: World cultures and the future of schooling.* Palo Alto, CA: Stanford University Press.

Bennett, S. & Kalish, N. (2006). *The case against homework: How homework is hurting children and what parents can do about it.* New York, NY: Three Rivers Press.

Brown, S. & Vaughan, C. (2009). *Play: How it shapes the brain, opens imagination, and invigorates the soul.* New York, NY: Avery.

Cooper, H. (1989, November). Synthesis on research of homework. *Educational Leadership, 47* (3), 85–91.

Cooper, H. (2001, April). Homework for all: In moderation. *Educational Leadership, 58* (7), 34–38.

Cooper, H. (2006). *The battle over homework: Common ground for administrators, teachers and parents* (3rd edition). Thousand Oaks, CA: Corwin Press.

Cooper, H., Robinson, J.C., & Patall, E.A. (2006). Does homework improve academic achievement? A synthesis of research 1987–2003. *Review of Educational Research, 76*(1), 1–62.

Csikszentmihalyi, M. (2007). *Creativity: Flow and the psychology of discover and invention.* New York, NY: HarperCollins.

Dudley-Marling, C. (2003). How school troubles come home: The impact of homework on families of struggling learners. *Current Issues in Education, 6* (4).

Gallagher, K. (2009). *Readicide: How schools are killing reading and what you can do about it.* Portland, ME: Stenhouse.

Gerver, R. (2010). *Creating tomorrow's schools today.* London, England: Continuum International Publishing.

Hofferth, S. & Sandberg, J. (2001). How American children spend their time. *Journal of Marriage and Family, 63* (2), 295–308.

Juster, F. T., Ono, H., & Stafford, F. (2004). *Changing times of American youth: 1981–2003.* Ann Arbor, Ml: University of Michigan Institute for Social Research.

Kohn, A. (2006). *The homework myth: Why our kids get too much of a bad thing.* Philadelphia, PA: DeCapo Press.

Kohn, A. (2007). Rethinking homework. *Principal, 86* (3), 35–38.

Pink, D. (2009). *Drive.* New York, NY: Riverhead Books.

Dorothy Suskind is a first-grade teacher in Richmond and an adjunct instructor for the University of Virginia and the University of Richmond.

EXPLORING THE ISSUE

Does Homework Lead to Improved Student Achievement?

Critical Thinking and Reflection

1. What, in your opinion, is the major issue with regard to homework effects and the difficulty in clearly understanding them?
2. In what way should the nature of the evidence be used to help frame a school district's policy discussion about whether or not to change their policy about homework?
3. If you were a building-level school principal, what kind of conversation should you have with your teaching staff regarding homework? How would this conversation differ if your school was an elementary school versus a high school?

Is There Common Ground?

The two articles selected to frame the issue are not that far apart; indeed they represent thoughtful perspectives from the practice community that converge on recognizing that there is more to the relation between homework and achievement than meets the eye.

From a practice perspective, the authors from both sides remind us there are also numerous value-related issues clouding the relation between homework and achievement that question the assumptions underlying the purpose of homework in the first place. Considerations paramount to this point of view include questions about why is homework assigned (goals), how "good" is the homework (quality), what is it used for (performance feedback). Equally important, from Suskind's perspective, is the concern about what is NOT happening because of homework; what are its potential disruptive effects—both at home and school.

From a research perspective (again, see Trautwein and colleagues referenced below), it is worth keeping in mind that several seemingly simple but complex issues and questions are raised including how is "homework" defined? How is "achievement" defined? Across what age groups/grade levels and student groups have the effects been obtained? Are the effects always uniform? etc. Take, for example, the matter of how homework is defined.

Create Central

www.mhhe.com/createcentral

Additional Resources

H. Cooper, J. C. Robinson, and E. A. Patall, "Does Homework Improve Academic Achievement? A Synthesis of Research, 1987–2003," *Review of Educational Research* (vol. 76, pp. 1–62, 2006).

H. Cooper and J. C. Valentine, "Using Research to Answer Practical Questions about Homework," *Educational Psychologist* (vol. 36, pp. 143–153, 2001).

U. Trautwein and O. Lüdtke, "Students' Self-Reported Effort and Time on Homework in Six School Subjects: Between Student Differences and Within Student Variation," *Journal of Educational Psychology* (vol. 99, pp. 432–444, 2007).

Ulrich Trautwein, Inge Schnyder, Alois Niggli, Marko Neumann, and Oliver Lüdtke, "Chameleon Effects in Homework Research: The Homework–Achievement Association Depends on the Measures Used and the Level of Analysis Chosen" *Contemporary Educational Psychology* (2009).

Internet References . . .

The Myth about Homework

http://www.time.com/time/magazine/article
/0,9 171,1 376208,00.html

How School Troubles Come Home: The Impact of Homework on Families of Struggling Learners

http://cie.ed.asu.edu/volume6/number

Dose Homework Improve Academic Achievement?—Harris Cooper

http://today.duke.edu/2006/09/homework_oped.html

Selected, Edited, and with Issue Framing Material by:
Leonard Abbeduto, *University of California, Davis*
and
Frank Symons, *University of Minnesota*

ISSUE

Does Grading Help Students Learn?

YES: Kyle Spencer, from "Standards-Based Grading" *The Education Digest* (vol. 78, September/October 2012)

NO: Alfie Kohn, from "The Case Against Grades" *Educational Leadership* (November 2011)

Learning Outcomes
After reading this issue, you will be able to: • Discuss the history and rationale of the grading system typically used in U.S. schools. • Understand the concept of standards-based grading. • Recognize the potential benefits and risks of the use of grades to support student learning.

ISSUE SUMMARY

YES: Kyle Spencer argues that grades provide useful information if they are linked to standards, or targeted competences to be acquired, indicating what competencies the student has mastered and which need more work. In fact, Spencer argues for more and more frequent grades than in the traditional approach to grading.

NO: Alfie Kohn argues that grades interfere with learning because they subvert the student's enjoyment of learning, or intrinsic motivation, instead leading the student to work for the grades rather than to learn. In addition, the focus on grades leads students to avoid intellectually challenging tasks.

Any of us who has grown up in the school system of the United States take for granted that our work will be graded. Concepts such as letters grades, grade point average (GPA), and the like are commonplace. In fact, many of us have found it more than a bit disconcerting if we took a class in which assignments were "checked in" but did not receive a letter grade or numerical rating. Moreover, even advanced professional training and employment options can be influenced by our school grades (e.g., many employers ask for college transcripts and consider GPA in their hiring decisions). But why do we grade? Are grades useful or harmful?

Grading systems can be traced in part to the influence of behaviorism in American psychology in the twentieth century. Although expressed in a number of seemingly distinct theories, the fundamental assumption of behaviorism—namely, that the behavior of any organism is controlled by forces that are external to it—is constant across its many manifestations. In Ivan Pavlov's theory of classical conditioning, a dog reflexively salivates in response to the sound of a bell that was previously paired with the delivery of food. In B. F. Skinner's theory of operant conditioning, a thirsty rat presses a bar when a light flashes because this results in the delivery of a few drops of water. In these examples, the organism's behavior is controlled by some feature of the world around it—the sound of a bell, the flash of light, the delivery of food or water. Despite its apparent complexity and the addition of a conscious mind, behaviorists have traditionally argued that human behavior, like the behavior of animals, is also controlled by external forces.

The influence of behaviorism has extended far beyond academic psychology to include the American classroom. This influence can be traced most directly to the work of Skinner (1904–1990), who emphasized the role of reinforcement in his theory of operant conditioning. According to Skinner, an event serves as reinforcement if it is contingent on an organism's response to a stimulus and increases the future likelihood of that response. If, for example, a student who is praised consistently by his teacher for completing assignments on time begins to meet deadlines with increasing frequency over time, the teacher's praise would be a reinforcer. It is important to note that, according to Skinner, we cannot know in advance whether praise, a gold star, a good grade, or any other stimulus will be reinforcing. In fact, he argued that we can only know that something is reinforcing if we observe that it leads to an increase in the target behavior. This was a critical point for Skinner. He felt that all too often teachers, parents, and cognitive psychologists expend too much effort "guessing" about what is going on inside a student's head: Is the student motivated? Will the student see my overture as positive or negative? Because we can never know for sure what is going on in another person's mind, Skinner believed that it is far more productive to analyze the consequences of a student's behavior. In short, according to Skinner, we can control a student's behavior by changing its consequences—removing the reinforcement for behaviors we see as negative and providing reinforcement for behaviors we see as positive. On this view, good grades serve to reinforce the behavior that preceded them (e.g., studying) and bad grades serve to punish, or at least not reinforce, the behaviors that preceded them (e.g., skipping class).

Other theories and approaches in psychology and education, however, have also been used to justify grading systems. On many theories of learning in cognitive psychology, grades can be useful for their informational value serving to provide corrective feedback. For example, many theories posit a construct of the mind labeled as the executive function, which is a set of conscious processes involved in planning cognitive activity. Receiving information in the form of grades would allow a student, through the use of executive function processes, to decide that a poor letter grade indicates the need for more studying, seeking additional assistance, reviewing previously studied material, etc. In short, the grade functions as feedback to change future behavior, presuming that the student is motivated to do well academically. On these theories, grades must be seen as having an informational value and thus are most effective when they are used systematically and coupled with a clear grading rubric or other feedback. If they are seen as arbitrary or assigned based on irrelevant or nontransparent criteria, their value to the learner is diminished.

Despite the different theoretical orientations supporting the use of grades, controversy remains. Grade inflation, variability in grading across classrooms and schools, and more general concerns about student achievement have generated considerable discussion about whether to use grades and if so, how. In the first selection, Kyle Spencer focuses on the potential informational value of grades. Spencer argues that grades provide useful information if they are linked to standards, or targeted competences to be acquired, indicating what competencies the student has mastered and which competences are lagging. Spencer notes that standards-based grading requires more frequent grades than does the traditional approach to grading. In the second selection, Alfie Kohn focuses on the potential motivational effects of grades. Kohn argues that grades interfere with learning because they subvert the student's enjoyment of learning, or intrinsic motivation, instead leading the student to work for the grades rather than to learn. In addition, the focus on grades leads students to avoid intellectually challenging tasks, according to Kohn.

YES ⤶

Kyle Spencer

Standards-Based Grading

A few years ago, it occurred to Frank Noschese, a physics teacher at John Jay High School in Westchester County, NY, that some of his 11th graders were able to get A's in his class without mastering complex concepts. They could solve exam problems that required them to plug in the right numbers but routinely missed the few questions that tested their understanding of more advanced concepts. Because Noschese's grading system didn't differentiate between those levels of knowledge, there was little incentive for students to focus on harder material.

Noschese wanted a method that would encourage students to move from easy concepts to hard ones and reward them for ultimately obtaining knowledge, no matter how long it took. So he designed a new grading system, inspired by the work of Robert J. Marzano and Jane E. Pollock. Now, every time Noschese's students take a quiz, they don't see one grade but three or four, each indicating whether they have demonstrated their understanding of a pertinent idea. Students who fail to grasp a concept have second and third chances to show they have finally mastered it, by retaking a quiz, conducting a lab experiment, or simply sitting with Noschese at his desk and explaining it.

Noschese is part of a growing band of teachers, schools, and entire districts that have put their faith in standards-based grading, an innovative, albeit complex and sometimes controversial, method that aims to make grades more meaningful. A standards-based report card contains an overall grade for each course but also indicates how well a student has mastered each of the class's several standards. As well, while traditional end-of-course grades are the final products of many factors, including quizzes, homework, behavior, and attendance, with standards-based grading nothing but mastery matters. Standards-based grades account for nonacademic elements very minimally or not at all.

Even if those "process" factors are important aspects of student development, says Ken O'Connor, author of *A Repair Kit for Grading: Fifteen Fixes for Broken Grades,* report cards need to separate them from academic attainment.

A Clearer Picture

Grading originally served to determine which students should be promoted to the next level, says Madhabi Chatterji, associate professor at Teachers College, Columbia University. Eventually, it was used as a sorting mechanism that allowed educators to rank students and establish classroom curves and hierarchies. Advocates of standards-based grading contend that traditional grades are often based on vague criteria and therefore unreliable. They can be used to reward or punish students for factors unrelated to competency and don't place enough emphasis on what is truly important: reaching proficiency in a subject so a student can pass state exams and perform well in higher-level classes.

Standards-based grading derives from the idea that teachers ought to have clearly defined academic goals for their students, be able to determine if they've met them, and then communicate that to students and parents. The approach has long been part of life at some elementary schools and was included in the No Child Left Behind Act as a suggested practice.

As states adopt Common Core standards in language arts and math, and as educators move toward a more uniform understanding of what students ought to know, this approach has grown popular among educators at all grade levels.

"There has been a national push to use standards to drive instruction and curricular development," says Kathleen Porter-Magee, a senior director at the Thomas B. Fordham Institute, an education think tank supportive of national standards. "Standards-based grading can seem like a natural extension of that movement," she says. It also "allows for a more nuanced conversation between parents and teachers about where students are strong, where they are weak, and how parents can help them."

Concern over how far American students lag behind other nations has also played a role in encouraging educators to more accurately assess student progress, as has the worry that too many high school graduates are heading to college unprepared.

Standards-based grading is just one of several experimental methods being tested in American classrooms. Another is narrative grading, in which teachers write lengthy reports on student progress. There are also digital badges, where students earn online certificates for accomplishing tasks that are eventually translated into grades. Some educators have moved toward a portfolio system, where students demonstrate progress through a series of projects they assemble and then review with their teachers. And in others there has been a move away from grades altogether.

Some states have encouraged districts to consider standards-based grading. In 2007, state officials in Massachusetts promoted the practice to teachers. The California Department of Education endorsed standards-based grading for improving middle school as early as 2001. And in 2010, Thomas R. Guskey, a professor at the University of Kentucky and coauthor of *Developing Standards-Based Report Cards,* developed a statewide standards-based report card for Kentucky and tested it in 20 schools.

Standards-based grading has become the rule in such districts as Montgomery County, MD; Minnetonka, MN; San Mateo-Foster City, CA; and Quakertown, PA. "There has been a real insurgence in this idea," says Guskey—evident by the proliferation of blogs, software firms, and consultants, all focused on helping schools embrace and adapt to the changes.

How Standards-Based Grading Works

To understand what standards-based grading means, . . . Like a traditional report card, it includes an overall grade or, for middle and high schoolers, a percentage grade for each class a student is enrolled in. But it goes much further, indicating up to six different marks for each subject, all pertaining to particular strands of learning identified by the Common Core State Standards (which Kentucky has adopted) as well as other national associations, such as the National Science Teachers Association. Rubrics that explain the marks are available online, as are guidelines for using the report cards for students with disabilities and English learners.

An Algebra 1 student, for example, might receive a 4 out of 4 in polynomials and quadratic equations, but only a 2—meaning partial proficiency—in linear equations. Typically, students may take several tries at mastering whatever areas they are weak in, and teachers count just the last or highest assessment.

In a separate box, the teacher can indicate if the student does homework, is punctual, cooperates, and participates. But on Guskey's report card, none of this is included in the student's grade. Shawn Cornally, a biology and calculus teacher at Solon (IA) High School, who uses a similar report card for his students, says separating the learning goals from the other factors is motivating. "It helps them to focus their energy and thoughts on the content of the course rather than the management," he says.

Teasing out topic-by-topic achievement results can be helpful for teachers, and doing so meshes with many districts' embrace of data-based decision making. In the Lindsay Unified School District in Tulare County, CA, which adopted standards-based grading in all of its schools, educators say the new system has changed how students view their time in school and how engaged they become in their mastery of material. This is because Lindsay takes a purist approach to standards-based grading, one that requires high school students to repeat courses until they have earned at least a 3 on their learning objectives.

Tom Blackmon, a world history teacher at Lindsay High School, says the new system has also allowed the school to provide more differentiated instruction, in large part because they track precisely what students know and don't know. Blackmon works with colleagues to group students according to what they've mastered. Through small-group instruction and independent or computer-based learning, students are given the chance to pick up concepts they are struggling with while other students move on.

Detractors of standards-based grading say the time, energy, and even math skills that the system requires can be a big impediment. By its very nature, it requires frequent assessment. Teachers who do this without a school-wide or district-wide initiative must sift through a year's worth of material and decide what the crucial knowledge points are and how to weigh them.

Overcoming Challenges

Ask proponents what they like about standards-based grading and they are likely to share an anecdote or two about a student who in years past slid by without ever quite mastering the pertinent curricular points. But they can't actually point to research that proves standards-based grading makes students more competent.

In 2004, Susan Pedersen and Doug Williams conducted a small, limited study of 77 7th graders to examine how student motivation was affected by various grading models. But the study's ultimate conclusion—that no matter how the students were graded, they fared more or less the same on the exam—is hardly a ringing endorsement for the need to change long-standing grading practices.

Teachers have acknowledged that instituting a standards-based grading system has its drawbacks. In a survey Guskey conducted in Kentucky during his standards-based grading pilot program, the majority of teachers who were handing out both standards-based report cards and traditional ones reported liking the new ones but not the extra time they took to fill out.

As well, parents have resisted the reform. Some parents in Kennewick, WA, which has been using the system in some middle schools for several years, became so disenchanted with it that they have fought to bring traditional grades back. Their concern: Students lose their motivation to study for tests when they know they will have multiple opportunities to make up for bad scores—something that they may not be able to do in high school and college. Parents have also taken issue with the premise that grading should ignore nonacademic factors, like whether or not children cooperate and do their homework.

And while it's more instructive for a 6th grader, and her parents, to know that she is "partially proficient" in multiplying fractions than that she has a B in math, it can be frustrating to read a report card with dozens of indicators, especially when parents may not know what to do with all that information. In 2005, when Montgomery County, MD, elementary schools piloted a new report card, parents were overwhelmed by the detail. Students had grades in 13 math subcategories—a number that grading experts consider overkill. As well, educators had yet to match up what they were actually teaching with what was on the report card.

The district is now rolling out a revised report card in the upper grades, with four to seven categories per subject and very specific links between classroom work and report card line items.

Educators say the Common Core State Standards have exacerbated this communication problem; many are written in language that seems arcane even to professionals, and there are simply too many to realistically track. Surveys like the one Guskey did in Kentucky discovered that parents respond best to report cards on which the authors have translated jargon-filled standards into language parents can relate to.

Advocates acknowledge that the staggering amount of information that standards-based grading produces, even on well-edited report cards, is really only as good as students' (and, in some ways, parents') ability and willingness to take advantage of it. "This is great for kids who want the chance to improve their grades," Noschese says. For those who are less interested in the challenge of really "getting it," he says, it's not so helpful.

But Douglas Reeves, founder of the Leadership and Learning Center, believes that such a view may be missing the point. Reeves assists educators on their grading practices and has seen that grades are more likely to match up to standardized test scores when schools use standards-based grading. "Standards-based grading makes people more honest," he says.

Kyle Spencer is a freelance writer who focuses on educational issues. He is based in New York.

Alfie Kohn  **NO**

The Case Against Grades

"I remember the first time that a grading rubric was attached to a piece of my writing. . . . Suddenly all the joy was taken away. I was writing for a grade—I was no longer exploring for me. I want to get that back. Will I ever get that back?"

—Claire, a student (in Olson, 2006)

By now enough has been written about academic assessment to fill a library, but when you stop to think about it, the whole enterprise really amounts to a straightforward two-step dance. We need to collect information about how students are doing, and then we need to share that information (along with our judgments, perhaps) with the students and their parents. Gather and report—that's pretty much it.

You say the devil is in the details? Maybe so, but I'd argue that too much attention to the particulars of implementation may be distracting us from the bigger picture—or at least from a pair of remarkable conclusions that emerge from the best theory, practice, and research on the subject: *Collecting information doesn't require tests, and sharing that information doesn't require grades.* In fact, students would be a lot better off without either of these relics from a less enlightened age.

Why tests are not a particularly useful way to assess student learning (at least the kind that matters), and what thoughtful educators do instead, are questions that must wait for another day. Here, our task is to take a hard look at the second practice, the use of letters or numbers as evaluative summaries of how well students have done, regardless of the method used to arrive at those judgments.

The Effects of Grading

Most of the criticisms of grading you'll hear today were laid out forcefully and eloquently anywhere from four to eight decades ago (Crooks, 1933; De Zouche, 1945; Kirschenbaum, Simon, & Napier, 1971; Linder, 1940; Marshall, 1968), and these early essays make for eye-opening reading. They remind us just how long it's been clear there's something wrong with what we're doing as well as just how little progress we've made in acting on that realization.

In the 1980s and '90s, educational psychologists systematically studied the effects of grades. As I've reported elsewhere (Kohn, 1999a, 1999b, 1999c), when students

from elementary school to college who are led to focus on grades are compared with those who aren't, the results support three robust conclusions:

- *Grades tend to diminish students' interest in whatever they're learning.* A "grading orientation" and a "learning orientation" have been shown to be inversely related and, as far as I can tell, every study that has ever investigated the impact on intrinsic motivation of receiving grades (or instructions that emphasize the importance of getting good grades) has found a negative effect.
- *Grades create a preference for the easiest possible task.* Impress upon students that what they're doing will count toward their grade, and their response will likely be to avoid taking any unnecessary intellectual risks. They'll choose a shorter book, or a project on a familiar topic, in order to minimize the chance of doing poorly—not because they're "unmotivated" but because they're rational. They're responding to adults who, by telling them the goal is to get a good mark, have sent the message that success matters more than learning.
- *Grades tend to reduce the quality of students' thinking.* They may skim books for what they'll "need to know." They're less likely to wonder, say, "How can we be sure that's true?" than to ask "Is this going to be on the test?" In one experiment, students told they'd be graded on how well they learned a social studies lesson had more trouble understanding the main point of the text than did students who were told that no grades would be involved. Even on a measure of rote recall, the graded group remembered fewer facts a week later (Grolnick and Ryan, 1987).

Research on the effects of grading has slowed down in the last couple of decades, but the studies that are still being done reinforce the earlier findings. For example, a grade-oriented environment is associated with increased levels of cheating (Anderman and Murdock, 2007), grades (whether or not accompanied by comments) promote a fear of failure even in high-achieving students (Pulfrey et al., 2011), and the elimination of grades (in favor of a pass/fail system) produces substantial benefits with no apparent disadvantages in medical school (White and Fantone, 2010). More important, no recent research has contradicted the earlier "big three" findings, so those conclusions still stand.

Why Grading Is Inherently Problematic

A student asked his Zen master how long it would take to reach enlightenment. "Ten years," the master said. But, the student persisted, what if he studied very hard? "Then 20 years," the master responded. Surprised, the student asked how long it would take if he worked very, *very* hard and became the most dedicated student in the Ashram. "In that case, 30 years," the master replied. His explanation: "If you have one eye on how close you are to achieving your goal, that leaves only one eye for your task."

To understand why research finds what it does about grades, we need to shift our focus from educational measurement techniques to broader psychological and pedagogical questions. The latter serve to illuminate a series of misconceived assumptions that underlie the use of grading.

Motivation: While it's true that many students, after a few years of traditional schooling, could be described as motivated by grades, what counts is the nature of their motivation. Extrinsic motivation, which includes a desire to get better grades, is not only different from, but often undermines, intrinsic motivation, a desire to learn for its own sake (Kohn 1999a). Many assessment specialists talk about motivation as though it were a single entity—and their recommended practices just put a finer gloss on a system of rewards and punishments that leads students to chase marks and become less interested in the learning itself. If nourishing their *desire* to learn is a primary goal for us, then grading is problematic by its very nature.

Achievement: Two educational psychologists pointed out that "an overemphasis on assessment can actually undermine the pursuit of excellence" (Maehr and Midgley, 1996, p. 7). That unsettling conclusion—which holds regardless of the quality of the assessment but is particularly applicable to the use of grades—is based on these researchers' own empirical findings as well as those of many others, including Carol Dweck, Carole Ames, Ruth Butler, and John Nicholls (for a review, see Kohn 1999b, chapter 2). In brief: the more students are led to focus on *how well* they're doing, the less engaged they tend to be with *what* they're doing.

It follows that all assessment must be done carefully and sparingly lest students become so concerned about their achievement (how good they are at doing something—or, worse, how their performance compares to others') that they're no longer thinking about the learning itself. Even a well-meaning teacher may produce a roomful of children who are so busy monitoring their own reading skills that they're no longer excited by the stories they're reading. Assessment consultants worry that grades may not accurately reflect student performance; educational psychologists worry because grades fix students' attention *on* their performance.

Quantification: When people ask me, a bit defensively, if it isn't important to measure how well students are learning (or teachers are teaching), I invite them to rethink their choice of verb. There is certainly value in *assessing* the quality of learning and teaching, but that doesn't mean it's always necessary, or even possible, to *measure* those things—that is, to turn them into numbers. Indeed, "measurable outcomes may be the least significant results of learning" (McNeil, 1986, p. xviii)—a realization that offers a refreshing counterpoint to today's corporate-style "school reform" and its preoccupation with data.

To talk about what happens in classrooms, let alone in children's heads, as moving forward or backward in specifiable degrees, is not only simplistic because it fails to capture much of what is going on, but also destructive because it may change what is going on for the worse. Once we're compelled to focus only on what can be reduced to numbers, such as how many grammatical errors are present in a composition or how many mathematical algorithms have been committed to memory, thinking has been severely compromised. And that is exactly what happens when we try to fit learning into a four- or five- or (heaven help us) 100-point scale.

Curriculum: "One can have the best assessment imaginable," Howard Gardner (1991, p. 254) observed, "but unless the accompanying curriculum is of quality, the assessment has no use." Some people in the field are candid about their relativism, offering to help align your assessment to whatever your goals or curriculum may be. The result is that teachers may become more adept at measuring how well students have mastered a collection of facts and skills whose value is questionable—and never questioned. "If it's not worth teaching, it's not worth teaching well," as Eliot Eisner (2001, p. 370) likes to say. Nor, we might add, is it worth assessing accurately.

Portfolios, for example, can be constructive if they replace grades rather than being used to *yield* them. They offer a way to thoughtfully gather a variety of meaningful examples of learning for the students to review. But what's the point, "if instruction is dominated by worksheets so that every portfolio looks the same"? (Neill et al. 1995, p. 4). Conversely, one sometimes finds a mismatch between more thoughtful forms of pedagogy—say, a workshop approach to teaching writing—and a depressingly standardized assessment tool like rubrics (Wilson, 2006).

Improving Grading: A Fool's Errand?

"I had been advocating standards-based grading, which is a very important movement in its own right, but it took a push from some great educators to make me realize that if I wanted to focus my assessment around authentic feedback, then I should just abandon grades altogether."

—New Jersey middle school teacher Jason Bedell (2010)

Much of what is prescribed in the name of "assessing for learning" (and, for that matter, "formative assessment") leaves me uneasy: The recommended practices often seem prefabricated and mechanistic; the imperatives of data collection seem to upstage the children themselves and the goal of helping them become more enthusiastic about what they're doing. Still, if it's done only occasionally and with humility, I think it's possible to assess for learning. But *grading* for learning is, to paraphrase a 1960's-era slogan, rather like bombing for peace. Rating and ranking students (and their efforts to figure things out) is inherently counterproductive.

If I'm right—more to the point, if all the research to which I've referred is taken seriously—then the absence of grades is a necessary, though not sufficient, condition for promoting deep thinking and a desire to engage in it. It's worth lingering on this proposition in light of a variety of efforts to sell us formulas to improve our grading techniques, none of which address the problems of grading, per se.

- It's not enough to replace letters or numbers with labels ("exceeds expectations," "meets expectations," and so on). If you're sorting students into four or five piles, you're still grading them. Rubrics typically include numbers as well as labels, which is only one of several reasons they merit our skepticism (Wilson, 2006; Kohn, 2006).
- It's not enough to tell students in advance exactly what's expected of them. "When school is seen as a test, rather than an adventure in ideas," teachers may persuade themselves they're being fair "if they specify, in listlike fashion, exactly what must be learned to gain a satisfactory grade . . . [but] such schooling is unfair in the wider sense that it prepares students to pass other people's tests without strengthening their capacity to set their own assignments in collaboration with their fellows" (Nicholls and Hazzard, 1993, p. 77).
- It's not enough to disseminate grades more efficiently—for example, by posting them online. There is a growing technology, as the late Gerald Bracey once remarked, "that permits us to do in nanoseconds things that we shouldn't be doing at all" (quoted in Mathews, 2006). In fact, posting grades on-line is a significant step backward because it enhances the salience of those grades and therefore their destructive effects on learning.
- It's not enough to add narrative reports. "When comments and grades coexist, the comments are written to justify the grade" (Wilson, 2009, p. 60). Teachers report that students, for their part, often just turn to the grade and ignore the comment, but "when there's only a comment, they read it," says high school English teacher Jim Drier. Moreover, research suggests that the harmful impact of grades on creativity is no less (and possibly even more) potent when a narrative accompanies them. Narratives are helpful only in the absence of grades (Butler, 1988; Pulfrey et al., 2011).
- It's not enough to use "standards-based" grading. That phrase may suggest any number of things—for example, more consistency, or a reliance on more elaborate formulas, in determining grades; greater specificity about what each grade signifies; or an increase in the number of tasks or skills that are graded. At best, these prescriptions do nothing to address the fundamental problems with grading. At worst, they exacerbate those problems. In addition to the simplistic premise that it's always good to have more data, we find a penchant shared by the behaviorists of yesteryear that learning can and should be broken down into its components, each to be evaluated separately. And more frequent temperature-taking produces exactly the kind of disproportionate attention to performance (at the expense of learning) that researchers have found to be so counterproductive.

The term "standards-based" is sometimes intended just to mean that grading is aligned with a given set of objectives, in which case our first response should be to inquire into the value of those objectives (as well as the extent to which students were invited to help formulate them). If grades are based on state standards, there's particular reason to be concerned since those standards are often too specific, age-inappropriate, superficial, and standardized by definition. In my experience, the best teachers tend to be skeptical about aligning their teaching to a list imposed by distant authorities, or using that list as a basis for assessing how well their students are thinking.

Finally, "standards-based" may refer to something similar to criterion-based testing, where the idea is to avoid grading students on a curve. (Even some teachers who don't do so explicitly nevertheless act as though grades ought to fall into something close to a normal distribution, with only a few students receiving As. But this pattern is not a fact of life, nor is it a sign of admirable "rigor" on the teacher's part. Rather, "it is a symbol of failure—failure to teach well, failure to test well, and failure to have any influence at all on the intellectual lives of students" [Milton, Pollio, & Eison, 1986].) This surely represents an improvement over a system in which the number of top marks is made artificially scarce and students are set against one another. But here we've peeled back the outer skin of the onion (competition) only to reveal more noxious layers beneath: extrinsic motivation, numerical ratings, the tendency to promote achievement at the expense of learning.

If we begin with a desire to assess more often, or to produce more data, or to improve the consistency of our grading, then certain prescriptions will follow. If, however, our point of departure isn't mostly about the grading, but about our desire for students to understand ideas from the inside out, or to get a kick out of playing with words and numbers, or to be in charge of their own learning, then we will likely end up elsewhere. We may come to see grading as a huge, noisy, fuel-guzzling, smoke-belching machine that constantly requires repairs and new parts, when what we should be doing is pulling the plug.

Deleting—or at Least Diluting—Grades

"Like it or not, grading is here to stay" is a statement no responsible educator would ever offer as an excuse for inaction. What matters is whether a given practice is in the best interest of students. If it isn't, then our obligation is to work for its elimination and, in the meantime, do what we can to minimize its impact.

Replacing letter and number grades with narrative assessments or conferences—qualitative summaries of student progress offered in writing or as part of a conversation—is not a utopian fantasy. It has already been done successfully in many elementary and middle schools and even in some high schools, both public and private (Kohn, 1999c). It's important not only to realize that such schools exist but to investigate *why* they've eliminated grades, how they've managed to do so (hint: the process can be gradual), and what benefits they have realized.

Naturally objections will be raised to this—or any—significant policy change, but once students and their parents have been shown the relevant research, reassured about their concerns, and invited to participate in constructing alternative forms of assessment, the abolition of grades proves to be not only realistic but an enormous improvement over the status quo. Sometimes it's only after grading has ended that we realize just how harmful it's been.

To address one common fear, the graduates of grade-free high schools are indeed accepted by selective private colleges and large public universities—on the basis of narrative reports and detailed descriptions of the curriculum (as well as recommendations, essays, and interviews), which collectively offer a fuller picture of the applicant than does a grade-point average. Moreover, these schools point out that their students are often more motivated and proficient learners, thus better prepared for college, than their counterparts at traditional schools who have been preoccupied with grades.

In any case, college admission is surely no bar to eliminating grades in elementary and middle schools because colleges are largely indifferent to what students have done before high school. That leaves proponents of grades for younger children to fall back on some version of an argument I call "BGUTI": Better Get Used To It (Kohn, 2005). The claim here is that we should do unpleasant and unnecessary things to children now in order to prepare them for the fact that just such things will be done to them later. This justification is exactly as absurd as it sounds, yet it continues to drive education policy.

Even when administrators aren't ready to abandon traditional report cards, individual teachers can help to rescue learning in their own classrooms with a two-pronged strategy to "neuter grades," as one teacher described it.

First, they can stop putting letter or number grades on individual assignments and instead offer only qualitative feedback. Report cards are bad enough, but the destructive effects reported by researchers (on interest in learning, preference for challenge, and quality of thinking) are compounded when students are rated on what they do in school day after day. Teachers can mitigate considerable harm by replacing grades with authentic assessments; moreover, as we've seen, any feedback they may already offer becomes much more useful in the absence of letter or number ratings.

Second, although teachers may be required to submit a final grade, there's no requirement for them to decide unilaterally what that grade will be. Thus, students can be invited to participate in that process either as a negotiation (such that the teacher has the final say) or by simply permitting students to grade themselves. If people find that idea alarming, it's probably because they realize it creates a more democratic classroom, one in which teachers must create a pedagogy and a curriculum that will truly engage students rather than allow teachers to coerce them into doing whatever they're told. In fact, negative reactions to this proposal ("It's unrealistic!") point up how grades function as a mechanism for controlling students rather than as a necessary or constructive way to report information about their performance.

I spoke recently to several middle and high school teachers who have de-graded their classes. Jeff Robbins, who has taught eighth-grade science in New Jersey for 15 years, concedes that "life was easier with grades" because they take so much less time than meaningful assessment. That efficiency came at a huge cost, though, he noticed: Kids were stressed out and also preferred to avoid intellectual risks. "They'll take an easier assignment that will guarantee the A."

Initially Robbins announced that any project or test could be improved and resubmitted for a higher grade. Unfortunately, that failed to address the underlying problem, and he eventually realized he had to stop grading entirely. Now, he offers comments to all of his 125 students "about what they're doing and what they need to improve on" and makes abbreviated notes in his grade book. At the end of the term, over a period of about a week, he grabs each student for a conversation at some point—"because the system isn't designed to allow kids this kind of feedback"—asking "what did you learn, how did you learn it. Only at the very end of the conversation [do] I ask what grade will reflect it . . . and we'll collectively arrive at something." Like many other teachers I've spoken to over the years, Robbins says he almost always accepts students' suggestions because they typically pick the same grade that he would have.

Jim Drier, an English teacher at Mundelein High School in Illinois who has about 90 students ranging "from at-risk to A.P.," was relieved to find that it "really doesn't take that long" to write at least a brief note on students' assignments—"a reaction to what they did and some advice on how they might improve." But he never gives them "a number or grade on anything they do. The things that grades make kids do are heartbreaking for an educator": arguing with teachers, fighting with parents, cheating, memorizing facts just for a test and then forgetting them. "This is not why I became a teacher."

Without grades, "I think my relationships with students are better," Drier says. "Their writing improves more quickly and the things they learn stay with them longer. I've had lots of kids tell me it's changed their attitude about coming to school." He expected resistance from parents but says that in three years only one parent has objected, and it may help that he sends a letter home to explain exactly what he's doing and why. Now two of his colleagues are joining him in eliminating grades.

Drier's final grades are based on students' written self-assessments, which, in turn, are based on their review of items in their portfolios. He meets with about three-quarters of them twice a term, in most cases briefly, to assess their performance and, if necessary (although it rarely happens) to discuss a concern about the grade they've suggested. Asked how he manages without a grade book full of letters or numbers, Drier replies, "If I spend 18 weeks with them, I have a pretty good idea what their writing and reasoning ability is."

A key element of authentic assessment for these and other teachers is the opportunity for students to help design the assessment and reflect on its purposes—individually and as a class. Notice how different this is from the more common variant of self-assessment in which students merely monitor their progress toward the teacher's (or legislature's) goals and in which they must reduce their learning to numerical ratings with grade-like rubrics.

Points of overlap as well as divergence emerge from the testimonies of such teachers, some of which have been collected by Joe Bower (n.d.), an educator in Red Deer, Alberta. Some teachers, for example, *evaluate* their students' performance (in qualitative terms, of course), but others believe it's more constructive to offer only *feedback*—which is to say, information. On the latter view, "the alternative to grades is description" and "the starting point for description is a plain sheet of paper, not a form which leads and homogenizes description" (Marshall, 1968, pp. 131, 143).

Teachers also report a variety of reactions to de-grading not only from colleagues and administrators but also from the students themselves. John Spencer (2010), an Arizona middle school teacher, concedes that "many of the 'high performing' students were angry at first. They saw it as unfair. They viewed school as work and their peers as competitors. . . . Yet, over time they switch and they calm down. They end up learning more once they aren't feeling the pressure" from grades.

Indeed, research suggests that the common tendency of students to focus on grades doesn't reflect an innate predilection or a "learning style" to be accommodated;

rather, it's due to having been led for years to work for grades. In one study (Butler, 1992), some students were encouraged to think about how well they performed at a creative task while others were just invited to be imaginative. Each student was then taken to a room that contained a pile of pictures that other people had drawn in response to the same instructions. It also contained some information that told them how to figure out their "creativity score." Sure enough, the children who were told to think about their performance now wanted to know how they had done relative to their peers; those who had been allowed to become immersed in the task were more interested in seeing *what* their peers had done.

Grades don't prepare children for the "real world"—unless one has in mind a world where interest in learning and quality of thinking are unimportant. Nor are grades a necessary part of schooling, any more than paddling or taking extended dictation could be described that way. Still, it takes courage to do right by kids in an era when the quantitative matters more than the qualitative, when meeting (someone else's) standards counts for more than exploring ideas, and when anything "rigorous" is automatically assumed to be valuable. We have to be willing to challenge the conventional wisdom, which in this case means asking not how to improve grades but how to jettison them once and for all.

References

Anderman, E. M., & Murdock, T. B., eds. (2007). *Psychology of academic cheating.* Burlington, MA: Elsevier Academic Press.

Bedell, J. (2010, July). Blog post.

Bower, J. (2010, March 28). Blog post.

Bower, J. (n.d.). Blog post. [Grading moratorium list]

Butler, R. (1988). Enhancing and undermining intrinsic motivation: The effects of task-involving and ego-involving evaluation on interest and performance. *British Journal of Educational Psychology, 58,* 1–14.

Crooks, A. D. (1933). Marks and marking systems: A digest. *Journal of Educational Research, 27*(4), 259–72.

De Zouche, D. (1945). "The wound *is* mortal": Marks, honors, unsound activities. *The Clearing House, 19*(6), 339–44.

Eisner, E. W. (2001, Jan.). What does it mean to say a school is doing well? *Phi Delta Kappan,* pp. 367–72.

Gardner, H. (1991). *The unschooled mind: How children think and how schools should teach.* New York: Basic Books.

Grolnick, W. S., & Ryan, R. M. (1987). Autonomy in children's learning: An experimental and individual difference investigation. *Journal of Personality and Social Psychology, 52,* 890–98.

Kirschenbaum, H., Simon, S. B., & Napier, R. W. (1971). *Wad-ja-get?: The grading game in American education.* New York: Hart.

Kohn, A. (1999a). *Punished by rewards: The trouble with gold stars, incentive plans, A's, praise, and other bribes.* Rev. ed. Boston: Houghton Mifflin.

Kohn, A. (1999b). *The schools our children deserve: Moving beyond traditional classrooms and "tougher standards."* Boston: Houghton Mifflin.

Kohn, A. (1999c, March). From degrading to de-grading. *High School Magazine,* pp. 38–43.

Kohn, A. (2001, Sept. 26). Beware of the standards, not just the tests. *Education Week,* pp. 52, 38.

Kohn, A. (2005, Sept. 7). Getting hit on the head lessons. *Education Week,* pp. 52, 46–47.

Kohn, A. (2006, March). The trouble with rubrics. *Language Arts,* pp. 12–15.

Linder, I. H. (1940, July). Is there a substitute for teachers' grades? *School Board Journal,* pp. 25, 26, 79.

Maehr, M. L., & Midgley, C. (1996). *Transforming school cultures.* Boulder, CO: Westview.

Marshall, M. S. (1968). *Teaching without grades.* Corvallis, OR: Oregon State University Press.

Matthews, J. (2006, Nov. 14). Just whose idea was all this testing? *Washington Post.*

McNeil, L. M. (1986). *Contradictions of control: School structure and school knowledge.* New York: Routledge & Kegan Paul.

Milton, O., Pollio, H. R., & Eison, J. A. (1986). *Making sense of college grades.* San Francisco: Jossey-Bass.

Neill, M., Bursh, P., Schaeffer, B., Thall, C., Yohe, M., & Zappardino, P. (1995). *Implementing performance assessments: A guide to classroom, school, and system reform.* Cambridge, MA: FairTest.

Nicholls, J. G., & Hazzard, S. P. (1993). *Education as adventure: Lessons from the second grade.* New York: Teachers College Press.

Olson, K. (2006, Nov. 8). The wounds of schooling. *Education Week,* pp. 28–29.

Pulfrey, C., Buch, C., & Butera, F. (2011). Why grades engender performance-avoidance goals: The mediating role of autonomous motivation. *Journal of Educational Psychology, 103,* 683–700.

Spencer, J. (2010, July). Blog post.

White, C. B., & Fantone, J. C. (2010). Pass-fail grading: Laying the foundation for self-regulated learning. *Advances in Health Science Education, 15,* 469–77.

Wilson, M. (2006). *Rethinking rubrics in writing assessment.* Portsmouth, NH: Heinemann.

Wilson, M. (2009, Nov). Responsive writing assessment. *Educational Leadership,* pp. 58–62.

ALFIE KOHN is a writer, lecturer, and commentator who focuses on education, child development, parenting, and human behavior.

EXPLORING THE ISSUE

Does Grading Help Students Learn?

Critical Thinking and Reflection

1. Consider the evidence Kohn cites against the use of grades. Can you use your own experiences in school to support or refute this evidence?
2. From your perspective as a student, do you think the informational value provided by standards-based grading would be more important than the potential "threat" to your intrinsic motivation? Why or why not?
3. Do you think that standards-based grading would be more effective for some types of students than other types? Which students would benefit most? Which would benefit least? Why?

Is There Common Ground?

Can we use empirical data to decide on whether grades have the detrimental impact on intrinsic motivation claimed by Kohn and other critics? In principle, it should be possible to compare classrooms or schools using traditional grading systems to those eschewing grades in favor of portfolio compilations, narrative assessments, or other more qualitative assessments. It should also be possible to compare classrooms or schools using different variants for traditional grading systems (e.g., those using a grading curve or criterion-based grading). Unfortunately, taking advantage of naturally occurring grading differences involves a correlational approach, which makes interpretation of cause and effect difficult. For example, there are likely to be many differences between a school that uses traditional grades and one using qualitative assessment techniques; thus, if we observe differences in student achievement, those differences may have nothing to do with grading systems but instead may reflect differences in student demographics, curriculum content, or teacher quality. Experiments have been conducted to address these issues, but they have often been quite artificial. In general, though, experiments have supported the idea that grades can diminish motivation when they seem arbitrary or are not linked to transparent criteria that provide useful corrective feedback.

Other issues further complicate the grading story. Some students may find grades motivating for the wrong reason (i.e., they work only for the grades), whereas others are motivated to learn but value the corrective feedback grades can provide. In addition, some students may appreciate the informational value of grades, but if they are not given the opportunity or, more importantly, the assistance needed to learn more effectively after a poor grade, they may become disheartened and lose interest over time. And finally, no system of evaluation can compensate for a poorly structured curriculum or an unskilled or disinterested teacher.

Create Central

www.mhhe.com/createcentral

Additional Resources

C. Pulfrey, D. Buch, and F. Butea, "Why Grades Engender Performance-Avoidance Goals," *Journal of Educational Psychology* (vol. 103, no. 3, 2011).

Thomas R. Guskey, "Five Obstacles to Grading Reform," *Educational Leadership* (November 2011).

Christopher S. Collins, "An Individual or a Group Grade: Exploring Reward Structure for Motivation and Learning," *Journal on Excellence in College Teaching* (vol. 28, 2012).

Internet References . . .

Center for Teaching—Vanderbilt University

http://cft.vanderbilt.edu/teaching-guides/

Teaching & Learning in Higher Ed

http://teachingandlearninginhighered.org/

Always Formative

http://alwaysformative.blogspot.com/

Selected, Edited, and with Issue Framing Material by:
Leonard Abbeduto, *University of California, Davis*
and
Frank Symons, *University of Minnesota*

ISSUE

Should Schools Decrease Class Size to Improve Student Outcomes?

YES: Bruce J. Biddle and David C. Berliner, from "Small Class Size and Its Effects," *Educational Leadership* (February 2002)

NO: Kirk A. Johnson, from "The Downside to Small Class Policies," *Educational Leadership* (February 2002)

Learning Outcomes

After reading this issue, you will be able to:

- Summarize the arguments for and against decreasing class size to improve student outcomes.
- Describe the issue with respect to the quantity and quality of evidence available to make an empirical decision about the effects of class size on student outcomes.
- Discuss class size issues in relation to historical and contemporary sociopolitical forces.

ISSUE SUMMARY

YES: Bruce J. Biddle and David C. Berliner argue that the gains from smaller classes in the primary grades benefit all types of students, and, importantly, that the gains are greatest for students traditionally disadvantaged in educational access and opportunity.

NO: Kirk A. Johnson argues that although the notion of reducing class size is popular among politicians, it is a costly initiative. The research suggests that in terms of raising achievement, reducing class size does not guarantee success.

Among the most common visual metaphors for public education in the United States is the one-room schoolhouse. Children of all ages and abilities were taught as a single class in one room under one roof. In a largely agrarian society, the arrangement was one of necessity. Following the arrival of the Industrial Revolution, rapid urbanization, and population growth compulsory education emerged, in part, to supply an educated labor force. School enrollments increased and children were stratified into graded classrooms by chronological age.

Concerns about class size in relation to student outcomes appear by as early as the 1920s and for the next four decades informal and opinion-based reviews seemed to support the generally held view that class size was unrelated to academic outcome. Then, a series of research method innovations led to quantitative reviews of the available research literature suggesting the opposite; student outcome and class size appeared to be positively related. At the same time, dramatic sociopolitical changes were occurring with respect to civil rights and equal access to education opportunities. Schools changed again with

further diversity and increasing enrollment. Open education became a prominent perspective, with issues related to student grouping and classroom arrangement practices receiving further scrutiny.

The argument concerning class size continues unresolved in contemporary education. There are many stakeholders with oftentimes conflicting points of view that involve rhetoric as much as research and values as much as facts. In general, proponents maintain on logical and empirical grounds that smaller class size makes sense because of increased opportunities for student–teacher interaction and therefore learning, reduced problem behavior because of a smaller student–teacher ratio, and overall improved classroom climate. Opponents, however, contend that there is little solid evidence supporting these claims, that reducing class size is a costly venture, and that student outcomes are better served by increasing the quality, not the quantity of teachers. The issue is never far from a political platform and in the late 1990s through the early part of the twenty-first century class size reduction moved through the legislative process and became a provision of the Elementary and Secondary Education Act (ESEA).

The debate between class size and student achievement is illustrated in the following selections. Critics of class size reduction contend that there should be tangible evidence of large benefits associated with reduced numbers. The standard should be high, the argument goes, because the financial costs underlying reducing class size are high. Even if there is some evidence that some students benefit, the majority of the evidence is mixed and policymakers should be reluctant to take up such measures in the absence of clear and compelling data. Johnson, for example, cites economic analyses arguing against large-scale policy change because the gains are either negligible or modest at best. In sum, the critics against reducing are not convinced that the evidence base unequivocally supports policy initiatives centered on reducing class size.

YES

**Bruce J. Biddle and
David C. Berliner**

Small Class Size and Its Effects

Studies of the impact of class size on student achievement may be more plentiful than for any other issue in education. Although one might expect this huge research effort to yield clear answers about the effects of class size, sharp disagreements about these studies' findings have persisted.

Advocacy groups take opposite stances. The American Federation of Teachers, for example, asserts that

> taken together, these studies . . . provide compelling evidence that reducing class size, particularly for younger children, will have a positive effect on student achievement. (Murphy & Rosenberg, 1998, p. 3)

The Heritage Foundation, by contrast, claims that "there's no evidence that smaller class sizes alone lead to higher student achievement" (Rees & Johnson, 2000).

Reviewers of class size studies also disagree. One study contends that "large reductions in school class size promise learning benefits of a magnitude commonly believed not within the power of educators to achieve" (Glass, Cahen, Smith, & Filby, 1982, p. 50), whereas another claims that "the . . . evidence does not offer much reason to expect a systematic effect from overall class size reduction policies" (Hanushek, 1999, p. 158).

That the American Federation of Teachers and the Heritage Foundation sponsor conflicting judgments is easy to understand. But why have reviewers come to such divergent views about the research on class size, and what does the evidence really say?

Early Small Field Experiments

To answer these questions, we must look at several research traditions, beginning with early experiments on class size. Experiments have always been a popular research technique because investigators can assign their subjects randomly to different conditions and then compare the results of those conditions—and this human intervention can appear to provide information about causes and effects. Experiments on class size, however, are nearly always done in field settings—schools—where uncontrolled events can undermine the research and affect results.

Small experimental studies on the effects of class size began to appear in the 1920s, and scores of them emerged

subsequently. In the 1960s, informal reviews of these efforts generally concluded that differences in class size generated little to no effect. By the late 1970s, however, a more sophisticated research method, meta-analysis, had been invented, which facilitated the statistical assembly of results from small-but-similar studies to estimate effects for the studies' populations. Reviewers quickly applied meta-analysis to results from early experiments in class size (Glass & Smith, 1979; Educational Research Service, 1980; Glass et al., 1982; Hedges & Stock, 1983) and eventually emerged with a consensus that short-term exposure to small classes generates—usually minor—gains in student achievement and that those gains are greater in the early grades, in classrooms with fewer than 20 students, and for students from groups that are traditionally disadvantaged in education.

Most of these early class size experiments, however, had involved small samples, short-term exposures to small classes, only one measure of student success, and a single education context (such as one school or school district). Poor designs had also made results of some studies questionable. Researchers needed to use different strategies to ascertain the effects of long-term exposure to small classes and to assess whether the advantages of early exposure to small classes would generalize to other successes and be sustainable.

Surveys

Survey research has provided evidence on the effects of class size by analyzing naturally occurring differences in schools and classrooms and by asking whether these differences are associated with student outcomes.

Well-designed surveys can offer evidence about the impact of variables that experiments cannot manipulate—such as gender, minority status, and childhood poverty—but survey research cannot easily establish relationships between causes and effects. For example, if a survey examines a sample of schools where average class size varies and discovers that those schools with smaller classes also have higher levels of student achievement, has the survey ascertained that class size generated achievement? Hardly. Those schools with smaller classes might also have had more qualified teachers, better equipment, more up-to-date curriculums, newer school buildings, more students from affluent homes, or a more supportive community environment—factors that may also have helped generate higher levels of achievement. To use survey data to make the case for a causal relation between class size and student outcomes, then, researchers must use statistical processes that control for the competing effects of other variables.

Serious surveys of education achievement in the United States began in the 1960s with the famous Coleman report (Coleman et al., 1966). Written by authors with impressive reputations and released with great fanfare, this massive, federally funded study involved a national sample and took on many issues then facing education. Today, most people remember the report for its startling claim that student achievement is almost totally influenced by the students' families and peers and not by the characteristics of their schools. This claim was widely accepted—indeed, was greeted with dismay by educators and endorsed with enthusiasm by fiscal conservatives—despite flaws in the report's methods that were noted by thoughtful critics.

Since then, researchers have conducted surveys to establish whether differences in school funding or in the reforms that funds can buy—such as small class sizes—are associated with desired education outcomes. Most of these surveys, usually designed by economists, have involved questionable design features and small samples that did not represent the wide range of U.S. schools, classrooms, or students.

In the 1980s, economist Eric Hanushek began to review these flawed studies and to discuss their supposed implications. Hanushek, committed to the notion that public schools are ineffective and should be replaced by a marketplace of competing private schools, concluded that differences in public school funding are not associated with education outcomes (see Hanushek, 1986, and various publications since).

Other analysts have challenged Hanushek's methods and conclusions on several grounds. Larry Hedges and Rob Greenwald, for example, have pointed out that Hanushek merely counts the number of effects that he believes are statistically significant, but because most of the studies that he reviewed had small samples, he has, of course, found few statistically significant effects. When researchers combine those effects in meta-analyses, however, they find that differences in school funding and the benefits that funds can buy—such as small classes—do, indeed, have an impact (see Hedges, Laine, & Greenwald, 1994, and other publications since).

Other commentators have noted that Hanushek's reviews include many studies that used inappropriate samples or did not employ controls for other school characteristics whose effects might be confused with those of class size. In addition, most of the studies did not examine class size directly but looked instead at student-teacher ratio—that is, the number of students divided by the number of "teachers" reported for a school or school district. Such an approach ignores the actual allocation of students and teachers to classrooms and includes as "teachers" such persons as administrators, nurses, counselors, coaches, specialty teachers, and other professionals who rarely appear in classrooms. Such a ratio does not tell us the number of students actually taught by teachers in classrooms.

Hanushek has not responded well to such criticisms; rather, he has found reasons to quarrel with the details and to continue publishing reviews claiming that small classes have few to no effects. These efforts have allied Hanushek with political conservatives who have extolled his conclusions, complimented his efforts, and asked him to testify in various forums where class size issues are debated. Because of these responses and activities, it is no longer possible to give credence to Hanushek's judgments about class size.

Fortunately, a few well-designed, large-scale surveys have investigated class size directly (see, for example, Elliott, 1998; Ferguson, 1991; Ferguson & Ladd, 1996; Wenglinsky, 1997). These studies concluded that long-term exposure to small classes in the early grades can be associated with student achievement; that the extra gains that such exposure generates may be substantial; and that such gains may not appear with exposure to small classes in the upper grades or at the secondary school levels.

Trial Programs and Large Field Experiments

Other types of small class research have addressed some of the shortcomings of early experiments and surveys. In the 1980s, state legislatures in the United States began political debates about the effects of small class size, and some states began trial programs or large-scale field experiments.

Indiana's Project Prime Time

In 1981, the Indiana legislature allocated $300,000 for a two-year study on the effects of reducing class size for the early grades in 24 randomly selected public schools. But initial results were so impressive that the state allocated funds to reduce class sizes in the 1st grade for all Indiana schools in 1984–85 and for K–3 by 1987–88, with an average of 18 students for each teacher.

Because of the statewide design of the initiative, it was impossible to compare results for small classes with a comparable group of larger classes. Some schools in the state had small classes before Project Prime Time began, however, so researchers compared samples of 2nd grade achievement records from six school districts that had reduced class size with three that had not. They found substantially larger gains in reading and mathematics achievement for students in small classes (McGivern, Gilman, & Tillitski, 1989).

These results seemed promising, but critics soon pounced on the design of the Project Prime Time study, decrying the fact that students had not been assigned to experimental and control groups on a random basis; pointing out that other changes in state school policy had also been adopted during the project; and suggesting that the state's teachers were motivated to make certain that small classes achieved better results because they knew how the trial program's results were supposed to come out. Indiana students probably did benefit from the project, but a persuasive case for small classes had not yet been made. A better experiment was needed.

Tennessee's Project STAR

Such an experiment shortly appeared in Tennessee's Project STAR (Student/Teacher Achievement Ratio), arguably the largest and best-designed field experiment ever undertaken in education (Finn & Achilles, 1990; Finn, Gerber, Achilles, & Boyd-Zaharias, 2001; Folger, 1989; Grissmer, 1999; Krueger, 1999, 2000; Krueger & Whitmore, 2001; Mosteller, 1995; Nye, Hedges, & Konstantopoulos, 1999).

In the mid-1980s, the Tennessee legislature funded a four-year study to compare the achievement of early-grade students assigned randomly to one of three conditions: *standard classes* (with one certificated teacher and more than 20 students); *supplemented classes* (with one teacher and a full-time, noncertificated teacher's aide); and *small classes* (with one teacher and about 15 students). The study began with students entering kindergarten in 1985 and called for each student to attend the same type of class for four years. To control variables, the study asked each participating school to sponsor all three types of classes and to assign students and teachers randomly to each type. Participating teachers received no prior training for the type of class they were to teach.

The project invited all the state's primary schools to be in the study, but each participating school had to agree to remain in the program for four years; to have the class *rooms* needed for the project; and to have at least 57 kindergarten students so that all three types of classes could be set up. Participating schools received no additional support other than funds to hire additional teachers and aides. These constraints meant that troubled schools and those that disapproved of the study—and schools that were too small, crowded, or underfunded—would not participate in the STAR program, so the sample for the first year involved "only" 79 schools, 328 classrooms, and about 6,300 students. Those schools came from all corners of the state, however, and represented urban, inner-city, suburban, and rural school districts. The sample population included majority students, a sizable number of African American students, and students receiving free school lunches.

At the beginning of each year of the study, the sample population changed somewhat. Some participating students had moved away, been required to repeat kindergarten, or left the study because of poor health. Other families moved into the districts served by STAR schools, however, and their children filled the vacant seats. Also, because attending kindergarten was not then mandatory in Tennessee, some new students entered the STAR program in the 1st grade.

In addition, some parents tried to move their children from one type of STAR class to another, but administrators allowed only a few students to move from a standard class to a supplemented class or vice versa. By the end of the study, then, some students had been exposed to a STAR class for four years, but others had spent a shorter time in such classes. These shifts might have biased STAR results, but Alan Krueger's careful analysis (1999) concluded that such bias was minimal.

Near the end of each year, STAR students took the Stanford Achievement Test battery and received separate scores for reading, word-study skills, and mathematics. Results from these tests were similar for students who were in the standard and supplemented classes, indicating that the presence of untrained aides in supplemented classes did *not* contribute to improving student achievement. Results for small classes were sharply different, however, with long-term exposure to small classes generating substantially higher levels of achievement and with gains becoming greater the longer that students were in small classes.

. . . STAR investigators found that the students in small classes were 0.5 months ahead of the other students by the end of kindergarten, 1.9 months ahead at the end of 1st grade, 5.6 months ahead in 2nd grade, and 7.1 months ahead by the end of 3rd grade. The achievement advantages were smaller, although still impressive, for students who were only exposed to one, two, or three years of small classes. STAR investigators found similar (although not identical) results for word-study skills and mathematics.

Small-class advantages appeared for all types of students participating in the study. The gains were similar for boys and girls, but they were greater for impoverished students, African American students, and students from inner-city schools—groups that are traditionally disadvantaged in education.

These initial STAR findings were impressive, but would students who had been exposed to small classes in the early grades retain their extra gains when they entered standard size classes in 4th grade? To answer this question, the Tennessee legislature authorized a second study to examine STAR student outcomes during subsequent years of schooling.

At the end of each year, until they were in the 12th grade in 1997–1998, these students took the Comprehensive Tests of Basic Skills and received scores in reading, mathematics, science, and social science. The results showed that average students who had attended small classes were months ahead of those from standard classes for each topic assessed at each grade level. . . .

Students who had attended small classes also enjoyed other advantages in the upper grades. They earned better grades on average, and fewer dropped out or had to repeat a year. And when they reached high school, more small class students opted to learn foreign languages, study advanced-level courses, and take the ACT and SAT college entrance examinations. More graduated from high school and were in the top 25 percent of their classes. Moreover, initial published results suggest that these upper-grade effects were again larger for students who are traditionally disadvantaged in education.

. . . Instruction in small classes during the early grades had eliminated more than half of the traditional disadvantages that African American students have displayed in participation rates in the ACT and SAT testing programs.

Taken together, findings from the STAR project have been impressive, but they are not necessarily definitive. The STAR student sample did not quite match the U.S. population, for example, because very few Hispanic, Native American, and immigrant (non-English-speaking) families were living in Tennessee in the middle-1980s. Also, news about the greater achievement gains of small classes leaked out early during the STAR project, and one wonders how this may have affected participating teachers and why parents whose children were in other types of classes did not then demand that their children be reassigned to small classes. Finally, the STAR schools had volunteered to participate, suggesting that the teachers and principals in those schools may have had strong interests in trying innovative ideas. Questions such as these should not cause us to reject the findings from the STAR project, but we should keep in mind that this was a single study and that, as always, other evidence is needed to increase certainty about class size effects.

Wisconsin's SAGE Program

Findings from Project STAR have prompted class size reduction efforts in other states. One type of effort focuses on increasing the number of small, early-grade classes in schools in disadvantaged neighborhoods. STAR investigators supervised such a program in Tennessee in 1989, reducing K–3 class sizes in 17 school districts where the average family income was low. The results of this and similar projects in North Carolina, Michigan, Nevada, and New York have confirmed that students from small classes generate higher achievement scores when compared with their previous performance and with those of students in other schools. Most of these projects, however, have been small in scope.

A much larger project focused on the needs of disadvantaged students is Wisconsin's Student Achievement Guarantee in Education (SAGE) Program (Molnar et al., 1999, 2000; Zahorik, 1999). Led by Alex Molnar, this program began as a five-year pilot project for K–3 classes in school districts where at least 50 percent of students were living below the poverty level. The program invited all schools in these districts to apply for the program, but it was able to fund only a few of these schools, and no additional schools were to be added during the pilot project. Schools received an additional $2,000 for each low-income student enrolled in SAGE classrooms. All school districts that applied were allowed to enter the program, and 30 schools in 21 districts began the program at the K–1 grade levels in 1996, with 2nd grade added in 1997 and 3rd grade in 1998.

The SAGE program's major intervention was to reduce the average K–3 class size to 15 students for each teacher. To assess outcomes of the program, researchers compared results from small class SAGE schools with results from standard class size schools in the same districts having similar K–3 enrollments, racial compositions, average family incomes, and prior records of achievement in reading. Findings so far have indicated larger gains for students from small classes—in achievement scores for language arts, reading, and mathematics—that are roughly comparable to those from Project STAR. In addition, as with Project STAR, African American students have made relatively larger gains.

Like project STAR, the SAGE program studied schools that had volunteered for the program and provided them with sufficient funds to hire additional teachers. The SAGE program, however, involved more Hispanic, Asian, and Native American students than had the STAR project.

After the announcement of findings from the initial effort, the Wisconsin legislature extended the SAGE program to other primary schools in the state. Therefore, what began as a small trial project has now blossomed into a statewide program that makes small classes in the early grades available for schools serving needy students.

The California Class Size Reduction Program

In 1996, California began a class size reduction program that has been far more controversial than such programs elsewhere. In earlier years, California had experienced many social problems, and major measures of achievement ranked California schools last in the United States. That year, however, a fiscal windfall became available, and then-governor Pete Wilson announced that primary schools would receive $650 annually for each student (an amount later increased to $800) if they would agree to reduce class sizes in the early grades from the statewide average of more than 28 students to not more than 20 students in each class (Hymon, 1997; Korostoff, 1998; Stecher, Bohrnstedt, Kirst, McRobbie, & Williams, 2001).

Several problems quickly surfaced. First, the California definition of a small class was larger than the size recommended in other studies. In fact, the size of small classes in California matched the size of standard classes in some other states. On the other hand, some California schools had been coping with 30–40 students in each classroom in the early grades, so a reduction to 20 students constituted an improvement.

The second problem was that the program's per-student funding was inadequate. Contrast the SAGE program's additional $2,000 for each student with the $650 or $800 offered by California. Nevertheless, the lure of additional funding proved seductive, and most California school districts applied to participate. This inadequate funding imposed serious consequences on poorer school districts, which had to abolish other needed activities to afford hiring teachers for smaller classes. In effect, then, the program created rather than solved problems for underfunded school districts.

In addition, when the California program began, many of its primary schools were overcrowded, and the state was suffering from a shortage of well-trained, certificated teachers. To cope with the lack of space, some schools created spaces for smaller classes by cannibalizing other needed facilities such as special education quarters, child care centers, music and art rooms, computer laboratories, libraries, gymnasiums, or teachers' lounges. Other schools had to tap into their operating budgets to buy portable classrooms, resulting in delays in paying for badly needed curricular materials or repairs for deteriorating school buildings. And to staff their smaller classes, many schools had to hire teachers without certification or prior training.

So far, results from the California program have been only modest. Informal evidence suggests that most students, parents, and teachers are pleased with their schools' smaller classes. And comparisons between the measured achievements of 3rd grade students from districts that did and did not participate in the early phases of the program have indicated minor advantages for California's smaller classes. These effects, however, have been smaller than those reported for the STAR and SAGE programs.

In many ways, the California initiative has provided a near-textbook case of how a state should *not* reduce class size. After failing to conduct a trial program, California adopted an inadequate definition of class size, committed insufficient funds to the initiative, and ignored serious problems of overcrowding and teacher shortages. This example should remind us that small classes are not a panacea for education. To be effective, programs for reducing class size need careful planning and consideration of the needs and strengths of existing school systems.

What We Now Know about Small Classes

What should we conclude about the effects of small classes? Although the results of individual studies are always questionable, a host of different studies suggest several conclusions.

- When planned thoughtfully and funded adequately, small classes in the early grades generate substantial gains for students, and those extra gains are greater the longer students are exposed to those classes.
- Extra gains from small classes in the early grades are larger when the class has fewer than 20 students.
- Extra gains from small classes in the early grades occur in a variety of academic disciplines and for both traditional measures of student achievement and other indicators of student success.
- Students whose classes are small in the early grades retain their gains in standard size classrooms and in the upper grades, middle school, and high school.
- All types of students gain from small classes in the early grades, but gains are greater for students who have traditionally been disadvantaged in education.

- Initial results indicate that students who have traditionally been disadvantaged in education carry greater small-class, early-grade gains forward into the upper grades and beyond.
- The extra gains associated with small classes in the early grades seem to apply equally to boys and girls.
- Evidence for the possible advantages of small classes in the upper grades and high school is inconclusive.

Tentative Theories

Why should reducing class size have such impressive effects in the early grades? Theories about this phenomenon have fallen largely into two camps.

Most theorists focus on the teacher, reasoning that small classes work their magic because the small class context improves interactions between the teacher and individual students. In the early grades, students first learn the rules of standard classroom culture and form ideas about whether they can cope with education. Many students have difficulty with these tasks, and interactions with a teacher on a one-to-one basis—a process more likely to take place when the class is small—help the students cope. In addition, teachers in small classes have higher morale, which enables them to provide a more supportive environment for initial student learning. Learning how to cope well with school is crucial to success in education, and those students who solve this task when young will thereafter carry broad advantages—more effective habits and positive self-concepts—that serve them well in later years of education and work.

The need to master this task confronts all students, but doing so is often a more daunting challenge for students who come from impoverished homes, ethnic groups that have suffered from discrimination or are unfamiliar with U.S. classroom culture, or urban communities where home and community problems interfere with education. Thus, students from such backgrounds have traditionally had more difficulty coping with classroom education, and they are more likely to be helped by a reduction in class size.

This theory also helps explain why reductions in class size in the upper grades may not generate significant advantages. Older students normally have learned to cope with standard classrooms and have developed either effective or ineffective attitudes concerning academic subjects—and these attitudes are not likely to change just because of a reduction in class size.

The theory also suggests a caution. Students are likely to learn more and develop better attitudes toward education if they are exposed to well-trained and enthusiastic teachers, appropriate and challenging curriculums, and physical environments in their classrooms and schools that support learning. If conditions such as these are not also present, then reducing class size in the early grades will presumably have little impact. Thus, when planning programs for reducing class size, we should also think about the professional development of the teachers who will participate in them and the educational and physical contexts in which those programs will be placed.

A second group of theories designed to account for class size effects focuses on the classroom environment and student conduct rather than on the teacher. We know that discipline and classroom management problems interfere with subject-matter instruction. Theories in this group argue that these problems are less evident in small classes and that students in small classes are more likely to be engaged in learning. Moreover, teacher stress is reduced in small classes, so teachers in the small class context can provide more support for student learning. Studies have also found that small instructional groups can provide an environment for learning that is quite different from that of the large classroom. Small instructional groups can create supportive contexts where learning is less competitive and students are encouraged to form supportive relationships with one another.

Theories such as these suggest that the small class environment is structurally different from that of the large class. Less time is spent on management and more time is spent on instruction, students participate at higher levels, teachers are able to provide more support for learning, and students have more positive relationships. Such processes should lead both to greater subject-matter learning and to more positive attitudes about education among students, with more substantial effects in the early grades and for those groups that are traditionally disadvantaged in education.

These two theories are not mutually exclusive. On the contrary, both may provide partial insights into what happens in small classes and why small class environments help so many students. Collecting other types of evidence to assess such theories directly would be useful, particularly observational studies that compare the details of interaction in early-grade classes of various sizes and surveys of the attitudes and self-concepts of students who have been exposed to classes of different sizes. Unfortunately, good studies of these effects have been hard to find.

Policy Implications and Actions

Given the strength of findings from research on small classes, why haven't those findings provoked more reform efforts? Although many state legislatures have debated or begun reform initiatives related to class size, most primary schools in the United States today do not operate under policies that mandate small classes for early grades. Why not?

This lack of attention has several causes, among them ignorance about the issue, confusion about the results of class size research and ineffective dissemination of those results, prejudices against poor and minority students, the politicizing of debates about class size effects and their implications, and practical problems associated with adopting small classes.

Recent debates about class size have become quite partisan in the United States, with Democrats generally favoring class size reductions and Republicans remaining hostile to them. Responding to President Bill Clinton's 1998 State of the Union address, the U.S. Congress set up a modest program, aimed at urban school districts with high concentrations of poverty, which provided funds for hiring additional teachers during the 1999 and 2000 fiscal years. This program enabled some districts to reduce class sizes in the early grades, and informal results from those cities indicated gains in student achievement.

Republicans have been lukewarm about extending this program—some apparently believing that it is ineffective or is merely a scheme to enhance the coffers of teachers' unions—and have welcomed President George W. Bush's call for an alternative federal program focused on high-stakes achievement tests and using results from those tests to apply sanctions to schools if they do not perform adequately.

The major problems standing in the way of reducing class sizes, however, are often practical ones. In many cases, cutting class sizes means hiring more teachers. With the looming shortage of qualified teachers, recruiting more teachers may be even more difficult than finding the funds to pay their salaries. Further, many schools would have to find or create extra rooms to house the additional classes created by small class programs, which would require either modifying school buildings or acquiring temporary classroom structures.

In many cases, meeting such needs would mean increasing the size of public school budgets, a step abhorred by fiscal conservatives and those who are critical of public education. The latter have argued that other reforms would cost less and be more effective than reducing class sizes. In response to such claims, various studies have estimated the costs of class size reduction programs or compared their estimated costs with those of other proposed reforms. Unfortunately, studies of this type must make questionable assumptions, so the results of their efforts have not been persuasive.

Nevertheless, reducing the size of classes for students in the early grades often requires additional funds. All students would reap sizable education benefits and long-lasting advantages, however, and students from educationally disadvantaged groups would benefit even more. Indeed, if we are to judge by available evidence, no other education reform has yet been studied that would provide such striking benefits. Debates about reducing class sizes, then, are disputes about values. If citizens are truly committed to providing a quality public education and a level playing field for all students regardless of background, they will find the funds needed to reduce class size.

References

Coleman, J. S., Campbell, E. Q., Hobson, C. J., McPartland, J., Mood, A. M., Weinfeld, F. D., & York, R. L. (1966). *Equality of educational opportunity.* Washington, DC: U.S. Government Printing Office.

Educational Research Service. (1980, December). Class size research: A critique of recent meta-analyses. *Phi Delta Kappan, 70,* 239–241.

Elliott, M. (1998). School finance and opportunities to learn: Does money well spent enhance students' achievement? *Sociology of Education, 71,* 223–245.

Ferguson, R. F. (1991). Paying for public education: New evidence on how and why money matters. *Harvard Journal on Legislation, 28,* 465–498.

Ferguson, R. F., & Ladd, H. F. (1996). How and why money matters: An analysis of Alabama schools. In H. F. Ladd (Ed.), *Holding schools accountable: Performance-based reform in education* (pp. 256–298). Washington, DC: Brookings Institution.

Finn, J. D., & Achilles, C. M. (1990). Answers and questions about class size: A statewide experiment. *American Educational Research Journal, 27*(3), 557–577.

Finn, J. D., Gerber, S. B., Achilles, C. M., & Boyd-Zaharias, J. (2001). The enduring effects of small classes. *Teachers College Record, 103*(1), 145–183.

Folger, J. (Ed.). (1989). Project STAR and class size policy. *Peabody Journal of Education* (Special Issue), *67*(1).

Glass, G. V., Cahen, L. S., Smith, M. L., & Filby, N. N. (1982). *School class size: Research and policy.* Beverly Hills, CA: Sage.

Glass, G. V., & Smith, M. L. (1979). Meta-analysis of research on class size and achievement. *Educational Evaluation and Policy Analysis, 1,* 2–16.

Grissmer, D. (Ed.). (1999). Class size: Issues and new findings. *Educational Evaluation and Policy Analysis* (Special Issue), *21*(2).

Hanushek, E. A. (1986). The economics of schooling: Production and efficiency in public schools. *Journal of Economic Literature, 24,* 1141–1177.

Hanushek, E. A. (1999). Some findings from an independent investigation of the Tennessee STAR experiment and from other investigations of class size effects. *Education Evaluation & Policy Analysis, 21*(2), 143–163.

Hedges, L. V., Laine, R. D., & Greenwald, R. (1994). Does money matter? A meta-analysis of studies of the effects of differential school inputs on student outcomes. *Educational Researcher, 23*(3), 5–14.

Hedges, L. V., & Stock, W. (1983). The effects of class size: An examination of rival hypotheses. *American Educational Research Journal, 20,* 63–85.

Hymon, S. (1997, July 7). A lesson in classroom size reduction: Administrators nationwide can learn from California's classroom size reduction plan and how districts implemented it. *School Planning & Management, 36*(7), 18–23, 26.

Korostoff, M. (1998). Tackling California's class size reduction policy initiative: An up close and personal account of how teachers and learners responded. *International Journal of Educational Research, 29,* 797–807.

Krueger, A. B. (1999). Experimental estimates of education production functions. *The Quarterly Journal of Economics, 114*(2), 497–532.

Krueger, A. B. (2000). Economic considerations and class size. Princeton University, Industrial Relations Section, Working Paper #447.

Krueger, A. B., & Whitmore, D. M. (2001). The effect of attending a small class in the early grades on college-test taking and middle school test results: Evidence from Project STAR. *Economic Journal, 111,* 1–28.

McGivern, J., Gilman, D., & Tillitski, C. (1989). A meta-analysis of the relation between class size and achievement. *The Elementary School Journal, 90*(1), 47–56.

Molnar, A., Smith, P., Zahorik, J., Palmer, A., Halbach, A., & Ehrle, K. (1999). Evaluating the SAGE program: A pilot program in targeted pupil-teacher reduction in Wisconsin. *Educational Evaluation and Policy Analysis, 21,* 165–177.

Molnar, A., Smith, P., Zahorik, J., Palmer, A., Halbach, A., & Ehrle, K. (2000). Wisconsin's student achievement guarantee in education (SAGE) class size reduction program: Achievement effects, teaching, and classroom implications. In M. C. Wang & J. D. Finn (Eds.), *How small classes help teachers do their best* (pp. 227–277). Philadelphia: Temple University, Center for Research in Human Development and Education.

Mosteller, F. (1995). The Tennessee study of class size in the early school grades. *The Future of Children, 5*(2), 113–127.

Murphy, D., & Rosenberg, B. (1998, June). Recent research shows major benefits of small class size. *Educational Issues Policy Brief 3.* Washington, DC: American Federation of Teachers.

Nye, B., Hedges, L. V., & Konstantopoulos, S. (1999). The long-term effects of small classes: A five-year follow-up of the Tennessee class size experiment. *Educational Evaluation and Policy Analysis, 21,* 127–142.

Rees, N. S., & Johnson, K. (2000, May 30). A lesson in smaller class sizes. *Heritage Views 2000 . . .*

Stecher, B., Bohrnstedt, G., Kirst, M., McRobbie, J., & Williams, T. (2001). Class-size reduction in California: A story of hope, promise, and unintended consequences. *Phi Delta Kappan, 82,* 670–674.

Wenglinsky, H. (1997). How money matters: The effect of school district spending on academic achievement. *Sociology of Education, 70,* 221–237.

Zahorik, J. (1999). Reducing class size leads to individualized instruction. *Educational Leadership, 57*(1), 50–53.

BRUCE J. BIDDLE is a professor emeritus of psychology and sociology at the University of Missouri, Columbia.

DAVID C. BERLINER is a Regent's Professor of Psychology in Education at Arizona State University.

Kirk A. Johnson

 **NO**

The Downside to Small Class Policies

From the attention and financial support given to class size reduction by politicians and the public, one might assume that research has shown small class size to be essential to positive academic outcomes. In fiscal year 2000, the U.S. Congress allocated $1.3 billion for the class size reduction provision of the Elementary and Secondary Education Act (ESEA). During the Clinton administration, class size received a great deal of attention through proposals to pump large sums of money into efforts to increase the number of teachers in public elementary schools, thereby decreasing the ratio of students to teachers (The White House, 2000).

Proponents of class size reduction claim that small classes result in fewer discipline problems and allow teachers more time for instruction and individual attention and more flexibility in instructional strategies (Halbach, Ehrle, Zahorik, & Molnar, 2001).

Do small classes make a difference in the academic achievement of elementary school students? Are class size reduction programs uniformly positive, or does a downside exist to hiring and placing more teachers in U.S. public schools?

The California Experience

In 1995, California enacted one of the broadest-reaching laws for ensuring small classes in the early grades. Strong bipartisan approval of the class size reduction measure in the California legislature reflected broad support among constituents for reducing class sizes. The program has been wildly popular over its short lifetime, but it has faced substantial obstacles to success.

California's class size reduction program has suffered from a lack of qualified teachers to fill classrooms. More or less simultaneously, nearly all elementary schools in the state demanded more teachers, and some schools—typically suburban—attracted far more teaching applicants than did those in the inner city.

A consortium of researchers from RAND, the American Institutes for Research (AIR), Policy Analysis for California Education (PACE), EdSource, and WestEd analyzed the effects of California's class size reduction initiative and outlined two basic problems. First, K–3 classes that remained large were "concentrated in districts serving high percentages of minority, low-income, or English learner (EL) students" (Stecher & Bohrnstedt, 2000, p. x). Second,

the average qualifications (that is, education, credentials, and experience) of California teachers declined during the past three years for all grade levels, but the declines were worst in elementary schools. . . . Schools serving low-income, minority, or EL students continued to have fewer well-qualified teachers than did other schools. (p. x)

Do Students Learn More in Small Classes?

Clearly, if billions of dollars are to be spent on reducing class size, tangible evidence should exist that students benefit academically from such initiatives. As yet, evidence of the efficacy of class size reduction is mixed at best.

One of the most frequently cited reports on class size is Mosteller's (1995) analysis of the Project STAR study of elementary school students in Tennessee. Mosteller found a significant difference in achievement between students in classes of 13–17 students per teacher and those in classes of 22–25.

University of Rochester economist Eric Hanushek, however, questioned Mosteller's results, noting that "the bulk of evidence . . . points to no systematic effects of class size reductions within the relevant policy range" (1999, p. 144). In other words, no serious policy change on a large scale could decrease class size enough to make a difference.

The current class size reduction debate often ignores the fact that class sizes have been dropping slowly but steadily in the United States over the course of many years. In 1970, U.S. public schools averaged 22.3 students per teacher; by the late 1990s, however, they averaged about 17 students per teacher—a result of a combination of demographic trends and conscious policy decisions to lower pupil-teacher ratios (U.S. Census Bureau, 1999).

Local and programmatic changes in class size can be illustrative, but does research indicate that, on a national level, students in small classes experience academic achievement gains superior to those of their peers in large classes?

The National Assessment of Educational Progress

The most useful database for analyzing whether small classes lead to better academic achievement is the National Assessment of Educational Progress (NAEP). First administered in 1969, the NAEP measures the academic achievement of 4th, 8th, and 12th graders in a variety of fields, including reading, writing, mathematics, science, geography, civics, and the arts. Students take the math and reading tests alternately every two years. For example, students were assessed in reading in 1998; they were tested in math in 1996 and 2000.

The NAEP is actually two tests: a nationally administered test and a state-administered test. More than 40 states participate in the separate state samples used to gauge achievement within those jurisdictions.

In addition to test scores in the subject area, the NAEP includes an assortment of background information on the students taking the exam, their main subject-area teacher, and their school administrator. Background information includes students' television viewing habits, students' computer usage at home and at school, teacher tenure and certification, family socioeconomic status, basic demographics, and school characteristics. By including this information in their assessment of the NAEP data, researchers can gain insight into the factors that might explain differences in NAEP scores found among students.

Results from the Center for Data Analysis

A study from the Center for Data Analysis at the Heritage Foundation examined the 1998 NAEP national reading data to determine whether students in small classes achieve better than students in large classes (Johnson, 2000). Researchers assessed students' academic achievement in reading by analyzing assessment scores as well as six factors from the background information collected by the NAEP: class size, race and ethnicity, parents' education attainment, the availability of reading materials in the home, free or reduced-price lunch participation, and gender.

Class size. The amount of time that a teacher can spend with each student appears to be important in the learning process. To address class size, the Center for Data Analysis study compared students in small classes (those with 20 or fewer students per teacher) with students in large classes (at least 31 students per teacher).

Race and ethnicity. Because significant differences exist in academic achievement among ethnic groups, the variables of race and ethnicity were included in the analysis.

Parents' education. Research indicates that the education attainment of a child's parents is a good predictor of that child's academic achievement. Because the education level of one parent is often highly correlated with that of the other parent, only a single variable was included in the analysis.

The availability of reading materials in the home. The presence of books, magazines, encyclopedias, and newspapers generally indicates a dedication to learning in the household. Researchers have determined that these reading materials are important aspects of the home environment (Coleman, Hoffer, & Kilgore, 1982). Essentially, the presence of such reading materials in the home is correlated with higher student achievement. The analysis thus included a variable controlling for the number of these four types of reading materials found at home.

Free and reduced-price lunch participation. Income is often a key predictor of academic achievement because low-income families seldom have the resources to purchase extra study materials or tutorial classes that may help their children perform better in school. Although the NAEP does not collect data on household income, it does collect data on participation in the free and reduced-price school lunch program.

Gender. Although data on male-female achievement gaps are inconsistent, empirical research suggests that girls tend to perform better in reading and writing subjects, whereas boys perform better in more analytical subjects such as math and science.

After controlling for all these factors, researchers found that the difference in reading achievement on the 1998 NAEP reading assessment between students in small classes and students in large classes were statistically insignificant. That is, across the United Sates, students in small classes did no better on average than those in large classes, assuming otherwise identical circumstances.

Such results should give policymakers pause and provoke them to consider whether the rush to hire more teachers is worth the cost and is in the best interest of students. In terms of raising achievement, reducing class size does not guarantee success.

When Irwin Kurz became the principal of Public School 161 in Brooklyn, New York, well over a decade ago, the schools' test scores ranked in the bottom 25th percentile of schools in Brooklyn's 17th District. Today, P.S. 161 ranks as the best school in the district and 40th of 674 elementary schools in New York City, even though a majority of its students are poor. The pupil-teacher ratio at P.S. 161 is 35 to 1, but the teachers make neither class size, nor poverty, nor anything else an excuse for poor performance. As Kurz likes to say, "better to have one good teacher than two crummy teachers any day."

References

Coleman, J., Hoffer, T., & Kilgore, S. (1982). *High school achievement.* New York: BasicBooks.

Halbach, A., Ehrle, K., Zahorik, J., & Molnar, A. (2001, March). Class size reduction: From promise to practice. *Educational Leadership, 58*(6), 32–35.

Hanushek, E. (1999). Some findings from an independent investigation of the Tennessee STAR experiment and from other investigations of class size effects. *Educational Evaluation & Policy Analysis, 21*(2), 143–164.

Johnson, K. (2000, June 9). *Do small classes influence academic achievement? What the National Assessment of Educational Progress shows* (CDA Report No. 00-07). Washington, DC: Heritage Foundation.

Mosteller, F. (1995). The Tennessee study of class size in the early school grades. *The Future of Children, 5*(2), 113–127.

Stecher, B., & Bohrnstedt, G. (Eds.). (2000). *Class size reduction in California: The 1998–99 evaluation findings.* Sacramento: California Department of Education.

U.S. Census Bureau. (1999). *Statistical abstract of the United States.* Washington, DC: Government Printing Office.

The White House (2000, May 4). President Clinton highlights education reform agenda with roundtable on what works [Press release].

Kirk A. Johnson is a senior policy analyst in the Center for Data Analysis, Heritage Foundation.

EXPLORING THE ISSUE

Should Schools Decrease Class Size to Improve Student Outcomes?

Critical Thinking and Reflection

1. Imagine you are in a position to set district policy regarding class size for the district's primary grade schools. What decision would you make with respect to the minimum and maximum number of students per grade? How would you calculate the adult per student ratio and how would you weight this information? What would be the primary factors influencing your decision regarding class size policy and why?
2. Why are Biddle and Berliner in support of a small-class size policy for U.S. schools? What are the major reasons they give to support their conclusion? Do you agree with the reasons they give and are you convinced by their argument?
3. Why is Johnson opposed to the use of small-class size policies in U.S. schools? Do you agree with his argument and his conclusion against smaller class sizes? Why, or why not?

Is There Common Ground?

In the first selection Bruce J. Biddle and David C. Berliner argue that the current best evidence, based on well conceived and controlled educational research studies, provides an increasingly strong platform from which to make several conclusions with respect to class size and educational outcomes, notably that early grade experience matters with greater gains associated with longer exposure to smaller classes. And, although all types of students benefit from smaller class sizes, the greatest gains are reported for historically disadvantaged groups of schoolchildren. They go on to explore policy implications of why, given the strength of the research findings, there are not more effective reform efforts underway in most primary schools in the United States. In the second selection, Kirk Johnson argues, however, the evidence is less than compelling that small class size is essential for positive academic outcomes and further, that the cost associated with reducing class size may be too high a price pay. The real difference maker, Johnson implies, is not more teachers but better teachers.

But what of those that benefit? Proponents argue that the current best evidence from well-designed studies does provide convincing and sufficient evidence that there are gains, they occur early, and are sustainable as a function of length of exposure. In other words, the earlier and longer a student experiences a small class size, the more pronounced the effects on later academic success. Moreover, these gains appear greater for traditionally disenfranchised student groups. As Biddle and Berliner point out, research studies addressing the issue of class size and student achievement may be among the most abundant in all of educational research and yet there remain no coordinated policies based on consensual agreement. They summarize several likely causes for this, including different perspectives of what is at issue, confu-

sion concerning research results and their interpretation, poorly disseminated findings, political agendas, and practical realities confronting local decision making to name a few. Perhaps the research agenda needs to continue forward with an even more refined eye toward exploring in greater detail the circumstances under which class size reduction is and is not beneficial and for which students. Presumably, as the evidence accrues from studies in which the design is agreed upon by both sides of the argument, there will be less room for disagreement about what the findings mean.

Create Central

www.mhhe.com/createcentral

Additional Resources

Readers interested in the original articles from the Tennessee STAR study should read "Answers and Questions about Class Size: A Statewide Experiment," by J. D. Finn and C. M. Achilles, *American Educational Research Journal* (vol. 27, 1990), and "Project STAR and Class Size Policy," by J. Folger, *Peabody Journal of Education* (Special Issue, vol. 67, 1989).

But, to see an alternative account of the findings, see "Some Findings from an Independent Investigation of The Tennessee Star Experiment and From Other Investigations of Class Size Effects," by E. A. Hanushek, *Education Evaluation & Policy Analysis* (vol. 21, 1999).

To learn more about the economics of achievement, see "How Money Matters: The Effects of School District Spending On Academic Achievement," by H. Wenglinsky, *Sociology of Education* (vol. 70, 1997).

For an historical account of many of the issues behind the contemporary viewpoints, review *Equality of Educational Opportunity,* by J. S. Coleman, E. Q. Campbell, C. J. Hobson, J. McPartland, A. M. Mood, F. D. Weinfeld, and R. L. York (Washington, DC: U.S. Government Printing Office 1966).

Internet References . . .

National Council of Teachers of English Position Statement on Why Class Size Matters

http://www.ncte.org/positions/statements /whyclasssizematters

Education Week: Class Size

http://www.edweek.org/ew/issues/class-size/

Class Size Matters

http://www.classsizematters.org/

Selected, Edited, and with Issue Framing Material by:
Leonard Abbeduto, *University of California, Davis*
and
Frank Symons, *University of Minnesota*

ISSUE

Should Student Time in School Be Changed?

YES: Elena Rocha, from "Choosing More Time for Students: The What, Why, and How of Expanded Learning," *Center for American Progress* (August 2007)

NO: Larry Cuban, from "The Perennial Reform: Fixing School Time," *Phi Delta Kappan* (December 2008)

Learning Outcomes

After reading this issue, you will be able to:

- Distinguish between historical and contemporary issues regarding school time.
- Describe at least three different approaches to changing time in school.
- Compare the different policy and practice issues regarding school start time.

ISSUE SUMMARY

YES: Elena Rocha, a scholar at the Center for American Progress and education consultant, uses multiple case examples and argues that the expansion of school learning time is necessary for meaningful school reform and improving student outcomes.

NO: Larry Cuban, a professor emeritus of education at Stanford University, provides a brief history of school reform efforts related to school time and argues that the call for expanding learning time in the form of lengthening the school day or year is not new and has little evidence supporting its effectiveness.

$\mathbf{C}$lassic (e.g., *A Nation at Risk*) and contemporary (e.g., *Prisoners of Time*) critiques of the U.S. public education system all recommend reform. And the reform recommended almost always requires changing school time—increasing the time a student spends in school daily, weekly, or annually. The issue of whether school time—the amount of time students spend in classrooms and school—should be changed by lengthening the school day or year is, in some sense, a barometer reflecting the current reform pressure the U.S. public education system is experiencing at any one point in time. Indeed, the history of debate over the issue parallels the history of U.S. public education itself reflecting various points along a timeline representing the evolution of the purposes of American public education.

The history of school time is often considered to be directly tied to an agrarian past in which time in school was limited because of time on the farm requirements. Although there is some truth to this, as with all issues in this volume, the issue is not that simple. In fact, there were and continue to be multiple forces at work determining the amount of time children and youth spend in school in the United States, which averages about 6 hours per day, 5 days per week, for approximately 180 days per

calendar year with a long summer break separating the school years. How these times were settled on has less to do with an ideal and more to do with a mix and compromise between material and political forces at work since the inception of public education in the United States—much like the early history of the automobile in which we forget that in addition to internal combustion engines running on gasoline there were also steam engine powered cars as well as electric cars in the early days of the automobile. Obviously, the internal combustion engine fueled by gasoline became the standard. Over the course of time it is easy to forget that there were alternative models and approaches. Similarly, in the early history of American public education there were different models and approaches used. It was, in fact, quite common to find year round schools operating in many urban areas. But, at the same time because of the heat of summers it was also just as common to find the school house closed for different periods of time throughout the summer months in urban settings as well as rural (it was easier to heat a building in winters than to cool it in summers; industrial pollution in some dense urban areas rendered schools virtually uninhabitable during warm summer months). As industrialization progressed and immigration increased, the need for some degree of uniformity and a standardized approach emerged within and across states.

It is also easy to forget that for much of the early days of the republic, education was primarily a local community-driven model with few compulsory attendance requirements. Following rapid industrialization after the Civil War along with changes in child labor laws and the political perspective that education could and should be used to create a civil citizenry committed to the ideals of the republic, the notion of compulsory education emerged and, along with it, the need for a standard length to the school day and year. Right up into the early part of the twentieth century, these arguments and compromises were ongoing in different legal statutes across the states. In one sense, considering the following selections, it could be said that the arguments are ongoing.

The above is not meant to be a comprehensive and exhaustive history of school time in the United States (for that, interested readers may turn to Rakoff, mentioned below in the further readings section) but, rather, was meant to provide a sense that the circumstances we find ourselves in have historical antecedents, often forgotten, that may have little obvious contemporary relevance. Indeed, this is a primary premise in the current arguments to change school time. Once practices become established, however, they can easily become part of the system's structure. To paraphrase an observation made by Ted Sizer, in the United States, the school schedule is "bred in the bone" (cited in H. Pennington's "Expanding Learning Time in High Schools" from the Center for American Progress, 2006). In the less distant pass, for example, strong forces and voices ranging from the tourist industry to teacher unions to parents—usually, demographically, upper middle class and above—have, in fact, argued for maintaining the status quo, that is, the long summer break for reasons related to revenue, respite, and recreation, respectively.

What then, are the contemporary arguments behind changing school time? One argument centers on the problem of summer learning loss or "summer slide." Here the issue is whether the extended summer break is detrimental to academic outcomes because material learned in the prior year is not retained and consequently has to be "retaught" at the beginning of the following school year. This issue is related also to the achievement gap between poor inner city urban student/school performance and affluent suburban student/school performance. The evidence, albeit limited, suggests that summer learning loss is more pronounced in the former. Another argument comes from comparative education in which student and school outcomes from other leading industrialized nations are compared with U.S. student and school outcomes and,

in almost all cases, are shown to be superior. Because almost all other industrialized nations require either longer school days or longer school years or both, time in school is considered a primary culprit in the gap between U.S. student and school performance outcomes and the rest of the industrialized world. The problem has taken a strong hold in political (state and federal) and business sectors, so much so that the purpose of public education is equated with producing a competitive workforce (but see Larry Cuban's comment on this). Taken together, these two issues represent essential elements in much of contemporary school reform efforts, so much so that almost all school reform efforts have changing (i.e., increasing) school time as a core feature. Indeed, it is argued that changing school time is essential for meaningful reform.

Given the above issue and arguments, what do we know about changing or expanding school time? What kinds of models are there? There are at least three general approaches (but there are certainly many variations of the theme). The first is simply extending the school day. The next is extending the school year. Different still is a year-round school year. Year round education (YRE) can take one of two primary forms—single- and multi-track calendars. As you might guess, each of these different approaches has different pros and cons or costs and benefits (for a good review see S. P. Johnson & T. E. Spradlin's Education Policy Brief mentioned below as well as E. Silva's *On the Clock: Rethinking the Way Schools Use Time* [Washington, DC: Education Sector, 2007]). By extending the school day and particularly the year it is argued that the United States will be brought in line with the rest of the industrialized world. There are significant costs associated with doing so, however, with no guarantee that it will produce the intended effect (a highly skilled competitive labor force). In the YRE models, the existing school days (approximately 180) are redistributed throughout the calendar year providing more continuous learning with the traditional long summer vacation broken up in shorter more frequent breaks throughout the school year (often referred to as "intersessions"). In this approach, part of the argument is that a more balanced calendar can offset the learning loss associated with long summer breaks. There are additional arguments associated with some YRE models that are based more on administrative issues and the effective use of limited space (i.e., resource management). From this perspective, it is expensive to have a relatively large facility sitting vacant for one-fourth of the calendar year, and YRE provides a more efficient use of space. Regardless of the model or approach adopted, common to all is the goal of changing time in school to improve outcomes.

YES

Elena Rocha

Choosing More Time for Students: The What, Why, and How of Expanded Learning

Setting the Stage

A crescendo of support from education researchers, analysts, reform advocates, and lawmakers about the need for additional learning time for our nation's under-performing students may well result in the coming months in meaningful reform. In fact, U.S. Secretary of Education Margaret Spellings believes that the expansion of learning time will be the next major push in school reform. The reason: our nation's public school students need to meet the demands and challenges of the 21st century but they simply cannot in public school systems that remain much the same as they were 50 years ago. The shift in educational rigor that globalization has ushered in is pushing policymakers to embrace systemic change in public education, with particular focus on closing achievement gaps between disadvantaged students and their peers.

In rethinking what it will take for our public schools to better serve students who are academically behind, wisdom tells us that a comprehensive approach that encompasses numerous options will provide the best opportunity to support student learning. The expansion of learning time can serve as one effective vehicle to modernize our schools because it allows teachers, principals, community organizations and leaders, and parents to build multiple curriculums to best educate our children to succeed in the 21st century. Expanded learning time turns dissatisfaction with the limitations of the current six-hour, 180-day school year into a proactive strategy that will create a new school structure for children.

Making more and better use of learning time by lengthening the school day, week, or year doesn't just change what happens between the hours of 3 p.m. and 5 p.m. Expanding learning time changes what happens from 8 a.m. and 5 p.m. and often encompasses additional days in the school calendar throughout the year to accelerate student learning and development. In short, expanding time for learning will revolutionize the way we teach our children.

To navigate through this forthcoming and thorough-going school reform effort, this paper will define what expanded learning time means, highlight what model programs look like when used effectively, and address how to successfully implement such reform efforts. As will become clear, expanded learning time is all about using time in ways that greatly benefit our students.

Choosing More Time for Students

What Is Expanded Learning Time?

Expanded learning time is a school-wide improvement strategy to boost student academic performance, close achievement gaps, and expand enrichment opportunities. The policy definition we prefer is the lengthening of the school day, school week or school year for all students in a given school. The purpose: to focus on core academics *and* enrichment activities to enhance student success. Such an increase in academic learning time requires an engaging, rigorous curricula as well as activities that expand the opportunities typically available to students. Because expanded learning time initiatives have the potential to result in substantial student achievement gains and other positive outcomes, it is widely considered an important strategy for low-performing, high-poverty schools.

At the core of expanded learning time is a critical and fundamental principle that cannot be overlooked—the complete redesign of the school's educational program. Successful implementation of expanded learning initiatives occur in tandem with other reform strategies and practices that take place through the redesign process. Without conjoining expanded learning time with the redesign principle, more time risks being "more of the same" and a promising school improvement strategy becomes a band-aid.

Expanded learning time schools formally incorporate the after-school hours into the official school day or add days to the official school calendar. These schools align rigorous academic and enrichment content with curriculum standards and student needs, are typically led by regular teachers and paraprofessionals, and frequently partner with successful community-based or other local organizations to provide enrichment opportunities and support.

Over the years, expanded or extended learning opportunities have been described as encompassing an array of activities, including before- and after-school programming, tutoring or summer programming, early childhood education, supplemental educational services, distance learning, and school-based or school-connected cultural and recreational activities. In addition, study hall, homework clubs, advanced coursework opportunities, and block scheduling or double periods have commonly been considered expanded learning time activities.

While such programs and activities extend learning time or use earmarked periods of time in new or non-traditional ways, they differ in format and content from expanded learning time initiatives that redesign a school's entire educational program.

Education advocates, researchers, and academics are currently assessing how much time is necessary to bring under-performing students to proficiency and put them on the path to long-term success. Although the debate continues, current thinking is that schools need to expand learning time by a minimum of 30 percent. The Center for American Progress, together with Massachusetts 2020, an educational nonprofit institution, is promoting the expansion of learning time for high-poverty, low-performing schools by no less than the equivalent of two hours per day, or 360 hours per year, to the districts' standard school schedule. This is roughly the equivalent of 30 percent more time. Other efforts, such as the Knowledge Is Power Program nationwide network of charter schools, are expanding learning time by as much as 62 percent.

Why Expanded Learning Time?

Expanded learning time is just one strategy with the potential to boost student achievement—but a promising one. It considers time a resource and capitalizes on the best uses of learning time while expanding it. This approach provides schools with added flexibility to exercise innovation in a very deliberate manner. Time, as a strategy, can be conceptualized in multiple ways. Four constructs of additional time are presented below.

Time as an Enabler
The expansion of learning time allows schools to do what is being asked of them—to help all students meet proficiency goals and prepare them for life after high school. Expanded learning provides more time and in-depth learning opportunities for students in the areas of math, science, literacy, and other core subjects to support academic excellence. More time also enables schools to expand the curriculum and integrate or maintain important enrichment activities in the school day and year, avoiding the crowding out of engaging programming such as art, music, sports, and drama. Together, greater attention to academics and enrichment can help to produce 21st century knowledge workers with technology, communication, problem-solving, critical thinking, and team-building skills—all skills necessary for life-long success in a global society.

Time as a Catalyst
Lengthening the school day, school week and/or school year for any significant amount of time requires leaders to rethink school reform in a way that is not incremental. Redesigning a school's structure to integrate additional learning time requires innovation and retooling from the ground up. It demands thoughtful consideration of all aspects of school-wide improvement such as curriculum development, teacher training and collaboration, and budgeting, as well as the technical components of large-scale reform such as transportation, program evaluation, and teacher contract negotiations. This school-improvement strategy allows community, school, and district leaders to put incrementalism aside in favor of comprehensive reform.

Time as a Unifier
Transforming the components of school redesign into a successful strategy necessitates the meaningful involvement of parents, teachers, and communities at-large throughout planning and implementation. Because expanded learning time is not an incremental strategy, outreach and inclusion of these actors in decision-making and design are central to the effort's success. As with most successful school reform initiatives, empowering and giving ownership to parents, teachers, and other valuable community members pays off. The process of expanding learning time therefore serves to unite these actors, giving them a role in the fundamental changes of their schools.

Time as a Preference
Student and school needs vary from community to community. Because there is no single reform strategy to improve student or school performance, multiple options must be available to families. Schools that expand learning time can broaden the choice options available. Presenting families with educational options for their children empowers them to choose the type of educational experiences and settings they feel will best meet the needs of their children. Although not a strategy for all students and schools, expanded learning time can be successful in many locations, such as larger school districts that may have greater capacity or access to other choice options.

How Has Time Historically Been Used?

The pursuit of challenging, extensive learning opportunities for students today is not unlike the ways in which privileged children have historically excelled. Boarding schools, study abroad, and the most rigorous academic and college preparation programs made different use of learning time, often by expanding it.

Today, many students are seeking additional opportunities to increase their academic growth and chances for success; they are taking advantage of extra academic opportunities during the traditional and non-traditional school hours. In doing so, these students use academic resources, particularly time, in different ways.

An increasingly common phenomenon is advanced students enrolling in summer school, after-school, intersession programs, and virtual learning courses to get a leg up on their academic progress. To hone their academic skills and increase their chances for acceptance into college, for example, students are attending summer classes to meet basic high school course requirements in order to take Advanced Placement or International Baccalaureate courses during the school year. Once considered prime time for remediation, these non-traditional learning blocks are becoming pre-requisites for high achievers.

These strategies, which have worked for so many privileged and academically advanced students, should not just be considered options for the elite. The lessons learned from alternative, innovative learning strategies that make more and better use of time are ripe for study and replication, particularly for struggling students and continually low-performing schools and districts, many of which lack access to expanded learning opportunities.

What Are the Benefits of More Time?

Initiatives that expanded learning time have facilitated school and classroom innovation to enhance teaching and learning. Through the expansion of learning time, teachers, for example, can provide students with more one-on-one instruction, teach in longer blocks to emphasize subject content, help students develop portfolios of their work, or utilize hands-on learning activities such as science labs and projects to help facilitate learning through application. The presence of more in-school time coupled with new and effective instruc-tional strategies can have great impact on student performance. Incorporating additional time into the school experience also helps to address the individual needs of students by providing them with extra supports such as working with specialists and by encouraging participation in engaging activities of interest.

But the benefits of expanded learning time reach beyond improvements in student academic performance, their personal development, and preparation for adulthood. Expanding time also serves teachers well by providing them with more time to engage in high-quality professional development, participate in support activities such as mentoring, plan and work collaboratively with others, and analyze data to improve instruction and student achievement. Providing substantial quality professional development opportunities for teachers results in higher quality education for students.

Schools, too, gain from the expansion of learning time by allowing community-based partnerships to play a critical role in the implementation and strengthening of educational curriculum. Community-based partnerships not only offer enrichment programming for students but also carve time out of the academic calendar for teachers to participate in training and planning activities. For instance, if there are seven learning periods in the school day, one of them may be led by a community partner such as the Boys & Girls Club or a community college. Or a local organization or institution such as a hospital or museum may teach a monthly class at their facility, providing students with an enriched learning opportunity outside of the school walls. These partner-led classes, in turn, free up teachers to participate in professional development or common planning activities while other skilled adults are working with students.

Beyond school boundaries, employers and post-secondary educational institutions also recognize the influence that additional learning time can have on workplace and college readiness. Both are looking for individuals with solid academic preparation as well as critical thinking and problem-solving skills. The business community in particular has been very vocal about their increasing need for 21st century knowledge workers. They caution that without significant school reform, businesses will be challenged even more than they are today to find skilled workers.

Parents and communities are also enthusiastic about the expansion of learning time and the ability for schools to focus on core academic content while engaging students in enrichment activities both inside and outside of schools. A longer school day or year provides children with a safe, supervised, and rich environment for a greater number of hours while parents are working.

While some efforts to expand learning time have been met with a degree of parental opposition, the Massachusetts experience reveals three important lessons. First, the more parents know about the benefits of additional learning time, the more in favor they are of the strategy. Second, lower-income parents who want their children to have the same academic and enrichment experiences as their more affluent peers are particularly in support of more learning time. And lastly, opposition to expanded learning time tends to come from a vocal minority of mostly middle-income parents who are able to provide individually tailored opportunities for their children like music lessons, horseback riding, or drama lessons.

Even students themselves seem to be open-minded to a longer school day, week, or year. Schools that have implemented greater learning time into the school calendar recognize that there is an adjustment period for students. School leaders, however, are finding that students, particularly those in elementary school, quickly adjust. An engaging curriculum and enrichment activities that interest students help to overcome the challenges in transitioning to additional learning time. When successful, reengaged students are more likely to stay in school and graduate.

What Role Does Research Play in Supporting Expanded Learning Time?

Admittedly, there is not a large body of research supporting the expansion of learning time. However, the concept of expanding learning time draws on decades of research on time and learning and whether and how time impacts student outcomes. This research, begun in 1963 with the work of educational psychologist John Carroll, concludes that instructional time is a determinant of academic outcomes and students achieve maximal learning when time spent learning matches time needed to learn. Additional research that contributes to the movement to expand learning time focuses on enrichment opportunities such as after-school programs. This research finds that participation in non-core academic activities raises engagement and academic outcomes.

The modern conceptualization of time and learning is captured by what is known as the Academic Learning Time, or ALT, model. Developed out of research conducted by David Berliner and Charles Fisher of Arizona State University, this model goes beyond the basic construct of time in an academic setting to address how time should be used in such a setting. In other words, academic learning time considers the quantity and quality of learning time, the level of student engagement, and measures of success or outcomes.

Further research on time and learning reveals that children lose some of what they've learned during the summer months in what is known as summer learning loss or the "summer slide." For many low-income children who lack engaging and enriching experiences during their time off, they can lose as much as two months of learning.

While much academic and scientific research exists on time and learning, brain development and cognitive abilities, and enrichment, it has yet to be directly linked to the concept of expanded learning time in school—although researchers and advocates are in the midst of developing a research agenda and design to directly study the impact of a longer school day, week, or year on academic achievement.

As the result of this lack of direct research, proponents of expanded learning time tend to rely on evidence from the schools and districts that have successfully implemented more time into the school calendar. The discussion below addresses the evidence and highlights four model expanded learning time programs.

Over the years, research has shown that poor and minority children tend to begin school at an academic deficit compared to their higher-income and white peers. Research also documents that students who start school behind academically are likely to stay behind. The reality is that too many disadvantaged children lack high-quality educational experiences and access to engaging, enriching programs during traditional school time, the after-school hours, and summer months, and consequently never catch up.

Unfortunately, too many schools have responded to this challenge by narrowing the curriculum in order to place greater emphasis on core subjects such as reading and math. Cognitive researchers, however, caution that this does greater harm than good by removing students from learning experiences that can actually help them gain broader knowledge and context to better understand what they are learning. Additional learning time used well can make school for these students about catching up and accelerating.

Are There Model Expanded Learning Time Programs?

The success of extended learning time is evident in a number of model programs. Several charter and public schools have implemented expanded learning time initiatives over a number of years, as have educational management organizations like New York-based Edison Schools that operate numerous schools for local school districts. Charter schools, however, appear to be the leading force in the movement to increase learning time and expand educational opportunities—perhaps because they have greater flexibility than public schools to develop and implement new programs. The Center for Education Reform conducted a national survey in 2005 of charter schools and found that 57 percent of respondents expand learning time: 13 percent expand the school day and year, 24 percent expand the school day, and 20 percent expand the school year.

But public schools are also embracing expanded learning time. School-based efforts to increase learning time have recently started to dot the country in growing numbers. Because these efforts are new, data may not yet reveal improvements in student achievement or result in schools making adequate yearly progress as required by the 2002 federal No Child Left Behind Act. Nonetheless, these schools should be carefully supported and their impact on student and school success documented.

Additional evidence of the growing popularity of expanded learning initiatives comes from media reports. Investigation of chronically low- or under-performing schools that are now showing signs of improvement often reveal the use of more learning time. For example, according to the Council of Great City Schools, the membership organization for leaders of the nation's largest school districts, several high-performing urban schools have implemented extended time programs and are seeing positive results. . . .

One of the most high-profile efforts is taking place in the state of Massachusetts. In 2005, it became the first state to undertake a state-wide effort to implement expanded learning time in multiple schools. Made possible by the appropriation of new state dollars, this effort is currently in place in 10 schools in five districts, with continued funds to grow the number of schools to 19 beginning in Fall 2007 (additional schools are also in the planning pipeline). New York City and school districts in Florida, California, and Pennsylvania have successfully implemented expanded learning time initiatives as well. Several other model programs in both schools and districts across the country that serve a variety of students will be profiled in an upcoming report by the Center for American Progress.

Although the search for schools that have successfully implemented greater learning time into the school calendar beyond the well-known KIPP Academies or Massachusetts school efforts, for example, is intensive, the practice of expanding time in schools is likely more widely used than known. In fact, there are several model expanded learning time programs, four of which are presented here.

Miami-Dade County Public Schools, School Improvement Zone

In 2004, Miami-Dade County Public Schools Superintendent Rudy Crew created the School Improvement Zone to help many of the district's most under-performing schools. He sought to improve student and school performance and remedy the low performance feeder patterns between primary and secondary schools in the district. To do so, he established criteria to identify the schools for inclusion in the School Improvement Zone. Selected schools had at least a three-year history of low performance, were high-poverty schools, were part of the district's low performance feeder patterns, and had strong school leadership.

The School Improvement Zone includes 39 schools: 20 elementary, 11 middle, and 8 high schools. Partial implementation of the Zone began with the 2004–2005 school year, with full-scale implementation the following year. Enrolling more than 43,000 students, the Zone's schools serve a student population that is 66 percent African American, 30 percent Hispanic, 78 percent low-income, and 17 percent English-language learners.

Schools in the School Improvement Zone expand the school day by one hour and lengthen the school year by two weeks. With a focus on literacy, the School Improvement Zone aims to enhance student comprehension and critical thinking skills while also focusing on mathematics. In addition, the School Improvement Zone emphasizes character development and enables students to participate in enrichment classes in what is known as the Academic Improvement Period.

Professional development is a major component of the School Improvement Zone and is offered to all teachers and staff. Professional development teams help to: guide reading, math and science instruction; analyze student-level data; provide content area support; and help teachers build learning communities. Teachers in the Zone are compensated for their extra time, receiving a 20 percent increase in pay.

While there have been gains in academic achievement, they are larger in elementary schools than middle and high schools. When the School Improvement Zone first began, there were nine schools ranked "F" and no schools ranked "A" under the Florida school grading system. Now there are three "F" schools and two "A" schools. Results also show other positive outcomes, such as increased attendance, decreased suspensions, increased parental involvement, and school improvement.

Fairfax County Public Schools

In 1997, Daniel Domenech became Superintendent of Fairfax County Public Schools in Northern Virginia. One of the first things he did in his new capacity was to identify the county's lowest performing schools and develop a strategy to turn them around. A significant part of the strategy for the 20 elementary schools identified was to expand learning time and focus on literacy.

Fairfax County Public Schools did so by first instituting full-day kindergarten and making Monday a full school day for all grades (originally they were half days to allow for teacher professional development). Making Monday a full instructional day did not interrupt professional development as the Superintendent worked professional training and development opportunities into the expanded school calendar.

Domenech then implemented an optional year-round school calendar that ran from August to the end of June to combat summer learning loss. To move to this schedule, the school community had to show overwhelming support of the idea through a parent vote. Those who did not support a modified school calendar had the choice to opt out, although very few did so. The year-round schedule allows for nine weeks in school followed by three weeks off. During these intersession breaks, additional learning opportunities are available to students on a voluntary basis.

Participation in intersession programs is approximately 70 percent. Currently, there are five Fairfax County Public Schools with a year-round calendar.

With the clear purpose of closing achievement gaps and improving school performance, Domenech sought to increase learning time across the whole school year. To do so, he had to make tough financial decisions and reallocate money to internally finance the expansion of learning time. Teachers in the schools with a modified calendar receive a 7.5 percent salary increase to compensate them for the additional 15 percent of time worked. Domenech's efforts to assist the district's low-performing schools continue today and have resulted in academic achievement gains over the years.

An Achievable Dream Academy

An Achievable Dream Academy in Newport News, Virginia, is a unique kindergarten through eighth grade public school that has successfully implemented expanded learning time and closed the academic achievement gaps with schools with more advantaged students. The school, created 12 years ago, grew out of an after-school tennis and tutoring program for local students. Well supported, it soon became an expanded learning school for the community's most underserved students. The school was developed through a partnership with the school district and the city of Newport News. It operates under the guidelines of the school district but is given additional flexibility that is traditionally afforded to charter schools.

Led by Director Richard Coleman, Sr., An Achievable Dream is a year-round school with four nine-week sessions followed by three weeks of break. Learning opportunities are available to students during the intersession breaks, two of which are mandatory. Students are tested during the nine-week session and the data is used to help teachers identify student's areas of need. These needs are then addressed during the intersessions.

In addition to a modified school calendar, the schedule expands the school day to eight and half hours. Half-day Saturday classes are available for students in the lowest quartile. The school currently enrolls almost 1,000 children. Ninety-nine percent of the students are African American, 96 percent qualify for free and reduced price lunch, and 75 percent are from single-parent homes.

Achievable Dream's mission is to promote social, academic, and moral education, known as S.A.M.E. To fulfill this mission, the school focuses on academic excellence and character development such as etiquette, conflict resolution, and healthy living. All students participate in tennis, in keeping with the history and tradition of the school. Students are taught reading and writing in 90-minute learning blocks that incorporate science and social studies. Students also participate in enrichment activities such as art, music, physical education, and computers and technology.

The school's program has received wide support from parents who understand the benefit of more time on student achievement. Parents are required to sign a contract to demonstrate their commitment and support of the school's S.A.M.E. mission. The school has also benefited from minimal teacher turnover. To be sure that teachers understand the demands of working in an expanded learning time school, the school's leaders clearly define what will be expected of them. To support the needs of these teachers, the school provides professional development and compensation for the additional time worked.

Achievable Dream expands learning time in a significant way. To do so, it receives funding from the city to compensate teachers for the expanded time, as well as funds from local businesses, grants from the U.S. Departments of Education and Justice, and money from fundraisers. But the school's efforts have paid off. Achievable Dream has successfully closed the achievement gap, exceeded federal and state annual yearly progress requirements, and has been a model for two additional area elementary schools that have recently transitioned to an expanded day school.

Amistad Academy and Achievement First Schools

Amistad Academy is a public charter school serving students in New Haven, Connecticut in the fifth through eighth grades. Founded in 1999, Amistad Academy is a college preparatory school that lengthens the school day by one and one-half hours to focus on mathematics and English language arts. The school has a mandatory 15-day summer academy to focus on core academics, and offers before and after-school programming and tutoring. Encore!, Amistad's after-school enrichment program, provides students with daily instruction in theater, karate, dance, and web design, for example. The program has been so successful that it has inspired other efforts such as that of Gompers Charter Middle School in San Diego, CA.

Amistad's student population, which is selected through a lottery system, is about 64 percent low income, 63 percent African American, 35 percent Hispanic and 2 percent Caucasian. During the school's initial years, leaders were focused on closing the learning gap, securing high quality teachers, and creating a supportive learning environment for students. These efforts paid off as the school saw its students make signifcant academic gains. Amistad students routinely score higher on state and national reading, writing, and math tests than many of their peers in wealthier school districts. In fact, Amistad has succeeded in closing the achievement gap of its students.

Amistad's success led to the creation and launch of Achievement First, a non-profit organization dedicated to sharing Amistad's secrets with other low-performing schools. Today, there are nine Achievement First schools in New Haven and Brooklyn, New York, serving students from kindergarten to 12th grade. Achievement First schools focus on both academics and character development. The core curriculum includes a daily three-hour reading block, additional time for math and writing each day, physical education or music, and history or science daily.

Teachers at Achievement First schools are assessed every six weeks and use the results to inform instruction. They also receive 13 days of professional development and work in collaboration with other teachers to provide strong learning opportunities to students. Teachers, parents, and students of Achievement First schools are required to sign a contract demonstrating their commitment to learning and student support.

What Have We Learned?

Clearly, school and district approaches to expanded learning time can vary in focus, structure, and content, among other things. Because expanded learning time is a choice and efforts to implement it are designed to meet the needs of specific students in particular schools, multiple strategies to expand learning time should be embraced. Although there is no single expanded learning time model, there are similarities among efforts.

Successful expanded learning time initiatives share a set of fundamental principles. In-depth analysis of new and existing initiatives and consultation with the individuals that led such initiatives identifes five key characteristics or pillars of success.

Bold Leadership

Visionary leadership is the foundation of any reform effort. To implement successful expanded learning strategies, school, district, and community leaders must be fully committed to moving in a new direction and fearless in taking a stand on the need for substantial change. Expanding learning time is a demanding strategy that requires careful planning before implementation. Leaders must therefore engage intensively in program design and clearly articulate the goals and expectations of the strategy. They must build and maintain the political will and support necessary for such change and as such serve as liaisons to all stakeholders. Engaging in continuous and meaningful public outreach is a critical component of leadership and necessary to support successful implementation.

Cases in point:

- Daniel Domenech, former Superintendent of Fairfax County Public Schools, created a Plan for Excellence in 1998.

  Part of the plan outlined a strategy to improve the district's lowest-performing schools by expanding learning time. Understanding that principal leadership was necessary to successfully implement more time on task, he developed support among school leaders. He then made the tough decisions that enabled him to financially support the expansion of learning time in 20 of the district's schools. His perseverance led to structural changes that still exist today to combat learning gaps.

- The founders of Amistad Academy visited successful schools around the nation to learn their secrets in order to apply them to a school improvement strategy to close achievement gaps. These visionary leaders then created Achievement First, a non-profit organization, to replicate the Academy in other low-performing schools in Connecticut and New York.

Teacher Participation and Leadership

Highly effective teachers delivering a rigorous curriculum in the classrooms of schools with extra time are a fundamental element of this strategy's success. Teachers in schools with more time should want to be there, be highly motivated, be dedicated to the school's mission and goals, and be well-trained. Teachers are leaders in the classroom and at school; they must be highly invested in student learning and school success. Because teacher support is critical to school success, they must play a vital role in the redesign process and reach consensus with school leaders about the vision for school improvement.

Cases in point:

- An Achievable Dream Academy places great importance on teacher-student relationships and the need for teachers to understand the needs of their students. As such, the school plays a pro-active role in conveying to teachers and potential teachers what is required of them to work in a year-round, expanded learning time school. During the interview and hiring process, administrators determine a teacher's passion for their work, gauge their understanding of the challenges they will have to undertake, and make sure that teachers understand what it takes to make and keep a high-performing school successful.

- The Massachusetts effort to expand learning time refects the various ways in which teacher contracts

can be constructed to support the needs of teachers in schools with expanded learning time. One school that extends the day by two hours requires all teachers to teach for the first of these two hours. The second hour is optional because community partners are brought in to lead activities. In a second school, teachers received a 30 percent increase in their salaries and were offered the option to transfer out of the school if they didn't want to extend their work day. A third school allowed existing teachers to opt out, but required new teachers or incoming teachers to teach for the additional time.

Use of Data

The use of data in expanded learning time efforts serves multiple functions. In the beginning, student-level data must be analyzed to inform leaders about the academic needs of students in the school. Doing so will demonstrate that schools and districts understand the needs of their students and are therefore designing a strategy of interventions around those students' needs. Assessment, portfolio, and other types of student performance data can also be used to influence student instruction and teaching methods, track academic growth over time, and connect students to teachers. Collecting and maintaining student, teacher, and school-level data also serves as educational research and development; it can provide researchers and education advocates with valuable information on the effect of systemic reform by linking educational strategies and inputs to student outcomes.

Case in point:

- Miami-Dade County Public Schools relied on school-level data to assess which schools were the lowest-performing and contributing to a low performance feeder pattern between elementary, middle and high schools. Based on this data, 39 schools were selected for inclusion in the School Improvement Zone: 20 elementary schools, 11 junior highs, and eight high schools. After three years of implementation, the Zone continues to use student- and school-level data to guide its intervention efforts and document its impact.

Community Support and Partnerships

Successful school reform efforts are those embraced by most stakeholders especially parents. Visionary leaders, and schools themselves, can't achieve reform on their own efforts alone. To sustain viable expanded learning time initiatives, they need broad-based community support and long-term commitment from partners. Actively involving communities in the design of the expanded school calendar will pay off with great dividends. Strategies that establish a balance between community outreach and involvement and the technical dimensions of program design are typically the most successful.

Case in point:

- Massachusetts 2020, the leading organization in the promotion of the state's effort to expand learning time, invested two years in the planning of this effort. In doing so, they conducted surveys to gauge public sentiment and support for education reform and the expanded learning time strategy, and embarked on a public education campaign aimed at parents and other members of the community. They also worked closely with teachers and the teacher unions—early on—and invested great care in helping to negotiate teacher contracts, when an objective voice was needed. In addition, the organization played a key role in securing community-based partners to work with schools that expanded their learning time.

Focused, Aligned Use of Time That Engages Students

At their core, schools that expand learning time must be focused and purposeful about how they do it. This focus begins with intentional choices about how to use time in ways that align with the school's goals and curriculum. Schools that expand learning time do not simply add enrichment courses such as art, music, or drama. Instead, they choose to offer courses that align academic content with enrichment programming and connect to student needs and interests. How these schools use expanded learning time must also align with state standards and appropriately relate to a state's school improvement plan. Such careful creation of a school's curriculum and use of learning time, and its fexibility to develop appropriately tailored interventions that will have lasting value for each student, is what makes expanded learning time a promising strategy that is far from "more of the same." Some expanded learning time schools have chosen to focus on being college preparatory institutions, while others focus on technology and science or communication and the arts.

Case in point:

- Miami's School Improvement Zone emphasizes literacy and enhancing student comprehension and critical thinking. The early elementary grades therefore focus on reading and writing skills. Later elementary and middle school grades participate in a Transition Academy, which expands the literacy focus and combines it with graduation and career preparation, character development, and study skills. Students in the later grades also participate in one-on-one tutoring if needed.

In addition to these fve pillars, successful expanded learning time initiatives also create a strong school culture to foster student learning. Development of the school's culture occurs organically through the redesign process which induces consideration by leaders of every aspect of schooling including the school's mission and goals—two primary components of institutional culture. As such, expanded learning initiatives are intentionally driven and applied. Successful initiatives provide students with a structured and supportive atmosphere to nurture learning. Such initiatives relate and connect to student needs and interests, are engaging and of high quality, include structured student and adult interactions, and maintain high expectations for student learning. Another component impacting school culture is parental engagement or involvement. Many schools with increased time ask parents to volunteer or sign contracts committing them to participate in their child's education through various activities like nightly reading logs.

As schools and districts explore the expansion of learning time, these five components should be thoughtfully considered and carefully incorporated into both planning and implementation efforts. Each one of them, however, involves more than just a slogan and brief defnition.

Conclusion

More and better use of learning time benefits *all* children, especially those who are academically behind and too often from low-income and minority families. Without comprehensive, school-wide reform, the challenge of getting under-performing students to grade level and beyond—while maintaining a rich, full curriculum—will remain difficult. Putting these students on a path to success will require nothing less than the best—the best teachers, the best principals, the best curriculum, the most time, the best supports, and the social security that accompanies a positive, strong learning environment. Well-implemented expanded learning time initiatives can provide all students in a school with the time, instruction, and structures necessary to achieve academic success and other positive outcomes.

ELENA ROCHA is a scholar at the Center for American Progress and education consultant.

Larry Cuban

 **NO**

The Perennial Reform: Fixing School Time

Education critics often call for longer school days and years. But there is little research to support such demands and several reasons why little will change.

In the past quarter century, reformers have repeatedly urged schools to fix their use of time, even though it is a solution that is least connected to what happens in classrooms or what Americans want from public schools. Since *A Nation at Risk* in 1983, *Prisoners of Time* in 1994, and the latest blue-ribbon recommendations in *Tough Choices, Tough Times* in 2007, both how much time and how well students spend it in school has been criticized no end.

Business and civil leaders have been critical because they see U.S. students stuck in the middle ranks on international tests. These leaders believe that the longer school year in Asia and Europe is linked to those foreign students scoring far higher than U.S. students on those tests.

Employers criticize the amount of time students spend in school because they wonder whether the limited days and hours spent in classes are sufficient to produce the skills that employees need to work in a globally competitive economy. Employers also wonder whether our comparatively short school year will teach the essential workplace behaviors of punctuality, regular attendance, meeting deadlines, and following rules.

Parents criticize school schedules because they want schools to be open when they go to work in the morning and to remain open until they pick up their children before dinner.

Professors criticize policy makers for allotting so little time for teachers to gain new knowledge and skills during the school day. Other researchers want both policy makers and practitioners to distinguish between requiring more time in school and *academic learning time*, academic jargon for those hours and minutes where teachers engage students in learning content and skills or, in more jargon, time on task.

Finally, cyberschool champions criticize school schedules because they think it's quaint to have students sitting at desks in a building with hundreds of other students for 180 days when a revolution in communication devices allows children to learn the formal curriculum in many places, not just in school buildings. Distance learning advocates, joined by those who see cyberschools as the future, want children and youths to spend hardly any time in K–12 schools.

Time Options

Presidential commissions, parents, academics, and employers have proposed the same solutions, again and again, for fixing the time students spend in school: Add more days to the annual school calendar. Change to year-round schools. Add instructional time to the daily schedule. Extend the school day.

What has happened to each proposal in the past quarter century?

Longer School Year. Recommendations for a longer school year (from 180 to 220 days) came from *A Nation at Risk* (1983) and *Prisoners of Time* (1994) plus scores of other commissions and experts. In 2008, a foundation-funded report, *A Stagnant Nation: Why American Students Are Still at Risk*, found that the 180-day school year was intact across the nation and only Massachusetts had started a pilot program to help districts lengthen the school year. The same report gave a grade of F to states for failing to significantly expand student learning time.

Year-Round Schools. Ending the summer break is another way to maximize student time in school. There is a homespun myth, treated as fact, that the annual school calendar, with three months off for both teachers and students, is based on the rhythm of 19th-century farm life, which dictated when school was in session. Thus, planting and harvesting chores accounted for long summer breaks, an artifact of agrarian America. Not so.

Actually, summer vacations grew out of early 20th-century urban middle-class parents (and later lobbyists for camps and the tourist industry) pressing school boards to release children to be with their families for four to eight weeks or more. By the 1960s, however, policy maker and parent concerns about students losing ground academically during the vacation months—in academic language, "summer loss"—gained support for year-round schooling. Cost savings also attracted those who saw facilities being used 12 months a year rather than being shuttered during the summer.

Nonetheless, although year-round schools were established as early as 1906 in Gary, Indiana, calendar innovations have had a hard time entering most schools. Districts with year-round schools still work within the 180-day year but distribute the time more evenly (e.g.,

45 days in session, 15 days off) rather than having a long break between June and September. As of 2006, nearly 3,000 of the nation's 90,000 public schools enrolled more than 2.1 million students on a year-round calendar. That's less than 5% of all students attending public schools, and almost half of the year-round schools are in California. In most cases, school boards adopted year-round schools because increased enrollments led to crowded facilities, most often in minority and poor communities—not concerns over "summer loss."

Adding Instructional Time to the School Day. Many researchers and reformers have pointed out that the 6 and 1/2-hour school day has so many interruptions, so many distractions that teachers have less than five hours of genuine instruction time. Advocates for more instructional time have tried to stretch the actual amount of instructional time available to teachers to a seven-hour day (or 5 and 1/2 hours of time for time-on-task learning) or have tried to redistribute the existing secondary school schedule into 90-minute blocks rather than the traditional 50-minute periods. Since *A Nation at Risk*, this recommendation for more instructional time has resulted only in an anemic 10 more minutes per day when elementary school students study core academic subjects.

Block scheduling in public secondary schools (60- to 90-minute periods for a subject that meets different days of the week) was started in the 1960s to promote instructional innovations. Various modified schedules have spread slowly, except in a few states where block schedules multiplied rapidly. In the past decade, an explosion of interest in small high schools has led many traditional urban comprehensive high schools of 1,500 or more students to convert to smaller high schools of 300 to 400 students, sometimes with all of those smaller schools housed within the original large building, sometimes as separate schools located elsewhere in the district. In many of these small high schools, modified schedules with instructional periods of an hour or more have found a friendly home. Block schedules rearrange existing allotted time for instruction; they do not add instructional time to the school day.

Extended School Day. In the past half century, as the economy has changed and families increasingly have both (or single) parents working, schools have been pressed to take on childcare responsibilities, such as tutoring and homework supervision before and after school. Many elementary schools open at 7 a.m. for parents to drop off children and have after-school programs that close at 6 p.m. PDK/Gallup polls since the early 1980s show increased support for these before- and after-school programs. Instead of the familiar half-day program for 5-year-olds, all-day kindergartens (and prekindergartens for 4-year-olds) have spread swiftly in the past two decades, especially in low-income neighborhoods. Innovative urban schools, such as the for-profit Edison Inc. and KIPP (Knowledge Is Power Program), run longer school days.

The latter routinely opens at 7:30 a.m. and closes at 5 p.m. and also schedules biweekly Saturday classes and three weeks of school during the summer.

If reformers want a success story in fixing school time, they can look to extending the school day, although it's arguable how many of those changes occurred because of reformers' arguments and actions and how many from economic and social changes in family structure and the desire to chase a higher standard of living.

Cybereducation. And what about those public school haters and cheerleading technological enthusiasts who see fixing time in school as a wasted effort when online schooling and distance learning can replace formal schooling? In the 1960s and 1970s, Ivan Illich and other school critics called for dismantling public schools and ending formal schooling. They argued that schools squelched natural learning, confused school-based education with learning, and turned children into obedient students and adults rather than curious and independent lifelong learners. Communication and instructional technologies were in their infancy then, and thinkers such as Illich had few alternatives to offer families who opted out.

Much of that ire directed at formal public schooling still exists, but now technology has made it possible for students to learn outside school buildings. Sharing common ground in this debate are deeply religious families who want to avoid secular influences in schools, highly educated parents who fear the stifling effects of school rules and text-bound instruction, and rural parents who simply want their children to have access to knowledge unavailable in their local schools. These advocates seek home schooling, distance learning, and cyber schools.

Slight increases in home schooling may occur—say from 1.1 million in 2003 to 2 to 3 million by the end of the decade, with the slight uptick in numbers due to both the availability of technology and a broader menu of choices for parents. Still, this represents less than 3% of public school students. Even though cheerleaders for distance learning have predicted wholesale changes in conventional site-based schools for decades, such changes will occur at the periphery, not the center, because most parents will continue to send their children to public schools.

Even the most enthusiastic advocates for cyberschools and distance education recognize that replacing public schools is, at best, unlikely. The foreseeable future will still have 50 million children and youths crossing the schoolhouse door each weekday morning.

3 Reasons

Reformers have spent decades trotting out the same recipes for fixing the time problem in school. For all the hoopla and all of the endorsements from highly influential business and political elites, their mighty efforts have produced minuscule results. Why is that?

Cost is the usual suspect. Covering additional teacher salaries and other expenses runs high. Minnesota provides one example: shifting from 175 to 200 days of instruction cost districts an estimated $750 million a year, a large but not insurmountable price to pay. But costs for extending the school day for instruction and childcare are far less onerous.

Even more attractive than adding days to the calendar, however, is the claim that switching to a year-round school will *save* dollars. So, while there are costs involved in lengthening the school calendar, cost is not the tipping point in explaining why so few proposals to fix school time are successful.

I offer two other reasons why fixing school time is so hard. Research showing achievement gains due to more time in school are sparse; the few studies most often displayed are contested. Late 20th-century policy makers seriously underestimated the powerful tug that conservative, noneconomic goals (e.g., citizenship, character formation) have on parents, taxpayers, and voters. When they argued that America needed to add time to the school calendar in order to better prepare workers for global competition, they were out of step with the American public's desires for schools.

Skimpy Research

In the past quarter century of tinkering with the school calendar, cultural changes, political decisions, or strong parental concerns trumped research every time. Moreover, the longitudinal and rigorous research on time in school was—and is—skimpy. The studies that exist are challenged repeatedly for being weakly designed. For example, analysts examining research on year-round schools have reported that most of the studies have serious design flaws and, at best, show slight positive gains in student achievement—except for students from low-income families, for whom gains were sturdier. As one report concluded: "[N]o truly trustworthy studies have been done on modified school calendars that can serve as the basis for sound policy decisions." Policy talk about year-round schools has easily outstripped results.

Proving that time in school is the crucial variable in raising academic achievement is difficult because so many other variables must be considered—the local context itself, available resources, teacher quality, administrative leadership, socioeconomic and cultural background of students and their families, and what is taught. But the lack of careful research has seldom stopped reform-driven decision makers from pursuing their agendas.

Conflicting School Goals

If the evidence suggests that, at best, a longer school year or day or restructured schedules do not seem to make the key difference in student achievement, then I need to ask: What problem are reformers trying to solve by adding more school time?

The short answer is that for the past quarter century—*A Nation at Risk* (1983) is a suitable marker—policy elites have redefined a national economic problem into an educational problem. Since the late 1970s, influential civic, business, and media leaders have sold Americans the story that lousy schools are the reason why inflation surged, unemployment remained high, incomes seldom rose, and cheaper and better foreign products flooded U.S. stores. Public schools have failed to produce a strong, post-industrial labor force, thus leading to a weaker, less competitive U.S. economy. U.S. policy elites have used lagging scores on international tests as telling evidence that schools graduate less knowledgeable, less skilled high school graduates—especially those from minority and poor schools who will be heavily represented in the mid-21st century workforce—than competitor nations with lower-paid workforces who produce high-quality products.

Microsoft founder Bill Gates made the same point about U.S. high schools.

> In district after district across the country, wealthy white kids are taught Algebra II, while low-income minority kids are taught how to balance a checkbook. This is an economic disaster. In the international competition to have the best supply of workers who can communicate clearly, analyze information, and solve complex problems, the United States is falling behind. We have one of the highest high school dropout rates in the industrialized world.

And here, in a nutshell, is the second reason why those highly touted reforms aimed at lengthening the school year and instructional day have disappointed policy makers. By blaming schools, contemporary civic and business elites have reduced the multiple goals Americans expect of their public schools to a single one: prepare youths to work in a globally competitive economy. This has been a mistake because Americans historically have expected more from their public schools. Let me explore the geography of this error.

For nearly three decades, influential groups have called for higher academic standards, accountability for student outcomes, more homework, more testing, and, of course, more time in school. Many of their recommendations have been adopted. By 2008, U.S. schools had a federally driven system of state-designed standards anchored in increased testing, results-driven accountability, and demands for students to spend more time in school. After all, reformers reasoned, the students of foreign competitors were attending school more days in the year and longer hours each day, even on weekends, and their test scores ranked them higher than the U.S.

Even though this simplistic causal reasoning has been questioned many times by researchers who examined education and work performance in Japan, Korea, Singapore, Germany, and other nations, "common sense" observations by powerful elites swept away such questions.

So the U.S.'s declining global economic competitiveness had been spun into a time-in-school problem.

But convincing evidence drawn from research that more time in school would lead to a stronger economy, less inequalities in family income, and that elusive edge in global competitiveness—much less a higher rank in international tests—remains missing in action.

The Public's Goals for Education

Business and civic elites have succeeded at least twice in the past century in making the growth of a strong economy the primary aim of U.S. schools, but other goals have had an enormous and enduring impact on schooling, both in the past and now. These goals embrace core American values that have been like second-hand Roses, shabby and discarded clothes hidden in the back of the closet and occasionally trotted out for show during graduation. Yet since the origins of tax-supported public schools in the early 19th century, these goals have been built into the very structures of schools so much so that, looking back from 2008, we hardly notice them.

Time-based reforms have had trouble entering schools because other goals have had—and continue to have—clout with parents and taxpayers. Opinion polls, for example, display again and again what parents, voters, and taxpayers want schools to achieve. One recent poll identified the public's goals for public schools. The top five were to:

- Prepare people to become responsible citizens;
- Help people become economically sufficient;
- Ensure a basic level of quality among schools;
- Promote cultural unity among all Americans;
- Improve social conditions for people.

Tied for sixth and seventh were goals to:

- Enhance people's happiness and enrich their lives; and
- Dispel inequities in education among certain schools and certain groups.

To reach those goals, a democratic society expects schools to produce adults who are engaged in their communities, enlightened employers, and hard-working employees who have acquired and practiced particular values that sustain its way of life. Dominant American social, political, and economic values pervade family, school, workplace, and community: Act independently, accept personal responsibility for actions, work hard and complete a job well, and be fair, that is, willing to be judged by standards applied to others as long as the standards are applied equitably.

These norms show up in school rules and classroom practices in every school. School is the one institutional agent between the family, the workplace, and voting booth or jury room responsible for instilling those norms in children's behavior. School is the agent for turning 4-year-olds

into respectful students engaged in their communities, a goal that the public perceives as more significant than preparing children and youths for college and the labor market. In elite decision makers' eagerness to link schools to a growing economy, they either overlooked the powerful daily practices of schooling or neglected to consider seriously these other goals. In doing so, they erred. The consequences of that error in judgment can be seen in the fleeting attention that policy recommendations for adding more time in school received before being shelved.

Teaching in a Democracy

Public schools were established before industrialization, and they expanded rapidly as factories and mills spread. Those times appear foreign to readers today. For example, in the late 19th century, calling public schools "factory-like" was not an epithet hurled at educators or supporters of public schools as it has been in the U.S. since the 1960s. In fact, describing a public school as an assembly-line factory or a productive cotton mill was considered a compliment to forward-looking educators who sought to make schools modern through greater efficiency in teaching and learning by copying the successes of wealthy industrialists. Progressive reformers praised schools for being like industrial plants in creating large, efficient, age-graded schools that standardized curriculum while absorbing millions of urban migrants and foreign immigrants. As a leading progressive put it:

> Our schools are, in a sense, factories in which the raw products (children) are to be shaped and fashioned into products to meet the various demands of life. . . . It is the business of the school to build its pupils to the specifications [of manufacturers].

Progressive reformers saw mills, factories, and corporations as models for transforming the inefficient one-room schoolhouse in which students of different ages received fitful, incomplete instruction from one teacher into the far more efficient graded school where each teacher taught students a standardized curriculum each year. First established in Boston in 1848 and spreading swiftly in urban districts, the graded school became the dominant way of organizing a school by 1900. By the 1920s, schools exemplified the height of industrial efficiency because each building had separate classrooms with their own teachers. The principal and teachers expected children of the same age to cover the same content and learn skills by the end of the school year and perform satisfactorily on tests in order to be promoted to the next grade.

Superintendents saw the age-graded school as a modern version of schooling well adapted to an emerging corporate-dominated industrial society where punctuality, dependability, and obedience were prized behaviors. As a St. Louis superintendent said in 1871:

> The first requisite of the school is Order: each pupil must be taught first and foremost to conform his

behavior to a general standard. . . . The pupil must have his lessons ready at the appointed time, must rise at the tap of the bell, move to the line, return; in short, go through all of the evolutions with equal precision.

Recognition and fame went to educators who achieved such order in their schools.

But the farm-driven seasonal nature of rural one-room schoolhouses was incompatible with the explosive growth of cities and an emerging industrial society. In the early 20th century, progressive reformers championed compulsory attendance laws while extending the abbreviated rural-driven short hours and days into a longer school day and year. Reformers wanted to increase the school's influence over children's attitudes and behavior, especially in cities where wave after wave of European immigrants settled. Seeking higher productivity in organization, teaching, and learning at the least cost, reformers broadened the school's mission by providing medical, social, recreational, and psychological services at schools. These progressive reformers believed schools should teach society's norms to both children and their families and also educate the whole child so that the entire government, economy, and society would change for the better. So, when reformers spoke about "factory-like schools" a century ago, they wanted educators to copy models of success; they were not scolding them. That changed, however, by the late 20th century.

As the U.S. shifted from a manufacturing-based economy to a post-industrial information-based economy, few policy makers reckoned with this history of schooling. Few influential decision makers view schools as agents of *both* stability and change. Few educational opinion makers recognize that the conservative public still expects schools to instill in children dominant American norms of being independent and being held accountable for one's actions, doing work well and efficiently, and treating others equitably to ensure that when students graduate they will practice these values as adults. And, yes, the public still expects schools to strengthen the economy by ensuring that graduates have the necessary skills to be productive employees in an ever-changing, highly competitive, and increasingly global workplace. But that is just one of many competing expectations for schools.

Thus far, I have focused mostly on how policy makers and reform-minded civic and business elites have not only defined economic problems as educational ones that can be fixed by more time spent in schools but also neglected the powerful hold that socialization goals have on parents' and taxpayers' expectations. Now, I want to switch from the world of reform-driven policy makers and elites to teachers and students because each group views school time differently from their respective perch. Teacher and student perspectives on time in school have little influence in policy makers' decision making. Although the daily actions of teachers and students don't influence policy makers, they do matter in explaining why reformers have had such paltry results in trying to fix school time.

Differing Views of Time in School

For civic and business leaders, media executives, school boards, superintendents, mayors, state legislators, governors, U.S. representatives, and the President (what I call "policy elites"), electoral and budget cycles become the timeframe within which they think and act. Every year, budgets must be prepared and, every two or four years, officials run for office and voters decide who should represent them and whether they should support bond referenda and tax levies. Because appointed and elected policy makers are influential with the media, they need to assure the public during campaigns that slogans and stump speeches were more than talk. Sometimes, words do become action when elected decision makers, for example, convert a comprehensive high school into a cluster of small high schools, initiate 1:1 laptop programs, and extend the school day. This is the world of policy makers.

The primary tools policy makers use to adopt and implement decisions, however, are limited and blunt—closer to a hammer than a scalpel. They use exhortation, press conferences, political bargaining, incentives, and sanctions to formulate and adopt decisions. (Note, however, that policy makers rarely implement decisions; administrators and practitioners put policies into practice.) Policy makers want broad social, political, economic, and organizational goals adopted as policies, and then they want to move educators, through encouragement, incentives, and penalties, to implement those policies in schools and classrooms that they seldom, if ever, enter.

The world of teachers differs from that of policy makers. For teachers, the time-driven budget and electoral cycles that shape policy matter little for their classrooms, except when such policies carry consequences for how and what teachers should teach, such as accountability measures that assume teachers and students are slackers and need to work harder. In these instances, teachers become classroom gatekeepers in deciding how much of a policy they will put into practice and under what conditions.

What matters most to teachers are student responses to daily lessons, weekly tests, monthly units, and the connections they build over time in classrooms, corridors, during lunch, and before and after school. Those personal connections become the compost of learning. Those connections account for former students pointing to particular teachers who made a difference in their lives. Teacher tools, unlike policy maker tools, are unconnected to organizational power or media influence. Teachers use their personalities, knowledge, experience, and skills in building relationships with groups of students and providing individual help. Teachers believe there is never enough time in the daily schedule to finish a lesson, explain a point, or listen to a student. Administrative intrusions gobble up valuable instructional time that could go to students. In class, then, both teachers and students are clock watchers, albeit for different reasons.

Students view time differently as well. For a fraction of students from middle- and low-income families turned off by school requirements and expectations, spending time in classrooms listening to teachers, answering questions, and doing homework is torture; the hands of the clock seldom move fast enough for them. The notion of extending the school day and school year for them—or continuing on to college and four more years of reading texts and sitting in classrooms—is not a reform to be implemented but a punishment to be endured. Such students look for creative shortcuts to skip classes, exit the school as early as they can, and find jobs or enter the military once they graduate. Most students, however, march from class to class until they hear "Pomp and Circumstance." But a high school diploma, graduates have come to realize, is not enough in the 21st-century labor market.

College for Everyone

In the name of equity and being responsive to employers' needs, most urban districts have converted particular comprehensive high schools into clusters of small college-prep academies where low-income minority students take Advanced Placement courses, write research papers, and compete to get into colleges and universities. Here, then, is the quiet, unheralded, and unforeseen victory of reformers bent on fixing time in school. They have succeeded unintentionally in stretching K–12 into preK–16 public schooling, not just for middle- and upper-middle class students, but for everyone.

As it has been for decades for most suburban middle- and upper-middle class white and minority families, now it has become a fact, an indisputable truth converted into a sacred mission for upwardly mobile poor families: A high school diploma and a bachelor's degree are passports to high-paying jobs and the American Dream. For families who already expect their sons and daughters to attend competitive colleges, stress begins early. Getting into the best preschools and elementary and secondary schools and investing in an array of activities to build attractive résumés for college admission officers to evaluate become primary tasks. For such families and children, there is never enough time for homework, Advanced Placement courses, music, soccer, drama, dance, and assorted after-school activities. For high-achieving, stressed-out students already expecting at least four more years of school after high school graduation, reform proposals urging a longer school year and an extended day often strike an unpleasant note. Angst and fretfulness become familiar clothes to don every morning as students grind out 4s and 5s on Advanced Placement exams, play sports, and compile just the right record that will get them into just the right school. For decades, pressure on students to use every minute of school to prepare for college has been strongest in middle- and upper-middle-class suburbs. What has changed in the past few decades is the spread of the belief that everyone, including low-income minority students, should go to college.

To summarize, for decades, policy elites have disregarded teacher and student perspectives on time in school. Especially now when all students are expected to enter college, children, youths, and teachers experience time in school differently than policy makers who seek a longer school day and school year. Such varied perceptions about time are heavily influenced by the socialization goals of schooling, age-graded structures, socioeconomic status of families, and historical experience. And policy makers often ignore these perceptions and reveal their tone-deafness and myopia in persistently trying to fix time in schools. Policy elites need to parse fully this variation in perceptions because extended time in school remains a high priority to reform-driven policy makers and civic and business leaders anxious about U.S. performance on international tests and fearful of falling behind in global economic competitiveness. The crude policy solutions of more days in the year and longer school days do not even begin to touch the deeper truth that what has to improve is the quality of "academic learning time." If policy makers could open their ears and eyes to student and teacher perceptions of time, they would learn that the secular Holy Grail is decreasing interruption of instruction, encouraging richer intellectual and personal connections between teachers and students, and increasing classroom time for ambitious teaching and active, engaged learning. So far, no such luck.

Conclusion

These three reasons—cost, lackluster research, and the importance of conservative social goals to U.S. taxpayers and voters—explain why proposals to fix time in U.S. schools have failed to take hold. Policy elites know research studies proving the worth of year-round schools or lengthened school days are in short supply. Even if an occasional study supported the change, the school year is unlikely to go much beyond 180 days. Policy elites know school goals go far beyond simply preparing graduates for college and for employability in a knowledge-based economy. And policy elites know they must show courage in their pursuit of improving failing U.S. schools by forcing students to go to school just as long as their peers in India, China, Japan, and Korea. That courage shows up symbolically, playing well in the media and in proposals to fix time in schools, but it seldom alters calendars.

While cost is a factor, it is the stability of schooling structures and the importance of socializing the young into the values of the immediate community and larger society that have defeated policy-driven efforts to alter time in school over the past quarter century. Like the larger public, I am unconvinced that requiring students and teachers to spend more time in school each day and every year will be better for them. How that time is spent in learning before, during, and after school is far more important than decision makers counting the minutes, hours, and days students spend each year getting schooled. That being said, I have little doubt that state and federal blue-ribbon commissions will continue to make proposals about lengthening time in school. Those proposals will make headlines, but they will not result in serious, sustained attention to

what really matters—improving the quality of the time that teachers and students spend with one another in and out of classrooms.

LARRY CUBAN is a professor emeritus of education at Stanford University.

EXPLORING THE ISSUE

Should Student Time in School Be Changed?

Critical Thinking and Reflection

1. Are "in-school time" and "learning time" the same thing?
2. What would you consider the pros and cons of changing school time to be in relation to each of the different models?
3. What kinds of evidence were discussed in relation to each of the arguments?

Is There Common Ground?

The two selections were selected because they were clear opinion pieces representing different sides of the argument. In some instances, similar citations are used but different conclusions are reached. Arguing for extending school time, Elena Rocha suggests that major school reform could and should start with altering the length of the school day and year. Alternatively, Larry Cuban reaches a different conclusion, suggesting that major reform efforts based on extending school time are not likely to be successful for a myriad of reasons related to the multiple purposes of U.S. public education and that very little research supports such changes. Based on the two selections it is clear that the issue of changing school time is a core component of educational reform. Thus, there are policy perspectives but also practice perspectives that are relevant. One way of reading the selections is to see Rocha's article as a call for what ought to be or could be, whereas Cuban's article reflects "what is." If the real overlying issue is education or school reform, then from that it follows that changing the school year is a part, but only one part, of a large school improvement strategy. To see changing school time as a "silver bullet" that will solve a set of interconnected problems in contemporary U.S. public education is misguided at best and naïve (neither piece suggested this, per se). As reform strategies go, steps can be taken (incrementalism) or a system can be overhauled (comprehensive). From both the selections, it is clear that there is more needed at a policy level than simply deciding to change time in school; there are community-level cultural issues, there are practice-level teacher implementation issues, etc. As one moving part among many, any significant changes in school time have to be integrated with the needs and preferences of a number of stakeholders (students, parents, educators, politicians).

In this era of evidence based practice (EBP), it should be second nature to ask what is the evidence supporting any policy decision with such a direct effect on practice. And, if there is evidence, how good is it? The majority of the evidence reviewed in Rocha's article was either anecdotal and/or based on cases (a specific school/district) in which the reform effort had been adopted. This kind of evidence provides "proof of principle" but by itself is not necessarily confirmatory. One general problem with anecdotal or case based evidence is that it is easy to include positive instances supporting a position and overlook negative instances contrary to a position. On the issue of changing school time, for example, it might be noted that the state of California—which has the largest number of YRE programs—will phase out almost all of their year-round schools by 2012 (for additional reading on California's "Concept 6" see B. M. Allen, *The Williams v. California Settlement: The First Year of Implementation* [San Diego, CA: ACLU Foundation of Southern California, 2005]). Positive and negative cases notwithstanding, the body of research evidence directly related to changing some aspect of school time is disappointingly small, with few well designed and executed research studies. This state of affairs leads to conclusions like that found in a review by H. Cooper and colleagues (mentioned below) that not enough dependable studies have been completed on which to base an informed policy decision for changing the school calendar. Part of the issue, however, as mentioned above, may be that if changing school time is really only one part of a larger school reform effort then evaluating calendar change in isolation from changing other components of the system is more than likely going to lead to mixed, modest, or no effects.

Finally, the notion of increasing time in school is treated, implicitly in most cases, as a synonym for the expansion of learning time. It is fair to wonder, then, what exactly is learning time? And, does a longer school day or year equal increased learning time? It turns out, as you might expect, that adding time and adding time learning are not necessarily synonymous (see, for example, K. R. Stanley and colleagues, "The Daily Schedule: A Look at the Relationship Between Time and Academic Achievement" in the *Education Policy Brief* from the Center for Evaluation & Education Policy, vol. 5, Summer, 2007). In one study examining student outcomes as a function on changing the daily schedule or calendar (longer blocks), J. McCreary and

C. Hausman found very small effects and concluded that there was limited evidence about the relationship between structural change and student outcomes (ERIC Document ED457590, 2001). Consistent with the notion mentioned above, it seems likely that it would be a mistake, based on the available evidence, to expect that changing school time would produce pronounced effects without simultaneously addressing professional development so that teachers can capitalize on the additional time. H. Pennington in "Expanding Learning Time in High Schools" (Center for American Progress, 2006) reaches the same conclusion and provides ample examples and models related to the component parts that must change simultaneously for meaningful school reform and changing school time is just one. It would seem, then, that there is a clear and important distinction between adding time to the school day or year and adding learning to the day or year (allocated school time, allocated class time, instructional time, and adding learning to the day are related but different concepts). Any informed discussion about expanding school time must recognize this distinction from the outset if there is to be a meaningful discussion and debate about the issue.

Create Central

www.mhhe.com/createcentral

Additional Resources

K. R. Stanley et al., "The Daily Schedule: A Look at the Relationship Between Time and Academic Achievement" in the *Education Policy Brief* from the Center for Evaluation & Education Policy (vol. 5, Summer, 2007).

H. Pennington, "Expanding Learning Time in High Schools" (Center for American Progress, 2006).

H. Cooper, J. C. Valentine, K. Chariton, and A. Melson, "The Effect of Modified School Calendars on Student Achievement and on School and Community Attitudes" *Review of Educational Research* (vol. 73, 2003).

S. P. Johnson and T. E. Spradlin provide a very informative overview of several aspects of the school time issue in their education policy brief in "Alternatives to the Traditional School Year" (Center for Evaluation & Education Policy, vol. 5, Spring 2007).

For a specific example of a study examining school time there is B. J. McMillen's report on "A Statewide Evaluation of Academic Achievement in Year Round Schools" in *The Journal of Educational Research* (vol. 95, 2001).

Internet References . . .

School Start Time

http://www.sleepfoundation.org/article/sleep-topics
/school-start-time-and-sleep

Fairfax School Start Time Slows

http://www.washingtonpost.com/local/education
/fairfax-school-start-times-effort-slows/2014/01/13
/028fc042-7c78-11e3-9556-4a4bf7bcbd84_story.html

The Impact of School Start Time on Adolescent Health and Performance

http://schoolstarttime.org/